‘Bringing together six of the most provocative of Muriel Dimen’s essays, editor Stephen Hartman wisely and playfully frames each with a team of invited commentaries that underscore Dimen’s unique way of mixing theory building, self-reflection, and political aims to enliven thinking and practices in the psychoanalytic field. The commentaries from a diverse set of interdisciplinary, intergenerational, international and intersectionally informed writers are offered with experiment in mind. Rendered with elegance, executed with care, and elaborated in friendship, they respond to Dimen’s call for a wild practice, a revolutionizing form of psychoanalytic reasoning that does not lose sight of collective concerns of race, gender, sexuality, ethnicity, and class. *Reading with Muriel Dimen/Writing with Muriel Dimen* is a real treat: a brilliant and passionate conversation in which Muriel’s vision and voice are given to us fresh with insight for these times.’

Patricia Tinceneto Clough, *professor of Sociology and Women’s Studies, psychoanalyst, and author of* The User Unconscious

Reading with Muriel Dimen/ Writing with Muriel Dimen

Reading with Muriel Dimen/Writing with Muriel Dimen: Experiments in Theorizing a Field is a collection of reading and writing experiments inspired by the late feminist psychoanalyst Muriel Dimen.

Each of the six projects that comprise this volume explores a stylistic and thematic manner of reading and responding to Dimen's work, challenging the field to write outside the standardized edition, and covering a remarkable breadth of essential analytic topics, such as sex, gender, money, love and hate, and boundary violations. As an homage to Dimen's quest to engage the personal and the political in the author's craft, and in collaboration with Dimen's endeavour to foster revolution across the psychosocial landscape that renders psychoanalysis its field, the authors offer readers a *wild analysis* of reading and writing.

Providing a clear introduction to and exploration of Muriel Dimen's groundbreaking work, this book will prove essential for scholars of psychoanalysis, cultural studies, and gender studies, as well as anyone seeking to understand Dimen's influence on psychoanalytic practice today.

Stephen Hartman is an Editor-in-Chief of *Psychoanalytic Dialogues* and a former editor of *Studies in Gender and Sexuality*, faculty at the Psychoanalytic Institute of Northern California and NYU, and author of over 40 articles and book chapters that explore the interface of technology and psychoanalysis through a psychosocial lens. Stephen practises in San Francisco and New York. His road bike and yoga mat are parked in Brooklyn.

Relational Perspectives Book Series

Series Editors: Adrienne Harris & Eyal Rozmarin
Founding Editor: Stephen Mitchell
Editor Emeritus: Lewis Aron

The Relational Perspectives Book Series (RPBS) publishes books that grow out of or contribute to the relational tradition in contemporary psychoanalysis. The term *relational psychoanalysis* was first used by Greenberg and Mitchell[1] to bridge the traditions of interpersonal relations, as developed within interpersonal psychoanalysis and object relations, as developed within contemporary British theory. But, under the seminal work of the late Stephen A. Mitchell, the term *relational psychoanalysis* grew and began to accrue to itself many other influences and developments. Various tributaries—interpersonal psychoanalysis, object relations theory, self psychology, empirical infancy research, feminism, queer theory, sociocultural studies and elements of contemporary Freudian and Kleinian thought—flow into this tradition, which understands relational configurations between self and others, both real and fantasied, as the primary subject of psychoanalytic investigation.

We refer to the relational tradition, rather than to a relational school, to highlight that we are identifying a trend, a tendency within contemporary psychoanalysis, not a more formally organized or coherent school or system of beliefs. Our use of the term *relational* signifies a dimension of theory and practice that has become salient across the wide spectrum of contemporary psychoanalysis. Now under the editorial supervision of Adrienne Harris and Eyal Rozmarin, the Relational Perspectives Book Series originated in 1990 under the editorial eye of the late Stephen A. Mitchell. Mitchell was the most prolific and influential of the originators of the relational tradition. Committed to dialogue among psychoanalysts, he abhorred the authoritarianism that dictated adherence to a rigid set of beliefs or technical restrictions. He championed open discussion, comparative and integrative approaches, and promoted new voices across the generations. Mitchell was later joined by the late Lewis Aron, also a visionary and influential writer, teacher and leading thinker in relational psychoanalysis.

Included in the Relational Perspectives Book Series are authors and works that come from within the relational tradition, those that extend and develop that tradition, and works that critique relational approaches or compare and contrast them with alternative points of view. The series includes our most distinguished senior psychoanalysts, along with younger contributors who bring fresh vision. Our aim is to enable a deepening of relational thinking while reaching across disciplinary and social boundaries in order to foster an inclusive and international literature.

Note

1 Greenberg, J. & Mitchell, S. (1983). *Object relations in psychoanalytic theory.* Cambridge, MA: Harvard University Press.

A full list of titles in this series is available at https://www.routledge.com/Relational-Perspectives-Book-Series/book-series/LEARPBS.

Reading with Muriel Dimen/ Writing with Muriel Dimen

Experiments in Theorizing a Field

Edited by Stephen Hartman

Routledge
Taylor & Francis Group
LONDON AND NEW YORK

Designed cover image: © Stephen Hartman and Christiaan Kuypers

First published 2023
by Routledge
4 Park Square, Milton Park, Abingdon, Oxon OX14 4RN

and by Routledge
605 Third Avenue, New York, NY 10158

Routledge is an imprint of the Taylor & Francis Group, an informa business

British Library Cataloguing-in-Publication Data
A catalogue record for this book is available from the British Library

Library of Congress Cataloging-in-Publication Data
Names: Hartman, Stephen, 1960–editor.
Title: Reading with Muriel Dimen / writing with Muriel Dimen: experiments in theorizing a field / edited by Stephen Hartman.
Description: Abingdon, Oxon; New York, NY: Routledge, 2023. | Includes bibliographical references and index. |
Identifiers: LCCN 2022039379 (print) | LCCN 2022039380 (ebook) | ISBN: 978-1-032-37086-6 (hbk) | ISBN: 978-1-032-37087-3 (pbk) | ISBN: 978-1-003-33525-2 (ebk)
Subjects: LCSH: Psychoanalysis and feminism. | Dimen, Muriel. | Political correctness. | Intersectionality (Sociology)
Classification: LCC BF175.4.F45 R45 2023 (print) | LCC BF175.4.F45 (ebook) | DDC 150.19/5082—dc23/eng/20221116
LC record available at https://lccn.loc.gov/2022039379
LC ebook record available at https://lccn.loc.gov/2022039380

ISBN: 978-1-032-37086-6 (hbk)
ISBN: 978-1-032-37087-3 (pbk)
ISBN: 978-1-003-33525-2 (ebk)

DOI: 10.4324/9781003335252

Typeset in Times New Roman
by codeMantra

for Muriel Dimen and Henry Urbach

Contents

Acknowledgements xvii
Credits List xix
Foreword by Virginia Goldner xxi

Among *Us*: Reading and Writing with Muriel Dimen **1**

STEPHEN HARTMAN

1 Politically Correct/Politically Incorrect—Redux and Revise **25**

Project One, Editor's Note 27
STEPHEN HARTMAN

Politically Correct? Politically Incorrect? 31
MURIEL DIMEN

To Capture the Frenzied Politically In/Correct? 41
KATIE GENTILE

ELA 44
ALMAS MERCHANT

Note 49
BETTINA VON LIERES

In Muriel Dimen's Footsteps—Five Notes on the Politically Correct and Politically Coerced in Current Israeli Contexts 51
CHANA ULLMAN

Note 54
FIONA ANCIANO

Note 56
GRIFFIN HANSBURY

Stars and Stripes Forever 58
JOANNA WHEELER

Making Life Accessible: A Note from the Suicidal to Society 61
J.R. LATHAM

The Limitations of White Liberal Discourse: Political Correctness as Dual Defense 65
LARA SHEEHI

The Unresolved Questions Muriel Dimen Helped Me Raise 71
LAURA TRAJBER WAISBICH

On Political Correctness: A Plea for an Intersectional Frame 75
LYNNE LAYTON

The Political Incorrectness of Feminism in the Wake of Calls for Decolonisation in South Africa 78
NOBUKHOSI NGWENYA

The Politically Correct and Incorrectness of Intersectionality in Feminist Discourse 83
SHIRI RAZ

Bring Back the Curbs on Political Incorrectness 87
SHYLASHRI SHANKAR

2 On Money, Love, and Hate **91**

Project Two, Editor's Note 93
STEPHEN HARTMAN

Money, Love, and Hate: Contradiction and Paradox in Psychoanalysis 95
MURIEL DIMEN

Good Night, See You Next Week 122
JUNE LEE KWON

The Empty Platter 130
JEFF JACKSON

3 Talking About *Sexuality and Suffering or the Eew! Factor*: What's a Nice Vanilla Analyst to Do? **133**

Project Three, Editor's Note 135
STEPHEN HARTMAN

Sexuality and Suffering, or the Eew! Factor 137
MURIEL DIMEN

What's a Nice Vanilla Analyst to Do? An Intergenerational Conversation on Muriel Dimen's "The Eew Factor" 150
LISA BUCHBERG AND EMMA KAYWIN

4 Wild Times/Wild Analysis/Wild Revolution **163**

Project Four, Editor's Note 165
STEPHEN HARTMAN

Inside the Revolution: Power, Sex, and Technique in Freud's "'Wild' Analysis" 167
MURIEL DIMEN

The Wild, the Revolution, the Abject Social Imaginary, the Racialized Psychoanalytic Setting a Conversation between Daniel G. Butler and Ken Corbett Inspired by Muriel Dimen's Contemplation of the Wild and the Heterodox in Sigmund Freud's Wild Analysis Held Amidst the 2020 American Summer of Social Discontent 187
DANIEL G. BUTLER AND KEN CORBETT

5 Rotten Apples – Talking About It/Them/Us 203

Project Five, Editor's Note 205
STEPHEN HARTMAN

Rotten Apples and Ambivalence: Sexual Boundary Violations through a Psychocultural Lens 207
MURIEL DIMEN

Paradise Lost: What Is Most Dangerous About Our Method – Muriel Dimen's "Rotten Apples and Ambivalence: Sexual Boundary Violations through a Psychocultural Lens" 218
VELLEDA C. CECCOLI

No Sex, Please. We're Psychoanalysts 231
ANN PELLEGRINI

6 Of Ghosts and Groups 241

Project Six, Editor's Note 243
STEPHEN HARTMAN

Ghosts and the Sexual Boundary Violation: The Limits of an Idea 246
BY MURIEL DIMEN (UNPUBLISHED MANUSCRIPT, 2015) WITH DISCUSSION BY THE WRITING GROUP KNOWN AS LOC 148:

FRANCISCO GONZALEZ; ORNA GURALNIK; STEPHEN HARTMAN; JULIE LEAVITT; JADE MCGLEUPHLIN; AND EYAL ROZMARIN.

Afterword 283
ADRIENNE HARRIS

Index 285

Acknowledgements

This project would not have been possible without the unflagging editorial support of Adrienne Harris on behalf of the Routledge Relational Perspectives Book Series, the comradery of my writing group LOC 148 — Francisco Gonzalez, Orna Guralnik, Julie Leavitt, Jade McGleuphlin, and Eyal Rozmarin, and constant encouragement from the executors of Muriel Dimen's literary and clinical estate: Virginia Goldner, Avgi Saketopoulou, and Velleda Ceccoli.

My deep gratitude goes to all the contributors to this volume whose enthusiasm and keenness to chart experimental territory honor Dimen's revolutionary spirit with unmatched verve. Rather than name each of you individually here, I want to simply say a very deeply felt, thank you.

My co-editors of *Psychoanalytic Dialogues*, Jack Foehl, Lauren Levine, and Amy Schwartz Cooney—with Jeff Jackson always at the ready—are the first-rate accomplices from page to print.

I am delighted to have the endorsements of Virginia Golder, Patricia Clough, and Adrienne Harris each of whom inspire me daily.

Finally, thank goodness for Kate Hawes, Georgina Clutterbuck, and Eleonora Kouneni, who skilfully guided me through the production process, and for Christiaan Kuypers' brilliant eye for design. A special thanks to my yoga teachers Nikki Vilella and Rebecca Ketchum for suppleness and strength in equal measure. And, of course, to my beloved mentor and friend Muriel Dimen: *namaste*.

Credits List

The editor also gratefully acknowledges the permission provided to republish the following materials:

'Money, love, and hate contradiction and paradox in psychoanalysis', Muriel Dimen, *Psychoanalytic Dialogues*, 1994, Taylor and Francis, reprinted by permission of the publisher (Taylor & Francis Ltd, http://www.tandfonline.com).

'Sexuality and Suffering, or the Eew! Factor', Muriel Dimen, *Studies in Gender & Sexuality*, 2005, Taylor and Francis, reprinted by permission of the publisher (Taylor & Francis Ltd, http://www.tandfonline.com).

'Inside the Revolution: Power, Sex, and Technique in Freud's "'Wild' Analysis"', Muriel Dimen, *Psychoanalytic Dialogues*, 2014, Taylor and Francis, reprinted by permission of the publisher (Taylor & Francis Ltd., http://www.tandfonline.com).

'Rotten Apples and Ambivalence', Muriel Dimen, *Journal of the American Psychoanalytic Association* (Volume 64, Issue 2), copyright © 2016 by (SAGE Publications). Reprinted by Permission of SAGE Publications.

'Ghosts and the Sexual Boundary Violation: The Limits of an Idea', Muriel Dimen, unpublished manuscript printed with the permission of the literary estate of Muriel Dimen, 2015.

Images of text edited in Muriel Dimen's hand were provided by the Dimen Literary Estate.

impersonal excitement that underlies psychic process and structure and that seeks discharge. Found among all human beings, it does not observe yet partakes of that natal divide between male and female (about which Freud was sometimes of two minds): although libido is "masculine," it nevertheless manifests in women (if perhaps with a reduced flow).

As a concept, libido does much theoretical work. To condense Person's (1986) admirable summary, it is not only an appetite demanding satisfaction, it has psychological power: It is a force that registers sexual instincts in the mind and thereby partners the emotion of sexual longing. Alternatively conceived, libido is an energy that accumulates to produce a tension Freud calls "unpleasure:" it mounts, surges, seeks release. Existing outside awareness, it nevertheless serves to excite consciousness, there to be transformed into something the psyche wishes to get rid of.

This original and very appealing psychoanalytic solution to the problem of defining or mapping that excess called sex nevertheless fell short of its goal. As Karen Horney (1926) would complain in regard to women's desire (a complaint Freud [1933] himself recognized but tendentiously negated), libido, if only masculine, may obscure more than

Foreword by Virginia Goldner

Muriel always said that Stephen understood her deepest intentions as an author. In this vibrant collection of papers, Hartman has honored Dimen's vision by sending her work around the globe – to be read not only by the 'usual suspects', but also by discussants of all shapes and sizes whose novel subjectivities could be felt making contact with hers.

The results are electric. Instead of Dimen's papers sandwiched in their time and place – slowly but surely becoming 'inert' in Hartman's terms – he has chosen discussants who will infuse her material with Corbett's 'More Life' by positioning her thinking in the 'rough and tumble' of today's present.

In these discussions, gender and sexuality, Dimen's first principles, no longer claim pride of place, since they have been complicated by the toxic hierarchies of race and colorism. 'Whiteness' can no longer be presumed, and it must be critiqued and decentred, a strategy that Dimen would find exhilarating.

Building on/against and from Muriel's work, these discussions ratify her restless sensibility and democratic instincts. She is still here. Talking – but also taking it all in.

Virginia Goldner, co-executor, Dimen Literary Estate and founding editor, *Studies in Gender and Sexuality*

Foreword by Virginia Goldner

Among *Us*

Reading and Writing with Muriel Dimen

Stephen Hartman

Writing matters. Reading matters. Who writes and who reads matters:

> To write means to want to be read. In the same stroke, it means to want to be understood. In the act of writing there is an effort being made; muddled and vague things are combatted, surpassed. It is about not enclosing yourself in wooly dreams.
>
> (Fanon, 2020, p. 166)

> There is a profound relationship between the personal and the political, between private and public life, between individual experience and culture: If you go deeply enough into one, you come upon the other.
>
> (Dimen, 1986, p. xv)

In the opening paragraphs of her 1986 memoire/novel *Surviving Sexual Contradictions*, Muriel Dimen is quick to let us know that she is on to something vital to the future of feminism. Speaking intimately from "author to reader", she takes off from this premise: "personal experience is engrained and contoured by culture; cultural experience is reciprocally informed and maintained by individuals and their personal principles and passions" (1986, p. xv).

With a simple semicolon that is crafted more sharply than a boomerang, Dimen stares down doctrinaire politics (or, in today's argot, virtue signaling) and changes the direction of causality. If you look closely enough at how public life structures private life you discover the importance of personal freedom. Never one to avoid controversy, Dimen elaborates: "Some things got polarized as the feminist movement probed this difficult and sometimes painful problem. Sometimes the personal was simply reduced to the political; the social context suddenly became the sole determinant of individual experience. At other times, the political was subsumed by the personal: Personal life—family, friendships, sex, therapy, personal development—was defined as the only viable reality while the constraints of the social world were all but neglected."

DOI: 10.4324/9781003335252-1

Ever-investigating how personal experience and social engagement reciprocally and recursively weave fabric into life, Dimen goes on to write an experimental memoire that has two narrative voices. The first is an imaginary character whose day, Dimen tells us, the author has invented. She is a character of strong mind, but her mind is also cluttered with the internalized voices of mother, father, friends, colleagues, neighbors, and passersby. Like Dimen, the protagonist is a social scientist and a psychotherapist who lives in New York and teaches at a university. Yes, she is divorced, yes, a feminist and yes, she cares deeply about sex. The events of her day and the fantasies that scroll through the protagonist's mind offer the second narrator, a commentator, the opportunity to examine *Muriel's* day as only an ethnographer or psychoanalyst might.

This narrator, Dimen as commentator, sees the protagonist from multiple points of view. She delves into the contradictions in the protagonist's actions and in her own reactions to them, so her voice (anticipating Dimen's postmodern psychoanalytic approach that will be crafted in the years ahead) has a quality of self-doubt that allows her (and hence the protagonist) room to maneuver as she wrestles with what she believes—given what society allows and given the relative privilege that her position in society provides. The jumble of personal and shared experience that can be theorized in this psychic easement, however tight the space and however prone to tripping over self-doubt anyone trying to hopscotch around an Other might be, Dimen will eventually name this generative space "the psychoanalytic field." At this point in her writing, it is a mine field. Each chapter is a writing experiment of sorts. A theme pops out of a quotidian scene: woman as-subject-as-object; power, gender, and desire; passion's wake; the strange relationship between sex and reproduction; women and hierarchy—each theme is then rendered as a dialogue between Dimen the protagonist, Dimen the author/commentator and, not one to lose track of her reader, Dimen imagining her reader reading her.

Dimen was quite clear that this narrative conceit risked positioning her character as if she were everywoman, a ruse germane to second-wave feminism that united all women in a common agenda. Yet everywoman, Dimen insists launching into her cherished mode of paradox, her character both is and is not. Women are aggregated as everywoman in masculinist fantasies that position females one-down. They are united, also, in certain feminist practices that delink the political from the many personal and sexual differences among women so that women may collectively gain foothold in the fight against patriarchy. True, to speak as everywoman is to take up the cause—but in the process of speaking in generalizations, Dimen finds herself brokering instructive doubts.

True, women share a common bond in experiences of discrimination, but women are also diverse and polyglot members of different races and classes who hail from an array of ethnic and religious backgrounds. Sexuality crosses these divides and, as with gender activism, sexuality can be amalgamated to affirm feminine desire while glossing over sexual difference. Or one register can seem to unite women at the other register's expense. The problem with the assumption that a gender theorist (or a sex advocate) may speak as everywoman, is that categorical *gender* has a way of blanching these differences to normalize hierarchy—volleying privilege to the gender theorist who speaks for, to, and above the theorized from the sought-after, one-up position of equality with men.

Dimen mines the odd pairing of gender and sexuality for contradictions in the first-person plural with the hope that every woman will find her voice within those contradictions. She works paradox here much as Kimberlee Crenshaw (1989, p. 140) parsed legal arguments that miss the mark with respect to Black women due to a failure to consider identity intersectionality: a Black woman on a witness stand will be esteemed female or Black to fit legal scrutiny; rarely can she be both. Crenshaw advocates for an intersectional legal accounting of the subject. She asks for the same nuance in how her feminist colleagues construe *women's* rights. Writing in the same heady moment between second- and third-wave feminism, at this point in her career, Dimen still identified as an academic feminist activist. In the manner that she and Crenshaw differently approach paradox, we can see Dimen edging toward the identity of *clinician* feminist activist.

Crenshaw argued that legal precedent speaks, as often do her feminist and racial justice colleagues, in a manner that denies the unique *compoundedness* of any woman's (and particularly poor Black women's) intersectional experience: "Black women are regarded too much as either like women or Blacks and the compound nature of their experience is absorbed into the collective experience of either group or as too different" from either protected class to merit legal distinction (1989, p. 150). Classification privileges white women and wealthier Black people. *Too different* women, i.e., poor Black women who don't typify the general category of women or Black people, are *intersectionally* erased. Crenshaw's project was to challenge, "the entire framework that has been used as the basis for translating 'women's experience' or 'the Black experience' into policy demands" (1989, p. 140).

Dimen, equally intent on challenging injustices that thrive within the framework of psychoanalysis, focused on interpersonal process. She supported the fight for civil rights at the policy level, but her bailiwick in the session and on the page was an idiosyncratic blend of ideology critique (2004), postmodern suspicion of metanarratives (Hartman, 2006), and Freud's conviction that the "talking cure" forges autonomy by bringing to the fore constraints on agency that are lived internally and reinforced socially (Dimen, 1997). Like her mentor Emmanuel Ghent, Dimen compelled us to dwell in the contradictions we encounter among the various subject positions we intersectionally inhabit, and not rush to resolve them. There, in the thicket of gender's "force field" (Dimen, 1991), Dimen prunes contradictions in our compound desires and identities. Surviving sexual contradictions seeds "the process that would allow one to climb into a new grasp of reality" (Ghent, 1992, p. 135).

Dimen's quest to frame clinical and political priorities with continuous attention to the socio-political and psychic structuralization (Ghent, 1992) of personal experience continues to vex psychoanalytic activists to this day. What one can grasp psychologically and achieve politically are rarely in synch. The intersection of psychic reality and material reality is as doggedly congested as the Oedipus Complex is never-waning (Loewald, 2009). Always on the lookout for room to maneuver, warry that the script falsely pits infinite regress vs. intervention and self-referential melancholia vs. an idealized picture of mourning, Dimen opted for a both/and. She took up pen and paper and put the protagonist of *Surviving Sexual Contradictions* to work. When Dimen the author of her readers' read espies Dimen the commentator speaking as everywoman, she volleys space on the page back to Dimen the protagonist who is then summoned to fumble or notch herself down in a way that opens space for difference.

It unfolds like this. Dimen the theorist has been waxing authoritatively about homophobia and heterosexual privilege. Her argument reaches its crescendo as she voices liberal cliches such as: "We all have trouble with intimacy" and "homophobia is harmful to all women whether straight or gay" (1986, p. 167); whereupon Dimen quickly course corrects.

No, some women face obstacles to intimacy that are encoded in cultural tropes such as the interpellation "dyke." Dimen adds: "Recoiling from part of their own possibility, women recoil from each other, thereby being deprived of the empathy and care underlying adult strength that women are trained to provide and of the solidarity generated when women group together to contest their second-class citizenship" (pp. 167–168). To sculpt the field of shared difference, Dimen turns to her protagonist who we find chatting about hairy legs and pantyhose with a dyke friend who is soon off to a party at a lesbian sex club.

Dimen has been flirty within the heterosexual zone of safety. The friend is nervous about the much-anticipated sexual adventure and wonders aloud if she should go to the party? Dimen reassures her: "'Absolutely,' I pat her shoulder for emphasis. 'It's the only way I'm going to find out exactly what goes on in them.'" (Dimen, 1986, p. 168). Neither woman has yet to take in that Dimen's quells sex panic by pulling rank. The friend wishes Dimen could come along assuming that she will not. Dimen tells the story of her first time in a lesbian bar, "I thought I would be raped or something, but, you know, for the first time in my life I thought I was accepted for just who I was" (p. 186). Ouch! Suddenly, the protagonist hears it, the friend hears it. Dimen and the friend work it out. Will we? Or will the banner of "we are all the same" blind us to the important safeguards in gender and sexuality that work to ensure we may not?

Sometimes mother or some other pesky internal critic is summoned to shatter everywoman Dimen's pretense. Sometimes, a simple contradiction in a thought bubble does the trick ('how dare that man in the street cat-call me. I'm a woman!'—exciting though it somehow was). Dimen plumbs her contradictions to sculpt personal and political freedom. Her two characters, one emergent in a novel, the other entrapped in a memoire, are bruised intimates to be sure. The take-down and the stand-back up that happens when the personal and the political collide, when the writer imagines herself in the position of the reader while also granting the reader her alterity, is for Dimen the work.

It's the work in the session and it's the work on the page. The matrix of contradictions that bring the compoundedness of identity to consciousness, this is the parched yet fertile ground where Dimen skillfully plants her flag in *Surviving Sexual Contradictions.* She will explore that space of encounter throughout a long and influential career. In time, barely speakable paradoxes that inhere in rogue bodies and sexual boundary violations will preoccupy Dimen (2000; 2011). Over time, she will draw closer to Crenshaw's intervention at the level of professional practice guidelines (Dimen, 2016). But for now, Dimen's task is an experiment in reading and writing that is an intervention in the social writ of a day in a life.

And such is a day in the life of an intellectual, white, Jewish, divorced professor, Dimen tells us, when a seductive male student flirts shamelessly with Dimen after class just before an exam he is otherwise doomed to fail. Lest the author or reader protest before imagining the mix of emotions the protagonist feels at that moment, a college friend of the narrator's surfaces from the collective unconscious to explode outrage by way of paradox. That friend worked sex to her advantage—though our protagonist isn't sure, was it to her advantage? Dimen as commentator steps in to note that there are women who "fuck their way to positions of power." Right then Dimen the protagonist walks into the department office and finds herself in a tilt-o-whirl when the handsome department chair one-ups the student whose hapless seduction he writes off as a lark, one-upping the boy so he may come-on to Muriel himself: let him off the hook, he advises with wink and nod, he's just a kid (unlike me who'd rather fuck you than hear about this insult). Obviously annoyed but also empowered by flirting back, Dimen invites the chair to read a draft of her paper, "Sexism and Authority in the Classroom." He hedges: "Sometimes I think you girls, sorry women, hate men," adding insult to injury (Dimen, 1986, p. 81). To which off-kilter Dimen chortles, "sometimes, I, we do."

Shame swirls and Dimen tries to recover by assigning the department secretary a rather menial task. It's the same assignment that the (probably) POC woman secretary has just agreed to perform for her (white) male boss. In the social climate of 2022, race would no doubt be an entry point to this scene. But in 1986, gender seemed to Dimen a more potent way to deconstruct the power relations that blanket microaggressions with a flavor of obviousness.

Dimen first turns to the secretary as a kindred female ally. Against her better judgment, Dimen asserts an inchoate brand of racial privilege by diverting the narrative to domesticity. This backfires, allowing the secretary to decline the request leaving Dimen high and dry. The protagonist is at first miffed, but she recovers by excoriating herself. Perhaps the secretary is overwhelmed by responsibilities *at home* (Black) and can't quite keep up with *her job* (white)? More shame and more circumspection: the domesticity angle might boost Dimen up the professional ladder, but it also universalizes the pair by locating their *pas de deux* in a woman's rightful place. Race and class go mostly unmarked because Dimen's layered tale is framed as a story about how gender fails to unite women who, indeed, have different needs. But race and class are prominent in Dimen the commentator's overriding critique. Catching the narrator having spoken as everywoman, Professor Dimen quickly chastises her for assuming privilege within the relatively safe and more elastic discourse of hierarchy among women at the racialized secretary's expense.

No fool when it comes to her own contradictions, and no apologist either, Dimen the commentator attempts to clean up this mess. There are hierarchies like gender that offer mobility within limits that can be stretched; and there are hierarchies like race that are obdurate and unremitting. When normative discourse compels "social reproduction" (Dimen, 1992, 2004) to ballast patriarchy, one social register often disguises the other's spoils. A "permanent hierarchy" casts women in relations of skin such that, in encounters of competition among women, race goes unmarked and political power may continue to accrue to the wealthy and the white among whom Dimen is enjoined to play professor to the secretary's lack.

Insofar as Dimen and the secretary fall into a social script that seems mundane (the white woman is after all the professor and the Black woman is of course her secretary), we hear here the *obviousness* that Althusser (1971) believed to be the kernel of power's solipsistic logic. Bourdieu (1977) elaborated this sleight of hand structural to the psyche as *the habitus*: "a subjective but not individual system of internalized structures, schemes of perception, conception, and action common to all members of the same group or class" (Bourdieu, p. 86) that renders "cultural capital" to the privileged class in the form of an internal object representation of oneself as normal (Layton, 2020).

In Dimen's vignette, ideology and the habitus are structuralized at the intersection of gender and race. An exchange of sorts takes the place of consciousness: sexuality, class, and race do not need to register in the interpersonal field because this is *obviously* a story about gender. Only when some gendery interaction is examined with Dimen-like precision (a skill Dimen attributed to her training in Interpersonal Psychoanalysis) do we have enough information to portray much of what gender talk elides.

Only then is gender in some sense restored to women. Dimen imagines a day in the life of another woman, a woman of color who is running for the vice-presidency. She "will be patronized, rather than straightforwardly confronted, by her male competitors and will be badgered by the press and public about her family's supposed faults" (Dimen, 1986, p. 78). Dimen's domestication of the secretary comes back to haunt her but her willingness to stay in the scene fosters a keen sense of future struggles. The female professor and the woman candidate may one day meet as professional equals. But the Black woman will be a representative of her domesticated caste; Dimen the white academic may disguise her contradictions by representing all women.

Time to step off the ladder. Trapped between personal needs and political aims, Dimen recounts how the quest for personal power locates women in a matrix of personal and political paradoxes whereupon differences in what woman may achieve mount in an intersectional array (Crenshaw, 1989). Trading places with men in the office would not ultimately supplant the cultural expectation that women be "relational" and men "individuated." Nor will it allow working-class women of color the opportunity to compete as everywoman, writes Dimen heralding nothing less than a revolution. The entire social structure must be taken apart and put back together again, she attests, because "the equal distribution of power and privilege and a fundamentally egalitarian, nonsexist structure of personal relations are mutually contingent...Only when people have no grounds to objectify each other will they no longer objectify themselves" (Dimen, 1986, p. 86–88).

If, for Dimen writing in 1986, a revolution in gender relations precedes a racial reckoning, I think it is fair to assume that Dimen experienced the maneuverability granted to gender to provide more wiggle room than she could easily imagine available in race. It was clear to Dimen that deconstructing gender brokers a new brand of agency that had the potential to stimulate a revolution in how we collectively and individually imagine *Us*. It was not clear in 1986 that racial struggles packed quite the same psychic punch. What we nowadays call "microaggressions," racist slips of the tongue and veiled snafus such as Dimen explored to unpack gender, are bolstered by unremittingly discriminatory material and legal structures that sustain the obviousness of race. Dimen couldn't imagine how a mental operation such as she outlined in 1986 and refined in her distinguished career could gather quite enough psychic heft to spawn the revolution in social consciousness that a newly invigorated feminism just might.

Flash forward and that reckoning, while not yet accomplished, is underway. The genre of memoire/novel that Dimen experimented with at a time when psychoanalysts were wont to share personal stories is now the stuff of book reviews and literary prizes. The form of personal/political interrogation that Dimen deployed in *Surviving Sexual Contradictions* has inspired—and continues to inspire generations of writers for whom personal narrative and political narrative combine to account for much more than collateral aspects of any one person's biography.

Dimen crafted a way of writing about the multivalent and chaotic forces in the interpersonal and intersubjective meeting of minds that allowed those who followed in her footsteps access to an *ultrapsychic* (Hartman, 2019) register: one that documents the relative mobility of psychic life in a zone where the personal and the political collide (*See, With Culture in Mind: Psychoanalytic Stories*, Dimen 2011, as an example). In that space brought to life by Muriel Dimen, Dimen's colleagues and students, many of whose work you will find in this volume, have thrived. Dimen's early writing is both portent and bellwether; it is timeless yet located so that we who read and write may aspire to be, together and each in her own way, revolutionaries. I am because we are and because Muriel was.

*****

The psychoanalytic landscape has shifted significantly since Muriel Dimen asked me to edit a volume of her collected papers, a book that was likely—as she knew with a heavy heart, to be published after her death. It is my great honor to be pairing this collection of six papers by Dimen with six projects by a collection of twenty-nine authors from six continents whose diverse writing practices, generational vantage points, theoretical orientations, and collectivity of life experience assembles here to queer the traditional form of the *collected works* text and to celebrate the incredible breadth of Dimen's visionary practice. Dimen's mastery of style and form is legend, and this collection of "reading and writing experiments" follows Dimen's lead in reaching toward a psychoanalytic horizon that is not constrained by convention nor by disciplinary, generational, or demographic boundaries. The permission to buck tradition, we thank Dimen for.

When Dimen passed away on February 13, 2016, Barack Obama was rounding out his presidency and Donald Trump's imperial ambitions were widely considered a sad joke. The #MeToo and #BlackLivesMatter movements and climate change were potent in the public mind and much discussed in psychoanalytic circles. Yet psychoanalysis, for the most part, carried on business as usual, couch-to-chair in the clinic and paper/discussions/reply in print. All the while, tumbling matriculation rates were giving psychoanalytic Institutes and professional associations cause for alarm. Suddenly, the status quo was circumspect. The general consensus was that "psychoanalysis" must rethink training requirements and recruit a younger and more racially diverse pool of analytic candidates and groom them to become faculty, writers, and journal editors lest the ongoing-being of the Field risk the spoils of irrelevance. Even the most stalwart Classical Institutes advertised a new look. The most venerable psychoanalytic societies and journals scrambled to populate dais and page with fresh faces—BIPOC when possible, more often white allies. I can hear Dimen chuckle at the International Psychoanalytical Association's much debated solution: training requirements for an analytic imprimatur could be relaxed from four to three times per week at local Institutes' discretion. "*Plus ça change*," she often quipped when struck by the fundamental immutability of institutions that claim dominion over practice.

Students of Dimen, whose work is generally charged by "the social" and reads the standard editions with a queer sensibility, began to move among the standard bearers of the Field. Still, peek behind the curtain and, despite the sprawl of Dimen's influence and her students' newfound platform to advocate for an inclusive psychoanalysis, experimentation with content and form—in the clinic and on the printed page—was a rare find.[1] Hasty demographic solutions that were meant to promote diversity and boost matriculation in Institutes began to ring hollow as BIPOC analysts described the pressure to assimilate in psychoanalysis (Gonzalez, 2021). A generation of psychoanalytic activists younger still than Dimen's students hailed a major overhaul of what "psychoanalysis" imagines itself to be given the insular guild that it had for so long been. Soon, a reckoning with Whiteness would churn Institutes right, left and center.

I am confident that Dimen would have joined in the call for the deinstitutionalization of the couch had she lived just a few years longer. She imagined a field comprised of multiple, nonhierarchical systems of practice each recursively invested in—but not determinative of—the other. Following a recursive logic, "the tradition" would be vested in its deconstruction just as the deconstruction of the Field evokes a more richly textured tradition. Francisco Gonzalez (2021) heralds a shift within institutional psychoanalysis from a guild structure that reifies its self-defined interests to a rhizomatic structure that invites multiple streams of psychoanalytic practice (from within and without Institutions) to coalesce in a "trans-mural psychoanalysis." I am sure Dimen would agree that it is a necessary condition for what Daniel Gaztambide (2019) terms a psychoanalysis *of and for* the people.

*****

Tradition lives larger in psychoanalysis than in most academic disciplines. So does hierarchy and generation. Albeit that Dimen worked indefatigably to pave the way for a new cohort of psychoanalytic activists to rise in the field, her vision for this book was fairly traditional. There were to be a dozen or more essays, most of them previously published but not gathered in a single volume. The collection would feature papers on class, gender, and sexuality from her early work and a focus on boundary violation in her later writings. Race and intersectionality were assumed important in several of Dimen's essays as registers within the social matrix, but as I described earlier, race was never Dimen's primary concern. Perhaps indicative of her subject position as a CIS white woman who came of age fighting for civil rights of all kinds, the struggle for racial justice was taken for granted and subsumed under the banner of feminism. The title of her (2003) award-winning book, *Sexuality, Intimacy, Power* speaks to Dimen's overarching interest in how psychic and social registers configure around—and are compromised by—power relations within intimate relations. In the new collection, a devoted reader of Dimen would recognize her trajectory from materialist anthropologist who sought a "Marx-Freud synthesis," to the feminist Foucauldian critic of heteronormative discourse, to the gender theorist intrigued by Laplanche and Stein's exploration of poignancy and enigma in sexuality, to the whistleblower whose life and work were forever changed after she recounted a sexual boundary violation that had occurred thirty years prior in her personal analysis. And, following this trajectory, the book was to be a testament to Dimen's contribution to the field.

Delighted as I was to have Dimen's confidence, I confess that I was apprehensive from the start. Not about Dimen, whose mentorship I cherish, or her writing that inspired me to jump from political theory to psychoanalysis. Somehow, Dimen's proposal for the book felt inert to me. I appreciated that it would be a valuable bibliographic resource, but I worried that the genre of collected works did not reflect Dimen's creative process which took shape, as Dimen (1999) wrote of Freud's footnotes, in the circumnavigation of the official text.

We never discussed my concerns. As Dimen grew increasingly ill and isolated in her New York apartment, I gathered that the solace she took in organizing her files ought not be challenged. She was dying, and this book was her lifeline. I dare not intercede. She would not have tolerated it; nor did I have the bandwidth to intervene. At the time, my life was in complete chaos. My husband was in the throes of his first full-throttle manic episode, and it was all I could do to keep everything we had built over thirty years from falling apart—never mind hold Dimen's legacy in a stack of PDFs. Avgi Saketopoulou and Virginia Golder, Dimen's literary executors, and Adrienne Harris, my editor, were gracious and encouraging as I ploddingly took the time I needed to settle into my appointed task. Then, Muriel died. And then, after six years of fighting for his dignity, my husband jumped to his death. You may have seen Henry before this all happened, sitting with Muriel in the back row of my first Division 39 conference talk beaming with pride. When Henry died, I had to reassess just about everything I ever took for granted. This book has profited from my struggle, and I am grateful for so much support and encouragement from friends and colleagues along the way.

*****

To do Muriel proud, I have changed course.

The mobilization within psychoanalytic communities around race and the phenomenon of disciplinary self-scrutiny located in the question "who speaks" swept across the psychoanalytic landscape after the killing of George Floyd in 2020. It is time to add the questions: "who reads?" and "who writes?" to this inquiry. At the time this book was first being compiled, the question of speaker privilege had yet to garner its current prominence. Psychoanalytic publishing was a rather predictable routine where, except perhaps for books in this imprint led by Dimen's comrade Adrienne Harris and in the journal *Studies in Gender and Sexuality* that Dimen stewarded for over a decade,[2] innovation was a rare event, authorship was notarized with an Institute affiliation, and the whiteness of the page was an oblivious point of departure. "Who publishes where?" was as unasked a question as its answer were obvious: in any given circle of influence, people who paid their dues plus a handful of ambitious upstarts who had the gumption not-to earned the right to print. Alas, the privilege to imagine oneself heard, to cop a phrase from Jessica Benjamin on the fallibility of mutual recognition, is always unevenly realized. "Who publishes?" was answered with a roster of aggregated authors' achievements.

The question "who publishes?" anticipates a break from the past. That said, this volume, still, is only as diverse as my network of contacts allowed me to make it. Perhaps the format I am developing here, inspired by Dimen's own experimentation with genre in *Surviving Sexual Contradictions*, will instigate a change in how the history of psychoanalysis is presented taking account of Dimen's vision and that of thinkers like Franz Fanon who are only now receiving their due.

As I write in the fall of 2021, COVID-19 is resurgent and psychoanalytic conferences still take place online. It seems ages ago that Dimen and her students were a mainstay in the back rows of psychoanalytic lecture halls, huddled with eyebrows akimbo while one or another of the field's illuminati prattle on about some psychoanalytic knot that Dimen had long since untangled. She had done so, to boot, in a tantalizing essay that the presenter had clearly read but never quite digested—which alternatively exhilarated and infuriated Dimen. "When will they learn!" she would audibly gasp with mock impatience—we would giggle—people around us never quite sure if they should "shush!" Muriel or join in the communal hilarity of Dimen's ebullient critique.

I count those moments among my education's finest, and I am ever grateful to Dimen for offering me this opportunity and for helping me advance as a writer and editor. Truth be told, I paid my dues—as did Dimen. We assumed privilege with a sour taste and a grain of salt. When I lived in New York just two blocks from Dimen, our cab rides home from professional meetings often featured banter about the trials and tribulations of filial piety in psychoanalysis. How to pay tribute to Dimen, I have asked myself time and time again, without blithely reproducing the hierarchical system that (I must admit) nurtured us? As I mentioned already, this text is not the text that Dimen imagined. I offer this introduction by way of due diligence, as explanation for why it is necessary to plot new coordinates as, I dare argue, Dimen would have wanted were she not confronting death.

Dimen was generous but precise. As a writer, clinician, teacher, and editor of psychoanalytic texts, she had an expansive view of "what matters" that stretched well beyond the canon. Her range of scholarly interests and curiosity about unconventional approaches reflected her training as an anthropologist who came to clinical psychoanalysis from the academy. Dimen applauded left-turns yet demanded rigor. She adopted a Freudian-relational notion of the unconscious along with Emmanuel Ghent's love for paradox and her clinical supervisor Edgar Levinson's exactitude in traversing the here and now, but she held tight to a cultural materialist read on social context (*See* M. Harris, 1968).

The baby is always already in the bathwater, so to borrow from Winnicott, there can be no baby without bathwater however polluted the bathwater may be with psychic effluvia of capitalism, racism, sexism, and homophobia. Perversely, conversely, and recursively, in the bathwater one may experiment with genre and form. And so Dimen did. Dimen read Lou Aron's visionary text on the internalized primal scene and found in Aron's ode to the infant's unconstrained imagination license to dream up a mutiny in the bathwater. She read Laplanche's description of the "General Theory of Seduction" and took license to dare translate nothing less than the sexual unconscious of Psychoanalysis itself.

Reading and writing are where dreams of revolution reside. So, reading and writing were consequential matters for Dimen, political matters. Dreams are constructed with an Escher-like recursive scaffolding that, like dreams once again experienced in the telling, are ever to be refreshed and reworked, parsed, analyzed, and refined. When one dreams as one writes, this recursive structure enlivens and makes the field, so the stakes are high. Every word counts. Dimen crafted some of our field's most trenchant critiques and visionary texts. Some were traditional papers and discussions. Others, she called *Notes* (2001). There were interviews, roundtables, editorial introductions to books and panels, keynotes, blog posts, op ed docs, and memoires, even fiction: an oeuvre unparalleled in style and generous with form, always noteworthy for its interdisciplinary scholarship and intergenerational appeal.

Those of us who had the good fortune to move from back-row huddle to the dais and then, thanks to Dimen's grooming, to the mastheads of journals understood Dimen's mission full well. In those back-row huddles, we learned that our manner of reading and writing psychoanalysis was a social practice that could change the way people inhabit gender, embody sexuality, and confront deeply personal experiences of class and race to encounter, in

Ken Corbett's apt phrase, "more life." Experiments with form challenge us to craft more space often in fewer words with greater access to affect. Experimentation with affect prompts us to dis-close what and to-whom may be disclosed. "Who speaks?" was for Dimen less a roster than an invitation, albeit one constrained by access to dais and page.

Alas, access to speech is itself a study in recursion. As a discipline, we push ahead, fall back, turn right, pivot left: we inevitably are back to where we started over-and-over again until something new happens. Perhaps this explains why Dimen determined to change psychoanalysis from the inside-out emphasizing the page on which Psychoanalysis both prints and omits who speaks. Harkening one of Fanon's (1955/2020, p. 175) journal entries: "You have to place yourself at the heart of the institution and interrogate it. If it is a generous source, it must enable multiple personalities to be manifest in it." Dimen's milieu, Dimen's community, Dimen's colleagues, her patients and her students, Dimen's readers and editors could only be as generous a source as *The Field* allows. Dimen held tight to the Discipline but championed inter-disciplinarity. All the while, she worried that she had gone too far, too fast, too furious. Had she been too much? Just as recursivity traces a line through Dimen's work, so too do affects stewed in too-muchness and, as we saw in *Surviving Sexual Contradictions*, painful albeit generative self-doubt.

In Dimen's persistent interrogation of a not-always generous forebear, perhaps we hear the influence of Laplanche on Dimen's thinking? Perhaps, again, in Dimen's self-conscious disclosure (call it a "translation" perhaps) of her repeated struggle with too-muchness, a Laplanchean hint about some origin story that helps us configure Dimen's relentless quest to proffer a more generous, creative, fair, and inclusive Field? When too much is too often translated as never enough, can any one person achieve more life? To this end, Dimen turned to the collective. Dimen was keenly aware that our dreams are constrained by historical forces and material conditions that render our subjectivity even as we strive to jump right over them. The question of too-muchness inevitably brings us back to our enigmatic past. But kerning forward, as one does when one types a manuscript, the spaces between words issue a summons: Who do I imagine I am when I speak? To whom do I write? Who reads me? Who do I speak for? Can we be a We? What are the stakes in "talking back" (Sheehi, 2020) to patriarchy given all that has heretofore been ruined or omitted in the Field as, likely also, in any One's life? Dimen was attentive to these concerns *avant la lettre* (to deploy a drole epithet in her uniquely queer argot). Nevertheless, as is inevitably the case, there were blind spots for Dimen. There were also sore spots. This book attempts to heal them as best a book that pays tribute might.

The best tributes have a quality that Katie Gentile (2020) calls *temporal tensegrity* (with a nod to the architect Buckminster Fuller whose tensile forms assemble space softly). Past, present, and future take current shape in a creative tension. Gentile explains:

> like the poles-canvas of a tent that are held in place only with their respective dynamic forces, temporal tensegrity enables a differentiating space within which pasts, presents, and futures, can be distinguished only through generative tensions. These differentiations emerge through the creation of tensions of accumulated times, the tensegrities of pasts, presents, and futures, always multiple.
>
> (2020, p. 142)

Dimen assumed temporal tensegrity and the imbrication of material, social, and psychic life in the assembly of self. So it was, Dimen (1999) explained, that lust meets libido in a tensile structure called *sexuality* that contrives agency from patterns that normative desire abides. And so, Dimen added (2001) with a wink and as a dare, perversion is *Us*.

Were it possible to search all of Dimen's oeuvre for the most often rehearsed phrase, I suspect a taxonomy of Dimen's writing would yield the hashtag: #CreativeTension. With that in mind, my hope is that this volume stands the test of times as it also pays tribute. In the years since Dimen and I first mapped out a collection of essays that she provisionally entitled, *A Field Theory of Its Own* (which eventually morphed into *Theorizing a Field: Psychosocial Landscapes from the Work of Muriel Dimen*), questions linking speech to privilege have gained traction and race has become the bulwark of efforts to chart a polyglot psychoanalysis. Race has become the lens through which we locate ourselves in a creative tension with *the field* much as, for Dimen's generation of psychoanalytic activists, gender and sexuality were the clarion call to progress. Intersectionality commands we note, nowadays and for good reason, what has been included and what has not as we launch our projects given the positionality we occupy at the time of writing. So, the project of a volume of collected works by a beloved mentor has become a collection of six projects, each inspired by a paper written by Dimen. Dimen appears as author and muse. Her interlocutors fill the page with an ear to tradition and an eye toward change. If a not-enough-ness and a too-muchness emerge in the process, so be it.

*****

Lara Sheehi (2020) opens an eloquent essay on decentering normative psychoanalysis by citing Sara Ahmed's *A Compliant Biography* (2019). Ahmed's words harken the conundrum Dimen repeatedly faced while championing innovation from the conference room's back row:

> For some to enter the room, to make a time, not just to proceed but to be there at all, you have to do something or say something that is heard

> as complaint. If a complaint is what you have to lodge, complaint can become a lodge, where you end up residing because residing requires changing how things are being done.

Dimen lodged in the field and no doubt changed it. It was not always a comfortable place, and Dimen was not afraid to dislodge what tradition wrought even when she felt evicted from the loggia of power consequent to her complaints.

In her late work, Dimen expressed a mix of determination and sadness that she insisted be represented in this book. Like Ahmed, Dimen accepted the psychic cost of talking back to power in psychoanalysis, and not without apprehension. Throughout her career, she lodged in the often-claustrophobic space where intimacy and power collide at warp speed even as she, paradoxically, held power and shared intimacy. As a clinician and scholar, Dimen parsed these terse moments for clues to map the democratization of intimacy. A private person who was determined to be never-shy, she reveled in a style of writing that maps affects both punchy and punched. Her writing has a "bring it on!" quality and Dimen was, no doubt, a force to reckon with. That said, those of us who knew her well remember how easily hurt Muriel could be when worry that her provocations had been misread and misunderstood overshadowed her achievement. Dimen carried on nevertheless; it was worth the psychic cost. Dimen's critique staged a battle for a future when no woman or queer or a person of color in psychoanalysis would ever to be consigned to the conference hall's back row.

Sheehi reminds us that the back row nonetheless long had a surfeit of empty seats that ought-yet be filled. In an eloquent credo in *Studies in Gender and Sexuality* (2020), Sheehi insists that the ideologically and systemically unseen warrant notice. By orienting our speech, locating our privilege, and grounding ourselves in the present-absences that haunt the field in plain sight, Sheehi occupies the position of critic with a lens on *the becoming* that is always already present in omission. Among that which marks any "*field of its own*" (Dimen's original title for this book) there are unheard rhythms to be accounted for, liminal elements among present company whose present-absence points to an elusive "in-common" (Mbembe, 2017) as well as the material and psychic damage that othering wrought. Dimen demanded that the sonorous voices of the queer and exiled be heard in the affects and "perverse" practices that those who are excluded bring to bear in the art of everyday suffering. Her version of "field theory" presumed the body's location in culture even while it was becoming *de rigueur* among Dimen's contemporaries to sculpt meaning in a space liminal to material culture at the juncture of container and contained. Dimen resisted this trend, and I believe it is possible to gather how Dimen would have addressed the problem of "who speaks" with reference to how she constructed "the field" in her theorization of boundary violation.

In Bionian Field Theory as in Laplanche's General Theory of Seduction, culture and material relations are bracketed in the service of an unconscious that is by-definition unknowable. Whether because of "containment" in the Bionian model or "unconscious intromission and implantation" for Laplanche, the individual only becomes articulate in relation to an Other's absent presence. To this end, the unconscious remains "unknowable" and the emphasis shifts from *knowing* to *translation*, that is from certainty to experience. Dimen admired theories that shift the psychoanalytic emphasis, in Ogden's account (2019), from an epistemological preoccupation to an ontological immersion in being-with an Other. Yet Dimen questioned *the ontological* turn's tendency to write the material body and, by extension, the body's position in culture out of primary experience. While she was intrigued by the search for meaning in relational space, she insisted on the body's received wisdom through its location and dislocation in culture. To bracket culture for the sake of "containment" or to foster efforts to fill in the gaps of a "hollowed-out transference" with silence is itself an act that rewrites history.

Gender and race are neither essentially true nor experientially found out for Dimen, they are recursively invested with meaning by the experiences that shape them and the disciplines that study and regulate them (Foucault, 1977). Embodiment greets us before we first come into the world. There is no being prior to memory and desire and no unconscious that lacks the footprint of the collective. In her proposal for this book, Dimen used a phrase that I that I coined to summarize her position on field theory (Hartman, 2021): "the body knows the mind's *rest.*"

The rest is an intentionally arcane and enigmatic synapse where the body holds cultural experience as it provides entry to "the field." In so being, *the rest* is the embodied flash point of experience, not the code used to translate experience but an inescapable aspect of perception itself. *The rest* is where too-muchness meets regulatory discourse in a dance with one's othered Self. Its boundary is ever unstable and restless, porous, or gilded by fate of enigmatic design. Dimen's "field theory of its own" relies on temporal tensegrity so as not to start the clock with a conceptual ruse of an unknowable unconscious and thus confuse the anxiety of influence for the boundary between self and other wherein "relation" happens (as in Civitarese & Berrini, 2022).

To describe a space denuded of culture and body as "relational" led, in Dimen's mind, to "the primal crime" of boundary violation (2015, this volumn, p. 167). Minus attention to sexuality, intimacy, and power, field theory turns its back on the speaker who speaks (whatever gobbled-gook they may have to say) in favor of the speaker who speaks-to the analyst with "symbolic" coherence. The scene of container/contained, thus risks inventing a field that demonstrates a patient who speaks, as did Dora, to a storm in her head and an author who, like so many in our lineage (Dimen & Harris, 1999) pays his dues to the institution that publishes him—an author who having been spoken-to and given voice to an Other, renders the patient's symbolic speech a product of analytic technique.[3]

By contrast, Dimen's *field of its own* finds relationality in psychosocial, which is to say, psychosexual commerce. The field is always already vested in a minefield of representations prior to first attempts at symbolization in the primal scene (Aron, 1995; Hartman, 2021). Even in its unrepresented form, this first psychic bonanza bonds one person to a social unconscious that parries more affect than a lone subject can communicate, more meaning than can be linked-to in a well-contained mind-field. The field is a "not yet embodied, not yet conscious, not yet symbolized movement among, toward and away from desire" that is in creative tension with an all the while embodied, acculturated and material body that is saturated with meaning (Hartman, 2020, p. 152).

What makes Dimen's version of field theory so clinically and politically astute is that Dimen links the in-between space wherein we observe *Who Speaks* to the boundary trouble (in psyche: mind, body, and culture) where *Who Speaks* is always already vested in what happens(ed). Dimen thus charts a deeply charged moment in the desire to speak or touch when a rupture between *who* and *speaks* is potent enough to map who may and/or does (not) speak (Saketopoulou, 2014). This is the transformational moment that Dimen recounts in her encounter with Dr. O. It's the moment that Guralnik and Simeon (2010) describe when the subject of interpellation sees herself in the I/eye of power (Foucault, 1980). Dimen believed psychoanalytic writing must chart the space in which it is possible to locate a mind of its own in creative tension with everything that censors what might have come to be said be its articulation preempted by parental interference, edict of the State, the "analytic police," the "normative unconscious" (Layton, 2020), traumatic dissociation, whiteness, etc. etc. in the service of desire. To be with others in-relation requires we flounder in the fields of *one's* own.

Dimen's field work looks like this. One minute a patient is a wordless plethora of disjointed affect; the next, they name Dimen the "landlady of time" (Dimen, 1994, p. 92). *Recursion* is the accelerator of this paradox: the flip side of airtight containment that animates insight except, that is, when dissociation holds sway. Recursively, the psychic makes the social which makes the psychic which makes the social in an ongoing chain of gestures among mismatched registers of meaning that are inflected with dynamics of who gets to speak about what just happened not to mention who pays for it. Dimen ardently believed there could be no psychoanalysis that brackets out the culture that imbricates the subject in a recursive array of experiences that are configured object-relationally and ranked intersectionally. When this is well described, theoretical inquiry and clinical experience recursively animate one another, giving psychoanalysis an ethical place in the public mind. For this location to command respect, it must demonstrate respect. Adamantly, Dimen urged we never forget "what psychoanalysis is only now starting to get: culture saturated subjective experience. Indeed, it is the business of psychoanalytic practice to document this approach to treatment" (Dimen, 2011a, p. 4).

These social known-unthoughts (to flip the couch on Bollas and on the current trend to prioritize negative capability in Bionian Field Theory) preoccupied Dimen. She was determined to expose them. When Dimen and I revisited the twenty or so papers that she intended to group in this volume, her goal was for *the field* to see *what* had been missing in plain sight. There was plenty that she tried to show us about plain sight that we had somehow missed. She died before the discourse shifted—ever so slightly and yet ever so tremendously—to an emphasis on *whom* the field had been missing in plain sight. Were Dimen alive today, I am certain she would see these blind spots as recursive twins: the what-missing marking the whom-missing so that whom-missing brings us back to the what-missing.

*****

This introductory essay works with Dimen's manner of hopscotching between self-reflection and theory building in style of what has come to be known as auto-criticism, a genre that Dimen penned in *Surviving Sexual Contradiction* long before the genre's current vogue. What follows is a collection of six projects, each a reading and writing experiment inspired by a paper of Dimen's, with teams of readers/writers constructed to evoke themes illustrative of Dimen's orientation to her readers, colleagues, students, family, and friends.

When I contacted the authors who graciously agreed to participate, I explained that the task was neither to write an authoritative text about Dimen, nor to feel confined to her text as they charted their own course. Each team was given a text to take off from and a format to write in. Beyond that, experimentation was the mission and Dimen the muse. Among *Us*, and with Dimen, we undergo a *wild analysis* of reading and writing.

I chose six papers of Dimen's that trace an arc from the 1989 essay, *Politically Correct/Politically Incorrect*, to an unpublished manuscript finished soon before her death in 2016, *Ghosts and the Sexual Boundary Violation*, that finds Dimen wrestling with her legacy. Sandwiched between these two relatively unknown papers are four of Dimen's most influential publications: *Money, Love, and Hate: Contradiction and Paradox in Psychoanalysis* (1994); *Sexuality and Suffering, or the Eew! Factor* (2005); *Inside the Revolution: Power, Sex and Technique in Freud's "'Wild' Analysis"* (2014); and *Rotten Apples and Ambivalence: Sexual Boundary Violations as a Problem of the Group* (2016).

Among the papers, op ed articles, book introductions, encyclopedia entries, and position statements that are missing from this collection are influential essays previously included in Dimen's book, *Sexuality, Intimacy, Power* (2011), published papers that document Dimen's journey *At the*

Crossroads: Feminism, Psychoanalysis, Politics (2004), while *Theorizing Social Reproduction: On the Origins of Decentered Subjectivity* (1992) comments on relational technique best summarized in *Reflections on Cure: I/Thou/It* (2010) and, of course, her masterful essay, *Lapsus Linguae or a Slip of the Tongue? A Sexual Boundary Violation in an Analytic Treatment and Its Personal and Theoretical Aftermath* (2011b) that has recently been republished in a two-volume work dedicated to Dimen's groundbreaking text, *Sexual Boundary Trouble in Psychoanalysis: Clinical Perspectives on Muriel Dimen's Concept of the Primal Crime* (2021a, 2021b), edited by Charles Levin.

As an editor, Dimen's careful read and margin note scrawl are infamous. At the suggestion of Ken Corbett and with the help of Virginia Goldner, co-executor of Dimen's literary estate, this book begins and ends with single-page samples of Dimen's editorial mastermind. The opening image finds Dimen lavishing the margins on a draft page from a typewritten text that Dimen and Goldner (2005) coauthored for the *American Psychiatric Publishing Textbook of Psychoanalysis*, a text that I have been privileged to teach more than a dozen times. The book closes with a page in Dimen's diagrammatic handwriting. Here, Dimen is editing notes from a conversation with Ken Corbett, Muriel Dimen, Virginia Goldner, and Adrienne Harris (2014) that would be published as the roundtable, "Talking Sex/Talking Gender", in *Studies in Gender and Sexuality*. In this fragment, Dimen's pen is alive on the page as editor, friend, reader, writer, admirer, co-conspirator and, speaking for the contributors to this book, legend.

I will introduce each of the projects that respond to a Dimen text with a description of "muse", "readers", and "form" where I explain the assignment as I conceived of it and how I chose the team that took it up. Here, allow me to explain that my goal in assembling teams to work with Dimen's papers was to foster experimentation and dialogue among an interdisciplinary, intergenerational, international, and intersectionally diverse array of readers and writers. This is most evident in Project One, Politically Correct/Politically Incorrect—Redux and Revise. Dimen's paper, first presented in 1984 at a feminist studies conference during her transition from academia to clinical psychoanalysis, was responded to by 13 authors from six continents who each in some way or another identify as a gender activist. Among these authors whose fields of study range from psychoanalysis to critical citizenship studies to anthropology, demography, and sociology, there is also an age range of three generations and an array of race and class subject positions. Katie Gentile took up the challenge of synthesizing this array of voices while also problematizing her role as an editor ever aware, as was Dimen when writing similar introductory texts, of the perils involved in assimilating liminal voices to a master discourse.

Two of the teams were organized to emphasize intergenerational dialogue with a twist. Lisa Buchberg, a psychoanalyst, and Emma Kaywin, a sexual health educator and activist are mother and adult child. In an earlier text (2019), Buchberg and Kaywin experimented with the interview format branching out from commentary on a text by Phillip Roth to an intergenerational meditation on sexuality. I invited them to take up the interview form again here with Dimen's *Sexuality and Suffering, or the Eew! Factor* appreciating that their deep dive into matters of abjection would also highlight the position of mother and adult child in a transgenerational dialogue on sexuality. Their conversation takes the form of a patchwork, recalling how Dimen wove recursive lessons that spring from multiple levels of engagement with the field, the literature, and the world into a collective narrative. Buchberg and Kaywin's subject matter sprawls from Dimen to Julia Kristeva to Monster Studies in search of interdisciplinarity and shamelessness.

Ken Corbett, long an office mate and close companion of Dimen, is a distinguished scholar whose work is widely read in psychoanalysis, cultural studies, and developmental psychology. He joins Daniel Butler, who never met Dimen, in a lively series of "blog posts" inspired by Dimen's Division 39 keynote address on Freud's *Wild Analysis*. Butler, who is completing a PhD in History of Consciousness at the time of this writing and was a clinical supervisee of mine when Dimen and I were first conceiving this book, finds his home in psychoanalysis among millennial voices who are transforming the field as they query its whiteness. He and Corbett share a great interest in thinking about race yet are also attentive to their subject position as CIS white queer men writing about race. Their pairing prompts consideration of the dynamics of race and generational hierarchy among psychoanalysts. Inspired by Dimen's keen interest in the emergence of online colloquia and the increasing use of the blog post thread as a literary form, I asked Corbett and Butler to experiment with the epistolary genre and, as you will see, allow themselves time and space to come to their project in the manner of a blog thread.

Jeff Jackson and June Lee Kwon responded to Dimen's essay on *Money, Love and Hate in the Countertransference* by contributing short fiction inspired by the characters in Dimen's essay. While not trained in psychoanalysis, Jackson has served as managing editor for several psychoanalytic journals. As a fiction writer, essayist, and performance artist, his work has won accolades and awards for its originality and experimental vision. Kwon, a candidate in psychoanalytic training at the New York University Postdoctoral Program, is a staunch advocate for diversity, equity, and inclusion in psychanalysis understood to include social justice work in community spaces. Her forays into fiction and poetry challenge the format of standard psychoanalytic representation. Jackson and Kwon's short stories speak to Dimen's text and to the field at large with wit, disgust, love, and hate in equal measure prompting us to imagine the ongoing life of the patients and analysts who are depicted in psychoanalytic texts as characters indistinguishable from the readers whose emersion in the text reanimates the characters in the context wherein they are read and assimilated to the master narrative of psychoanalysis.

Reading and discussing papers has long been the mainstay of psychoanalytic publishing, and this volume would be remiss not to acknowledge that much of Dimen's enduring contribution adopted the standard journal format. For a project on Dimen's last published paper, *Rotten Apples and Ambivalence* (2016), Velleda Ceccoli and Ann Pellegrini worked from texts that they had earlier presented at a colloquium on Dimen's paper at New York University in 2017. Here, Ceccoli offers what on first gloss seems a traditional precis of Dimen's paper and Pellegrini responds with a canny discussion that locates Dimen in lineage with Foucault and other cultural critics whom Dimen admired.

In a very subtle way, these papers query the traditional format of paper/discussion/reply in response to Dimen's absence. Ceccoli and Pellegrini are keenly aware that the question, "who speaks," is all the more nuanced when one must speak on behalf of someone who cannot reply. The task is to interpret Dimen without displacing Muriel as the author of her own text. Ceccoli speaks at times as if Muriel, understanding all the while that her rephrasing of Dimen remakes Dimen in Ceccoli's words. Pellegrini's self-conscious placement of Dimen in heroic lineage similarly disrupts the manner by which the standard format routes Who Speaks into Who Publishes noting, along the way, Who Cites and, of course, who is remembered. I am reminded of Ahmed's (2019) witty quip about an author who: "sited himself because he cited himself." Ceccoli and Pellegrini are keenly aware of the seduction of citation. They were both dear friends of Dimen's, and the slippery boundary that this project traces between homage and appropriation while also paying tribute is no doubt contextualized by the authors' admiration for Dimen.

Finally, perhaps the most challenging project in this book was also the one I felt most necessary. Dimen tutored many of my generation of psychoanalytic writers in groups that she nurtured tirelessly culminating in the book *With Culture in Mind, Psychoanalytic Stories* (2011). Dimen was keenly aware of group dynamics yet ever determined to keep the focus on reading and writing. To reproduce that tension in the service of a reading and writing experiment by a group, I turned to my own writing group, known among the six of us (Francisco Gonzalez, Orna Guralnik, Julie Leavitt, Jade McGleuphlin, Eyal Rozmarin and myself) as LOC 148. Our collaboration began with choosing which text to work with and proceeded through more than fifteen hours of conversation about Dimen's unpublished essay "Ghosts and the Sexual Boundary Violation: The Limits of an Idea" (2015). Not thinking of this as a "roundtable", LOC 148 transcribed and painstakingly edited the text to enact reading and writing as a group activity. Words of Dimen's guided our quest. She writes: "I do not really know how I came to know I could speak. Once again, I can recount the sequence of events. But the emotional process remains illegible." Legibility being, as LOC 148 experienced through this encounter, a problem of and for the group.

Finally, I am grateful to Adrienne Harris whose afterward note invites ever more experimentation, provocation, collaboration, and diversity in the way psychoanalysis reads and writes.

Notes

1 Community psychoanalysis initiatives that would capture much attention in just a few years were just beginning to coalesce into a movement. *See* Gonzalez and Peltz (2021).
2 Dimen was especially proud when *SGS* published a graphic essay (Reis, 2007): perhaps the first ever in a psychoanalytic journal.
3 This problematic in writing is beautifully explored by McGleughlin (2020), Del Mar Miller (2021) and Leavitt (2021).

References

Ahmed, S. (2019). *What's the Use: On the Uses of Use*. Durham, NC: Duke University Press.

Althusser, L. (1971). *Lenin and Philosophy*. New York: Monthly Review Press.

Aron, L. (1995). The internalized primal scene. *Psychoanalytic Dialogues*, 5: 195–237.

Bourdieu, P. (1977). *Outline of a Theory of Practice*. New York: Cambridge University Press.

Buchberg, L. & Kaywin, E. (2019). *On Misogyny: An Interdisciplinary Mother-Daughter Conversation*. Panel presented at the Congress of the International Psychoanalytic Association, London, July 25, 2019.

Civitarese, G. & Berrini, C. (2022). On using Bion's concepts of point, line, and linking in the analysis of a six-year-old child. *Psychoanalytic Dialogues*, 32: 17–35.

Corbett, K., Dimen, M. Golder, V. & Harris, A. (2014). Talking sex/talking gender: A roundtable. *Studies in Gender and Sexuality*, 15: 295–317.

Crenshaw, K. (1989). Demarginalizing the intersection between race and sex: A black feminist critique of antidiscrimination doctrine, feminist theory, and antiracist politics. University of Chicago Legal Forum, vol. 1, article 8.

Del Mar Miller, K. (2021). A radically open analysis: Writing as wrapping, video as skin. *Psychoanalytic Dialogues*, 31: 528–544.

Dimen, M. (1986). *Surviving Sexual Contradictions: A Startling and Different Look at a Day in the Life of a Professional Woman*. New York: Macmillan.

Dimen, M. (1989). Politically Correct? Politically Incorrect? In: C.S. Vance, ed., *Pleasure and Danger: Exploring Female Sexuality*. Boston, MA: Routledge & Kegan Paul, pp. 138–148.

Dimen, M. (1991). Deconstructing difference: Gender, splitting, and transitional space. *Psychoanalytic Dialogues*, 1: 335–352.

Dimen, M. (1992). Theorizing social reproduction: On the origins of decentered subjectivity. *Genders*, 14: 98–125.

Dimen, M. (1994). Money, love, and hate: Contradiction and paradox in psychoanalysis. *Psychoanalytic Dialogues*, 4: 69–100.

Dimen, M. (1997). The engagement between psychoanalysis and feminism. *Contemporary Psychoanalysis*, 33: 527–548.
Dimen, M. (1999). Between lust and libido: Sex, psychoanalysis, and the moment before. *Psychoanalytic Dialogues*, 9: 415–440.
Dimen, M. (2000). The body as Rorschach. *Studies in Gender and Sexuality*, 1: 9–39.
Dimen, M. (2001). Perversion is *us*?: Eight notes. *Psychoanalytic Dialogues*, 11: 825–860.
Dimen, M. (2003). *Sexuality Intimacy Power*. Hillsdale, NJ: The Analytic Press.
Dimen, M. (2004). Between mind and matter: In search of the Marx/Freud synthesis. *Culture and Society*, 9: 52–62.
Dimen, M. (2005). Sexuality and suffering: Or, the "Eew!" factor. *Studies in Gender and Sexuality*, 6: 1–18.
Dimen, M. (2010). Reflections on cure: Or, "I/though/it". *Psychoanalytic Dialogues*, 20: 254–268.
Dimen, M. (2011a). Introduction. In: M. Dimen, ed., *With Culture in Mind: Psychoanalytic Stories*. New York: Routledge, pp. 1–10.
Dimen, M. (2011b). Lapsus lingue, or, a slip of the tongue?: A sexual boundary violation in an analytic treatment and its personal and theoretical aftermath. *Contemporary Psychoanalysis*, 47: 35–79.
Dimen, M. (2014). Inside the revolution: Power, sex, and technique in Freud's "Wild Analysis." *Psychoanalytic Dialogues*, 24: 499–515.
Dimen, M. (2015). Ghosts and the sexual boundary violation: The limits of an idea. Unpublished manuscript.
Dimen, M. (2016). Rotten apples and ambivalence: Sexual boundary violations through a psychocultural lens. *Journal of the American Psychoanalytic Association*, 63: 361–373.
Dimen, M. & Goldner, V. (2005), Gender and Sexuality. In: E.S. Person, A.M. Cooper & G.O. Gabbard, eds., *The American Psychiatric Publishing Textbook of Psychoanalysis*. Washington, DC: American Psychiatric Publishing Inc., pp. 93–102.
Dimen, M. & Harris, A., eds. (1999). *Storms in Her Head: Freud's Women Patients Revisited*. New York: Other Press.
Fanon, F. (2020). *The Psychiatric Writings from Alienation and Freedom*. New York: Bloomsbury Academic Press.
Foucault, F. (1977). *Discipline and Punish: The Birth of the Prison*. New York: Pantheon.
Foucault, M. (1980). *Power/Knowledge: Selected Interviews and Other Writings, 1972–1977*. New York: Vintage.
Gaztambide, D.J. (2019). *A People's History of Psychoanalysis: Fromm Freud to Liberation Psychology*. New York: Lexington Books.
Gentile, K. (2020). Kittens in the clinical space: Expanding subjectivity through dense temporalities of interspecies transcorporeal becoming. *Psychoanalytic Dialogues*, 31: 135–150.
Ghent, E. (1992). Paradox and process. *Psychoanalytic Dialogues*, 2: 135–159.
González, F.J. (2021) "The Edifice Complex: Towards a Trans-Mutual Psychoanalysis," Plenary Address, Psychology and the Other Conference, Sept 17, 2021.
González, F.J. & Peltz, R. (2021). Community psychoanalysis: Collaborative practice as intervention. *Psychoanalytic Dialogues*, 31: 409–427.

Guralnik, O. & Simeon, D. (2010). Depersonalization: Standing in the spaces between recognition and interpellation. *Psychoanalytic Dialogues*, 20: 400–416.
Harris, M. (1968). *Cultural Materialism: The Struggle for a Science of Culture.* New York, Vintage.
Hartman, S. (2006). Introduction to the roundtable on bringing the plague. *Studies in Gender and Sexuality*, 7: 309–319.
Hartman, S. (2019). Hashtag mania or misadventures in the #ultrapsychic. *Studies in Gender and Sexuality*, 20: 84–100.
Hartman, S. (2020). Introduction to "The Internalized Primal Scene". In: G. Atlas, ed., *When Minds Meet: The Work of Lewis Aron.* New York: Routledge, pp. 48–51.
Hartman, S. (2021). When the body knows the mind's rest. In, Levin, C. ed. *Social Aspects of Sexual Boundary Trouble in Psychoanalysis.* New York; Routledge, pp. 151–174.
Layton, L. (2020). *Towards a Social Psychoanalysis: Culture, Character, and Normative Unconscious Process.* New York: Routledge.
Leavitt, J. (2021). A letter to Kathleen Del Mar Miller: Skin to skin, bone to bone. *Psychoanalytic Dialogues*, 31: 551–563.
Levin, C. (2021a). *Sexual Boundary Trouble in Psychoanalysis: Clinical Perspectives on Muriel Dimen's Concept of the Primal Crime.* New York: Routledge.
Levin, C. (2021b). *Social Aspects of Sexual Boundary Trouble in Psychoanalysis.* New York; Routledge.
Loewald, H. (2009). *Papers on Psychoanalysis.* New Haven, CT: Yale University Press.
Mbembe, A. (2017). *Critique of Black Reason.* Durham, NC: Duke University Press.
McGleuphlin, J. (2020). The analyst's necessary nonsovereignty and the generative power of the negative. *Psychoanalytic Dialogues*, 30: 23–138.
Ogden, T. (2019). Ontological psychoanalysis or what do you want to be when you grow up? *Psychoanalytic Quarterly*, 88: 661–664.
Reis, B. (2007). Fetish: A graphic essay. *Studies in Gender and Sexuality*, 8: 303–311.
Saketopoulou, A. (2014). To suffer pleasure: the shattering of the ego as the psychic labor of perverse sexuality. *Journal of the American Psychoanalytical Association*, 15: 254–268.
Sheehi, L. (2020). Talking back: Introduction to the special edition: Black, indigenous, women of color talk back: Decentering normative psychoanalysis. *Studies in Gender and Sexuality*, 21: 73–76.

Project One

Politically Correct/ Politically Incorrect—Redux and Revise

Project One

Editor's Note

Stephen Hartman

Muse

Dimen, M. (1989). Politically Correct? Politically Incorrect? In: C.S. Vance, ed., *Pleasure and Danger: Exploring Female Sexuality*. Boston, MA: Routledge & Kegan Paul, pp. 138–148.

Dimen's thoughts on political correctness and political incorrectness, published originally in 1984 and reprinted in Carole Vance's 1989 book, *Pleasure and Danger: Exploring Female Sexuality* begins with a provocative vignette. A lover cajoles Dimen up against a wall and slowly and explicitly describes how he is going to fuck her. "And when I'm done," he explains tracing the parts of her body that he imagines needing attention with a drunken hand, "you'll look a lot better" (Dimen, 1989, p. 138). It is all Dimen can do not to laugh at the man's feeble attempt to inscribe doubts about his own sexual prowess onto Dimen's body. Still, she desires him plain and simple despite a feminist embargo on seduction by machismo.

Dimen turns to her audience (who are presumed to be women of several academic disciplines and a variety of ages who can at times feel oppressed by feminist orthodoxy) and asks:

"Question 1. How do you define politically correct?"

She goes on to answer this question plus four more reaching toward the ultimate ask: "what is bad about politically correct ideology and behavior?"

Questions and answers organized in a series of vignettes. This experiment in style and form resembles the way academics often organize presentations as "notes." Notes are a first gloss, often inconclusive, often pointing out research that is yet to be done but all the while alerting us to a problem that needs to be addressed.

Readers

For this project, I have assembled a group of 14 authors from around the world and a variety of academic disciplines whose investment in political correctness finds them at the crossroads of personal and professional

DOI: 10.4324/9781003335252-3

commitment. Like Dimen's presumed audience, they are people whose subject positions at times come in conflict with what is deemed "politically correct." Their task is to collectively offer a picture of what constitutes politically correct and politically incorrect at this moment in a variety of social, political, and academic contexts. Katie Gentile graciously agreed to collate the responses and represent them in some sort of a synthesis—aware all the while that the task of summary is rife with problems of representation.

Form

Authors were asked to write a short note on political correctness and incorrectness such as they might offer at a conference or research meeting. The essays were not intended to be finished or polished but rather works in progress, voices in search of dialogue. During her career as an editor, Dimen wrote several introductions to journal panels and books where her task was to orient the reader to the problem at hand and provide a synthetic overview of the range of contributions. This is a particularly complicated task when the roster of authors is diverse in opinion and life experience, and when the editor's synthetic choices are inflected with questions about the assimilation of minority authors into a master narrative. Gentile's introduction to the project works with this premise. We then present the panelists' contributions in alphabetic order determined by their first name rather than the patronymic family name.

Bios

Fiona Anciano, Ph.D., is Associate Professor of Political Studies, and Deputy Dean of Teaching and Learning, at the University of the Western Cape in Cape Town, South Africa. She researches urban governance and democracy in informal settlements, spending time with students doing fieldwork, to understand how to improve democratic representation and accountability in cities in South Africa.

Katie Gentile, Ph.D., is Professor and Chair of the Department of Interdisciplinary Studies at John Jay College of Criminal Justice (City University of New York). She is the author of *Creating bodies: Eating disorders as self-destructive survival* and the 2017 Gradiva Award winning *The business of being made: The temporalities of reproductive technologies, in psychoanalysis and cultures*, both from Routledge. She is editor of the journal *Studies in Gender and Sexuality*, on the faculty of New York University's Postdoctoral Program in Psychotherapy and the Psychoanalysis and the Critical Social Psychology program at the CUNY Graduate Center.

Griffin Hansbury, MA, LCSW-R, is a psychoanalyst in private practice in New York City. A recipient of the Ralph Roughton Award from the

American Psychoanalytic Association, his writing has appeared in several journals, including the *Journal of the American Psychoanalytic Association*, *Psychoanalytic Dialogues*, and *Studies in Gender and Sexuality.* As an urban critic, writing under the pen name Jeremiah Moss, he is the author of *Vanishing New York* and *Feral City.*

J.R. Latham, Ph.D., is a queer theorist from Melbourne, Australia. His work combines critical concepts of "drugs," ageing and narrative with bioethics, queer theory, and science and technology studies (STS) with a focus on improving healthcare for marginalized people.

Lynne Layton, Ph.D., writes, speaks, and teaches about how the social world is psychically lived, both consciously and unconsciously. She has been a psychoanalytic feminist scholar and activist since the 90s, challenging normative theories and working to create more inclusive psychoanalytic spaces. A member of the Grassroots Reparations Campaign organizing team, she is also an activist in the movement for reparations for African Americans.

Ally Merchant, Ph.D., is a clinical psychologist in New York, USA. She practices and supervises in her private practice, STEPS, as well as in community mental health at Sun River Health. Currently, she is receiving psychoanalytic training at NYU and she seeks to make psychoanalysis and psychoanalytic training available and accessible in the public sector.

Nobukhosi Ngwenya, Ph.D. (c.), is a Junior Research Fellow in the African Centre for Cities, at the University of Cape Town, South Africa. Her research interests include housing, the urban land question, and bottom-up planning praxis.

Shiri Raz, Ph.D., is a therapist for couples and individuals, specializing in work with vegans and mixed couples (vegans and non-vegans) in private practice in Rishpon, Israel. She is an animal rights activist and writer.

Shylashri Shankar, Ph.D., is a senior fellow at the Centre for Policy Research, New Delhi. She is the author of: *Scaling justice – India's Supreme Court, anti-terror laws and social right*; *Battling corruption: Has NREGA reached India's rural poor?*; and *A secular age beyond the West*. Her non-fiction book *Turmeric Nation: A Passage through India's Tastes* won the AutHer award for the best non-fiction in 2020–2021.

Lara Sheehi, Psy.D., is Assistant Professor of Clinical Psychology at the George Washington University Professional Psychology Program. She is a scholar-practitioner and a decolonial abolitionist. She is co-author with

Stephen Sheehi of *Psychoanalysis under occupation: Practicing resistance in Palestine* (Routledge, 2022).

Chana Ullman Ph.D, is a clinical psychologist and training psychoanalyst at the Tel Aviv institute of Contemporary Psychoanalysis. She is a faculty at the school of psychotherapy, and at the doctoral program in Psychoanalysis, Tel Aviv University. She has also been the president of IARPP. Ullman writes about the personal and political and witnessing in Israeli contexts.

Bettina von Lieres, Ph.D., is a scholar and activist teaching and researching in the field of critical citizenship studies at the University of Toronto, Scarborogh. Her publications include *Domains of freedom: Justice, citizenship and social change in South Africa* (co-edited with Thembela Kepe and Melissa Levin, UCT Press, 2016).

Laura Trajber Waisbich, Ph.D., works on citizenship and development issues in the Global South. She is an activist-researcher with an initial training in International Relations and Political Science and a PhD in Geography. Laura is currently affiliated with the Brazilian Centre of Analysis and Planning (Cebrap), the South-South Cooperation Research and Policy Centre (Articulação SUL) and the Igarapé Institute, all based in Brazil.

Joanna Wheeler, Ph.D., is founder and director of Transformative Story and a senior research fellow at the University of Western Cape. She has been working with creative methodologies and critical approaches to participation for the last 20 years.

Politically Correct? Politically Incorrect?

Muriel Dimen

Drink in hand, he leaned against the wall with an air of teasing, self-mocking arrogance, eyes soft from intoxication. His sensual anticipation was all-enveloping. "When we get home, I want to fuck you," he said lovingly. "I'm going to put it in you, and go in and out, in and out, real slow, for a long time." He jerked his hips slightly. "That's how I'll fuck you," he said softly. "And when I'm done, you'll look a lot better." It'll perk things up here, "lightly touching her breasts," and make things smaller here, "patting her waist," and smooth things out here, "caressing her hips."

An ancient ache cramped her thoughts and all she could do was laugh. She wished he were taller and looser. Knowing he was sensitive about his miniature body, she consciously fed his vanity, telling him of the lean precision of his proportions, the beauty of his classic face, the grace of his genitals. Indeed, his body awed her, even as his insecurity stimulated in her a luxuriant contempt. Their love-making was wonderful that night – as always. He did all the work – as always. He was hurt that she was not more grateful.

Which of the following shall we say to the preceding story?

Because men can abuse women in one way or another, women should sleep only with women.

Or, women should educate men not to hurt women.

Or, women should discuss their sexuality in their CR groups in order to understand why they engage in masochistic behavior and get support for not doing it anymore.

Or, if pornography is the theory and rape is the practice, then women should not write stories like the one above, which just encourage rape and are therefore anti-feminist.

This story, and others like it, bring up the question "What is to be done?" It thereby evokes judgments about politics, sexuality, and "politically correct" behavior. We may put five questions to the issue of politically correct/incorrect behavior:

Question 1: How do you define politically correct?

Answer: Politically correct is an idea that emerges from the well-meaning attempt in social movements to bring the unsatisfactory present into line with

DOI: 10.4324/9781003335252-4

the utopian future, in fact, to make the "revolution" happen. Although ideas about what is acceptable behavior develop in any political organization, left or right, the express phrase, politically correct, seems to be associated with the left. The phrase is charged, because the left, in its conception of itself, stands for freedom, yet finds itself in a contradictory situation: in order to realize its goal, it finds itself telling people how to behave and therefore interfering with their freedom.

Politically correct behavior, including invisible language and ideas as well as observable action, is that which adheres to a movement's morality and hastens its goals. The idea of politically correct grows naturally from moral judgments (which any political ideology or philosophy contains) that deem certain aspects of the present way of living bad. It is this moral evaluation that fuels visions of better ways of living and energizes attempts to realize them. In the light of the resulting politico-moral principles, certain behaviors and attitudes can come to seem not only "bad," because they are harmful to society or to people, but "wrong," because they hinder social transformation.

Question 2: What is politically correct?

Answer: I don't know: anything, including seeming opposites, can be correct in different groups, movements, or societies. The Talmud requires intercourse; the Shakers prohibited sexual activity; Marx, Engels and Freud celebrated (but did not practice) monogamy; Bohemianism advocates promiscuity and multiple sexualities, but disdains fidelity.

The ideology of political correctness emerges in all sorts of movements, applying to behavior, social institutions, and systems of thought and value. For example, various socialist and utopian movements have identified the nuclear family as a breeding ground for a socially destructive individualism, and propose communal living because it would promote a collectivist spirit. At various periods in Western history, then, social movements have instituted communes as a desirable first step in creating the good society they envisioned for the future. In the 1960s (which spilled into the 1970s), certain sectors of the left found the nuclear family and its bedrock, monogamous heterosexual marriage, to be both bad and wrong, i.e., politically incorrect, while communes and non-monogamy (for which no positive term ever developed) came to seem good and right, that is, "left," in other words, politically correct.

The appearance of political correctness in feminism creates a contradiction. One of feminism's tenets is an individualism (sometimes bourgeois, sometimes anarchistic) that proclaims self-determination for women, translating into "every woman for herself." However, feminism is also a mass movement based on collective struggles against the state in such areas as reproductive rights and the workplace. Such a political movement can be successful only if it is founded on shared moral and political principles. In some sense, it is this movement that constitutes the social context which makes feminism's individualistic principles possible. It is not feasible, however, for both these tendencies, one toward the individual, the other toward the social web, to be simultaneous guides to politically correct behavior.

Feminists have made judgments about political correctness particularly in the area of sexual behavior. This is because of the special cultural tension between sexuality and feminism: desire, of which sexuality is one very privileged instance, pushes and pulls at all people. Yet because it is in the domain of the subjective, desire tends to be associated with things female in the patriarchy of the twentieth-century nation-state where women, subjectivity, and sexuality share the same symbolic space. This shared symbolic space creates a second contradiction for feminists. On the one hand, since women have been traditionally defined as sex objects, feminism demands that society no longer focus on their erotic attributes, which, in turn, feminism downplays. In this way it becomes politically correct not to engage in any stereotypically feminine behavior, such as putting on make-up, wearing high heels, shaving legs and arms, or coming on to men. On the other hand, because women have been traditionally defined as being uninterested in sex, they have been deprived of pleasure and a sense of autonomous at-one-ness, both of which are necessary to self-esteem. Feminism therefore demands sexual freedom for women. In this way it becomes politically correct for women to be sexual explorers, visiting, if not settling down in, homosexuality or polysexuality; experimenting with cock-sucking or anal intercourse or tantric sex; trying out orgies or, perhaps, even celibacy. In consequence, these judgments about the correct path are as contradictory as the situation which gave rise to the feminist critique in the first place.

Question 3: Why do people want to say and do politically correct things?

Answer: Politically correct ideology and behavior are attractive, because they proceed from acute and visionary perceptions of political oppression. If people create visions of what is good, it seems sensible and self-respectful to try to live them out. Politically correct ideology and behavior attempt to escape the manifestly harmful, and to avoid things that damage, even if they feel good. In addition to these rational reasons, there are irrational forces which motivate political correctness, springing, for example, from the fear of separateness that makes conformity compelling. Conformism, present in any social group, can have an important role in making members of out-groups feel selfrighteously stronger.

Question 4: What is good about politically correct ideology and behavior?

Answer: It is empowering; by psychological and ideological means, it creates the space for people to organize politically. It becomes a basis for organization and communication between people so that political structure may thrive. It also disrupts the identification with the aggressor, dispelling an individual and collective sense of victimization and providing a shared vision that guides behavior. Finally, it taps into a deeply rooted wish to belong to a collectivity in which what one desires to be is also moral to be.

Question 5: What is bad about politically correct ideology and behavior?

Answer: When the radical becomes correct, it becomes conservative. The politically correct comes to resemble what it tries to change. For it plays on the seductiveness of accustomed ways of living, the attractiveness of orthodoxy. Its social armoring can lead the person away from self-knowing authenticity and the group toward totalitarian control. It makes a misleadingly clean cut between personal experience and old, but still powerful, social practices, and draws a misleadingly neat circle around experience and a new set of supposedly completely acceptable practices.

The application of politically correct ideology and behavior to sexuality therefore founders on a double contradiction, the first in the relation between person and society, and the second in the relation between conscious and unconscious forces. The discovery/creation of sexual pleasure is very much an individual journey, even as your craft pushes off from received notions of gender, and is sped on or becalmed by concurrently developing notions of what is possible and permissible. No matter how carefully charted by conscious intentionality, the journey's course is determined finally by a complex mix of conscious and unconscious, rational and irrational currents that represent a swirling together of personal desire and cultural force.

Her tongue slid along the soft involuted folds of her labia. Her tongue slid along the soft involuted folds of her labia. She licked her clitoris; she licked her clitoris. They came together, not knowing who was who.

"Your name came up," she said, later, "but I told them I didn't want you in the group." "Why not?" she asked. "Because I want to keep my personal life and my public life clearly differentiated."

Sexuality is simultaneously highly individualized and highly socially constructed, subject to will and at the mercy of compulsion. Erotic sensation, like any feeling, is experienced personally. It is as idiosyncratic as any aspect of character, perhaps seeming even more so because spoken language, the means of adult communication, is so poor a vehicle for sharing bodily experience and its meaning. Yet sexuality, like character, is socially contextualized. The overt rules that shape sexual possibility, form, and feeling are common knowledge, but they are made more compelling by almost invisible, nearly insensible politico-moral judgments. For example, the incest prohibition is familiar enough, yet it is less commonly recognized that the heterosexual, Oedipal taboo presumes a prior, unspoken one on homosexuality.

The 1960s produced a critique of the privatization of sexual experience, which our society portrayed as both unique and unmentionable. Privatization isolated people from each other, leaving them to feel alone in the confusion that arose in the space between what they wanted and what they were supposed to want. Privatization prevented change, it was thought, because it encouraged people to act individually on what seemed to be their own idiosyncratic, personal problems originating in specific family histories. The critique examined the social construction of personal sexuality, and envisioned one more open, including openness to multiple desires in oneself and to others' experimentation, open public discussions of sexuality, and open relationships (non-monogamy, swapping, group sex).

For sexuality is by its nature an experience that benefits from a stance that anything goes, that any avenue may (but not "must") be explored. Erotic pleasure mushrooms when there are no musts. But this accessibility means that sexual experience can be affected by anything. Sexual intimacy is too generous an experience to exclude anything, including the forces of the unconscious and the forces of hierarchy. When you get into bed with someone, you bring all of you: your past, remembered or forgotten; your present, including parts of it which you think your rational mind can keep out; your hopes for the future. Sexual intimacy is therefore particularly resistant to rules of political correctness, or, rather, when it succumbs to rules, passion disappears. Its very non-rationality allows the politically incorrect to enter.

The sexual explorations of the 1960s ventured often into homosexual desires. Lesbianism, spurred on by the radical and feminist critiques of sexuality, emerged as a public, empowering, and passionate option for many, despite overt and covert homophobia in major branches of the bourgeois women's movement. The judgment that patriarchy contaminates heterosexual relations suggested that homosexuality was the safest and most enhancing form of erotic experience (a form that, for the previous generation, represented the most frightening, yet most intriguing, variety of bad and wrong sexuality). Indeed, by contrast with the pain and anger infusing most straight relationships, lesbian ones came to seem idyllic, promising the realization of honesty, equality, mutuality, and love, in the midst of a dishonest, disloyal, hierarchical, and hate-filled culture of death. To have believed this promise, however, that any relationship could be Edenic in a hellish culture, was to have forgotten what the 1960s said: the personal is political. Since social rules, structure, and language shape not only social interaction but personal experience, which accumulates as people mature, rational conscious will may not be their best adversary. What may be required as an effective adversary is the force of irrational passion, sexual and otherwise, unearthed from the repression/oppression of past and present.

She is 8. Her father, 41, and her brother, 5, are about to take a shower together. "Me, too," she cries, eager to see her father's genitals. "No, no, dear, little girls don't take showers with their fathers," says her mother, 40. Since when? she wonders. She knows what she wants. They know too. Do they know that she knows that they know that she knows?

In seventh grade, if you wear green on Thursday, they call you a dyke. If you wear a black sweater any day, they call you a whore. Somehow, she forgets and wears green on Thursdays and black sweaters when she likes. At a party in a suburban basement rec-room, she finds herself suddenly alone, the only girl in the room, when the lights go out and all the boys jump her and feel her up everywhere you can imagine. The girls giggle in the laundryroom.

A girl from another crowd tells her she looks nice in her black sweater. They become friends, sort of. She sleeps over at her friend's house one night. They bake chocolate chip cookies and listen to opera. Later her friend invites her into her bed to do what her friend's crowd has been doing for a while. She feels nothing, is frightened, and goes back to her own bed.

She starts kissing boys on the mouth at 11 and likes it a lot. She doesn't pet above the waist with boys until 15; she doesn't like it but does it anyway to be grown up. She won't pet below the waist until 17; then she doesn't want to admit that she likes the orgasms.

She starts masturbating at 18. At 23, she has intercourse for the first time; she likes the fact that she's doing it; it takes her 15 years to like doing it.

The crisis of self vs society explodes in sexual experience. Sexual arrangements provide an important set of terms by which we negotiate, as we mature, the relation between who we are and want to be, and who we are told and allowed to be. The negotiation is complex and long, indeed unending, because sexuality is multi-faceted and changes with age. Notions of political correctness therefore constitute psychological footbinding.

As a married woman, she is monogamous and heterosexual for 15 years.

She and a woman friend have a seemingly endless series of seemingly emergency discussions about whether the two of them should sleep together.

She keeps wondering why she is so scared to have an affair.

She has a one-night stand with a man and feels liberated. Her marriage ends.

She becomes promiscuous.

She imagines that every affair will end in marriage and children.

She loves men even when they hurt her.

"I love to fuck with you," she says to her. "We don't call it fucking, my dear," the other one answers.

Gender should not exist and everyone should sleep with everyone and everything.

Commitment is possible and necessary.

Erotic experience is extraordinary, lying somewhere between dream and daily life. Although sex is not amenable to mechanistic tinkering, it is not as safely private as dream (which, fortunately, cannot be controlled by political fiat). When you try to change passion piece by piece, it dissipates. Sexuality therefore differs from those domains, for example, politics or housework, in which it may make sense to pull behavior into line with ideology. Part of what makes sex tick is its very irrationality. It brings the crazy passions of infancy into adult experience, a welcome relief, much like that brought by dreams from ordinary, rational, waking control.

Sexuality lies between things; it borders psyche and society, culture and nature, conscious and unconscious, self and other. It is intrinsically ambiguous. Ambiguity confers on sexuality an inherent novelty, creativity, discovery, and these give it its excitement, its pleasure, its fearsomeness. Sexual experience entails loss of self-other boundaries, the endless opening of doors to more unknown inner spaces, confusions about what to do next, or who the other person is, or what part of the body is being touched, or what part of the body is doing the touching, or where one person begins and the other ends. This is sometimes pleasurable, sometimes painful, always unsettling.

Ambiguity makes sex difficult to deal with. Take, for example, part and whole relations with which we play in sex, sometimes being or relating to a part – a breast, penis, buttock – sometimes being or relating to wholeness. Parts and wholes come in bodies and in social roles. Infants have no conception of another human as a whole being. Mother, for example, is solely the nurturer, not the scientist or secretary or dreamer or lover she may be to the adults whom she knows. Were an adult to treat her in terms of only one part, it would be cruel, thoughtless. Adulthood, in our society, ideally entails seeing the other's multi-dimensionality. Adulthood also includes being receptive to one's own multi dimensionality which paradoxically includes the parts left from infancy, such as the interest in and the ability to relate to parts. Therefore could not adulthood include in some enriched way this lost aspect of the self?

Women are taught to relate to sexuality as whole beings in a society that celebrates parts, for example, measuring women by their breasts and men by their penises. "Women are so nice," my analyst once observed, "they never say, 'You call *that* a penis?'" Whereas men can and do ask for better breasts, hips, thighs. Now, this expectation of thoughtful, feminine wholism may have hampered women's exploration of their own and others' parts, as well as their feelings about them. To the degree that this expectation becomes politically correct for feminists, it may limit each woman's exploration of herself.

More: perhaps the ability to make part-objects of others, to take the part for the whole, can be helpful in coming to know and manage the world. For example, my friend Peggy says that the best way to get rid of a flasher is to say, "Oh, that looks just like a penis, only smaller."

Still more: perhaps this ability can be fun. For example, what does it feel like to make part-objects of men? Here is a preliminary classification from years of crotch-watching:

1 A slight bulge just to one side of and two-thirds of the way down the fly
2 A long, skinny cylinder slanting across the fly almost to the other thigh
3 A loose dangle way down the inner thigh
4 A horizontal ridge straight across the bottom of the fly
5 A faded spot right next to the bottom of the fly
6 A little bump centered on a little hump
7 A big bump centered on a big hump
8 Gay fourth button bulge
9 Tight with no bulge at all
10 Preppy-loose, denying everything
11 Packed so full, with so little differentiation, you wonder if it's real

12 A neat round wet spot which dries quickly after he returns from the bathroom
13 Huge balls stretching the pants on the thigh; you can see this as he sits with his legs spread on the subway.

Here are some feelings I had watching these crotches: Curiosity: what exactly lay beneath the blue denim, the chinos, the wool? Excitement: what might be the relation between surface, contents, and performance? Empathic discomfort: do they feel as ambivalent about being observed as we do? Shame: you are not supposed to poke into people's private business.

The whole is greater than the sum of the parts. But the more we know of the parts, the more we know of the whole. The clitoral orgasm became public knowledge in 1969 because feminism made it so. But then the clitoral orgasm became the only politically correct orgasm to have, consequently foreshortening exploration and, at best, confusing, at worst, marginalizing, those who had a different experience. Now the news of the G-spot makes it seem like there is some truth to reports of the vaginal orgasm after all.

Within the movement, it is easy for the socially correct – monogamy or nuclear families or vaginal orgasms – to be denounced as politically incorrect; for the socially incorrect – promiscuity or polysexuality or clitoral orgasms – to become politically correct; and for the once-correct, now-incorrect to disappear from politically correct history. To take another example: the conference offered no workshops on sex in a longterm relationship, perhaps suggesting its political incorrectness. Long-term monogamous relationships are sometimes taken as models of wholeness, which they most assuredly are not. But an awful lot of people live in them even while wanting out, and an awful lot of people who are out want in, even when they know better.

Indeed, sexual ambiguity may be responsible for the sexual boredom that sometimes emerges in long-term relationships. This boredom is born of the fright we feel when we reach the end of the routine pathways to intimacy, and the unknown looms before us. In thus confronting the problem of creation and of the new, we become anxious and then, to calm ourselves, bored. It is hard for us to go off into the emotional wilds with another person, because we are socially and psychologically stunted in ways, and due to forces, too complex to go into here. However, given that it is difficult to connect with anyone at all, it is not unreasonable that, rather than tolerate the uncertain provocation of sharing ever more intense inner experience with another person we seek the seductive comfort of the monogamous routine, or the familiar excitement of one-night stands.

Where does this leave us? In an ambiguous, uncertain spot. The idea of political correctness masquerades as eternal truth which we would all like to believe is possible, because it makes us feel much more secure. But everything changes – except the existence of contradictions. With social transformation come new ones. I do not believe that an eternally true consciousness of what is politically correct in sexuality, or in anything, is possible. Or, to say the same thing in other words, the road to false consciousness, no matter how you wish to define it, is paved with politically correct intentions.

Sexuality is not the route to revolution. But sexuality is a prime shaper of desire, and constraint of desire leads directly to selfbetrayal and social bad faith. We suffer not from too much desire, but from too little. One reason we fail to rebel, or have incomplete revolutions, is because our hopes have been truncated, particularly by sexism whose core is sexual oppression. Sexual oppression resembles other kinds of domination, like class or race. Yet it is different, because it goes for the jugular of all social relatedness and psychological integration – desire.

We wish, we want, we are in a state of longing – this is the experience of desire, the unconscious fount of activity, creativity, and subjectivity. It is not confined to the sexual passion that arises from and speeds it. Born in the space between wish and possible satisfaction, desire is potentiated by social experience, which also gives it form. Our infant souls absorb, through our skins, its social shapes that cradling adult hands transmit. It may mean power or weakness, purity or evil, hope or despair; we learn to want to want, or not to want.

But desire always rushes beyond its psychocultural channels. It is what moves us, in our personal uniqueness, toward both intimacy and collectivity, and back to self, and again toward society. Since sexuality is the sculptor of desire, since gender organizes sexuality and shapes part of desire into the self, since gender as we know it is born of sexual oppression, then feminism, for me, must be a struggle for sexual emancipation. For we must make sure that we desire all we can so that we will be able to create, and therefore get, all we desire.

Note

Some of the material contained in this paper will receive fuller treatment in the author's forthcoming book, *Surviving Sexual Contradictions,* New York, Macmillan[1].

1 Editor's note: Dimen's note predates her publication of the book, *Surviving Sexual Contradictions,* in 1986.

Suggested Reading

Kathy Acker, *Kathy Goes to Haiti,* Toronto, Rumour, 1978.
John Berger, G., New York, Pantheon, 1972.
Angela Carter, *The Bloody Chamber,* Harmondsworth, Penguin, 1981.
Janine Chasseguet-Smirgel (ed.), *Female Sexuality,* Ann Arbor, University of Michigan Press, 1970.
Colette, *Earthly Paradise,* New York, Farrar Strauss, 1966.
Muriel Dimen, "Notes Toward the Reconstruction of Sexuality", *Social Text,* vol. 6, 1982, pp. 22–31.
Deirdre English, Amber Hollibaugh, and Gayle Rubin, "Talking Sex", *Socialist Review,* vol. 58, 1981, pp. 43–62.

Susan Griffin, *Women and Nature,* New York, Harper & Row, 1980.
Heresies, *The Sex Issue # 12,* vol. 3, no. 4, 1981.
Masud Khan, *Alienation in Perversions,* New York, International Universities Press, 1979.
Joel Kovel, *The Age of Desire,* New York, Pantheon, 1981.
Gayle Rubin, "The Traffic in Women: Notes on the 'Political Economy' of Sex", in Rayna Reiter (ed.), *Toward* an *Anthropology of Women,* New York, Monthly Review Press, 1975, pp. 157–210.
Robert Stoller, *Sexual Excitement,* New York, Simon & Schuster/Touchstone, 1979.

To Capture the Frenzied Politically In/Correct?

Katie Gentile

It was 1987 and I was assigned pieces from *Pleasure and danger: Exploring female sexuality* (Vance, 1984) as a radical gesture by a women's studies professor at the University of Michigan. It felt subversive and untethering to enter into a world of feminism without boundaries. If nothing was in/correct, how would we know misogyny when we came/orgasmed to it?

The book was a collection from a conference held at Barnard College in 1982, an annual gathering of feminist scholars, this one focused on women's sexuality. While having an entire conference dedicated to women's sexuality would still be novel, almost 40 years ago, it led to protests identifying splits in feminist activists. (It still would.) The conference was discussing danger; not just the dangers in liberating what was identified as "female" sexuality in a patriarchal society, but danger in terms of what happens when one comes into being as a recognizable, legitimate subject in a culture where one breathes in sexualized violence on a daily basis. Under such conditions, can sexuality pulse, breath, come to life in any gratifying way, without the spark or glint of chaffing misogyny? Because the conference would include discussions of S-M and pornography, the group Women Against Pornography picketed. This split became articulated as one between pro-sex or anti-porn feminists, a clear inheritance of the Madonna-whore binary.

In many ways, the book was ahead of its time in theorizing pleasure-dangers from gender transitions, S-M play, and heterosexual, lesbian, and bi-nonmonogamies. Interdisciplinary writers and activists from Hortense Spillers, Cherrie Morega, hattie gossett, Kate Millett, Gayle Rubin, Alice Echols, Oliva Espin, Roberta Galler, and Dorothy Allison theorized or/and performed the deconstruction of a "politically correct" "female" sexuality. Many of these chapters have become standards in women's and gender studies classes, and Galler's "Myth of the perfect body" is one of the groundbreaking essays in dis/ability studies.

The collection also enacted the white supremacy that can still course through feminism, in that whiteness remains unmarked and seemingly invisible, and any identification of race or ethnicity is confined to discrete chapters by BIPOC authors. There are no intersectionalities.

DOI: 10.4324/9781003335252-5

I lay out this limited context to place Muriel's essay in a history where to be included in this volume, was to be identified as a radical feminist, a cutting edge killjoy (Ahmed, 2010) shaping debates within academic and activist feminist circles. Although not yet publishing in psychoanalysis, Muriel's chapter shows she is working to articulate the powers of the political on not just the personal but the psyche, and the ways sexual desire enfolds longings for group recognition. So the power of the politically in/correct can be enshrined and worn like cozy armor (or perhaps a horned fur hat as exhibited by white supremacists terrorizing the capital on January 6, 2020). She couldn't know at this point that railing against political correctness could be a radical feminist stance in 1984, but a fascistic, white supremacist dog-whistle shortly after.

As Muriel playfully describes the tensions of desire that are not politically correct or feminist enough, she also cloaks the whiteness from her musings. When she reflects on political correctness acting as a form of "psychological foot-binding" (p. 144) we see the malignancy of a colonial anthropology at work. Sexual desire, as she writes, is the "unconscious fount of activity, creativity, and subjectivity…between the wish and the possible satisfaction" (p. 147) and countering the tamping down, snuffing, out and constraint of such desire is a central tenet of feminism. To embrace and articulate sexual desire, though, is to bring into being different encounters for a white, Jewish woman than for a BIWOC. But by writing emancipation as occurring through sexual desire and power, Muriel seals her fate as a future radical feminist psychoanalyst.

Even in this early chapter, Muriel's inability to be confined to one form of analysis, one disciplinary frame or narrative structure, was clear. Muriel welcomed and facilitated chats that associated freely across boundaries of content, process, and structure. So it is fitting to have this collection of 13 writers muse about this essay, the politically in/correct, and the empty spaces or erasures of experiences in Muriel's essay. Here politically in/correct endures, but with the consequences of "cancel culture" as the sword looming above us at all times. The politically in/correct is interrogated from multiple perspectives and forms: The refuge of splitting for psycho-social regulations and the unconscious roots of violence in language (Layton), memoirs of embodied in/correctnesses (Shankar; Wheeler), #MeToo in Brazil (Waisbich), and being a privileged potential wielder of the damning sword of cancel culture (Anciano); the suicidal consequences of being canceled and the un-being of embodying what is beyond cultural symbolization (Latham; Hansbury); an enraged/ing repetition of all one BIWOC is forced to swallow for any semblance of inclusion, echoes over and over in the reader (Merchant); brilliant "take-downs" of Dimen's essay (1984), using it to complicate disavowals and seductions of white supremacy (Sheehi), speciesism (Raz), and feminist decolonizations where activist appeals for women's equity are cast as colonial tools (Ngwenya); the moralism of being correct in the context of Israel (Ullman). All of these essays continue the intellectual and embodied struggle to resist the structural through the interpersonal (von Lieres) recognizing that these experiences are of course, co-emergent. From prose, to clinical case material, to a poetry-based quiz, the writers in this section gift not a collection of essays but a labyrinth of possibilities best read through as one paper that fluidly moves through spaces and times-geographies, continents, generations, races and ethnicities, genders, building on, against, and from, Muriel's work.

References

Ahmed, S. (2010). Killing joy: Feminism and the history of happiness. *Signs, 35* (3): 571–594.

Dimen, M. (1984). Politically Correct? Politically Incorrect? In, C.S. Vance, ed., *Pleasure and danger: Exploring female sexuality,* pp. 138–148. Boston: Routledge & Kegan Paul.

Vance, C. S. (1984). *Pleasure and danger: Exploring female sexuality.* Boston: Routledge & Kegan Paul.

ELA

Almas Merchant

(Read carefully: There will be a quiz at the end.)

This is a story about race.

This is a story about class.

This is a story about racing…racing hearts.

This is a story about race.

This is a story about class.

This is a story about racing… thoughts.

This is a story about race.

This is a story about class.

This is a story about racing… against time.

Is… this… a story?

Thisisastoryaboutaprosewriterturnedpoetbecauseanideaneededtobeconveyedfast.

This is a story about race.

"*This is history.*"

This is a story about class.

This is a story about racing…sirens.

I am… in this story?

This is bad poetry because good prose is not enough.

This is a story about ~~anger rage impotence~~ cancel culture?

This is a story about race.

This is a story about class.

Are… you…in this story?

This is a story about race.

This is a story about class.

DOI: 10.4324/9781003335252-6

"Why the FUCK are you in this story?"
This is a story about race.
"Are you bored?"

Quiz:

This is a story about:

a. Race
b. Class
c. Your inability to listen to others' suffering and constant need to inject your own, unprocessed death anxiety onto others using specific racial tropes (and the weight of your seniority) so no one can question the validity of your words even though they are dog whistles via the means of a professional listserv.
d. All of the above.

Psst…when in doubt, the answer is like, *ALWAYS* C.

<u>ELA</u> 1
(Read carefully: There will be a quiz at the end.) 2
This is a story about race.
This is a story about class. 3
This is a story about racing…racing hearts.
This is a story about race.
This is a story about class.
This is a story about *race & class.* 4
This is a story about racing… thoughts.
This is a story about race.
This is a story about class. 5
This is a story about racing… against time.
Is… this… a story? 6
Thisisastoryaboutaprosewriterturnedpoetbecauseanidea
neededtobeconveyedfast. 7
This is a story about race.
"This is history." 8
This is a story about class.
This is a story about racing…sirens.

I am... in this story?
This is bad poetry because good prose is not enough. **9**
This is a story about ~~anger rage impotence~~ cancel culture?
This is a story about race.
This is a story about class.
Are... you...in this story?
This is a story about race.
This is a story about class.
"*Why the FUCK are you in this story?*" **10**
This is a story about race.
"*Are you bored?*"

Quiz:

This is a story about:

a. Race
b. Class
c. Your inability to listen to others' suffering and constant need to inject your own, unprocessed death anxiety onto others using specific racial tropes (and the weight of your seniority) so no one can question the validity of your words even though they are dog whistles via the means of a professional listserv. 11
d. All of the above.

Psst...when in doubt, the answer is like, *ALWAYS* C. **12**

Notes:

1. The title of this poetic essay is inspired by school closures and the turn to remote learning in order to "flatten the curve" of the spread of coronavirus in New York. The complete form of ELA is "English Language Arts." I am struck by the demand upon *children* to be resilient and apply reading comprehension skills while adults continue to feign their surprise that the virus is not a "great equalizer."
2. One of the many "rituals" of adolescence in the United States is the taking of standardized tests, particularly the Scholastic Aptitude Test (SAT) as a requirement for application to colleges. The SATs this spring were canceled with many universities opting out of using the SATs as a determination of an applicant's capacity for success. The ways in which class and race intersect around the SATs and the capacity for wealthier

folks to avail of paid classes to ensure success for an "aptitude" test continues to widen the gap between "haves" and "have-nots". I am using the idea of a "quiz" to alert the reader to this.

3. Kimberle Crenshaw wrote her seminal piece on intersectionality in 1989, seven years after Dimen's piece, "Politically Correct, Politically Incorrect." Intersectionality is a word that was not taken up in common parlance until the second decade of the 2000s. Dimen makes no mention of race or class in this piece on sex and gender and that seems appropriate given the context of the time. In 2020, however, it feels essential (and personally inescapable), then, as a queer non-Black WOC, to explicitly write (and repeatedly state) the importance of race and class rather than staying with gender and sexuality. This is especially true in psychoanalysis which *continues* to have difficulties in contending with its history of racism.
4. In early March, 1 billion Indians have been placed on lockdown. Over 60 days later, homeless migrants are still walking across my home country to get home as police beat them and deny access to food provided by soup kitchens. "India's Coronavirus Lockdown Leaves Vast Numbers Stranded and Hungry https://nyti.ms/33RzrDI." The images of this migration remind me of the migrations post partition. As people who have the luxury to stay home, I am haunted by images of dying migrant workers (of all ages) in India and the racially disproportionate deaths in the US by this "great equalizer."
5. In thinking about the partition of India, I have been inspired by movies such as Deepa Mehta's *1947 Earth* which brutally depicts the harnessing of rage using horizontal violence against a colonized people. I also have been drawn to native New Yorker, Phillip Glass's 1979 opera, *Satyagraha*, about the Indian freedom, which was revived in 2011 at the Lincoln Theater. Not only has the content been important for me to consider but also the music has a repetition that I find myself inspired by in the repetition here.
6. The linguistic devices in this writing were also inspired by feminist writer Gertrude Stein's short story: "The wife has a cow. A Love Story."
7. In writing this, in early March 2020, I was aware of the urgency with which New York would have to change to ensure the least amount of lives are lost. I was also aware of how much easier it would be for those with resources to change while poor folks who are mostly Black in this city would not have the same luxury and ease. Everything I believed then is true today in June, 2020.
8. All lines in quotes are directly lines from my patients the week of March 16, 2020.
9. As someone who suffers from severe asthma, I often find myself breathless. The images of lungs being destroyed by the respiratory illness that is COVID-19, a virus that disproportionately kills Black and Latinx folk

due to the structural racism that leads to lack of access to healthcare and nutritious food, the screams of "I Can't Breathe" by Black men murdered by police in this country all coalesce into breathless, activated, speedy sentences.

10. Carly Simon's 1972 song, "You're so vain" (https://youtu.be/j13oJajXx0M) kept playing in my mind when this sentence was uttered in my practice. The song is about a woman singing to a man but my patient was talking about Whiteness and the ways it infuses itself into conversations, even those that have nothing to do with Whiteness.
11. Professional listservs are like mini social networks and serve as a litmus test for a culture. The ways in which these (mostly white) listservs can violate and overwhelm a person of color remind me of Dimen's 2006 paper, "Lapsus Linguae". I am struck by the many years between "Politically Correct, Politically Incorrect" and "Lapsus Linguae" because it is at this point that Dimen finally names the experience I have when virulent racism, denials about said racism, closing of ranks around the person making a racist comment finds its way into my inbox. It feels, I imagine, like an unwelcome, non-consensual tongue in my mouth with no conversation about it later.
12. Once again, a tongue-in-cheek joke about multiple choice tests.

Note

Bettina von Lieres

I am drawn to Muriel Dimen's fourth question: what is good about politically correct ideology and behaviour? I have no problem with political correctness. I associate it with a politics of inclusion. I am always on the look-out for new words and practices that address problems of marginalization. I find this question the most compelling because it focuses our attention on how politically correct ideologies potentially infuse the social with new possibilities. What do I mean by this?

I associate politically correct language with strategic practices which re-define the boundaries of the political. Politically correct discourses often emerge when the political is rooted in a relentless logic of exclusion. In the South African anti-apartheid movement, we, as activists, quickly adopted new languages and practices of political mobilization in order to collectively oppose institutionalised racism. We used politically correct language to hold together a complex social movement. Words like "non-racialism" were quickly assimilated on the basis that they helped us to forge new critical alliances. While there was protracted debate on the meanings of "non-racialism", there was little time to contest its strategic usages. Activists were disappearing and dying. We learnt how to be nimble and how to rapidly accept new political words in the name of unity and solidarity. I thus view politically correct words as a strategic means to an end – the end of inclusive social movements capable of social action in a time of profound crisis and violence.

I find the other questions in Muriel's chapter less compelling. Asking about the bad side of political correctness can only be done from a position of political privilege – a position in which people have the time and resources to think about themselves politically. The majority of people in the world do not have this privilege. Living a life of unrelenting material indignity and non-recognition by those in power, often only becomes bearable through dissociating from expectations of rights and dignity. It comes with shutting down expectations of citizenship, and with it, expectations of the right to political language itself. For most people in the world, it is only through forms of collective action that allow for the presentation of

DOI: 10.4324/9781003335252-7

political perspective that political language becomes meaningful. Collective action becomes the arena in which political agency, subjectivity, and political language emerges. Collective action gives delinked political experiences a scaffolding to hang on. Learning a new political language of collective offers opportunities to shift dissociated experiences of citizenship into undissociated ones. Asking whether or not politically correct language is bad is not the most interesting question. What is more interesting is asking about the possibility of collective action as an arena for the emergence of political subjectivity, and with it, the possibility of a political language in the first place.

In Muriel Dimen's Footsteps—Five Notes on the Politically Correct and Politically Coerced in Current Israeli Contexts

Chana Ullman

1. In this bold yet nuanced paper Muriel Dimen (1984) defines politically correct as the attempt to "Bring about the revolution, bring the present into line with utopian future." The politically correct, she says, confounds moral judgment with left-wing ideology: acts of speech or deeds are judged as wrong because they hinder left-wing ideology. In light of this definition, there is currently no PC in Israel. In fact, current PC that attempts to bring the present into utopian future defines wrong as that which hinders right-wing ideology. The Israeli right-wing majority currently marches to the drum of a Utopian future and dictates the correct and incorrect in language. What has been accepted and mainstream liberalism becomes impermissible. PC becomes an effective policing of speech advancing right-wing hegemony. Language changes. For example, the terms "Occupied territories", like the term "Occupation", gradually disappeared from public discourse. It is not banned, no rule is necessary, it is simply not used publicly. The Hebrew biblical terms "Judia" and "Sameria" are now widely used for the territories occupied by Israel since 1967.

   In 2016 Miri Regev, the minister of culture, attempted to turn right-wing PC into a law. She declared a new amendment to the law [*] —"loyalty in culture": those theatrical or other artistic endeavors that "speak against the Jewish state" will not be funded. Eventually the law did not pass, but those artists who depend on government support, realized that they better censor themselves. The Politically correct became politically coerced by the right-wing government of the time. This is not to say that there are no different voices within Israel, those who refuse to abide by this collective voluntary censorship, but those stand out as radical and courageous.
2. Muriel Dimen writes that PC cannot be defined by content. Yet people on the left find PC regulations attractive because they emanate from acute perceptions of oppression. PC stems from the decent motivation to protect those who are the target of contempt and discrimination. The Politically correct appears where there is a recognition of a social split

DOI: 10.4324/9781003335252-8

between the privileged and the disadvantaged. In Israeli contexts, PC is relevant in addressing the schism between Aschenazi and Oriental Jews.

Three days preceding the elections of 1981, a well-known celebrity of the time, Dudu Topaz, speaking to the crowd at a rally supporting the Labor party, said "fortunately we do not have Chachchachim here to interfere with our rally, they all stayed at the Likud's (right-wing party) headquarters". The term "Chachchach" is a derogatory term for young people of Moroccan origin. The uproar following this insult, some say, cost the Labor party the elections that year. The PC regarding Ashkenazi vs. Oriental origins has been a powerful PC struggle supporting equality within Israel and (I say this with caution), did meet utopian goals of bringing about change. In a turn of events, still ongoing terms previously used to humiliate are now adopted proudly by young Israeli writers of Moroccan and other African-Arab origins, revolutionizing Israeli poetry and literature.

3. The PC is necessary in domains of trauma. One assumes a moral superiority of those who survived or "paid the highest price" of losing a family member. In the Israeli contexts of war and terror and the legacy of the Holocaust, there are things one should not say or do because they will hurt the feelings of bereaved families or of survivors. Television series (e.g., "the Boys"), art works or meetings of groups that recognize a Palestinian narrative, are vehemently protested as hurting the feelings of bereaved parents or survivors. Similarly, the "no comparison" argument is regularly used to silence criticism of inhumane practices.

   The often-genuine claim of hurting someone's feelings, becomes an indictment of multiplicity, banning different and complex views of the legacy of the Holocaust or of placing horrible losses in the Palestine/Israel conflict in a wider context.

4. Muriel Dimen is acutely aware of the danger of self-righteousness, of PC becoming the dogma, attempting to control impure thoughts, and looking for this impurity in the other. Muriel goes a long way to avoid this danger, by revealing the impurity of her own thoughts.

   Political correctness that turns into moralism erases the possibility of drawing distinctions. Context and intentions do not matter. Some words become taboo and should not be uttered regardless of context. Some people, e.g., those who agree with my left-wing perspective, become automatically "good" regardless of their claims or actions. Gideon Levi, a courageous Israeli journalist who consistently exposes Palestinian suffering under Israeli occupation, wrote a glowing portrait of Jeremy Corbyn dismissing all claims of rising anti-Semitism in British Labor. PC may become rigid binaries, in this case if you are with me in protecting Palestinian rights than you can do no wrong.

5. Dimen points to the paradox of blurring the distinctions between left-wing ideology and moral judgment: in the name of advocating moral

good do we take away the freedom of thought and speech and the acknowledgment of variability that is inherent in left-wing ideology? This is a challenge that requires our constant attention. If we allow this kind of limitations of speech and thought, what happens when it is practiced by a different dominant ideology? As Dimen writes, "Everything changes in the world except contradictions". Her legacy is in the protection of contradictions and paradoxes, and of freedom to continue to explore and commit despite them. This legacy is now more crucial than ever: Can we protect a Utopian vision that recognizes contradictions and ambiguity in a world full of binaries going in the opposite direction?

Reference

Dimen, M. (1984). Politically Correct? Politically Incorrect? In, C.S. Vance, ed., *Pleasure and danger: Exploring female sexuality,* pp. 138–148. Boston, MA: Routledge & Kegan Paul.

Note

Fiona Anciano

I am writing this note less from the point of view of someone who 'experiences' political correctness but rather as someone who feels responsible for 'delivering' it. I am a white, female, 44-year-old associate professor of Politics at a historically disadvantaged (politically correct for black and poor) university in Cape Town, South Africa. I love my job. Every year I get to teach the first term of 'Introduction to Politics' to 500 new students at the start of their degrees. This is a position of privilege and power. However, to paraphrase Voltaire (and the uncle of a famous arachnid), with power comes great responsibility.

In my unending state of white guilt I feel I hold the responsibility to ensure I am focused on never consciously or unconsciously mirroring the racial prejudices of the past. To do this I clutch to waves of political correctness. The problem is, as Muriel Dimen points out, what is politically correct can be subjective, and can certainly change with the times.

I face this conundrum in my class on a regular basis. One of my most interesting years, however, was when the concept of 'White Monopoly Capital' (WMC) took hold of the public discourse. Students' social media – their Facebook, and Twitter and Instagram – was filled with images and statements about the evils of WMC and how 'it' was forcing then South African President Jacob Zuma to step down. WMC became a catchphrase for everything that was wrong with the country, to the extent that the leader of a movement called *Black First, Land First*, blamed WMC for a severe storm that hit Cape Town in 2017.

How do I deal with this in the classroom? Is it politically incorrect for me to question the legitimacy of these claims, especially as the only white person in the room? I teach politics. Race and capital and power are not concepts we can, and nor should we, skirt over in our discussions. However in my attempt to be sensitive to racial oppression, and in this sense politically correct, I was losing my ability to engage authentically with students.

During the WMC phase the class was so heightened to racial profiling that in one lecture where I apologised for not seeing a hand at the back of the auditorium as, I stated: 'its dark back there', the students all burst into

DOI: 10.4324/9781003335252-9

shocked laughter. There was an assumption that I had made a reference to the race of the student. I was perplexed – was it now politically incorrect to use the word dark? Must I start saying 'there is a lack of light'?

In the months that followed it transpired that a UK public relations firm, Bell Pottinger, was behind the WMC 'fake news' media campaign. They had been funded by close associates of President Zuma, the Gupta brothers, to destabilise narratives in South Africa and created antipathy for those calling for Zuma's removal. Evidence has shown that Zuma did engage in the politics of corruption and patronage, and he is indeed facing trial. These are the issues I need to analyse with my students. This presents an ongoing reflective quest: to teach students with sensitivity, and awareness of their context and history, without losing the ability to engage robustly and authentically.

Dimen notes that 'sexuality, like character, is socially contextualised'. I would argue that race too is socially contextualised, if not socially constructed. While apartheid created systemic racial oppression in South Africa, it also led to fixed categories of belonging and othering, where your skin colour too easily defines you. Fixating on fixed racial categories and ignoring their social construction does not allow for the reality that social transformation is a continuing process. So in some sense I agree with Dimen that 'the road to false consciousness, no matter how you wish to define it, is paved with politically correct intentions' (p. 147). Particularly, politically correct intentions than maintain an 'us vs them' stance. However, there is also the historical fact of oppression and inequality. Surely, we need to be politically correct to ensure sensitivity to this reality and to not (unconsciously) perpetuate bias? The challenge is how to straddle these tensions; how to be sensitive to the history of political racial oppression and the current reality of economic racial inequality, while not being derailed by the banner of political correctness. This is a challenge I will face each year in my teaching, and one, that I must remind myself I take on from a position of power.

Note

Griffin Hansbury

Many of my young queer patients come out of college and into treatment with a chorus of internalized voices that shame them for their bodies, desires, and identities. While I expect such a chorus to come from the hetero- and cis-normative, queer-phobic world, more and more, in the anxious era of the Trump presidency, those policing voices come from within the queer community. This phenomenon feels like an echo of the past, an artifact of the Reagan/Bush 1980s, and I find myself flashing back to the painful political correctness of the lesbian sex wars that yielded to sex-positive third-wave feminism during my own time in college when I was coming out as trans, hoping for freedom and a utopian future during what Dimen called an "unsatisfactory present."

A patient assigned female at birth is trying out genders, moving from butch to nonbinary and then, tentatively, to transgender man. When he tells his queer friends he's a trans man, they tell him that this identificatory shift grants him male privilege, the kind that cis men have, and all the toxic masculinity that goes with it, even though he is not taking testosterone and still reads as female. Is trans male privilege equivalent to cis male privilege? For his friends, this is not a question; passing privilege is simplistically flattened into cis male privilege. His friends tell him he must be quiet and stop "taking up space." My patient has been quiet and small his whole life, but he does not want to be toxic. He shifts away from a male identity and collapses into uncertainty.

A cisgender lesbian patient worries she might be a misogynist. Her friends have told her that simply looking at women's bodies with sexual desire is an act of misogyny. My patient takes this injunction into the bedroom with her female partner. Afraid to desire, filled with guilt and shame, she forfeits her sex drive.

A young transgender man regularly misses sessions. He tells me he shouldn't "take up space" in treatment because he's privileged – white, middle-class, masculine, and cisgender-passing. He is severely depressed and fantasizes about suicide. However, he explains, "trans women of color suffer more" and his depression doesn't measure up on the hierarchy of

DOI: 10.4324/9781003335252-10

pain. He drops out of treatment, concluding that it would be wrong to continue when the needs of others are so much greater than his.

A cisgender man worries he's a misogynist because he enjoyed sex with women before he came out as queer. Now, when he has sex with men, he enjoys topping but worries about being too vigorous and taking too much pleasure. He's afraid he'll be accused of rape, even though he is diligent about affirmative consent. He can't maintain an erection and avoids sex with his partner.

In each of these cases, and many others, the patient relents to a policing that masquerades as "good queer politics," giving up (for now) aspects of their gender identities and sexualities. Internalizing the logic of their peers (and might this internalization be a capitulation to the normativizing logics of white, capitalist, hetero-patriarchy?) they will not forgive themselves for being incorrect, messy and human, impure in thought and deed. "When the radical becomes correct," wrote Dimen, "it becomes conservative. The politically correct comes to resemble what it tries to change."

What is it about this moment in history, like the conservative Reagan/Bush 1980s, that incites many queers to police their peers? We are living through another far-right backlash, this time against the Black Lives Matter movement and an unprecedented groundswell of transgender/nonbinary youth that threatens to upend the gender hegemony. For those of us outside the center, the backlash is frightening. (When Trump was elected, many of my trans patients worried about being sent to concentration camps.) Have we defensively slipped into a collective paranoid-schizoid position, in which the only options are to be all-good or all-bad? Are queers so frightened by the existential threats (real, unreal, and as yet unrealized) that we resort to surveillance and punishment, the weapons of our own jailers, to ensure that our queer siblings (and our queer selves) do not fall to the wrong side of the all-good/all-bad split? Most of us living in queer bodies understand that we are outlaws, unruly and dangerous. We have already, somewhere in our psyches, submitted to control and containment and that primes us for shame and guilt, easy targets, receptive to accusations of sin. We want so badly to be good.

Stars and Stripes Forever

Joanna Wheeler

It was a sweltering morning in Rio de Janeiro. I hadn't slept well, tossing and turning in damp sheets. From the balcony, I could see a haze that hung low over the city, so that only the mountain tops were clear. The phone rang and I answered. "Joanna, this is Sonia. Turn on the television. New York is under attack." I couldn't make sense of the words. Everything felt surreal. The images on the television, of smoke rising from the World Trade Centre, the haze over the city. I watched as the second plane hit the tower. I watched as the towers collapsed. My body felt number with horror, the sound of blood rushing through my ears a pulsing hum. I didn't leave the room for the whole day. I sat, in suffocating heat, watching CNN and trying to call my closest friends in New York. I couldn't get through. I couldn't eat. I couldn't look away.

I never celebrated being American. After years of living in Argentina and Brazil, I did everything I could to subdue my American-ness—to speak flawless Spanish and then Portuguese. To question American imperialism and to sympathise with hatred for what America represented for many people I met. But on that day, I wanted to find an American flag and drape it over my balcony to publicly signal our collective grief and mourning. I wanted to claim my American-ness, in that moment of destruction. But I had no flag apart from the Brazilian one I carried for carnival earlier that year. Late, in the blue light of the endless CNN feed, I finally fell asleep, dreaming of smoke and screams.

The next day came and I finally found the ability to move again. I felt disconnected, disjointed, separate from my body. My mind was in New York, in America. I was anxious and restless. I finally spoke to my closest friend who worked in the same block as the World Trade Centre. She was safe but so many were not. I went to the local café. I sat down at the table and on the wall next to me were postcards and drawings that anyone could pin up. Staring straight at me was a cartoon drawing. Osama Bin Laden, his head scarf wound neatly around his head, had his tunic lifted up around his waist as he anally raped a woman who looked like the Statue of Liberty. She was bent over on her hands and knees; he stood behind her, towering over her.

DOI: 10.4324/9781003335252-11

On his face was a massive grin. On her face were tears, and over her body the remnants of a burned American flag. Someone had smeared actual shit on her ass. I could smell the reek of it over the bitter smell of my coffee. On any other day, I might have felt a small frisson of disgust at this image. I might have smiled and pretended to understand why this image would be drawn. But on that day, what I felt was rage, deep and burning. I wanted to tear down the drawing and rip it to shreds. Around me, other people in the café noticed the drawing too and started laughing, sharing their amusement. I sat, silent, as my coffee grew cold.

A year later, I moved to London. Leaving Brazil was sad and difficult but an offer on a doctoral programme beckoned. My boyfriend was English, and we decided it was time to give things a try in the UK. For the first few months, I missed Rio desperately. I felt lost in London. I couldn't read people or situations as I was used to in Rio. I could understand the language but not the social queues. I spent six months applying for jobs, so that I could afford to live in London and take up my PhD place. One afternoon, I sat on a train on the way to a meeting. A group of a few people sat in the next set of seats. Their conversation drifted over to me. "Do you know her? The loud one, the American. I hate Americans." I had heard this before, about me, too. After a few months of living in the UK, I modulated my voice, I spoke with a different cadence, I used phrases and words that sounded more British. I only realised I did it when I spoke to my family in the US. They would mock me for sounding English. To them, it sounded like a deception. To me, it sounded like survival; it sounded like acceptance. It sounded like subduing my American-ness again. Back on the train, I sat silent, as their conversation moved on. When my stop came, I got up and walked off the train without looking at them.

Years passed. I married my English boyfriend. I had two babies, born with the help of midwives and the National Health Service. I found work and finished my PhD. I went back to Brazil for months at a time. My job took me to many countries and places: India, Bangladesh, Nigeria, South Africa, Mexico, Bosnia and Herzegovina, Ethiopia. I breathed in what it was to be in those places. I breathed out my American-ness. In an event in a village in Nigeria, we were welcomed by the local chief, who asked us to introduce ourselves. "Where are you from?" he asked. I didn't say: I'm American. I said, "I live in the UK." It wasn't shame of being American that I felt, it was alienation. After so many years in other places, what part of me was still American? What was more honest: to say that I lived in the UK or to say that I was American? Would anyone really care? But in Nigeria, I knew that the sense of where one is from is strong—it is not a minor detail, but it is something that is felt in every part of you. I realised I didn't feel like I was from anywhere anymore.

As a family, we moved to Cape Town. I'd done it before. The packing, the sorting, the endless lists and forms. Arriving, feeling at once lost but excited. Making the repeated choice to try, to reach out, to understand what was different, to accept it. To let go of what came before, to let go of being sure, to let go of American-ness. This time was different because I was going through the whole process with my children. My children, with their American passports and English accents, flattening over the years to sound South African. Like all the places I lived before, I absorbed as much as I could of the place around me. I worked with storytelling, listening to stories from people living in townships in many varieties. With work, I travelled to even more places: Indonesia, Colombia, Zambia, Ghana, Kenya, Mozambique, Namibia. And I loved Cape Town deeply.

At one storytelling workshop with health activists from a township, a Black woman looked at me with tears running down her face. She'd been remembering the marriage forced on her by her family, the violence of her husband, the loss of her child, and underneath it all the enduring pain of apartheid. "You white people," she said, "who do you think you are, to come here and ask us to tell you about our pain." Yes, I thought, with a sense of conviction. She is right. The very fact of who I am is pouring salt on her wounds. On what basis can I sit here with her and help her to tell her story? Just because she has said that she wants to do this, and I know I can help her to find and tell her story in a way that she wants, is that enough? In that moment, it was not.

I'm back in the UK again. Leaving Cape Town was incredibly hard. Making my way in the UK is also fraught with questions and worries: modes of politics in the UK are drawing stark lines between who can belong and who cannot. Right and left-wing populism are gaining ground. After 20 years of living outside of the US, I wonder what part of me is still American. And I realise, in part through my time in South Africa, that I carry my privilege with me, into every space and moment. I can't subdue my American-ness and I can't embrace it. It haunts me like a ghost, an uneasy shadow that I step through, coating me with the residue of home.

Making Life Accessible

A Note from the Suicidal to Society

J.R. Latham

I used to cry on the way to work. Every day. I would get on the tram, find a place to rest my back, if possible, and slowly, silently, let tears roll down my cheeks. I wished all the pain and hurt and injustice could wash away: down my face, dripping onto the streetcar floor and leave this world forever. It was never forever but it gave me the solace to survive the day. I would sometimes wear sunglasses, sometimes a hat, but I hardly hid, or tried to. Always I had with me, wrapped around my skull like a life-giving hug, my noise-cancelling head phones: blasting a soundtrack to my misery – life, or death. No one ever seemed to notice. Two to four tracks later, I step onto the road and stride into work: I HAVE A PURPOSE. I'M AN AUTHORITY. *I'M NOT WORTHLESS*.

To endure the daily practices of being constituted as **worthless**, however, requires such extraordinary self-belief as to cast across one's mind-body a kind of Kryptonian resistance to the forces of this Earth. That's what I attempted to do for something like two years. My powers declined over time. Their harms began to penetrate: creeping self-doubts at the end of the day; waking frights at 4 am; new intolerances to all kinds of foods; and I lost the ability to ride a bike – a loss I felt deeply since bike-riding was one of my first tools of freedom and autonomy. But I persisted. I continued to exist. "What is to be done?"

> Don't take it personally!
> You need a thick skin!
> Water off a duck's back!
> This is not for the faint-hearted!

I am not faint hearted. I am sensitive to the world around me and my place in it. This is a prodigious asset that none of my work would be possible without. To be bureaucratized into nothingness; told minute by minute in every moment of your daily work-life that *what you are* is a number on a page; reduced solely to a check box that's been ticked… Even here and now I can't describe to you the voices in my head screaming: YOU CAN'T WRITE

DOI: 10.4324/9781003335252-12

THAT. WHO GIVES A FUCK ABOUT WHAT YOU HAVE TO SAY? YOU SOUND LIKE A WHINGING WHITE FUCK. NO ONE CARES.

Here are some feelings I have about crying on the tram: Loneliness: surrounded by all these people, I am alone. Curiosity: will anyone ever say or do anything? Shame: you are not supposed to cry, and certainly not in public. Different: No one is like me; I am not like them, and, I do not want to be. I don't do it to make a spectacle of myself. It began, like so much does, as an accident. I couldn't help myself. And I may well have been mortified had anyone ever attempted to show me some compassion. This, however, is retrospective speculation. Because it never happened, I do not know.

I hate the description "suicidal ideation." It's not *ideal*-izing. It's not ceiling-staring or naval-gazing. It's hardly a choice. Those "rational," note-leaving suiciders are a fucking minority in my opinion. A tragic one, to be sure. And I by no means intend to denigrate the memories of these devastating losses. But I am trying to describe something else. What if it is *not* "the **formation of ideas** or concepts" ("ideation") but rather its opposite: "A break with reality." For someone who theorizes reality, this is truly terrifying.

The first person I knew jumped in front of train, they said – though I don't know how much "jumped" is really the right or accurate verb to use here. I imagine it as more of a fall, a letting go of the bullshit of the world and a slip to embrace its end. And we have a lot to lose from romanticizing such events and I by no means intend to do so. I'm trying – and surely failing – to articulate a kind of desperation that simply has no words:

> **Can't handle it**
>
> Have to be around people
>
> Don't want to
>
> Can't be alone – can't be around people – can't stand them – can't be alone at work – have to be around people; subjected to that unanswerable classic – "How are you!?"

Great!

I've spent almost a decade writing a book about the importance of possibilities to making life liveable. And now I find myself seeing everywhere the possibilities for my own demise. I stop driving. I stop walking along some of my usual routes that cross bridges over creeks and highways. These are good moves – but I cannot protect myself. I increasingly see my own death in everything: expanses of water, oncoming traffic, heights of all kinds, train-lines, kitchen knives and gardening tools, lighters, poisons, medicines and drug dealers, a redback spider. My overwhelming desire is really something quite simple: RELIEF. To feel helpless, to feel trapped, to feel the desperate pain of **IMPOSSIBILITY.**

It does not feel like a **choice** to me. It feels instinctive; like a natural, biological imperative to *self-protection*: YOU CANNOT GO ON SUFFERING LIKE THIS!

The most infuriating euphemism is that exemplar: "do something stupid." STUPID! Stupid is thinking you can actually endure this situation indefinitely. What a cruel, callous, vicious and brutal analysis of someone else's pain. To call someone so desperate '**stupid**' is precisely the inhumane logic that seems to rule our thinking on suicide. I'm beginning to understand the preparedness of note-leavers.

It was December. A hard time of year for so many. And across my screen came post after post of an interview by Zackary Drucker with Sandy Stone, one of my key intellectual influences; who made my own work possible. A beautiful portrait of Stone's life, I felt no longer trapped by the suburban hell I sat in but rather catapulted across the world with her: kayaking down the Kobuk river, criss-crossing the USA via that "wonderful parallel subculture-or superculture" of 1960s lesbian adventuring, to the polis of Santa Cruz's women's organizing, out on the road with Olivia Records and thrust, one might say, into the academy. And at that place, "away from everyone I knew, [...] away from home, [...] in a hostile environment", Stone recounts:

> They didn't believe in cultural theory or critical theory, they were hostile to me and they later in fact threw me out. And I developed a strategy. There was an elevator in the humanities and social sciences building, which had eight floors. The sociology department was on one of the top ones. The elevator was very slow. I'd get in, the doors would close, I'd pick a time of day when there were few people in the building or traveling in it, and if I was lucky enough to be alone in the elevator, the doors would close, I'd lean against the wall of the elevator and I'd cry. I'd cry and cry 'til I got to my floor and the doors would open, and I'd be on! I'd go in and do whatever the hell needed to be done. I wound up doing that for almost five years.

In these moments of desperation and anguish and solitary peace, whatever kinds of ways we each are suffering, I found myself united in the alleviation of that infuriating pain with someone of great political importance to me. She was like me. I was like her. We endured, we persisted, **we survive** through one of the most beautiful displays of humanity I can imagine. I am not alone anymore. I can be in the elevator with Sandy Stone every day.

Stone: "you just put your head down and you keep fucking moving forward. That's the only thing I know. And it's terrifying and exhausting and if you're very, very lucky, you break through into something eventually."

I can hardly bear to wonder what might have happened if someone tapped me on the shoulder and told me to turn it down. And this is vital, *I* may well have been this person. **How inconsiderate!** These were moments when I let myself feel all the hurt of the night before, the day before, the rejection before, the lifetime before. To have been shown another act of repudiation, another endorsement of my inability to participate *properly* in the world around me; another confirmation that I don't fit in: that what I do/WHO I AM (these are the same thing) is **wrong**. I simply may not have survived it. So it was dangerous to cry on the tram, and I knew that. But I could find no less treacherous alternatives to that commute. I've tried to find headphones that don't have this projecting effect. But that's a luxury I have now that I have a salary. So I'll just leave you with this: when you find yourself on a tram or a train or a street beside some seemingly inconsiderate fuckwit whose music is too loud, he very may well be such an entitled prick. Or it might be me, just trying to get to work without dying.

Suggested Reading

Best, Susan. "Driving Like a Boy: Sexual Difference, Embodiment and Space." In *Imagining Australian Space: Cultural Studies and Spatial Inquiry*, edited by Ruth Barcan and Ian Buchanan, 93–101. Nedlands: University of Western Australia Press, 1999.

Bishop, Elizabeth. "One Art." *Poems: The Centenary Edition*, 198. London: Chatto & Windus, 2011.

Drucker, Zackary. "Sandy Stone on Living Among Lesbian Separatists as a Trans Woman in the 70s." *Vice*, December 19, 2018. https://www.vice.com/en_us/article/zmd5k5/sandy-stone-biography-transgender-history.

Latham, J.R. *Making Maleness: Trans Men and the Politics of Medicine*. Minneapolis: University of Minnesota Press. Forthcoming

Lewinsky, Monica. "The Price of Shame." TED Talk, March 2015. https://www.ted.com/talks/monica_lewinsky_the_price_of_shame?language=en.

Madonna. "Woman of The Year Acceptance Speech." *Billboard Women in Music*. New York, December 9, 2016. https://www.youtube.com/watch?v=c6Xgbh2E0NM.

O'Dwyer, Siobhan, Sarah Pinto and Sharon McDonough. "Self-care for Academics: A Poetic Invitation to Reflect and Resist." *Reflective Practices* 19, no. 2: 243–249, 2018.

Sedgwick, Eve Kosofsky. "Teaching/Depression." *The Scholar and Feminist Online* 4, no. 2 (Spring 2006). http://sfonline.barnard.edu/heilbrun/sedgwick_01.htm.

Stone, Sandy. "The Empire Strikes Back: A Posttranssexual Manifesto." In *The Transgender Studies Reader*, edited by Susan Stryker and Stephen Whittle, 221–35. New York and London: Routledge, 2006.

Wurtzel, Elizabeth. *More, Now, Again*. New York: Simon & Schuster, 2002.

The Limitations of White Liberal Discourse

Political Correctness as Dual Defense

Lara Sheehi

I write from the occupied land of the Pamunkey people, in the heart of "colonial Williamsburg", two miles from Jamestown Settlement. Political correctness, or its more recent instantiations, progressive identity politics and "cancel culture", do not extend their armor to those who were genocided on this land; they also do not extend to the enslaved peoples who built William & Mary, also two miles from my home. Political correctness does not extend because its alleged protective potency is only truly afforded to those who already have power. Those in power—not only Focauldian power, but systemic, real, material power (economic, social, political)—unlike those constitutively oppressed by that power, exercise an ability to simultaneously bemoan the functionally demonstrative mechanisms of political correctness and at once exploit its perceived power to defend their own systemically endowed positionality. This is not a polemical statement or assertion. Rather, I make this argument with specific intent to exercise an arm of psychoanalysis that seems to become eclipsed in such discussions: the reality principle.

As a framework and concept, political correctness can selectively constrain and surveil language and behavior, adjectives and nouns, but does not account for tense—historical reality—preferring to conceptualize oppression as representative of a "past time" vs. grappling with the present-day instantiations of that oppression faced by people who are decidedly not of the past, whether indigenous or black. In this way, political correctness, especially as it is weaponized, materializes as a dual defense in the white liberal discourse, and most especially as deployed by white liberal progressives. On the one hand, when deployed to sanction, usually on behalf of an Other/collective, and usually within the framework and parameters as decided on by that individual-acting-on-behalf-of, it acts as a defense against aggression—a move toward innocence (Tuck & Yang, 2012; Razack & Fellows, 1998), a salve that works to pacify one's own complicity in systems of oppression while ceding nothing. This is especially the case if the deployment lacks, as it often does, any systemic analysis of imperialism, colonialism, settler colonialism, and capitalism. This type of deployment also has decided limits, posing a technical difficulty in conceptualizing it as truly

DOI: 10.4324/9781003335252-13

in service of liberation, rather than a liberal attempt at diversification and inclusion. One cannot but conjure up countless examples where white liberal progressives hit upon the limits of digestible content, regressing into the split against which they may have been internally working against—what might be understood as performative allyship.[1] For example, I have written elsewhere (Sheehi, 2018) how the mere whisper of Palestine has the capacity to shut down analyzable space, the utterance itself unmetabolizable even if one's ability to speak of Palestinian self-determination should be included under the rubric of political correctness. The same can be seen when factions of the Black Lives Matter movement articulate and commit to explicitly anti-capitalist, anti-imperialist, and anti-jingoistic rhetoric and praxis; similarly, the limits of white liberal progressive stewardship ends the moment indigenous folks articulate the necessity of Land Back as a nonnegotiable starting point to collective working through.

On the other hand, when deployed antagonistically to champion "freedom" and defend "free speech"[2], it is done so to shore up a disavowal of historical truths and displace one's desire for spaces that allow sadistic, though often disavowed, pleasure in hate, racism, sexism, ableism, transphobia, fatphobia, etc. (Carter Carter personal communication, June 27, 2020). Take for example the utterly sanctimonious debacle of a letter published in Harper's in 2020[3] by hundreds of prominent intellectuals, journalists, and, for better or worse, people who aspire to be either. The swift counternarratives to the auspicious display of power by the self-appointed Freedom Vanguard highlighted the gross exploitation of seemingly liberal values in service of individualistic and reactionary ends that, in its most insidious form, sought itself to stifle meaningful dissent, the most powerful of which has played out on the global stage, and in opposition to which most of the signatories stand. Indeed, a quick glance at the signatories highlights the bad faith position that constitutes the anti-political correctness/identity politics and cancel culture opposition brigade, many of whom are ardent Zionists who have engaged in deliberate threat campaigns against Palestinian academics (Bari Weiss[4]), activists, and anyone who dare advocate global Boycott, Divestment, and Sanction (BDS) efforts to pressure Israel. Likewise, one can discern trans-exclusive radical feminist (TERFs) signatories and explicit transphobes who have themselves lobbied for the firing of prominent trans journalists (Jesse Signal[5]) and who have advocated for crypto-conversion therapy for trans individuals (JK Rowling[6]). The concern over the death of debate and freedoms, then, emerges as a defense against reality, both historic and material, and more so, a re-entrenchment of power by positioning oneself as victim—perhaps the biggest delusion of white liberal progressiveness that is, not incidentally, also shared by right-wing conservatism. As Tuck and Yang (2012) remind us, this repetitive move is particularly insidious because, "pain is the token for oppression, [and] claims to pain then equate to claims of being an innocent non-oppressor" (p. 16).

In other words, both white liberal progressives, who Osita Nwanevu calls "reactionary liberals", shore up a *normativity* shaped by white supremacy, just as readily as their so-called despised archenemies, the most obvious of which was on display in the Harper's letter. Nwanevu describes this normativity with piercing clarity: "All of their supposed enthusiasm for debate and heterodoxy is typically marshaled in defense of a handful of opinions—on transgender identity, feminist sexual politics, and the nature of racial disadvantage—which, far from having been chased into some intellectually 'dark' corner, are relatively common and largely shared by the most politically powerful people in America today" (Nwanevu, 2020, Paragraph 24). Normativity, then, as espoused by both "left" and "right" constitutes a win for ["Western"] "civilization" and its eternally ignoble plight for democracy. Both work toward the same end: to shore up the sanctity of whiteness and further imbricate white supremacist structural functioning.

This is the perspective from which I come to understand Dimen's warning, "the road to false consciousness, no matter how you wish to define it, is paved with politically correct intentions" (1984, p. 147), though I know, by deduction, this is not what she meant. Perhaps she could not anticipate the limits of her own white progressive worldview and how this position, as black feminists like Audre Lorde, bell hooks, doris davenport, and countless others, came to see, would shore up the "cultural wars" that were being activated at that time. While white liberal and radical feminism codified a particular position doing work to push back against Reagan, rampant homophobia during the AIDS crisis, the war on poverty, etc.—these spaces still precluded or only provided narrow spaces for black, indigenous and other women of color. This remains true today, of course, and especially true of our psychoanalytic circles, training institutes, and organizations (*See* recent examples, Steele 2021; Merson, 2021; Dadlani, 2020; Merchant, 2020; Crane, 2020; Jones, 2020; Holmes, 2020; Haddock-Lazala, 2020).

An example might help concretize the sting of reality.

Kirkland Vaughans, the first black male keynote of a major psychoanalytic conference, was on stage 10 min into his keynote speech, that year held in New Orleans. I was rushing from a meeting and opened the grand ballroom doors to a room packed with folks; it was already "standing room only". I made my way to the furthest most right wall, taking a seat on the floor next to many others who had also missed the window for formal seating. Kirkland was showing a video: a black girl getting assaulted in her school by a "resource officer", pushed out of her seat, brutalized. The audience gasps, visibly shaken, actively registering their dissent against the violent imagery. He continues to speak; folks are enthralled. Out of the group huddled along the wall with me emerges a white person, femme, probably in their mid-thirties, tall. She later takes a seat in the aisle, directly in front of me. Let me contour the spatial dynamics for ease: the wall, me, white person, chairs full of folks, the middle aisle at the end of which stood Kirkland at the podium, more people in chairs, left wall with more standing folks.

I initially think nothing of it. Perhaps she is planning to leave, making a half-way step to the door, so as not to disturb anyone.

But, instead, she starts to do yoga.

Yes, *yoga*. Not stretching. Not back cracking or working out a kink. Pigeon pose, on both sides, downward dog, tree pose, yoga.

I find myself more than distracted; I am distinctly aware that *something is happening*. Something *real* is happening, unfolding before me, and I also recognize I have to retain the ability to think—to not be seduced into the individual encounter, but rather understand this as but one tiny example in a panoply of systemic violence. In this moment, I work against the white liberal discourse of political correctness, even as I am keenly aware of not wanting to act impulsively out of ableist notions of body constriction. Kirkland's voice cuts through my internal debate, and I am grounded in the reality-based intervention I need to make. I lean over and ask her in a whisper if she would mind stopping her yoga, as it was very distracting. She glares at me and says she is "just stretching". I say, "perhaps you can do that in a way that is not disrespectful to the speaker". She says, "no one else seems bothered", gesturing to the unperturbed white faces in the audience. She is right. How does nobody *feel* what is happening? This is visceral for me. Realizing that she is not quite getting the codes I am speaking, I respond: "I find myself incredibly disturbed that you are doing this, in an aisle, while a black man is speaking". Her face contorts, angered, she leans into me and through polite-aggression whispers to me, "you are oppressing *me*".

A white progressive liberalism might warn me not to intervene in that moment, as I would be interfering with the body autonomy of a woman, something that has long been policed. That historical reality is true, and a necessary factor with which to contend against the continued crush of patriarchy. And, yet, perhaps here the curiosity of nuance and a psychoanalytic praxis of holding multiple meanings is most crucial, but so often crumbles precisely as a function of white progressive liberalism, the aim of which is to fundamentally retain power, even in contradiction to espoused liberal values.

Take for example, a different psychoanalytic conference at which I was presenting (are we tuning into a repetition compulsion yet?), where an elderly white woman—self-identified as a liberal feminist—during question and answer demanded that my sister, Annie Lee Jones, "prove" to her the racial enactment Annie Lee had recounted had happened earlier in the day. After our talk, the same elderly white woman approached me and screamed that the intervention I had made (pointing out the process that was unfolding between she and Annie Lee) was "unacceptable!! Don't you know that us white women have been enslaved far longer than ANY black or brown women! We were slaves before you! We are STILL slaves! We weren't allowed to work!". This banal protestation shows us what historical reality has taught us in far more brutal ways: white women, including liberal feminists, have subjugated especially black and indigenous women and upheld patriarchy in support of social, economic, and political supremacy (a recognition that has been documented assiduously by scholars, and recently by Rafia Zakaria in her book *Against White Feminism*, 2021; and Ruby Hamad's *White Tears, Brown Scars*, 2019). Had I remained ensconced in the white feminist liberal progressive mindset of body autonomy alone, I would have missed the sociopolitical reality.

In that moment of my intervention with yoga-practitioner, then, I chose historical reality over white liberal discourse on political correctness. It is important to note that my intervention itself was also not about politically correct saviorism in service of Kirkland; indeed, this is the crucial working piece that works *against* white progressive liberal rigidity. In fact, I do not believe that this white woman would not have done yoga had it been another white person on stage. Rather, in her structurally secured whiteness, that moment provided her the *luxury* to disavow the sociohistorical meaning, the unconscious meanings, and that, as Gauttari (1972/1967) reminds us, "the dominant classes will have an increasing hold on the unconscious determinations of individuals" (as cited in Herzog, 2016).

In that moment, whiteness allowed her to place her *individual* self above the raced and gendered structural dynamics at play. In doing so, she vacated her embodied responsibility to that reality, not coincidentally, into me, a brown, immigrant, Other, in a white professional space, who *viscerally* registered the violence of that moment, only to be received as the aggressor myself, the *oppressor*, victimizing her in my disciplining "political correctness". My intervention then came to be simultaneously read as personalized, ahistorical, and depoliticized, and also encroaching on her embodied personal freedoms, as though freedom itself is just granted and equitably distributed to all (let alone within *my* reach to wrench from her).

We might be seduced into reading this merely as an enactment or a projective identification, and perhaps it was. But, the volume at which these types of encounters happen, the repetitiveness, the predictably, far more readily lends itself to a *structural* diagnostic, one that isolates a white supremacist underpinning as the root purveyor of all subsequent symptoms.

This seems to be what Dimen misses herself when she states: "when the radical becomes correct, it becomes conservative" (p. 141). This stance is less about *correctness* and more about a refusal to disavow nonnegotiable historical and material truths, a denial of which obfuscates a proper working through and instead supports a reliance on archaic—conservative—defenses. In this way, the seduction of a dual defense that recalibrates a social order affording comfort through rigidity to the few vs. fluidity and generativity for the collective feels far more of a threat than the shared fear of political correctness or an elusive "cancel culture".

Notes

1 For more on this notion, *See* Klutz, J., Walker, J. & Walter, P. (2020) Unsettling allyship, unlearning and learning towards decolonising solidarity. *Studies in the Education of Adults*, *52*(1), 49–66.

2 A more in-depth discussion of issues regarding free speech, especially within psychoanalysis and psychology is beyond the scope of this paper. See for example, Berger, E., & Jabr, S. (2020). Silencing Palestine: Limitations on free speech within mental health organizations. *International Journal of Applied Psychoanalytic Studies*, *17*(2), 193–207.
3 Found at: https://harpers.org/a-letter-on-justice-and-open-debate/.
4 For more information, see Glenn Greenwald's pieces in the intercept: https://theintercept.com/2017/08/31/nyts-newest-op-ed-hire-bari-weiss-embodies-its-worst-failings-and-its-lack-of-viewpoint-diversity/andhttps://theintercept.com/2018/03/08/the-nyts-bari-weiss-falsely-denies-her-years-of-attacks-on-the-academic-freedom-of-arab-scholars-who-criticize-israel/.
5 For more information, see Julia Serano's piece: http://juliaserano.blogspot.com/2017/12/my-jesse-singal-story_11.html and trans journalist, Katelyn Burn's Twitter thread: http://archive.is/8lePc.
6 For more information, see JK Rowling's own sanctimonious account: https://www.jkrowling.com/opinions/j-k-rowling-writes-about-her-reasons-for-speaking-out-on-sex-and-gender-issues/.

References

Crane, L. S. (2020). Invisible: A mixt Asian woman's efforts to see and be seen in psychoanalysis. *Studies in Gender and Sexuality*, *21*(2), 127–135.

Dadlani, M. B. (2020). Queer use of psychoanalytic theory as a path to decolonization: A narrative analysis of Kleinian object relations. *Studies in Gender and Sexuality*, *21*(2), 119–126.

Dimen, M. (1984). Politically Correct? Politically Incorrect? In, C.S. Vance, ed., *Pleasure and danger: Exploring female sexuality,* pp. 138–148. Boston: Routledge & Kegan Paul.

Haddock-Lazala, C. M. (2020). X'ing psychoanalysis: Being LatinX in psychoanalysis. *Studies in Gender and Sexuality*, *21*(2), 88–93.

Herzog, D. (2016). Desire's politics: Félix Guattari and the renewal of the psychoanalytic left. *Psychoanalysis and History*, *18*(1), 7–37.

Holmes, N. (2020). The motherland, my ancestors, and me: My experience navigating psychoanalytic spaces. *Studies in Gender and Sexuality*, *21*(2), 113–118.

Jones, A. L. (2020). A Black woman as an American analyst: Some observations from one woman's life over four decades. *Studies in Gender and Sexuality*, *21*(2), 77–84.

Merchant, A. (2020). Don't be put off by my name. *Studies in Gender and Sexuality*, *21*(2), 104–112.

Merson, M. (2021). The whiteness taboo: Interrogating whiteness in psychoanalysis. *Psychoanalytic Dialogues*, *31*(1), 13–27.

Steele, J. (2021). Fear of blackness: Understanding white supremacy as an inverted relationship to oppression. *Psychoanalysis, Culture & Society*, *26*, 338–404.

Sheehi, L. (2018) Palestine is a four-letter word. *DIVISION/Review*, *18*, 28–31.

Razack, S. & Fellows, M. L. (1998). The race to innocence: Confronting hierarchical relations among women. *Journal of Gender, Race & Justice*, *335*, 343.

Tuck, E., & Yang, K. W. (2012). Decolonization is not a metaphor. *Decolonization: Indigeneity, Education & Society*, 1, 1–40.

The Unresolved Questions Muriel Dimen Helped Me Raise

Laura Trajber Waisbich

It was a hot afternoon in Sao Paulo several years ago. I was walking with my mum in what was then our neighbourhood heading nowhere worth remembering. A white car approaches us. It was one of those Volkswagen Kombis, so commonly seen in Brazilian cities. The driver slows down, opens his window and stares at me in a lascivious way rolling his tongue around his lips. I, infuriated, immediately shout at him: 'fuck off, son of a bitch'. Did I curse his mum? Possibly. Or was it just an angry 'go fuck yourself?'. Not sure. My mum looks at me half-appalled, half-angry, and says: 'What happened to you? Why are you so out of your senses?' I responded that he deserved my anger and nothing else. Was she mad at me for cursing strangers on the street? Was she mad at me for responding violently to a man's appreciation of my body, of me as a woman? I don't know.

I completely forgot this episode until a couple of years later when, in 2015, a wave of feminist campaigns bloomed in Brazil, some of them cyberfeminist campaigns. Among the most vibrant hashtag campaigns there was one called #MyFirstHarrassement (*#Meuprimeiroassedio*) where people would narrate their first experiences of being harassed. This campaign was launched as a response to paedophilic comments targeting a 12-year-old girl who appeared on TV in a junior edition of the world-famous cooking show Masterchef. I had no particular memory about a first harassment, nothing especially dramatic or traumatising to share. But many people did. A recent study showed that the average age of first harassment among stories told on social media in response to that campaign was 9.7 years old.[1] But I kept quiet. Shared nothing. Just silently read the numerous stories told by my female friends and colleagues about their first-hand experiences with sexual abuse or harassment when they were kids. My male friends and colleagues shared nothing. Maybe out of respect for what was a women-led action, empowering women's standpoint (or 'lugar de fala' as we call in Brazil). Maybe because child-abuse of boys remains a largely overlooked issue, another taboo. A few months later, a new hashtag campaign was launched: #MySecretSanta *(#Meuamigo secreto)*. Secret Santa is a very popular tradition in Brazil among friends and even work colleagues at Christmas time. The idea

DOI: 10.4324/9781003335252-14

behind this virtual campaign was to allow for stories of daily experience with misogyny to be shared, concealing the name/identity of the 'perpetrator' and making light of it just like Secret Santa. Rather than a campaign of open naming and shaming, Secret Santa was, at the individual level, a safe(r) way to pass along the message. Collectively, it was also about creating a pool of more-or-less general, generalisable stories several women could identify with. We all got our Secret Santas and unsurprisingly they kind of looked alike.

This time I decided to share my story with them. And I secretly named my mum as my Secret Santa. I named a woman rather than a man: a woman who I thought had behaved in a misogynistic way with me, perhaps acting out the structural misogynist pressures that she, I and all women are subject to. I felt like raising the structural issue. That was my Secret Santa speech. Days later, I asked myself (feeling guilty in that recurrant social-media sorta way), whether I had been stupid to name a woman rather than a man secretly. And worst: to have secretly named my own mum. No one knew at the time my Secret Santa was my mum because the Secret Santa stories had no names attached. But still, was it correct, or appropriate or fair to denounce what it felt to me as a certain kind of women's misogyny when men, or the patriarchy some would say, are the main source of this violence in the first place? I also asked myself several other questions about that afternoon in Sao Paulo. Had she blamed me, years before, for responding to a very uncomfortable cat-call? To my harassment in the street? Did she see in me one of those men-hating feminists, and felt it was appropriate to blame me rather than blaming the guy for approaching us in a sexually violent way? But I decided not to deeply dig into those questions, or even raise the issue with my mum. I just carried on.

As the #MeToo movement unfolded first in the United States and then globally, 1 or 2 years later,[2] we all started to listen to more personal and collective stories. We re-engaged in our own private and collective discussions, online and offline, and re-opened that box of painful, interesting and/or challenging conversations around the movement and what it meant to be feminist. But also on what the naming-and-shaming and criminally denouncing meant to our contemporary 'punishment societies'. At the time I was working for a human rights NGO in Brazil, whose work focused, among other things, on challenging mass incarceration in Brazil, which is so prevalent. A social phenomenon that Brazil shares with other unequal societies, such as the United States, in appallingly similar ways[3].

For someone embedded in the human rights movement in Brazil at the time, the punishment discourses and legal turns of the #MeToo mattered a lot to me, maybe as much as the gender and sexuality discussions. Those were not easy questions. Not easy questions to ask and discuss among different generations and types of feminist movements cross-cutting age, class, race. Not easy questions to ask and not easy discussions to have among

Brazilians, who live in one of world's most unequal and violent societies in the world. People's perception of the (politically) correct and the incorrect, right and wrong, as much as of the violent and non-violent, were often too diverging. Shaped by our own most subjective experiences and by what in social sciences we often referred to as our 'positionalities'.

Reading Muriel Dimen's *Politically Correct? Politically Incorrect?* (1984) brought me back to this story again. I started thinking about those weird blame-games again with my mum and with myself in terms of politically correct and incorrect. In terms of expectations and mutual judgements from woman-to-woman on what is right and appropriate behaviour, including when one is faced with harassment on the street. But also what are the limits to what we call and understand by sexuality, sexual freedom and violence? And the ways in which those boundaries change according to our own subjective lived experiences and context? Whereas I have not exactly changed my feelings and appreciation about what happened in that hot afternoon in Sao Paulo, I can see where my mum, who is a psychoanalyst, is coming from. Where her concern with my anger was coming from.

As the #MeToo unfolded, a first fissure from within came from a group of French feminists, from the so-called May '68 generation. They were worried about the framings of the #MeToo movement in the United States. Framings, they said, that confined women to always be the victim in society: something they saw as being at culturally at odds with their French way of approaching the issue. They claimed a 'freedom to bother'. However, to me this 'bothering' framing sounds more unsettling than appealing particularly when thinking about extremely violent societies like Brazil or the US. Moreover, I certainly don't buy into the hard cultural relativist approach that separates French women from North American, South American or Brazilian women. But I could also see what was bothering this group of French feminists in that much of the #MeToo discussion went global initially through the lenses and repertoires of American feminists. This framed sexual abuses and victimhood with an American accent, and they, those French women, felt the need to dispute the American framing of politically correct and incorrect as well as ideas of women's sexualities and violence. There is a parallel to be drawn between this conversation – on context and appropriate framings and repertoires for feminist movements – and the anti-racist movements, particularly in the Americas. Much been said about ways that US Black and anti-racist movements' framings and conceptualisations travel across geographies, including to countries like Brazil[4], and the imposition of those 'global scripts' on local struggles, as much as the 'translation', 'localisation' and/or 'hybridisation' strategies employed by local groups to create their own scripts. The circulation of narratives, repertoires, concepts is a very frequent phenomenon, even more so in times of accelerated globalisation and of social media. Yet, is also important to recognise that this circulation of the #MeToo is a process that connects different feminist voices around the world and their struggles while simultaneously generating friction and debate between them. Circulation is a deeply politicising process.

Undeniably, the #MeToo movement and the countless other feminist campaigns, such as those in Brazil, opened many doors to talk about sexuality and violence, but also about intersectionality and privilege and how those might influence what we name and perceive as appropriate/inappropriate or behaviour and how then we differentiate those socially correct/incorrect behaviours from the criminal ones. To me what is most interesting about those disputed notions of appropriate/inappropriate is how we then imagine our societies will function in the future. Yes, #MeToo is about women seeking justice for past violence they suffered. But it is also asking what kinds of societies and sociabilities, including gendered relations, we might build to replace the broken ones we currently have. The more I think about this topic, the more I realise that I hold a weird mix of strong beliefs of morally/politically/socially right-and-wrong with unsettling uncertainties. Muriel Dime's 1984 piece offered me an opportunity to come back to some of those questions with the tranquillity of not having to arrive at final answers.

Notes

1 *See* Natansohn, L. and Reis, J. (2017). 'Com quantas hashtags se constrói um movimento? O que nos diz a "Primavera Fe-minista" brasileira'. *Dossiê Tríade*, Universidade Federal da Bahia.

2 The #Metoo campaign (or #Metoo movement) peaked in the US in late 2017, although the first use of this expression dates from much earlier.

3 *See*, for instance, Alexander, M. (2010). *The new Jim Crow: Mass incarceration in the age of colorblindness*. New York: New Press.

4 It was a Brazilian friend and social scientist that opened my eyes to this parallel and suggested me to expand on this topic. I thank her and all my generous and attentive readers for sharingtheir thoughts with me on this vignette.

On Political Correctness

A Plea for an Intersectional Frame

Lynne Layton

"Politically Correct/Politically Incorrect". I really never use the terms. As Dimen (1989) suggests, "notions of political correctness… constitute psychological foot-binding" (p. 142). My experience of well over 50 years in activist movements suggests that although the term "politically correct" started life ambiguously within the feminist movement – for some, a proud affirmation, for others a put-down of zealous comrades – it is currently largely deployed as a weapon by people who are not on the left to demean people on the left whose positions they don't like. Part of what makes political correctness psychologically foot-binding, whether used within or against the left, is the way it often does the cultural work of denying the force of interlocking oppressions, its failure to analyze issues in an intersectional frame.

Back in the 70s, I remember labor organizers in a feminist group repeatedly lamenting the fact that there were no working-class women in the group, without of course ever thinking that perhaps there was something in their own analysis that kept working-class and all women of color away from our all white middle-class group. These Marxist feminists were usually the ones who used the term "politically correct" to describe their own platform, unaware that their white, upper-class positionalities were often performed in such a way as to make the resulting politics alienating to anyone not occupying those positions. Both then and now, within the left, a derogatory comment like "She's so PC" is used precisely to describe someone who you think has flattened out a complex and even sometimes contradictory set of issues. In such cases, being politically correct boils down to operating in a frame that is not intersectional.

I wish I had always practiced my politics within an intersectional framework, but in my 70s and 80s feminist activism I was fairly oblivious of my race/classed position and how it informed my political views. I was fairly oblivious of U.S. history. The value of doing politics in an intersectional, historically informed frame was brought home to me during the 2018 blow-up that led to the split in the Women's March movement. I of course am not aware of all the internecine details, but the movement seems to have split over an incapacity to hold the complexities of intersecting oppressions.

DOI: 10.4324/9781003335252-15

Founder Vanessa Wruble apparently felt that some of the women of color she had hoped would lead the movement held anti-Semitic views and supported anti-Semitic movements (this and the following details are drawn from Stockman, 2018). Wruble, who is a white Jew, said that, at a first meeting, two other organizers, Tamika Mallory (African-American) and Carmen Perez (Latina) suggested that Jews need to look into the large role they played in the slave trade and now in the prison industry. Wruble researched the claim and found that Nation of Islam (NOI) leader Farrakhan was behind the false theory that the Jews had orchestrated the slave trade. Wruble was also disturbed to find that NOI members had been hired to provide security for the march. Perez and Mallory, the latter of whom acknowledges admiration for Farrakhan and the NOI, disagreed with Wruble's construction of the events. Eventually, Wruble was asked to leave the group, and, as so often happens on the left, she started a new and somewhat competing group, March On. In the December 2018 *New York Times* article, Mallory reflected that, in the wake of the controversy, the non-Jewish group members did research that rendered more complex their view of Jews; they realized that Jews not only play a role in upholding white supremacy but are often also the targets of white supremacy. Mallory's report of doing some intersectional and historical homework made me hopeful, but that work did not prevent the split. The more reports I read about the events, the less I understood them and the sadder I got; they largely add up to a confusing "she said/she said." I felt there was little to no grieving for what had been politically lost in this not uncommon situation marked by denial of the ways that the identity-formation of different groups within a given culture occurs in relation. Political correctness often entails seeking refuge in split, essentialized identifications.

All that said, I rarely hear charges of political correctness/incorrectness within the left today. The bigger current threat to the left, it seems to me, is the wholesale attack from both liberal and right-wing quarters against a perceived tyranny of left-wing political correctness. An excellent case in point is a piece by Lionel Shriver (2019) in *Harper's Magazine*. Typical of this genre of left bashing, Shriver ridicules terms like "privilege," "cisgender," "people of color," "enslaved people," "microaggression." One begins very soon to understand why she has been characterized as "dripping in privilege" (p. 5): for example, she uses the royal liberal white bourgeois "we" to opine that, since Lyndon Johnson, "we've expressed concern for the 'underprivileged.' Shining a spotlight on the 'privileged' fosters resentment in people who feel shafted and an impotent guilt in people at whom the label is hurled" (p. 5). Funny, but impotent guilt is not at all what I feel when I reflect on the unearned privileges I've enjoyed simply by virtue of being seen as white. Shriver's stance exemplifies what Solnit (2017) has described as the "willed obliviousness of privilege."

The same royal "we" declares that since there is no linguistic or meaningful difference between "colored people" and "people of color," it is an idiotic nod to political correctness to use the latter term – Shriver exhibits not an ounce of awareness or care that it is "people of color" who have asked to be referred to as such. "Cisgender," she says, is not a necessary word; it "feels forced and inorganic" (p. 6); it is a misuse of language, an unnecessarily "freighted neologism" (p. 6) – to her. She hears no voice but her own, she who reportedly changed her name from Margaret Ann to Lionel because her given name didn't adequately reflect her tomboy gendered experience. Shriver calls the use of these terms "linguistic skullduggery – that is, winning an argument without the bother of actually having one…" (p. 6). Yet it is she who shuts down argument with comments such as: "Reflexive resort to this argot therefore implies not that you think the same way as others of your political disposition but that you don't think" (p. 7). Is that an argument?

For Dimen, the tension in left feminism's politically correct/politically incorrect wars of the 70s and 80s lay in the movement's commitment to freedom and to a collective project of dismantling patriarchy. Shriver's attack on various parts of the left as "politically correct," like most such attacks, shows a complete obliviousness to collective claims, to history, and to interlocking oppressions. She experiences the left's "political correctness" as an organized assault on her individual right to use the word "slave." "Privilege," she writes, is something that can be "acquired through merit" (p. 5) not something you ARE (i.e., "white"). Having been engaged for several years in racial equity work, I recognize most of Shriver's rhetorical moves – call me "politically correct" if you wish – as a manifestation of white fragility. Indeed, while at first glance she seems to speak only the language of individualism, her voice is in fact representative, consciously, or, more likely unconsciously, of a white collective that is terrified that marginalized communities are daring to tell them not, as she puts it, to shut the fuck up, but to LISTEN, to attend to something beyond the sound of their own "linguistically correct" voice.

References

Dimen, M. (1989) Politically Correct? Politically Incorrect? In C.S. Vance (ed) *Pleasure and Danger: Exploring Female Sexuality* (New York, NY: Pandora), pp. 138–148.

Shriver, L. (2019) Lefty lingo. *Harper's Magazine*, pp. 5–7.

Solnit, R. (May 30, 2017) The loneliness of Donald Trump. Retrieved from http://lithub.com/rebecca-solnit-the-loneliness-of-donald-trump.

Stockman, F. (2018) Women's march roiled by accusations of anti-semitism, *New York Times*, December 3. https://www.nytimes.com/2018/12/23/us/womens-march-anti-semitism.html.

The Political Incorrectness of Feminism in the Wake of Calls for Decolonisation in South Africa

Nobukhosi Ngwenya

History repeats itself:

> Women have played a role in every revolution in human history. And once the revolution is over, they are sold down the river every single time.
>
> (Russell-Swart, 2014: 218)

In the past decade or so, we have seen a resurgence of these debates, many of which often culminate in some form of mass action by womxn. For example, in January 2019 five million womxn formed a wall of protest in Kerala, India, to assert their rights to enter the Sabarimala temple.[1] In so doing, these womxn join millions of womxn in the history books who have been fighting for womxn's rights to be recognised and upheld. From the 1789 women's march in Versailles, to the 1913 women's suffrage parade in Washington, D.C., the 1929 Women's Riot in Nigeria and the 1956 Women's March in Pretoria, South Africa, to the more recent January 2019 women's march in Kerala, India women have been at the forefront of efforts to bring about social, economic and political change. Whilst we may not have (yet) achieved complete social transformation as envisioned by earlier feminist movements, we have managed to secure a "thousand tiny empowerments" (Sandercock, 1998: 129; Snyder-Hall, 2010) over the years. It is upon these 'small wins', so to speak, that I, and many young womxn across the globe, have built lives and careers that our great-grandmothers could never have imagined for themselves.

But, with the revolution seemingly over – after all we have a world-renowned Constitution that has rendered gender equity an unassailable right – womxn, particularly feminists, are being sold down the river once again as Phoebe Russell-Swart observes in the quote above. Calls for decolonisation made primarily by student movements across the country have, surprisingly, placed us, namely black, African womxn, in the crosshairs of keyboard activists (again!). There has been an upswing in voices – of various genders – lamenting that feminism is unAfrican. In so arguing, those who

DOI: 10.4324/9781003335252-16

believe feminism is unAfrican are in essence arguing that possession of political, physical, spiritual power by womxn in Africa is new. Subsequently, the voices and actions of previous generations on the continent and their hard-won victories for gender equality are erased.

With the erasure of the victories of previous generations, and amidst calls for decolonisation feminism and the identification of one's self as a feminist is now politically incorrect. How does a socio-political ideology such as feminism, which advocates for gender parity become politically incorrect? More so, how does feminism become politically incorrect in a country which has one of the highest rates of gender-based violence in the world.[2] Dimen (1984: 138–139) uses the term "politically correct" with reference to the:

> [I]dea that emerges from the well-meaning attempt in social movements to bring the unsatisfactory present into line with the utopian future, in fact, to make the 'revolution' happen [...] The idea of politically correct grows naturally from moral judgements (which any political ideology or philosophy contains) that deem certain aspects of the present way of living bad.

The question that I have been trying to answer for some time now is: what is the utopian future that social movements calling for decolonisation are working towards? What are the moral judgements that have been made to determine that feminism – as a way of living and an identity – is bad (or at the very least contributing to the maintenance of the current and undesired state of affairs)? At the heart of calls for decolonisation in South Africa, particularly in South African institutions of tertiary education, is a call to not only interrogate how knowledge is produced but also who produces knowledge. The calls have a strong anti-Eurocentric undercurrent that is manifested in calls for de-westernisation. According to Mignolo (2009: 161): "de-westernisation means, within a capitalist economy, that the rules of the game and the shots are no longer called by Western players and institutions". It follows then that calls for decolonisation (read de-westernisation), were accompanied by calls for the rejection of Western concepts, which feminism is but one. It is within this context that feminism has become a "dirty word, even among those who support the advancement of professional careers for women" (Schiebinger, 2000: 1173).

There is on the one hand, amongst those who are pro-decolonisation, for whom feminist ideology is unAfrican and, therefore, politically incorrect. Bowler (2018: online) argues that the adage "feminism is unAfrican' is, thus, an attempt to dictate the borders and applicability of feminism – without, conveniently, having to inhabit the experience that is at the centre of the reason feminism exists". On the other hand, there are those for whom the term – not what it signifies – is unAfrican. But if not 'feminism', what other term(s) can be used to signify this concept and the many ways – both visible and invisible (Bowler, 2018) – of being feminist? Is there a term in one or several African languages to denote the concept of feminism? Is feminism by another name still feminism? This is the question which we need to begin finding an answer to, bearing in mind that it is not simply a matter of translating the term from English to any one of a number of African languages. Whilst the word 'feminism' may be new in the African context, feminism itself as an ideology, a practice or a way of life is not. Pilane (2016: online) states that the "beauty of feminism in Africa is that it has existed long before the word even reached our shores". There are numerous examples of matrilineal societies which are still in existence. There are also several matriarchal African societies, which afforded women a number of social and sexual freedoms in the pre-colonial era (The African Report, 2017). This is disputed however. Several authors argue that there were no matriarchies in pre-colonial Africa. Ms. Afropolitan (2012) argues that the notion of the existence of matriarchal societies in pre-colonial times serves to curb and control feminist activism. It also has the effect of, one, masking the existence of patriarchy in pre-colonial African societies. Second, the argument that there were matriarchal societies in pre-colonial Africa, shifts the blame for patriarchy on colonialism to such an extent that we "forget about the African patriarchs [despite] historical evidence of male-dominant systems in precolonial Africa" (Ms. Afropolitan, 2012: online).

The debate around whether or not feminism is 'African' is quite surprising given the current wave of wokeness[3] that has swept across the globe. But, still the debate lingers. As Chioke (2019: online) muses: "If I had a penny for every time I've heard 'feminism is unAfrican', I would probably be on [a] yacht finishing this article". Whilst I might not have heard the adage enough to be finishing this piece on a yacht, I have certainly heard it enough to believe that it "disrupts the identification [of decolonial activists] with the aggressor" (Dimen, 1984: 141). Perhaps, it is also an indication that feminism, or some version of it, which was once considered radical (and politically correct), now "resemble[s] what it tries to change" (ibid.). Nevertheless, we cannot ignore that at the root of feminism is (personal) choice (Pilane, 2016) and self-determination, which is also one of the fundamental principles of decolonisation movements. Herein lies a contradiction within the decolonisation movement. Whilst advocating for self-determination of individuals in former colonies, the right to self-determination is denied to those who self-identify as feminists. This contradiction is equally present within feminist movements, some of which infringe on womxn's choices specifically those that are judged to maintaining a patriarchal status quo and colonial structures.

The swell in the number of voices arguing that *feminism is unAfrican* has stirred much needed debate and political engagement not only amongst feminists but from activists with similar (perhaps overlapping) agendas, namely advocates of decolonisation. But the extent to which these debates will lead to a reimagining of either or both movements remains to be seen.

Notes

1 The Sabarimala Sree Dharma Sastha temple (Sabarimala temple for short) is a Hindu pilgrimage site dedicated to Lord Ayyappa.

2 The high rates of gender-based violence in South Africa, which have been characterised as a "state of gender civil war" (Moffet, 2014: 218), have had a significant impact on the country's health, economic and social development (Jewkes et al., 2009).

3 The term 'woke' is a political term whose origins can be traced back to the 1960s. Literally the term refers to 'staying awake'. However, the non-literal meaning of the term – "being conscious of racial discrimination in society and other forms of oppression and injustice" (Dictionary.com, n.d.: online) – is used more often. It is a call-to-action by Black activists, which entered popular culture in 2008 when the artist Erykah Badu used it in her song titled *Master Teacher*. The term has since gained traction and has deviated from its original meaning and purpose as a call-to-action to become derogatory, internet slang (Sanders, 2018; Schneider, 2019). This deviation in meaning has led to a number of authors such as Pulliam-Moore (2016) arguing that the era of wokeness is drawing to a close, well, online at least.

References

Bowler, D. (2018). Whatever You Choose to Call It, Feminism Is Not Un-African. [Online]. Available: https://www.africanliberty.org/2018/11/05/feminism-is-not-un-african-or-irrelevant-by-danielle-bowler/.

Chioke, E. (2019). Is Feminism Really 'unAfrican'? [Online]. Available: https://blog.usejournal.com/is-feminism-really-unafrican-de28a51fa67c?gi=54ed0eed105f.

Dimen, M. (1984). Politically Correct? Politically Incorrect? In C.S. Vance, (ed.), *Pleasure and Danger: Exploring Female Sexuality*. London: Pandora Press, pp. 138–148.

Jewkes, R., Abrahams, N., Matthews, S., Seedat, M., van Niekerk, A., Suffla, S. & Ratele, K. (2009). Preventing Rape and Violence in South Africa: Call for Leadership in a New Agenda for Action. MRC Policy Brief. [Online]. Available: https://jliflc.com/wp-content/uploads/2014/06/Preventing-rape-and-violence-in-SA-MRC-2009.pdf.

Mignolo, W.D. (2009). Epistemic Disobedience, Independent Thought and Decolonial Freedom, *Theory, Culture & Society*, 26(7–8): 159–181.

Moffet, H. (2014). Feminism and the South African Polity: A Failed Marriage. In P. Vale, L. Hamilton & E.H. Prinsloo, (Eds), *Intellectual Traditions in South Africa: Ideas, Individuals and Institutions*. Pietermaritzburg: University of KwaZulu Natal, pp. 218–241.

Ms. Afropolitan. (2012). There were no Matriarchies in Pre-colonial Africa. [Online]. Available: https://www.msafropolitan.com/2012/06/the-myth-of-matriarchy-in-africa.html.

Pilane, P. (2016). Feminism Has Always Been African. [Online]. Available: https://mg.co.za/article/2016-05-06-00-feminism-has-always-been-african/.

Pulliam-Moore, C. (2016). How 'Woke' went from Black Activist Watchword to Teen Internet Slang. [Online]. Available: https://splinternews.com/how-woke-went-from-black-activist-watchword-to-teen-int-1793853989.

Sandercock, L. (1998). *Towards Cosmopolis: Planning for Multicultural Cities*. New York: John Wiley & Sons.

Sanders, S. (2018). Opinion: It's Time to Put 'Woke' to Sleep. [Online]. Available: https://www.npr.org/2018/12/30/680899262/opinion-its-time-to-put-woke-to-sleep.

Schiebinger, L. (2000). Has Feminism changed Science? *Signs,* 25(4): 1171–1175.

Schneider, C. (2019). What Does it Take to be Woke, Stay Woke, and Live Woke? [Online]. Available: https://www.yahoo.com/lifestyle/does-woke-stay-woke-live-140000186.html.

Snyder-Hall, R.C. (2010). Third-Wave Feminism and the Defence of 'Choice', *Perspectives on Politics,* 8(1): 255–261.

The African Report. (2017). Is Feminism Un-African? [Online]. Available: https://www.theafricareport.com/815/is-feminism-un-african/.

The Politically Correct and Incorrectness of Intersectionality in Feminist Discourse

Shiri Raz

"...By the mid-17th until the end of the 19th century, wet nursing by black women slaves had become very popular in Europe and America. Hundreds and thousands of young black women in both continents were forced to breastfeed white babies while simultaneously prohibited from breastfeeding their own babies, who were dying of malnutrition and related diseases."

Kate paused and took a deep breath before she continued her presentation to her local feminist club. She had prepared for today but knew that what she had to say next would not be easily received by the women in the audience. Despite the social price she was about to pay, she felt that while she identified with the truth and goals of the movement, its political correctness had to be challenged.

"The similarity between the violent exploitation of these women and the practices used to exploit cows in the dairy industry on a mass scale, day by day, should not be overlooked. Not by us. They are all victims of violence, just because they are females in an industry based on the exploitation of the female body...."

"Stop! Enough! I won't sit here and listen once again to your outrageous and demagogic attempt to humiliate women of color by comparing them to beasts!"

Susan shouted impatiently, storming out of the room. Some other women in the crowd followed suit and left the room. The remaining women did not seem particularly eager to hear the rest of what she had to say, trying as hard as they could to avoid Kate's eyes. Kate had to stop and walk off the stage, feeling misunderstood, helpless, and ashamed.

Intersectionality is a prevailing attitude in contemporary feminism. Coined in 1989 by Kimberle Crenshaw, the term was a call to unite struggles in order to eliminate gender-based and racial discrimination altogether. Evolving through the years, the term had become a well-established consensus in the feminist movement; an approach which today encompasses more than just the intersection of race and gender. Today, intersectionality is a term used widely by academics and human rights activists alike to illustrate the interplay of any kind of discrimination – whether based on gender, race, age, physical or mental ability, sexual identity, religion, nationality, or ethnicity. Over the past few decades, intersectionality has dramatically

DOI: 10.4324/9781003335252-17

expanded the limits of feminist discourse. It has granted an audible voice for silenced groups worldwide but has nevertheless failed, to date, to provide such a voice to the world's single largest oppressed community – animals.

Animals in general, specifically animals produced in the agriculture and meat industries, are the largest caged and violently abused population – today and throughout the history of all living beings. Every year, approximately 56 billion chickens, cows, goats and pigs are slaughtered for food – a figure that does not include male chicks and unproductive hens killed in egg production, as well as the infinite number of fish and other ocean creatures killed by the monstrous fishing industry, which is almost impossible to calculate and therefore estimated in tons.

Painfully understandable, the majority of land animals utilized in the animal food industries are females. Female animals in the food industry suffer the most – quantitatively and qualitatively. For years they are exploited violently, only then to be blessed with the dubious salvation of slaughter. The egg and dairy industries – each with its atrocious practices – are based on the exploitation of the reproductive systems of female cows, goats and chickens. To produce milk, a female mammal must give birth. She is, therefore, artificially and forcibly impregnated. Then, after several long months of gestation (in cows, like human women, gestation takes about nine months), she is separated from her baby calf, against her will, so her milk may be used for human profit. Her female calf shall endure a similar fate, eternalizing the chain of exploitation, while male calves are sent directly to the meat industry. In the dairy industry, female cows or goats undergo this cycle of forced pregnancy and heartbreaking separation about five times during the course of their lives until they are slaughtered. Females in the egg industry suffer a similarly horrendous fate. Only a few days old, baby chicks undergo the appalling procedure of debeaking – where the tips of their beaks are cut off to avoid injury and infection – and then, with five other chicks, are locked in a tiny cramped cage, unable to spread their wings or turn around for the remainder of their lives. Rows and rows of such cages lay among countless identical pens in dark storerooms. Her eggs will never be fertilized, and she will never have the opportunity to incubate them. After two years of such torture, she will be saved from further agony by death via poisonous foam or electrocution. The exploitation in these industries is not limited to animal females alone. Ironically, of the 600 million keepers of livestock – in itself, an oppressed and poverty-stricken population – approximately two-thirds are women (FAO, 2011; Thornton et al., 2002).

It is therefore undeniably clear that females in the food and agricultural industries are violently exploited – for merely being female. Nevertheless, the politically correct use of the term "intersectionality" has clear limits that exclude females of other species from any discourse of freedom or rights. Voices that call for a new perception of intersectionality are criticized or treated as esoteric. Such are the voices of eco-feminists Josephine

Donovan (1990) and Carol Adams (1990, 1994, 1996, 2004). For over three decades, both have argued that there is a dangerous and robust link between the continuing subjugation of women and human domination of nature. While Adams focuses on the similarity of cultural and lingual mechanisms which serve to construct the perception of a subject with feelings and rights, whether woman or animal, as an object (the term she coined for this was "absent referent"), Donovan points out the absurdity of fighting to end repression on one hand while being actively involved in another kind of oppression on the other (Adams & Donovan, 1995, 2008). Both, with the aid of eco-feminist thinkers such as Gaard (1993), Gruen (1996), Mallory (2010) and others, call for a new feminist perspective, one that recognizes the injustice and violent exploitation of animals and that can identify with their plea for freedom.

"We should not kill, eat, torture, and exploit animals because they do not want to be so treated, and we know that. If we listen, we can hear them" (Donovan, 1990, p. 375).

These voices were and still are being strongly countered by many – intentionally and unintentionally standing guard to keep non-human females (or males) excluded from the politically correct discourse about gender discrimination. The most influential and most common critique came from anti-essentialist feminists such as Janet Biehl who claimed that eco-feminists biologize the personality traits assigned to women by the patriarchy. According to their view, "the implication of this position is to confine women to the same regressive social definitions from which feminists have fought long and hard to emancipate women" (Biehl, 1991, p. 3). With a strong tailwind from others (Faber & O'Connor, 1988, 2011; Sargisson, 2001), this effort to avoid patriarchic hierarchy serves as a solid argument for maintaining a violent ethnocentric species-based and politically correct hierarchy where men and women together stand above all other beings.

A few weeks after her failed attempt to make her friends see the similarity between what she perceived as two different but analogous oppressions, Kate left the club. It was too painful and frustrating for her to stay. As she explained to one of her friends:

"Watching the most courageous women I know as they battle for justice and social equality while simultaneously indulging in a café latte is heartbreaking. I am leaving yet hold on to the desperate hope that one day you too will be able to hear the silent pleas of the present-day oppressed and caged wet-nursing slaves".

References

Adams, C. (1990). *The Sexual Politics of Meat: A Feminist-Vegetarian Critical Theory.* New York: Continuum.

——— (1994). *Neither Man Nor Beast: Feminism and the Defense of Animals.* New York: Continuum.

——— (1996)."Ecofeminism and the Eating of Animals", in *Ecological Feminist Philosophies*. K.J. Warren (ed.), Bloomington: Indiana University Press: 114–136.
——— (2004). *The Pornography of Meat*. New York: Continuum.
Adams, C. and J. Donovan (eds.). (1995). *Animals and Women: Feminist Theoretical Explorations*. Durham, NC: Duke University Press.
——— (eds.). (2008). *The Feminist Care Tradition in Animal Ethics: A Reader*. New York: Columbia University Press.
Biehl, J. (1991). *Rethinking Ecofeminist Politics*. Boston, MA: South End Press.
Crenshaw, K. (1989). Demarginalizing the Intersection of Race and Sex: A Black Feminist Critique of Antidiscrimination Doctrine, Feminist Theory and Antiracist Politics. University of Chicago Legal Forum: Vol. 1989: Issue. 1, Article 8.
Daniel Faber, D. and O'Connor, J. (1998). *Ecological Politics: Ecofeminists and the Greens*. Philadelphia, PA: Temple University Press.
——— (2011). "Ecofeminism Revisited: Rejecting Essentialism and Re-Placing Species in a Material Feminist Environmentalism". *Feminist Formations*, 23(2): 26–53.
Donovan, J. (1990). "Animal Rights and Feminist Theory". *Signs*, 15(2), 350–375. Retrieved from www.jstor.org/stable/3174490.
FAO (2011). *The State of the World's Land and Water Resources for Food and Agriculture (SOLAW) – Managing Systems at Risk*. Rome/London: Food and Agriculture Organization of the United Nations/Earthscan, URL: http://www.fao.org/nr/solaw/en/.
Gaard, G. (ed.). (1993). *Ecofeminism: Women, Animals, Nature*. Philadelphia, PA: Temple University Press.
Gruen, L. (1996). "On the Oppression of Women and Animals". *Environmental Ethics*, 18(4): 441–444.
Mallory, C. (2010). "What Is Ecofeminist Political Philosophy? Gender, Nature, and the Political". *Environmental Ethics*, 32(3): 306–322.
Sargisson, L. (2001). "What's Wrong with Ecofeminism". *Environmental Politics*, 10(1), 52–64. DOI: 10.1080/714000513.
Thornton P. K. (2010). "Livestock Production: Recent Trends, Future Prospects". *Philosophical Transactions of the Royal Society of London. Series B, Biological Sciences*, 365(1554): 2853–2867. DOI: 10.1098/rstb.2010.0134.

Bring Back the Curbs on Political Incorrectness

Shylashri Shankar

If political correctness implies the attempt to bring the unsatisfactory present into line with the utopian future, which in the case of a modern, democratic India implies infusing the values of equality, fraternity, and freedom into how citizens live, think, and act, then I come from a country and a society that was and continues to be intrinsically politically incorrect in its make-up. As a Hindu, I am born into a caste that is ranked hierarchically with other castes, and am part of a religion that forms the majority in the country, and this accident of birth determines my worth in the eyes of others.

Looking back at my childhood and teenage years, I did not have any friends who were from the lowest castes, and I had only a couple of Muslim friends. But this was more because my world revolved around where I lived (few Muslims lived in our neighbourhood) and in my convent school (my classmates came from a similar background where our parents either followed a profession or were in business).

In my teenage years, the politically incorrect statement echoed by the neighbourhood 'aunties' and my relatives (but not my parents) was – whatever you do, don't marry a Muslim. Why? Because they can have three wives and they can divorce you instantly just by uttering 'talaq, talaq, talaq'. It did not seem to me then to be a politically incorrect statement, but simply a factual one about Muslim marriage and divorce laws. Or so I thought then. But looking back, I see how that statement about not marrying a Muslim had a subtext of prejudices – they are violent because their religion proselytises and so on. In conversations at home with relatives (most of my aunts, two of my favourite uncles and a great-uncle were rabidly anti-Muslim) and with some of my parents' friends, I was used to being branded as a 'Paki sympathiser', as an 'apologist for Muslims' and so on. Growing up with lots of visits with cousins, aunts and uncles, I was accustomed to challenging these prejudices (which were about other religions and other castes), and sometimes ignoring them, but never letting

DOI: 10.4324/9781003335252-18

these views colour the affection that bound us. I was unaware that words have the power to infiltrate and shape prejudices. Political correctness was not required in private spaces – you said what you thought, and if the other person did not agree with you, both ignored that fact. It came from living in insular bubbles where hierarchy and inequality were taken for granted.

Later, at Cambridge University where I read for a social and political sciences Tripos, my close friends were Pakistani, with whom I shared common cultural and literary sensibilities. When I returned to India in the early 1990s, I was struck by the rise of anti-Muslim rhetoric in public discourse; Hindu nationalists were encouraging the 'Hindu' voter to reclaim India from the Muslims. But what shocked me were some friends who had never uttered anti-Muslim sentiments, but were doing so now. The debates I used to have with my relatives were now also occurring with friends.

Meanwhile, a close English friend converted to Islam and married a British Muslim of Pakistani descent. My mother, who was very fond of her, was upset and expressed her concern about the Damocles sword of three wives and the quick divorce. My friend changed her name and asked me to call her by her new Muslim name. That's when I resisted, telling myself that by erasing her old name, she was erasing my memories too that were connected with it. It took me time to say her new name, but even now, I still find myself thinking of her by her old name. I am not as sure now that my resistance is unconnected to the Muslim name. Would I have had the same resistance if she had become a Hindu? Was I really not influenced by the politically incorrect statements I grew up hearing?

In England, I realised that I was 'brown' or a 'blackie' to the white English who were as familiarly insular as my relatives in India. This was the first time I experienced 'political correctness' in the glances when they first encountered me or the careful way in which race was discussed by acquaintances in my presence. But I was also informed that since I came from India and was a foreigner, the local prejudices did not apply to me. But the political incorrectness was evident in the manner and thoughts masked by these politically correct utterances. But this experiencing of racism did not make me question my self-worth because that had already been fashioned and established by my birth in a high caste. Nor did it make me realise the loss of self-worth and dignity experienced by a low caste person.

After university, I went to work at the World Bank in Washington DC where I saw and disagreed with the high levels of political correctness when referring to African Americans. I felt then that political correctness was blocking the ability of a non-African American to see the African

American as a human being first rather than as a category. It was blocking friendship. It annoyed me when I too was seen as a category – a woman, a minority, a foreigner, an Indian brought up in a traditional society. In Austin, Texas, where I moved to teach at the university, each time I would enter a restaurant or a bar with my American-Greek friend, everyone would turn to look at us, as if I were an insect pinned to a board. Politically incorrect behaviour, but politically correct words and conversations. It reinforced my fervent belief that if we wanted to treat one another as human beings and not as categories, we should not be politically correct. But I had not examined what we would be if we were not politically correct. I thought if we openly shared our political incorrectness, we would have put it out there, and then we could move through and towards seeing the other as a human. I would have agreed with Muriel Dimen that the road to false consciousness, no matter how you wish to define it, is paved with politically correct intentions.

Now, circa twenty-first century, I ask myself, is false consciousness such a bad thing? I live in an India where, in the name of allowing everyone the right to freedom of speech, horrible slurs are being uttered about Muslims in public and in the internet space. India has changed. Those elements of political incorrectness that disturbed me in the early 1990s are now seen as legitimate everyday-speak in public and in private. Our decades of living in insular bubbles, and where we either ignored or were matter of fact in our encounters with others not like us, was now coming apart.

I began to revise my view on political correctness. Now I think this: it is better to treat someone respectfully even if one did not really respect them, than treat someone as disrespectfully as one felt about them. The habit of public respect could, hopefully, percolate into our private behaviours, but even if it did not, it would not be as harmful as the present situation of a giddy liberation from the obligation to be 'politically correct'.

What is to be done? There is a concerted move by a democratically elected government to draw a misleadingly neat circle around Hindu religion and Indian nationality, and blend personal experience and old and still powerful social practices, in this case the divide between Hindus and Muslims. New amendments to citizenship laws privilege the non-Muslim immigrant, and when applied in conjunction with the government's stated objective to carry out a compilation of a national register of citizens, carries a grave threat to those Muslims in India who do not possess the documentary evidence of citizenship. Our long struggle to corral politically incorrect sentiments in private spaces has been torn down. We live in a politically incorrect world with complete freedom of speech and expression. The question facing us is how to tackle the contradiction between what a collective stands for (e.g., individualism in feminism) and what they have to do to realise this goal (curb freedom by telling people how to behave). Dimen is right that it is not feasible for both these tendencies to be simultaneous guides to politically correct behaviour. I choose to return India to the curbs on the freedom to express politically incorrect sentiments in public spaces.

Project Two

On Money, Love, and Hate

Project Two

Editor's Note

Stephen Hartman

Muse

Dimen, M. (1994). Money, love, and hate: Contradiction and paradox in psychoanalysis. *Psychoanalytic Dialogues*, 4: 69–100.

Paradox guided Dimen's clinical ear. Contradiction inked her pages. In this sprawling essay on hate and love in the countertransference, at every step of the way, Dimen brings complex theory to life with reference to the characters (be they Freud or a patient of Dimen's or, for that matter, Dimen herself) whose precarious relationship with money, love, and hate gives psychoanalysis its casting call. While this essay is not typically read as a character study, I have often found in its dramatis personae a guide to the complexity contained in any debt as framed in every fee.

Readers

Asymmetry is often thought to be a boon to psychoanalysis. The power differential between analyst and patient as demonstrated in the frame and fee has been theorized to invoke the negative transference as much as it has been predisposed to provide a measure of separateness, betoken commitment, and conjure reciprocity. For this team, I chose two authors who are very differently positioned and, depending on their intersectional identification, (a)symmetrically aligned in "the field" of psychoanalysis. Jeff Jackson is an accomplished white CIS male novelist and performance artist (not a psychoanalyst though no stranger to the field) whose experimental fiction has won accolades. June Lee Kwan is an early career psychologist and activist, a woman of color whose use of fiction offers respite from the canonical form of the case vignette that is often imposed on psychoanalytic candidates. Each was asked to respond to Dimen's cast of characters. Given the *psychoanalytic* frame of this writing experiment, I was interested to see how authority would accrue in each *reader's* voice in the position of *writer.*

DOI: 10.4324/9781003335252-20

Form

The initial task was for each author to sit with Dimen's paper and then write a short story that brings to life a character (loosely defined) or a problem (interpreted as they wish) with no necessary reference to Dimen's paper other than an ear to money, love, and hate. The authors then traded their stories with the option to write a follow-up story that was influenced by their counterpart's intervention. They decided against a second round of text given the way these two very different stories combine to tell a singularly pointed story.

Bios

June Lee Kwon is a licensed clinical psychologist with a private practice in lower Manhattan. Her essays on journals of psychoanalysis have been frequently described as literary, as her clinical and academic endeavors focus on enlivening of experiences that are oppressed and disavowed.

Jeff Jackson is the author of the acclaimed novels *Mira Corpora* (Two Dollar Radio) and *Destroy All Monsters* (Farrar, Straus & Giroux). He has been a finalist for the *Los Angeles Times Book Prize* and his work has been translated into several languages. He lives in Charlotte, N.C.

Money, Love, and Hate

Contradiction and Paradox in Psychoanalysis

Muriel Dimen

The way analysts talk, behave, and feel in relation to money is replete with an uneasiness that is the surface manifestation of a deep, psychocultural contradiction between money and love that cannot be thought, willed, or wished away. For the clinical project to succeed, this contradiction can and must find a temporary, reparative resolution in the paradox between love and hate. This essay takes up the question of money in the spirit of the Marx–Freud tradition, in postmodern perspective, and through several languages, not only psychoanalysis, but social theory, anthropology, and less centrally, feminist theory as well. It addresses money's unconscious and emotional resonance, and its cultural meanings; money's clinical and theoretical vicissitudes in the context of cultural symbolism and economic change, as well as the class position of psychoanalysis and the psychology of class itself; and money's relational meaning in transference and countertransference.

SINCE MOST PSYCHOANALYTIC DISCOURSE about money takes place informally, it seems appropriate to begin in anecdotal style. When I first mentioned to colleagues my intention to write about this topic, I was greeted with what you might call a less than enthusiastic response. "Why are you talking about money?" asked one, quite startled. Another found the proposed title a bit inappropriate and wondered if it oughtn't be changed to something like "Between Commerce and Trust." It's almost as though money were in fact not quite a suitable topic for our distinguished community. Something we don't talk about, at least in public? A little unsavory, perhaps? Or vulgar?

This was not the first time I'd met with psychoanalytic unease about money. Consider Dr. French, as I am calling him, a colleague to whom, many years ago, I referred a patient's husband. The man had a cash business (no, he wasn't dealing drugs) and, like his wife, paid his analyst in cash, just as anyone in his subculture did whenever buying anything. Shocked, Dr. French shook his hands as if to rid them of dirt and said to me with an embarrassed smile, "It's, well, money just doesn't *belong* in the consulting room."

It begins to look as though Freud was right, doesn't it? Recall his (1913) ubiquitously quoted observation: "Money matters are treated by civilized people in

DOI: 10.4324/9781003335252-21

the same way as sexual matters—with the same inconsistency, prudishness and hypocrisy" (p. 131).

Freud and his contemporaries might not have shared Dr. French's feelings about cold, hard cash. If they had, they probably would have written about it; to my knowledge, the only classical reference to the matter is Abraham's (1921) certainly accurate diagnosis of severe anality in people who insist on paying not only analysts' bills but even the smallest sums by check (p. 378). Nevertheless, our forebears, themselves uneasy about money, recognized the deep desire that its dilemmas simply vanish. They thought hard about money's relation to development, character, and pathology. Abraham's (1921) and Jones's (1918) attention to its place in anal characterology develops Freud's (1908) original insights about its psychosexuality, "the sexual and especially the anal erotic significance of money" (Aron and Hirsch, 1992, pp. 39–40), ideas that are certainly familiar enough and to which I return later. Ferenczi (1914) augments this line of reasoning by assigning money a role in development; he argues that the adult attachment to money represents a socially useful reaction formation to repressed anal eroticism. Fenichel (1938) suggests that anal-erogeneity is made use of, and strengthened, by a social system based on the accumulation of wealth and competitiveness.

The approach to money taken by Ferenczi and Fenichel was political as well as psychoanalytic. Ferenczi (1914), for example, concludes that the "capitalistic instinct ... contains ... [both] an egoistic and an analerotic component"; standing at the disposal of the reality principle, "the delight in gold and the possession of money ... also satisfies the pleasure-principle" (p. 88). Fenichel (1938) points out that what he identifies as the drive to amass wealth is born with capitalism, adding that in precapitalist, tribal society it did not exist, while, in a future classless society, it would have disappeared (p. 108). They were not the only classically trained psychoanalysts who wanted to unite two of the three great and diverging arteries of 19th-century European thought, Marxism, and psychoanalysis (to put them in their chronological order; the third and temporally intermediate one is Darwinian evolutionary theory). While it is unlikely and probably not desirable that these two grand theories will meld into a single perspective encompassing nothing short of human life itself, nevertheless the dialogue between them has been fruitful and remains compelling. Not only Ferenczi and Fenichel but such luminaries as Edith Jacobson, George Gero, and Annie Reich received their intellectual formation during a time heady with progressive politics and psychoanalytic discovery. While some, like Wilhelm Reich and Erich Fromm, kept striving for synthesis, others abandoned their politics, a yielding impelled more by their Holocaust-driven escape to an anticommunist United States (with its medicalized and anti-intellectual psychoanalysis) than by the inherent incompatibility of two cherished and imaginative comprehensions of human possibility (Jacoby, 1983).

Taking up the question of money in the spirit of the Marx–Freud tradition (a project already called for by Rendon, 1991) but adding a postmodern perspective, I consider money's vicissitudes in the psychoanalytic relationship a topic that is theoretically immediate as well. Freud's discussions about money as a practical matter (1913) and money as a psychological matter (e.g., 1908) may appear in separate essays (see Whitson, n.d., p. 3). But their distance in print represents only the map of his thought, not their lived geography. In the light of recent psychoanalytic and social thought, money's clinical and theoretical locations turn out to be more proximate than might at first appear. Developments in psychoanalytic theory—such as the Kleinian understanding of love and hate, the Winnicottian notion of paradox, the interpersonal assessment of countertransference, and contemporary relational arguments about the simultaneity of one-person and two-person psychologies—and developments in social theory—such as social constructionism, critical theory, and postmodernism—permit a synthetic and evolving interpretation of money in the psychoanalytic relationship that is both clinically relevant and theoretically responsible.

On reflection it becomes clear that a theory of money cannot derive from psychoanalysis alone. Consider Freud's only partially theorized perspective. His ideas on the psychosexuality of money, which predate his instructions about its handling in the clinical setting, in essence constitute the sole intellectual frame for his practical considerations. Money is, Freud (1913) says, to be approached in the consulting room with the same matter-of-factness as sex, for while money has a narcissistic dimension, being "in the first instance … a medium for self-preservation and for obtaining power, … powerful sexual factors are [also] involved in the value set on it" (p. 131). The way analysts address it ought then to serve psychotherapy. By speaking with frankness, Freud says, he furthers the educative project of psychoanalysis; he shows patients that "he himself has cast off false shame on these topics, by voluntarily telling them the price at which he values his time" (p. 131).

As for the rest, for the principles on which Freud bases his policy of leasing his time and setting his fee, he speaks from "ordinary good sense" (p. 131). He speaks as a practical man of the world who must consider his material existence by charging for all time leased and regularly collecting his debts (pp. 131–132). The arrangement of leasing one's time, he observes, is "taken as a matter of course for teachers of music or languages in good society" (p. 126). He is faithful to his beliefs, not only his own theory of treatment but what is closely related, his ethics. In elaborating his ethical position, he reviews the behavior of other professionals, concurring in, or distinguishing his own practice from, theirs. He has, he tells us, desisted from taking patients without charge or extending courtesy to colleagues' kin for three reasons. For one thing, free treatment stirs up resistances to, say, the erotic transference in young women and to the paternal transference in young men, who rebel against any "obligation to feel grateful" (p. 132). For another, charging a fee preempts countertransferential resentment of patients' selfishness and exploitativeness (pp. 131–132). Finally, he finds it "more respectable and ethically less objectionable" to avoid the pretense to philanthropy customary in the medical profession and to acknowledge straightforwardly his interests and needs (p. 131).

The common sense from which Freud reasons is, however, like any informal system of "folk" or cultural knowledge, embedded in unexamined presuppositions. It combines, in effect, the expectations and prejudices customary for his class with his personal needs and predilections, and thus contains unarticulated ideas about issues that are only now being theorized in psychoanalysis—such as the patient's experience of the analyst's subjectivity (Aron, 1991) or the relation between one-person and two-person psychologies (Ghent, 1989; Aron and Hirsch, 1992)—or have, only since Freud's time, been anatomized by social thought, like the economic and political place of the helping professions, the social class of analysts and patients, and the psychology of class (Sennett and Cobb; 1972, Ehrenreich, 1989). Such vantage points being absent either from classical theory or from psychoanalytic thought altogether, it is not surprising that, until recently, so few analysts have considered the matter of money systematically. Whatever the other resistances to this topic (and I get back to them shortly), the intellectual tools to study it have been missing.

I want here to refurbish the intellectual tool kit by conversing in several languages, not only psychoanalysis but social theory, anthropology, and, less centrally, feminist theory as well. I decode money's unconscious and emotional resonance, as well as its cultural meanings. I track its clinical and theoretical vicissitudes in terms of cultural symbolism and economic change, as well as the class position of psychoanalysts and the psychology of class itself. Through both an examination of Freud's dicta and feelings about money and a clinical example, I render its relational meaning in transference and countertransference.

Money in Psychoanalytic Question

If Freud and his contemporaries were laconic on this matter, his followers have become exponentially voluble as the psychoanalytic century has worn on. The bibliographical entries in the anthology *The Last Taboo: Psychoanalysis and Money* (Krueger, 1986) are few and far between until the 1960s, when they begin to cluster; and then in the 1970s and 1980s they positively blizzard. Here we are in the 1990s, trying to climb out of what has been termed a "recession" but has really been a depression, which has nipped at, if not bitten into, the practices and pocketbooks and psyches of most psychoanalysts in private practice. Just in the last three years, there have appeared two more books on the question, one a general anthology (Klebanow and Lowenkopf, 1991) and the other about the fee (Herron and Welt, 1992). All cover quite a range of topics, from fee setting, personal philosophies about fee policies, and the relation between gender and money to managed health care and the effects of free treatment.

The snowballing discussion of money has a history, part of which is cultural. Psychoanalysis's "last taboo" fell during a period when a lot of other icons were being broken too, as, simultaneously, the class position of professionals was subtly but permanently shifting. If the 1960s (the "we decade") saw the blossoming of sexual expression and the 1970s of narcissism (the "me decade"), then the

1980s (the "greed decade") made the admission of the desire for money and the accumulation of wealth at least more common if not more socially acceptable. But, we might ask, acceptable to whom? Surely not stockbrokers and corporate raiders. Wall Street's expression of greed may well have had to do with the wildest financial party since the roaring twenties, a party perhaps even more avaricious than the age of the robber barons. But people who trade in money are supposed to be on good terms with selfishness; helping professionals are not. Instead, they are supposed to value money only for its ability to serve a modest standard of living. What was surprising in the 1980s, then, was the seemingly sudden acquaintance with covetousness on the part of professionals.

Psychoanalysts' heightened interest in money, not to mention their greed, had, however, more than a decade behind it. It was, in fact, a response to, and expression of, a long, slow slide in their socioeconomic fortunes. The 1960s were a watershed in a century-long trend; until then, the gap between rich and poor in the United States had been steadily decreasing. After that, the gap began to yawn. The middle class, from which traditionally have come most analysts and analysands, began to shrink, indeed, to decline; presently, middle-class people can no longer count on owning their homes or sending their children to college without impoverishing themselves (Newman, 1988; Ehrenreich, 1989). By the same token, the insurance reimbursements that subsidized their psychoanalytic treatment have dwindled, bruising both those in need of therapeutic help and those who make their living by providing it.

This decline in middle-class fortunes coincided with a boom in the helping professions, which in turn further reduced professionals' share of the pie. The extension of parity to psychologists and social workers by insurance companies, the increasing participation of social workers in the psychoanalytic profession, the proliferation of "media shrinks," and the flood of self-help books—these belong to the expansion of psychotherapy to all levels of the middle class, even to the working class. Part of the democratizing trend in psychoanalysis (Havens, 1989, p. 142; Zaphiropoulos, 1991, p. 242), this growth also belonged to a cultural change that might be called the "therapization of America." The evolution of a therapy-sensitive culture in which people are knowledgeable about, and receptive to, psychotherapy, in which consumers assume the right to question and choose among all medical authorities, and in which psychotherapy is packaged by managed health care has, ironically, also reduced analysts' incomes. The more competition there is among providers of mental health care, the fewer the patients and the lower the fees for each privately practicing analyst (Chodoff, 1991, pp. 254–256; Drellich, 1991, pp. 159–161; Aron and Hirsch, 1992); the more knowledge consumers have, the more they question analysts' authority and resist the imposition of what have sometimes seemed to be arbitrarily high fees (see also Herron and Welt, 1992, p. 171).

As psychoanalytic pockets slowly emptied, psychoanalytic journals began to fill up with articles on money. Comparisons would be interesting. In other countries, say, Sweden, where the middle class remains or has become economically secure, as it was in Freud's time, are these issues handled differently? Are they addressed systematically? Or are they ignored, as, in fact, they were in Europe and the United States until, for all intents and purposes, 30 years ago? Or take the obverse: will psychoanalysts in Eastern Europe begin formally to consider the clinical and theoretical problems money presents as their practices leave the public domain of (medical) hospital care and enter the private market?

The Disturbance of Money

In responding, if only unconsciously, to this recent (and perhaps permanent) downturn in the American economy, however, analysts are noticing merely what has been there all along. In saying this, I am revising Durkheim's (1930) classic sociological position, codified in his paradigmatic study of suicide. Durkheim (1938) drew a parallel between medical and social science: if studying illness reveals the nature of health (as, indeed, Freud himself, 1905, argued), then, he said, studies of social pathology should reveal the basis for social order and hence the true nature of social life. That social life is normally orderly, however, can no longer go unquestioned. A deconstructive, postmodern approach, which, perhaps not strangely, finds a harbinger in Freud, suggests otherwise. Taking a Foucauldian tack (Flax, 1990, p. 36), I argue that studying social disorder reveals instead the normal lines of discontinuity and conflict that are the fault lines along which cultural evolution and changes in inner life occur.

So with money and psychoanalysis: just as we learn from "hysterical misery" about "common unhappiness" (Freud, 1895), so if we look into disrupted economics, we come upon money's ever-present, complicated meaning in psychoanalysis and, thence the normal difficulties of the work. Several recent papers teach us a lot about the underrecognized countertransferential effects of analysts' economic dependence on their patients that these parlous times make visible. While their work allows us to see that you and your patients want you to *be* as invulnerable as a tenured full professor, you actually *feel* about as secure as a part-time adjunct. Yet, analysts have been so uncomfortable with their own feelings of need and greed (Aron and Hirsch, 1992, p. 255) that they have tended to treat money as a psychological problem for patients and merely a practical one for analysts (Whitson, n.d., p. 3). Indeed, analysts' dystonic relation to their own dependence may constitute the biggest single counterresistance in regard to money (Aron and Hirsch, 1992, p. 243; Whitson, n.d., p. 3). Herron and Welt (1992) concur and develop the theme: "The issue ... isn't that greed exists [among psychoanalysts]; rather, it is how that greed is responded to; how it is aroused, frustrated, or met" (p. 48; See also Shainess, 1991).

Analysts' pecuniary need of their patients, however, is not only a discrete countertransference problem. As we can see from Freud's by now well-known financial preoccupations, it is an inevitable thorn in their sides that demands as much inspection as their other basic needs *vis-à-vis* patients, their needs for, for example, love and respect, power and gratitude. Throughout his 17-year correspondence with Fliess (Masson, 1985), Freud writes periodically about his money-related worries, as well as about the times when his income feels to him adequate. It's quite clear not only that his cash flow is uneven but that this unpredictability breeds cynicism. For example, he prefers American patients for their hard currency (Gay, 1988) and writes, on January 24, 1895, "Mrs. M. will be welcome; if she brings money and patience with her, we shall do a nice analysis. If in the process there are some therapeutic gains for her, she too can be pleased" (Masson, 1985, p. 107). Notice also his reference to his wellborn, well-to-do patients as "goldfish," once on September 21, 1899 (p. 374) and another time on September 27, 1899: "The goldfish (L. von E., an S. by birth and as such a distant relative of my wife) has been caught, but will still enjoy half her freedom until the end of October because she is remaining in the country" (p. 375). Such mordant humor ought not gainsay Freud's famous largess toward some of his patients, for example, the Wolf Man (1918). Still, since he complains, on September 15, 1898, of sleeping during his "afternoon analyses" (Masson, 1985, p. 303), can we not imagine that, sometimes, the most desirable capacity of a patient's purse may have detoxified her less alluring capacity to make him nod off? In any event, Freud's pervasive, if intermittent, focus on money and its ups and downs of anxiety, cynicism, optimism and the like suggests that the roller coaster of comfort and fear about income so familiar to contemporary analysts is doubly determined: the product of hard times, this anxiety may also be an aggravated variant of a pattern actually inherent to the work not only of psychoanalysts but, as we see in a moment, of most helping professionals.

In the last generation or two, analysts have had a far smoother economic ride than Freud, and those made anxious by money were more likely to be in the beginning stages of practice. For example, at the beginning of the affluent 1980s, when my practice was relatively new and supplemented by an academic position, I made my anxiety known to my supervisor, a very senior and well-known analyst of interpersonal persuasion. His reply was, "You can do your best work only when it's become a matter of indifference to you whether you gain or lose an hour." While he seemed to be saying that one can work well only when money is out of the picture, I would now put it another way. It's not that money is relevant to analytic work only when times are bad. When times are good, it's relevant by its absence; then, we're like TAPS, which is what the disabled call the rest of us, "temporarily abled persons." From our present perspective of financial doubt, then, we might wonder whether the mid-century lack of competition among analysts was simply a constant or, instead, an active agent of countertransference. For example, if financial uncertainty now unsettles analysts, can financial security make them smug? Was it such smug sincerity, as well as, perhaps, character, that led another prominent analyst, during the ironically but wistfully termed "golden years" of psychoanalysis (the late 1950s/early 1960s to the stock market crash of 1987), to decline patients older than 40 because he thought them less able to change? Can complacency distort analysts' respect for patients' neediness, transforming empathy into pity? Could such a countertransference amplify the vexing popular mistrust of psychoanalysis itself?

These questions intersect another vital clinical issue, the countertransference symbolism of money. Do psychoanalysts not face a dilemma of safety that money actually symbolizes? If feeling unsafe threatens to impede the analyst's confidence and hence competence, is it also possible to feel too safe (Greenberg, 1986)? There's a necessary insecurity: psychoanalysts cannot guarantee their method will work, for success depends on a relationship being established and maintained, and the sustenance of relatedness is a day-to-day affair (P. Bromberg, personal communication). More. Current emphases on clinical process, on the importance of not knowing too precisely where you are in a session suggest a need for analysts to tolerate a certain amount of danger (Bion, 1980; Eigen, 1986). Indeed, they develop Freud's insistence on not pressing the patient for linear sense: In explicating the value of the fundamental rule, Freud (1913) cautions, "A systematic narrative should never be expected and nothing should be done to encourage it" (p. 136). Only in this atmosphere of unsafety can we expect to come upon the new and/or the forgotten. Hence money's rollercoaster effect becomes a convenient, rationalized, and inevitable container for the nonrationality and uncertainty of psychoanalytic process.

While not arguing that the uncertainty of earning a living in capitalist society guarantees the feeling of risk necessary to analytic process, I insist that the anxiety money generates cannot be banished from the consulting room. On the contrary, it is endemic to the particular sort of *work* analysts do (*See*, e.g., Chodoff, 1986). Analysts, it turns out, are not alone in their unease about money matters. They share it with everyone else in their class, a class called the "professional-managerial class" (Ehrenreich and Ehrenreich, 1979; Ehrenreich, 1989) that came into being between 1870 and 1920 (the birth period, note, of psychoanalysis, as well as the robber barons). Professional-managerial work ranges from law and medicine to middle management, from social work and psychotherapy to education, from academe to journalism. It entails what is crudely called mental labor but is better characterized as labor that combines intellect and drive with considerable, although not total, autonomy and self-direction (Ehrenreich, 1989, pp. 38, 78).

Professional-managerial work is not only a livelihood. It is also a means of power and prestige, and a shaper of personal identity. Because it involves conceptualizing other people's work and lives (Ehrenreich, 1989, p. 13), it confers authority and influence. Indeed, it was arguably the chisel that the then-emerging middle class used "to carve out" its own socioeconomic place, its own "occupational niche that would be closed both to the poor and to those who were merely rich" (p. 78). Finally, by providing the opportunity for creativity and discovery in regard not only to one's work but also to one of its chief instruments, one's self, it enters—indeed, expresses, reflects, and generates—one's identity.

This kind of work renders the professional-managerial class an elite. But, and this is Barbara Ehrenreich's main point in *Fear of Falling,* it is a highly *anxious* elite. For one thing, members of this class know that their power, privilege, and authority can make their clients envy, resent, and hate them (and, analysts would add, idealize them). For another, they, like their clients, also sometimes suspect, even if secretly, that because they do not produce anything visible or tangible, they do not actually do anything real; as such, not only does their work seem worthless, it also cannot match their own or their clients' idealization. Because their only "capital," so to speak, is, as Ehrenreich writes, "knowledge and skill, or at least the credentials imputing skill and knowledge" (p. 15), their high status is insecurely founded. She continues, unlike real, material capital, skill, and knowledge cannot be used to hedge inflation, nor can they be bequeathed. They must be renewed by and in each person through hard work, diligence, and self-discipline. Consequently, members of the professional-managerial class, like anyone in any class but the highest, fear the misfortunes that have overnight sent even middle-income people sliding into homelessness and indignity, a fear that Melanie Klein and Joan Riviere (1964), to whom I shall return, liken to that of children who imagine being orphaned or beggared as punishment for their unconscious aggression (p. 109, *n*1). They fear falling through the economic and moral safety net, hence Ehrenreich's aptly titled *Fear of Falling*. They fear "falling from grace," the title of another book by Kathy Newman (1988) on a similar topic; they fear losing their financial status, their elite position of authority, the work they love and their identity as moral, beneficent persons. Rooted in the very work of professionals, then, this anxiety about felt fraudulence and looming loss is actually built into the role of analyst in a class-structured society.

Class, Countertransference, and Alienation

Like all social institutions, class has powerful unconscious resonance. In the most general sense, class refers to the material aspect of society and the way it divides and joins people along a ladder of economic and political power. By definition, class is hierarchical; the relation between classes is determined by their economic and political superiority or inferiority to one another. To put it more crudely, class distinctions are about money and its unequal distribution in society. Conversely, money represents the veritable or potential differences in power among individuals and among groups. It indicates not only differences of class but those constituting other hierarchies, like race, ethnicity, gender, sexual preference, and so on. Money, in other words, is symbolic of the fault lines webbing and cracking a psychological and social reality in which difference is the nucleus of hierarchy (Dimen-Schein, 1977, pp. 88–92). The hierarchy of privilege organized by class, status distinctions, the unequal amounts of money people have—these trigger not only greed but envy, excite questions of self-esteem, invite oedipal competitions.

The fault lines of class and other hierarchies show up systematically in transference and countertransference. To return to our exemplar: if, in his most despondent moments, Freud felt greed and cynicism toward his "goldfish," he was unreflectively contemptuous of the middle class and benevolently condescending toward those poorer than he. Addressing the petit bourgeois reluctance to pay for psychoanalysis, Freud (1913) argued that the restored health and increased "efficiency and earning capacity" afforded by treatment made therapy less expensive than it appeared. Therefore, he concluded; "We are entitled to say that the patients have made a good bargain. Nothing in life is so expensive as illness—and stupidity" (p. 133).

As for the poor, he opined that the best psychoanalysis could supply was "a practical therapy of … the kind which … used to be dispensed by the Emperor Joseph II" (p. 133). Known as the "emperor of the beggars" (1780–1790), Joseph, in good Enlightenment fashion, used on occasion to live among the poor so he could come to know at firsthand what they needed (C. Fink, personal communication). It would not, of course, have occurred to either the emperor or the physician what we take for granted today, that poor people might actually have been able to articulate at least some of their own needs. Still, while Freud (1913) regrets the inaccessibility of psychoanalysis to the impecunious, he acknowledges that "one does occasionally come across deserving people who are helpless from no fault of their own, in whom unpaid treatment does not meet with any of the obstacles [including secondary gain] that I have mentioned and in whom it leads to excellent results" (p. 133). Nevertheless, in his relation to such poor patients as he might have taken on, his paternalism would have had to be analyzed. That it would not have been is a foregone conclusion. As we have known from his unconscious sexism, the emotional structure of socioeconomic hierarchy does not appear on his map or on that of classical psychoanalysis.

From a psychoanalytic perspective, one might see in Freud's intermittent dyspepsia about his patients a symptom of what has been called the "money neurosis" suffered by the bourgeoisie in Vienna and other European cities in the late nineteenth century (Warner, 1991). From a political perspective, one could label it "classism," or class prejudice. If we put psychoanalysis and politics together, however, what we discern in Freud's heart is the social malaise called "alienation." What I mean by alienation is not so much estrangement or disaffection but the cause of these feelings. Hear, for example, the dysphoria of a supervisee who reported thinking, during a difficult session, "I wouldn't be sitting here if I weren't doing it for the money." His guilt, bewilderment, loss, hate, and self-hate proceed from the way money, which permitted him to do his work, nevertheless stole from him its pleasures and meaning. When money is exchanged in a capitalist economy, both buyer and seller—patient and analyst—come to be like commodities, or things, to one another because they enter into relation with each other through the mediation of a third thing (money) that, simultaneously, separates them. As money wedges them apart, so it estranges them from themselves, a distancing that creates anxiety in both (Amar, 1956, p. 286; Marx, 1964, p. 113; Mészáros, 1975, pp. 178, 186). This theft of the personal satisfaction you take in work and in your relationship to those with whom you work is alienation, the process by which your labor and its fruit become alien to you because of the very socioeconomic structure that lets them be (a defining point that deserves particular emphasis here because it tends to be omitted from psychoanalytic discussions [e.g., Fromm, 1966; *See* Struik, 1964, pp. 50–52; Mészáros, 1975, p. 36]).

Alienation, in short, is the estrangement of people from their activity, their products, other people, and themselves (Oilman, 1976, p. 135). An occupational hazard of modem life, it is core to psychoanalysis. As Masud Khan (1979) writes in the preface to *Alienation in Perversions*: "In the nineteenth century two persons dictated the destiny of the twentieth century, Karl Marx and Sigmund Freud. Each ... diagnosed the sickness of the western Judaeo-Christian cultures: Marx in terms of the alienated person in society; Freud, the person alienated from himself" (p. 9). And, of course, we would add today, "herself." Elsewhere, Khan (1972) calls psychoanalysis the "inevitable result of a long sociological process of the evolution and alienation of the individual" in the West. Freud's genius, he declares, was "to evaluate the situation and give it a new frame in which [the alienated] could find [their] symbolic, therapeutic speech and expression" (p. 131). Extending Khan's point, I think of psychoanalysis as the perfect therapy for a culture of alienation, for in it you pay a stranger to recover yourself. Paradoxically, psychotherapy that is bought and sold under conditions of alienation generates a "dis-ease" in both the person who pays the stranger and the stranger who is paid, and that needs treatment too. In a way, then, my goal is to explicate how alienation filters into transference and countertransference and how clinical process, by exploiting it, transcends it in a momentary, utopian, and reparative fashion.

Commerce and Psychoanalysis

This explication requires a further and ethnographic inquiry into money's cultural and psychological significance. As the agent of alienation, money has acquired many kinds of meaning. One psychoanalyst observes that it "is esteemed, yet ... condemned" and traces this familiar ambivalence to twin polarities—one, the dichotomy between the "altruistic, selfless, humanistic sacrificing ethic" of the Judaeo-Christian tradition and the acquisitional, individualist values of capitalism; and two, Puritanism's conflict, in which hard work and thrift are valued, but their material rewards may not be enjoyed (Krueger, 1986, p. 4). Another notes the contradiction between the philanthropic inclinations of psychoanalysis and the custom of fee for service (Gutheil, 1986, p. 182); he thus echoes Freud's admonition that the analyst be immune to demands for charity routinely placed on the medical profession lest they obstruct one's ability to make a living.

But what *is* money? Money is so deeply embedded in our culture, daily life, and history that it tends to stay just out of definition's reach. Indeed as many years of teaching anthropology showed me, one's own culture is often intangible until it is compared with another. Like any institution, psychoanalysis has its own subculture. Let me, then, switch the conversational perspective once again and look at money anthropologically. A most important conclusion from the lengthy anthropological debate about money is that money objects are not present in all cultures (Dimen-Schein, 1977, pp. 197–199). Money, in other words, is not cultural bedrock. Instead, it comes into being under particular political, economic, and/or ecological conditions. For example, under some circumstances, the circulation of goods and services does not require money but instead is carried out by barter or by conventionalized equivalences. In other situations, different kinds of money have evolved, varying not only in substance (rock, shell, bead, metal, paper) but in their use and function.

After much cross-cultural comparison, then, anthropologists have come up with a universal definition of money, that, spelled out, helps us see, as if anew, money's meaning in psychoanalytic context: Money is any material object that performs one or more of the following five functions—a medium of exchange, a standard of value, a unit of account, a store of value, and a standard of deferred payments. While there may be different objects serving each different function in any one society, the first function tends to be controlling; whatever is the medium of exchange likely serves the other functions too. Finally, money itself may be a commodity, as it is in capitalism, where you buy it with what we call interest, that is, with more of the same (LeClair and Schneider, 1968, p. 468).

According to this less than exciting definition then, there's nothing mystical about money; it is, among other things, a matter of commerce. As Freud saw, however, this plain fact notoriously renders clinicians uneasy. After all these years, psychotherapists still "want to nurture their image as beneficent purveyors of good rather than as individuals who are at least partially involved in commerce" (Tulipan, 1986, p. 79), suffering its alienating effects as much as their customers. Even the notion of fee for service goes gently by the rough implications of trade, civilly suggesting the fair-and-squareness of being paid for the work you do so that you, like your patients, may use what you earn by your labor to buy what you need to live. But commerce? No. That we find tawdry and petty, the very opposite of the trust and professionalism on which psychoanalysis depends (Herron and Welt, 1992, p. 4).

Still, commerce is a cornerstone of the psychoanalytic edifice. It is not the only cornerstone, but it is a primary one. We sell our services to make our living. Oh, yes, sometimes analysts see patients for free. Some even argue that it may be necessary not to charge certain kinds of patients in order to treat them at all (Jacobs, 1986). But even to say "for free" suggests the norm, that analysts engage in trade (See also Homer, 1991, p. 177).

Without money, then, there's no psychoanalysis at all. But with it comes an unavoidable anxiety, an anxiety to which I attribute my colleagues' initial disgruntlement, as well as Dr. French's shock. Indeed, I would be quite surprised were anyone able to think through this topic without a moment or two of anxiety. Just in case that anxiety has in the present instance proved elusive, perhaps I may offer some assistance. Think, for instance, of that moment when you learn that your analytic patient who comes four times a week has been fired and will have to discontinue treatment. That first dip on the Cyclone at Coney Island has nothing on it. Or turn it around: You have taken on a new patient at your very highest fee for a long-term analysis. To take a milder example, you find out that a colleague's practice has doubled while yours has only maintained, or even dropped an hour or two. Suppose it's even the reverse, and you feel merely the queasiness of dismayed triumph: You have got more hours, income, or both than a friend who badly needs the money.

Are these suggestions extreme? Perhaps there are clinicians to whom the loss (or gain) of, let us say $600 a week or about $25,000 a year has no emotional resonance. If so, then the extremity of these examples may have something to do with the history recounted earlier: analysts who came of age before and just after the middle class began its recent, but silent, descent in the 1960s are likely to be very differently positioned and to have been initially less worried than those whose practices began in the last 15 or 20 years. The original work experience of the last generation may well have created a basic sense of ease, financial optimism, and professional security no matter what the current economy.

Nevertheless, psychoanalytic anxiety in relation to money has always sufficed to create the tacit prohibition on asking people how many hours they carry or what fees they charge unless you know them *very* well. Of course, it's never in the best of taste for professionals to inquire about each other's income. The traditional ideology of the professional-managerial class is that they work for love, not money or power—although, as we have seen, the 1980s saw some segments of this class reverse their priorities. Still, I do not suppose it would surprise anyone to find that in order to protect themselves from their anxiety about money and the alienation contextualizing it, psychoanalysts depict their pecuniary practices in ways that are, at best, confusing. Let me illustrate with an anecdote. I remember an informal and anonymous survey about fees taken at a retreat sponsored by the New York University Postdoctoral Program in Psychotherapy and Psychoanalysis. One of the obstacles to evaluating the results of this most unscientific investigation is the difference between what people say they do and what they actually do, and sometimes this difference is further complicated by gender. While I can't here anatomize the question of gender difference in presentation of professional self, it's absolutely true that in answering the questionnaire, all the women said they had a sliding scale, while each man declared one bold fee. Yet, we all know male analysts, both senior and junior, who "reduce" their fees, to use that rather cool and complacent euphemism for bargaining. The alleged tendency of women to charge lower fees (Herron and Welt, 1992, p. 174; *See* Liss-Levenson, 1990) may be at times a fact, and at others, an artifact of the same asymmetrical self-presentation: although men may charge the same fees as women, offer sliding scales, and the like, saying so publicly is probably inconsistent with their gender identity, in contrast to women, whose self-sacrifice accords more with cultural and intrapsychic expectations of women. To let the men off the hook I also have a female colleague who, in order to conquer her own anxiety about her recently increased expenses (as well as, perhaps, to make me anxious), rather loftily announced that she was now "taking" patients at higher fees. (And I always think, "How nice of her!")

The Contradiction between Money and Love

The point is critical: the way analysts talk, behave, and feel in relation to money is replete with uneasiness, an uneasiness that is the surface manifestation of a deep, psychocultural contradiction that cannot be thought, willed, or wished away. In the marrow of our culture, this contradiction is embedded in the matrix of our work. It inhabits our souls. And it will not disappear until the very bones of our society change, for like all social contradictions, it is a relation between contraries that are historical and therefore mutable but only by a political change that resolves their opposition. All we can do in our work is to find a temporary and utopian resolution to it, and I return to that later.

For now, let us proceed with the contradiction between money and love, for that is what I am talking about. Money and love, the twin engines that make the world go round, at least the world as we know it, do not go together at all. Worse. They negate, undo one another, and their contradiction funds alienation. While money may be a matter of commerce, it is, like any material object, social practice, or cultural symbol, simultaneously a matter of primitive passion. Freud knew this. He called money the "Devil's gold," an image he found in European folklore. The Devil, say the tales, gives his lovers a parting gift of gold, which, upon his going, turns to excrement (Freud, 1908, p. 174). (By the way, witches were said to have made a similar present to their lovers; neither gender has a monopoly on love's cruelties.) Freud's psychosexual interpretation of this extravagant and primal metaphor addressed what it means to consort with what he called "the repressed instinctual life." For example, he noted how the image contrasts the most precious and the most worthless of substances, money and feces, and considered how this contrast sublimates anal eroticism (whence Ferenczi's discussion). This interpretation is, of course, right, brightly illuminating, for example, Dr. French's distress about the mess that base and dirty money made in his office, the scene of noble motives and high-minded encounters.

The aspect of Freud's interpretation that awaits elaboration, however, is the *relation* between the gift and the act; what needs unraveling is the relation between the Devil and his lovers so that we may, in turn, decipher the relation between money and love, as well as the relation between those who exchange both, and therefore the place of money in psychoanalysis. Freud and the European folktales had something very subtle in mind, and if you have ever been loved by the Devil, you will know what I mean. Shakespeare did. Recall sonnet #129, which begins:

> The expense of spirit in a waste of shame
> Is lust in action,

and ends with this couplet,

> All this the world well knows; yet none knows well
> To shun the heaven that leads men to this hell.

Follow me, if you would, through a brief exegesis of this poetry, which takes us where we must go, along the nonlinear road from love to hate. When the Devil has left you, you know not that you have been fooled, but that you have fooled yourself. Your feelings, yearnings, longings have betrayed you. You now see you knew all along that what you thought was pure gold was false, that what you thought would uplift you only degrades you. You have searched to be better than you are, in fact, to be the best you can be. The Devil's betrayal crumbles your dreams, destroys the ideal self into which you have breathed life by imagining it in the other's form. In the end, you become less, not more, than you hoped to be. This degradation, then, is the Devil's gold: the Devil's gold is a gift, not a payment. It is a gift given after passion is spent. But, instead of honoring an encounter that, we must assume, was glorious, as glorious as love, this gift degrades it. Gold given to mark love becomes worse than nothing, degraded desire and lost illusions. Hopelessness.

That capacity to make everything less than it is and so to make us doubt what it was we had in mind when we worked so hard to get it that capacity, says Freud, is what money has. That's why it's the Devil's gold. Money is a pact with the Devil. That's what Marx (1964) said expounding on Goethe (and having also just quoted Shakespeare):

> That which is for me through the medium of *money*—that for which I can pay (i.e. which money can buy)—that am I, the possessor of the money. The extent of the power of money is the extent of my power. … Thus, what I *am* and *am capable* of is by no means determined by my individuality. I *am* ugly, but I can buy for myself the most beautiful of women. Therefore I am not ugly, for the effect of *ugliness* its deterrent power—is nullified by money. I, as an individual, am *lame,* but money furnishes me with twenty-four feet. Therefore I am not lame. … Money is the supreme good, therefore its possessor is good.
>
> (p. 167)

If, as Marx goes on to tell us, money can "transform all [your] incapacities into their contrary," why would you not sell your soul to get it? If money can get you whatever you need, then it "is the bond binding [you] to *human* life, … the bond of all bonds" (p. 167). But then what can you get yourself? Money can create all that we are and desire and, by the same token, destroy it. Marx therefore asks, "Can it not dissolve and bind all ties? Is it not therefore the universal *agent of separation?* It is the true agent *of separation* as well as the true *binding agent* … of society" (p. 167). The agent of alienation, it absorbs all creative power into itself, robs people of their own potential; just as money transforms imperfections into powers, so it "transforms the *real essential powers of* [human beings] *and nature* into what are merely abstract conceits" (p. 168–169). In a way, money occupies the place in modem society that kinship has in premodem culture; it is the cultural nerve center, the institution that organizes economic life, structures social relations, underlies political power, and informs symbol, ritual, and systems of meaning. Kinship, however, unlike money, can't be taken away from you; as the aphorism has it, Home is, when you go there, they gotta take you in." In contrast, "money … is the alienated *ability of* [hu]*mankind*" (p. 167). That's why it's the Devil's gold.

In our culture, money has the same unconscious effect no matter in what trade it is used. By reducing everything to a common denominator, it robs everything and every person of individuality and thereby debases what it touches. That is one reason we like to separate it from love and distinguish the profane, public sphere of work, trade, and politics from the sacred, private space of intimacy, love, and relationship. Perhaps that is also one reason that, in the families with which we are familiar and in which men have conventionally been the breadwinners in the public sphere that has traditionally been their province, men, more than women, have tended to think of the money they bring home as their nurturing gifts; decontextualizing money, they can thereby deny the alienation that otherwise robs them of their integrity (Rapp, 1978; Dimen, 1986). As feminism has taught us, of course, these domains mix in a way that makes the personal political, so that men, too, feel about money and love the way a blue-collar worker, described by Richard Sennett and Jonathan Cobb (1972) in *The Hidden Injuries of Class*, felt about having to put in overtime to send his son to college: aghast to find himself hating his kid, he said, "*Things were touching that shouldn't touch*" (p. 200).

Money degrades because it makes everything the same. Some kinds of money are called by anthropologists "special-purpose" money, because they can be used in exchange only for particular objects or services; they are contrasted with the "general-purpose" money to which we are more accustomed, money that can buy anything that can be bought. One of the most famous ethnographic examples of special-purpose money is the jewelry used in the system of ceremonial exchange known as the Kula Ring and practiced in the Trobriand Islands of New Guinea; it was studied by Malinowski (1922), who had quite a lot to say to psychoanalysts. Through ritualized ceremonies of bargaining, chiefs of different villages or islands would exchange with regular trading partners bracelets and necklaces made of shells. With any given partner, a chief would give necklaces and receive bracelets, or vice versa; necklaces would go clockwise from island to island and bracelets counterclockwise. The individual's aim in this exchange was to acquire prestige, of which each shell ornament carried a different amount created by, and registered in, the history of the exchanges it had undergone.

This special-purpose money could not be used in any other direct exchange. For example, the chiefs' trading expeditions also occasioned market trade in utilitarian goods in which the ornaments played no role. Commoners would accompany the chief on his voyages, in return for the chance not only to bask in his glory but also to haggle for food, tools, and the raw materials that they could not produce or forage at home. On the trading voyages, the jewelry and the utilitarian goods circulated in completely separate spheres; voyagers could not buy oars with necklaces, for example. Commoners were not, however, excluded from prestige circulation. On certain ceremonial occasions, to demonstrate political loyalty, they would transfer some of their own goods to the chief, in return for which he, on still later and formally unrelated occasions, would give back ornaments that could then become the basis for a commoner's climb up the prestige and political ladder (Dimen-Schein, 1977, pp. 215–217; Malinowski, 1922).

There is a crucial distinction between special-purpose and general-purpose money: whatever is transacted with special-purpose money tends to retain its individuality, indeed, is embedded in the relationship governing the transaction; general-purpose money, in contrast, is a "universal equivalent; since everything becomes translatable into it," it makes everything symbolically the same (Dimen-Schein, 1977, p. 197). For example, in Manhattan (as of this writing), $1.25 can buy, and thus means, both a subway token (itself a sort of special-purpose money) and, let us say, a frozen yogurt. While special-purpose money is linked only in particulars, general-purpose money measures everything by the same standard; we may think, for example, that a frozen yogurt has the same price as a token, say, $1.25, but we won't think that $1.25 and the yogurt cost the same, that is, that each can be exchanged for a token. While tokens will always represent one's relationship only to the subway or a subway clerk (or, perhaps, the taxi driver who will occasionally accept a token as a tip in lieu of the change a passenger cannot find), that $1.25 will indiscriminately represent one's relationship to everyone and everything, from the subway and yogurt clerks one gives the money to, to the bank and the (automated) tellers one gets it from; from the Sunday paper for which one pays the newsdealer $1.25, to that most appealing pair of shoes of whose less than appealing $250 price it is a mere half of 1 percent.

General-purpose money, or a universal medium of exchange, nullifies the particular meaning of any object or transaction, destroying its individuality:

> As money is not exchanged for any one specific quality, for any one specific thing or for any particular human essential power but for the entire objective world ... from the standpoint of its possessor it therefore serves to exchange every property for every other, even contradictory, property and object; it is the fraternization of impossibilities. It makes contradictions embrace.
>
> (Marx, 1964, p. 169)

In capitalism, money is a universal medium of exchange. Although everything is not in fact for sale, in principle it is. Since the same standard, whether the dollar, ruble, or yen, quantifies everything, then money erases all differences between things, levels all qualities, and eliminates all particularity. Money reduces everything to its abstract capacity to be exchanged. The car assembled in Detroit, the hamburger flipped at the Moscow McDonald's, the ad created for a candidate or dish detergent in Tokyo—what these things signify is not anyone's desire for, or consumption of, them but what they have in common, their cash value.

The Paradox between Love and Hate

We come to what happens when that most general of things, money, pays for that most personal of experiences, the psychoanalytic journey. The psychoanalytic relation, like love, is highly particular. So particular is it that, at its most intense, in the heat of an analytic encounter, no generality seems to apply to it at all. For example, one has to work very hard to *think* about what is happening, to recall or develop the theory or construct suited to clarify the complex relation that is transpiring. In fact, this doubled tension, the struggle to engage and the struggle to conceptualize, is one mark of the curative power of psychoanalysis, making it quite distinct from ordinary intercourse.

This particularity, however, is regularly undercut by the money that permits it. As analysts, we all know how rapidly our narcissism or, as Freud would have called it, our self-preservative instinct leads us to equate the loss of an hour with a bill we'll have to find some other way to pay; how disjunctive, that is, contradictory, this thought is to the personal relation that we are also about to lose, with the feeling of loss that looms; and how dysphoric the hunch that our patients perceive these feelings (Aron and Hirsch, 1992; Whitson, n.d.). As patients, who of us has not wondered just which of our analysts' bills our own treatment services? Or thought that we are replaceable by some other patient with enough money to pay the fare for their own personal journey? What's so personal and particular then? In fact, it's so painfully bizarre to go from the feelings of special love, meant only for one's analyst or one's patient, to the money that allows those emotions to flower but could also be used to buy many other things or could disappear in a flash, that one represses the connection and asks, as did my colleague, Why are we talking about money? That monthly bill rasps against the poignant longings for love that bloom in the psychoanalytic contact. It threatens to destroy them, turn them to shit. Like the man said, things touch that shouldn't.

When love turns to hate, it seems wise to move from Freud to Klein. In the psychoanalytic contact, as in the psyche, as, indeed, in our culture, the contradiction between money and love threatens to transform love into its seeming opposite; hate in turn threatens to annihilate relatedness altogether; and analysts, not unlike infants, feel the paralysis of terror. Money incites hate, if only because there is never enough of it to go around. But, according to Melanie Klein and Joan Riviere (1964) in *Love, Hate and Reparation*, this twist of social fate resembles the vicissitudes of dependency that they see as the understructure of society, relatedness, and love. Riviere stresses,

> the degree of *dependence* of the human organism on its surroundings. In a stable political and economic system there is a great deal of apparent liberty and opportunity to fulfill our own needs, and we do not as a rule feel our dependence on the organization in which we live—unless, for instance, there is an earthquake or a strike! Then we may realize with reluctance and often with deep resentment that we are dependent on the forces of nature or on other people to a terrifying extent.
>
> (p. 5)

While this emergency recognition of dependence may typify only our own culture and even only certain groups within it, what Riviere goes on to say is probably universal. Not only, she says, does dependence become awful when external events deprive us of what we need. Such terror also inheres in love. The "possibility of privation" tends "to rouse resistance and aggressive emotions," a murderousness that forebodes doom (p. 7). What such loss feels like to the infant is what it unconsciously feels like to the adult: Your world "is out of control; a strike and an earthquake have happened ... and this is *because*" you love and desire. Your "love may bring pain and devastation" to you and to those you love, but you "cannot control or eradicate" either your desire or your hate (p. 9). Hate is a condition of love, as love is a condition of life. You must love in order to live, but loving also means hating.

This, then, is the paradox of my title, the paradox of love and hate to which Klein, and later Winnicott and Guntrip, introduced us. I do not hold, with Klein and Riviere, that these primal passions of love and hate are constitutional. Nor do I hold with Guntrip (1969, p. 24) that only one of them, love, is what we begin with. I prefer what I call the big bang theory, in which love and hate are co-born. Their mutual birthing is what makes their relation paradoxical, for paradox denotes the indissoluble tension between contraries that themselves never change, are transhistorical, atemporal, universal. The paradox of love and hate comes into being through the primal relationship; these passions take their shape and meaning from their passage through the emotional and structural net of that intimacy in which they likewise participate. Love and hate, emerging together, become mutually meaningful in the context of failure, when babies and mothering persons disappoint each other, when, as the earlier Klein seemed to argue, babies, in hating the primary caretaker, also first sense their love, and when, as Winnicott (1947) taught us, parents, to their often denying dismay, feel for their babies what they long ago learned to disavow, the dreaded hate that portends the death of their newborn and miraculous and reparative love.

That we must absorb, indeed, relish this paradox so as to do our best work, we have learned from Winnicott (1945) and from Searles (1965), as well as from Khan (1970), who says: "One could argue that what is unique about the clinical situation is that the analyst survives both the loving and the hating of the patient as a person, and the patient as a person at the resolution of the relationship survives it, too, and is the richer for it" (p. 111).

The Landlady of Time

That paradox is an acquired taste we've all learned from our clinical work. For example, last year, I moved my office to a new and, I would say, upscaled location; while my furnishings are substantially the same, the setting itself is far more elegant and professional than the old one. Most of my patients, including Ms. Rose, as I will call her, were pleased with their new environment. They read it as a sign of surging hope for their therapeutic progress and, not coincidentally, a sign of hardiness in me, an ability to survive their aggression.

About six weeks after this move, Ms. Rose, whose low fee is nevertheless a struggle for her to pay, took the opportunity to push on with her analytic work. She missed an appointment, one she had rescheduled because of an upcoming conference. The next time she came, she sat up on the couch and looked me in the eyes. With icy fury, she challenged me: "Suppose someone has an accident?" she asked. Suppose they were in the hospital? Would I charge them? I should note here that Ms. Rose had been in treatment with me for slightly over five years. She then explained that she had missed her session because her alarm clock had failed to work. Rageful that she would have to pay anyway, she declined to call to tell me what had happened; I should say that I tried to telephone her but never reached her. Her diatribe intensified. Must she, she wanted to know, be responsible for everything? Could we not share the responsibility? Somewhere in here, I said that the basis for my charging her was my commitment of time. "Of course," she said, "I understand this is a business; you have to guarantee yourself an income. But what about *my* interests?" The schedule was for my convenience, not hers. It's often inconvenient for her. Oh, she knew the answers: she had to conform to my schedule because I wanted her to face the reality principle. I would not change it, so she had two choices, to pay or not to pay. Anyway, why should she rely on my judgment that she needed more than one session a week? Then, like an archer at last loosing her bow, she let fly her final question: "What are you, the Landlady of Time?"

Ms. Rose is a poet as well as a graduate student in political studies, and if her rage made my heart beat in anger, her metaphor hit me right in the solar plexus. I felt all the emotions of the rainbow—guilt, recognition, anxiety, excitement, hate. After all, Freud said that analysts lease their time. And one of the dilemmas with which I am trying to deal here is what happens when money turns our work into a commodity just like any other. Indeed, it did not escape my notice that Ms. Rose had granted me a perfect illustration of my present argument, which I had already begun to think about. Her knowledge of my inner life was, in certain respects, as unerring as her poetic aim.

At this, for us, unprecedented point of mutual hate, we continued. I said that while she appeared to be asking about my policies, she in fact often seemed to assume my reply. She agreed. She also concurred with my view that she was treating this clash like a pitched battle and added that her anger meant not that she would not continue to analyze this situation with me but that she was no longer letting her relationships go unquestioned. She then observed that it was odd to feel the same way about our relationship, since, of all the people she had been questioning, I was the one who had been kindest to her. I asked, by way of interpretation, Where else should she bring her anger? Where hate but where she loves? She nodded in agreement. I added, correctly but in a fit of bad timing that spewed straight from my anger, that it was about time she was doing this, to which she coldly replied that she knew I would say that. She then began to list my unfairnesses in regard to money, some of which I acknowledged, others of which I contested. At session's end, I wished her a good trip. Her scornful smile said, "Who needs your good wishes?" Two weeks later, when she returned, she gave me a cartoon, in which a therapist is saying to a naked turtle, "I see you're coming out of your shell."

Every clinical moment is overdetermined, and many elements had fused to make Ms. Rose's rage combust. What I would like this vignette to illustrate is my contention that in the psychoanalytic contact, the contradiction between money and love can be resolved only if we transform it into the paradox between love and hate. The Devil's gold turns love to shit only when you cannot live out the hate with the one you love. What Ms. Rose and I did was to live the contradiction together, risking the hate that seemed to be killing us, tolerating imminent annihilation until she found a way to survive it, until the paradox of love and hate presented itself to her in what Ghent (1992) has characterized as the "somewhat altered consciousness that prevails in a spontaneous moment of creativity" (p. 9).

While the disparity in our financial, social, and ethnic status (I am white, Jewish, and a full-fledged member of the professional-managerial class, to which Ms. Rose, fair-skinned, Afro-American, and from a lower-middle-class family, aspires) had always been apparent and sometimes attended to, the envy, greed, fear, and hate stimulated by these economic and cultural differences had become far more accessible in my new surroundings. Until now, Ms. Rose had denied the contradictory dimension of our strange intimacy and could feel only fragments of her love and hate. My new office, which flagged not only my standing and authority but her own aspirations for the best for herself, now permitted her to move the contradiction between money and love into the center of the relationship, where it produced the hate that it always does. There were precursors. For example, shortly after I opened the new office, we began to discuss her ways of skirting shame. One day, she noticed a most offensive but, in this context, strangely appropriate odor emanating from the lovely garden onto which my casement windows open. Sniffing carefully, she said, "Why, it smells like cats." Then she giggled. I asked her about the giggle. She tentatively answered, "Well I just thought, *you* smell like a cat."

Once the river of hate began to rage, once she finally woke up, opened her eyes, and, in shock, saw me for who I am, that is, the Landlady of Time, not only the money-hate but all the others, all hate itself, could fill the space between us. Her rage was the sound of her shell cracking, heralding the emergence of the self we had previously called the waif in the cave. Naked, that waif emerged, angry yet/and still loving. Her discovery of the paradox, that it was strange to doubt me, even though I was the one she had felt to have been most caring during her years of personal and professional difficulty and struggle, created this utopian moment in which there began to grow another kind of love, the kind of bond you have with someone only when you have shed blood together. Since then, Ms. Rose has let me in on her thought that perhaps analysis is not always the most important thing in her life. She has owned more of the analytic work and, in return for permitting me to write about this encounter between us in a way that disguises her identity, has asked to see this paper; she has, in fact, read this version. Finally, she is no longer my tenant in the cave of psychoanalysis; she has also made us into an interracial and otherwise nontraditional family: in her last dream, she wondered what I saw in the little black girl I had adopted when there were so many white ones around. Hate having been accepted along with differences and inequities between us, she could begin imagining her own, still untenanted loveliness.

Conclusion: From Contradiction to Paradox, and Back

Money, along with its coordinates, space and time, belongs conventionally to what has been labeled the analytic "frame." I would like, in concluding, to argue that the frame, which Langs (1973) calls "ground rules," ought to be treated as part of the picture too (*See* also Homer, 1991; Herron and Welt, 1992, p. 11). While analysts and patients often find the ground rules irritating, not only their outlining of, but their presence inside, the consulting room in fact potentiates the utopian moment that makes treatment work. They enter the symbolic play the frame permits: "When there is a frame it surely serves to indicate that what's inside the frame has to be interpreted in a different way from what's outside it. … Thus the frame marks off an area within which what is perceived has to be taken symbolically, while what is outside the frame is taken literally" (Milner, 1957, p. 158). Because money while a constituent of the frame is also in the picture, it can be played with as symbol as well as literally exchanged. Thus, in bourgeois culture, as I have argued, a money relation is thought not to be a love relation. Money appears to negate love, producing the hate that signs their contradiction.[1] But the psychoanalytic situation is a case where money permits love, where, for a moment, the culture can be upended, where you can love even where you would most expect to hate, where you would not get to love unless money were exchanged, where money in fact guarantees the possibility of love, and where, therefore, the contradiction between money and love, and the hate it generates become safe.

We know this from Freud, even though, in this instance, he did not appear to know what he knew. His own case histories reveal that the money relation and, hence, alienation entered his patients' lives through their families. Gallop (1982), a Lacanian feminist literary critic, points out that "the closed, cellular model of the family used in ... psychoanalytic thinking is an idealization.... The family never was, in any of Freud's texts, completely closed off from questions of economic class. And the most insistent locus of that intrusion into the family circle ... is the maid/governess/nurse" (p. 144).

The governess, an omnipresent and essential member of most bourgeois European families, was always from the lower class. She symbolizes, in the unconscious and text alike, the very "financial distinction" that also comes to characterize the relation of Freud and all analysts to their patients. Gallop reminds us, in this context, of Dora's dismissal of Freud, the two weeks' notice she gave him with the same courtesy she would have used upon firing a servant (or a servant, on quitting, would have given her). Gallop argues that for psychoanalysis to provide the radical encounter of self with self it promises and to contend, I would add, with alienation, "Freud must assume his identification with the governess" (p. 146), because, rather "than having the power of life and death like the mother has over the infant, the analyst is financially dependent on the patient" (p. 143).

To put it more concretely, unless money may leave the frame and enter the picture, psychoanalysis must renege on its promise. The very economic transaction that distinguishes the psychoanalytic relationship from ordinary intimacies renders the transference sensible; money mediates one-person and two-person psychologies, their ambiguous, paradoxical, and contingent interface made possible and manifest by money's unavoidable but necessary and definitive arbitrariness, by what, in a way, Freud would have called the reality principle (Ms. Rose, it turns out, was right). "The fact that the analyst is paid ... proves that the analyst is ... a stand-in" (p. 143). Payment, in other words, grounds the possibility of genuinely new experience in the analysis, as well as that of remembering, repeating, and working through the past: the old happens with a newcomer who would never, without money, have been known and whose job it is to interpret both the old and the new. Reciprocally, the money relation also unveils the countertransference, in the service of whose understanding analysts must be willing to confront, internally and, when indicated, interpretively, both the discomforts and the pleasures of money's powerful place in psychoanalysis.

In a respectful view of psychoanalysis as seduction, Forrester (1990), another Lacanian literary critic, argues:

> Psychoanalysis treats money as if it truly were the universal means of exchange, and patients do behave as if they could buy love.... The analyst ... plays on the fact that patients do not know what they mean, nor do they know what money will buy. It is insofar as they do not know these things that seduction begins. And with seduction, the questioning of the contract and the calling into question of authority ... begins.... The original seduction is thus that offered by the contract—namely that it is *just* a contract....

> Its means of accomplishment is the free speech whereby one of the parties will contract the disease of love that the other will cure by treating the proffered seductive words as if they were simply the universal means of exchange.
>
> (p. 47)

At the heart of psychoanalysis, this most private of encounters, lies society, just as at the heart of public life lies the alienation psychoanalysis tries to cure. Psychoanalysis is not revolution, and it doesn't make the contradiction between money and love go away. But for a brief, utopian moment, it permits transcendence. In the psychoanalytic contact, the contradiction between money and love, a relation between contraries that can be transformed, finds a temporary, reparative resolution in the paradox between love and hate, a relation between contraries that never changes. The possibility of transformation distinguishes contradiction from paradox: contradiction bears resolution; paradox does not. Or, rather, as Ghent (1992) has recently said, the only resolution of paradox is paradox itself, here to inhabit, without rushing to relieve, the tension between love and hate, a tension that also preserves the memory of the contradiction between money and love it resolves.

The lesson of contradiction is perhaps easier to remember than that of paradox, which is, in turn, one of the easiest to forget. That money negates love, this we know preconsciously and needs, I think, only to be surfaced to stay in consciousness. But paradox is different; it is relearned each time it is lived. This is perhaps what Freud (1923) was trying to capture when he said that "love is with unexpected regularity accompanied by hate (ambivalence)" (p. 43). That love and hate go together, this is an analytic commonplace. But that, in the hot moment of loving or hating, we never remember that they do, this, perhaps, is wisdom.

Note

1 That the dichotomy between money and love may also define love as we know it is a consideration that is important but not possible to take up here.

References

Abraham, K. (1921), Contributions to the theory of the anal character. In: *Selected Papers of Karl Abraham, M.D.*, trans. D. Bryan & A. Strachey. New York: Basic Books, 1953, pp. 370–392.

Amar, A. (1956), A psychoanalytic study of money. In: *The Psychoanalysis of Money*, ed. E. Borneman (trans. M. Shaw). New York: Urizen Books, 1976, pp. 277–291.

Aron, L. (1991), The patient's experience of the analyst's subjectivity. *Psychoanal. Dial.*, 1:29–51.

Aron, L. and Hirsch, I. (1992), Money matters in psychoanalysis: A relational approach. In: *Relational Perspectives in Psychoanalysis*, ed. N. Skolnick & S. Warshaw. Hillsdale, NJ: The Analytic Press, pp. 239–256.

Bion, W. R. (1980), *Key to Memoir of the Future.* Perthshire: Clunie Press.
Chodoff, P. (1986), The effect of third-party payment on the practice of psychotherapy. In: *The Last Taboo,* ed. D. W. Krueger. New York: Brunner/Mazel, pp. 111–120.
Chodoff, P. (1991), Effects of the new economic climate on psychotherapeutic practice. In: *Money and Mind,* ed. S. Klebanow & E. L. Lowenkopf. New York: Plenum Press, pp. 253–264.
Dirnen, M. (1986), *Surviving Sexual Contradictions.* New York: Macmillan.
Dimen-Schein, M. (1977), *The Anthropological Imagination.* New York: McGraw-Hill.
Drellich, M. (1991), Money and countertransference. In: *Money and Mind,* ed. S. Klebanow and E. L. Lowenkopf. New York: Plenum Press, pp. 155–162.
Durkheim, E. (1930), *Suicide,* ed. G. Simpson (trans. J. A. Spaulding & G. Simpson), New York: Free Press, 1951.
Durkheim, E. (1938), *The Rules of Sociological Method.* Glencoe: Free Press.
Ehrenreich, B. (1989), *Fear of Falling.* New York: Pantheon.
Ehrenreich, B. & Ehrenreich, J. (1979), The professional-managerial class. In: *Between Labor and Capital,* ed. P. Walker. Boston: South End Press, pp. 5–48.
Eigen, M. (1986), *The Psychotic Core.* Northvale, NJ: Aronson.
Fenichel, O. (1938), The drive to amass wealth. In: *The Collected Papers of Otto Fenichel,* 2d series, ed. H. Fenichel & D. Rapaport. New York: Norton, 1954, pp. 89–108.
Ferenczi, S. (1914), The ontogenesis of the interest in money. In: *The Psychoanalysis of Money,* ed. E. Borneman (trans. M. Shaw). New York: Urizen Books, 1976, pp. 81–90.
Forrester, J. (1990), *The Seductions of Psychoanalysis:* Cambridge: Cambridge University Press.
Flax, J. (1990), *Thinking Fragments.* Berkeley: University of California Press.
Freud, S. (1895), Psychotherapy of hysteria. *Standard Edition,* 2:253–305. London: Hogarth Press, 1955.
Freud, S. (1905), Three essays on the theory of sexuality. *Standard Edition,* 7:125–245. London: Hogarth Press, 1953.
Freud, S. (1908), Character and anal erotism. *Standard Edition,* 9:167–175. London: Hogarth Press, 1953.
Freud, S. (1913), On beginning the treatment. *Standard Edition,* 12:123–144. London: The Hogarth Press, 1958.
Freud, S. (1923), The ego and the id. *Standard Edition.* 19:3–68. London: Hogarth Press, 1961.
Fromm, E. (1966), *Marx's Concept of Man.* New York: F. Ungar.
Gallop, J. (1982), *The Daughter's Seduction.* Ithaca, NY: Cornell University Press.
Gay, P. (1988) *Freud.* New York: Norton.
Ghent, E. (1989), Credo: The dialectics of one-person and two-person psychologies. *Contemp. Psychoanal.,* 25:200–237.
Ghent, E. (1992), Paradox and process. *Psychoanal. Dial.* 2:135–159.
Greenberg, J. (1986), Theoretical models and the analyst's neutrality. *Contemp. Psychoanal.,* 22:87–106.
Guntrip, H. (1969), *Schizoid Phenomena, Object-Relations and the Self.* New York: International Universities Press.
Gutheil, T. A. (1986), Fees in beginning private practice. In: *The Last Taboo,* ed. D. W. Krueger. New York: Brunner/Mazel, pp. 175–88.
Havens, L. (1989), *A Safe Place.* Cambridge, MA: Harvard University Press.
Herron, W. G. & Welt, S. R. (1992), *Money Matters.* New York: Guilford Press.

Homer, A.J. (1991), Money issues and analytic neutrality. In: *Money and Mind*, ed. S. Klebanow & E. L. Lowenkopf. New York: Plenum Press, pp. 175–182.

Jacobs, D. H. (1986), On negotiating fees with psychotherapy and psychoanalytic patients. In: *The Lost Taboo,* ed. D. W. Krueger. New York: Brunner/Mazel, pp. 121–131.

Jacoby, R. (1983), *The Repression of Psychoanalysis.* Chicago: The University of Chicago Press.

Jones, E. (1918), Anal-erotic character traits. In: *Collected Papers.* Boston: Beacon Press, pp. 438–451.

Khan, M. M. R. (1970), Montaigne, Rousseau and Freud. In: *The Privacy of the Self.* New York: International Universities Press, 1974, pp. 99–111.

Khan, M. M. R. (1972), On Freud's provision of the therapeutic frame. In: *The Privacy of the Self.* New York: International Universities Press, pp. 129–135, 1974.

Khan, M. M. R. (1979), *Alienation in Perversions.* New York: International Universities Press.

Klebanow, S. & Lowenkopf, E. L, eds. (1991), *Money and Mind.* New York: Plenum Press.

Klein, M. &. Riviere, J. (1964), *Love, Hate and Reparation.* New York: Norton.

Krueger, D. W. (1986), Money, success and success phobia. In: *The Last Taboo,* ed. D. W. Krueger. New York: Brunner/Mazel, pp. 3–16.

Langs, R. (1973), *The Technique of Psychoanalytic Psychotherapy.* Northvale, NJ: Aronson, esp. pp. 89–215.

LeClair, E. E., Jr. & Schneider, H. K. (1968), Some further theoretical issues. In: *Economic Anthropology,* ed. E. E. LeClair, Jr. & H. K. Schneider. New York: Holt, Rinehart & Winston, pp. 453–474.

Liss-Levenson, N. (1990), Money matters and the woman analyst: In a different voice. *Psychoanal. Psychol.,* 7 (Supplement):119–130.

Malinowski, B. (1922), *Argonauts of the Western Pacific.* New York: Dutton, 1961.

Marx, K. (1964), *The Economic and Philosophical Manuscripts of 1844,* ed. D. Struik (trans. M. Milligan). New York: International Publishers.

Masson, J.M. (1985), *The Complete Letters of Sigmund Freud to Wilhelm Fleiss, 1987-1904).* J. M. Masson, ed. New York: Belknap Press.

Mészáros, J. (1975), *Marx's Theory of Alienation,* 4th ed. London: Merlin Press.

Milner, M. (1957), *On Not Being Able to Paint.* New York: International Universities Press.

Newman, K. S. (1988), *Falling from Grace.* New York: Free Press.

Oilman, B. (1976), *Alienation,* 2d ed. New York: Cambridge University Press.

Rapp, R. (1978), Family and class in contemporary America: Notes toward an understanding of ideology. *Science & Society* 42:278–300.

Rendon, M. (1991), Money and the left in psychoanalysis. In: *Money and Mind,* ed. S. Klebanow & E.L. Lowenkopf. New York: Plenum Press, pp. 135–148.

Searles, H. (1965), *Collected Papers on Schizophrenia and Related Subjects.* New York: International Universities Press.

Sennett, R. & Cobb, J. (1972), *The Hidden Injuries of Class.* New York: Vintage.

Shainess, N. (1991), Countertransference problems with money. In: *Money and Mind,* ed. S. Klebanow & E. L. Lowenkopf. New York: Plenum Press, pp. 163–175.

Struik, D. J. (1964), Introduction. In: *The Economic and Philosophical Manuscripts of 1844: Karl Marx,* ed. D. J. Struik. New York: International Publishers, pp. 9–56.

Tulipan, A. B. (1986), Fee policy as an extension of the therapist's style and orientation. In: *The Last Taboo,* ed. D. W. Kreuger. New York: Brunner/Mazel, pp. 79–87.

Warner, S. L. (1991), Sigmund Freud and money, In: *Money and Mind*, ed. S. Klebanow & E. L. Lowenkopf. New York: Plenum Press, pp. 121–134.
Whitson, G. (n. d.), Money matters in psychoanalysis: The analyst's coparticipation in the matter of money. Unpub. ms.
Winnicott, D. W. (1947), Hate in the countertransference. In: *Through Paediatrics to Psychoanalysis*. New York: Basic Books, 1975, pp. 194–203.
Zaphiropoulos, M. L. (1991), Fee and empathy: Logic and logistics in psychoanalysis. In: *Money and Mind*, ed. S. Klebanow & E. L. Lowenkopf. New York: Plenum Press, pp. 235–244.

Good Night, See You Next Week

June Lee Kwon

To mothers and their children

I

The boy grins while touching my inner thighs. His thin lips give me the creeps. I pull his hands off me, but they are stuck to my thighs. "Get off me!" I try to yell, but each word seems to implode in my mouth. My gut pounds hard each time I pull his hands away from me. I start smacking his back ruthlessly. His back is just the size of my palm. He is small. I feel mad.

I wake up shuddering from panic and guilt.

It is already past noon. Maybe the melatonin I took the previous night put me into a deep sleep. I needed that sleep. I just wish I did not sleep deep enough to have a vivid and memorable dream. Everything has a cost. I fucking paid for that good night sleep.

The pile of black hair and crumpled dust balls scattered around my bedroom floor sicken me a bit. She used to say my room looks haunted. I do not disagree. The pink stuffed bunny is fallen from the shelf, looking back at me with its shiny plastic eyes. I still smell the faint mixture of piss and shit veiled with Clorox when I look at the thing in the eyes. My room is haunted. I am haunted. She was haunted too.

I tumble out of my bed.

12:50

I can never seem to leave on time. It takes me so long to get going. I can never quite get going. But she will be surprised to know how many places I have visited and left. Or how many places I stop by each day. She will certainly be surprised to know how many things I have going for me. I guess she

DOI: 10.4324/9781003335252-22

will never know. No matter how many times I tell her. She will never quite know what I have, where I go, whom I hang with, and all that junk. They are all junk. They do not make her happy nor proud. I am just latching onto her thighs.

1:10 PM

I have missed airline flights several times. I admit that it may have something to do with my reluctance for departure. Some people seem to have no problems getting up and leaving, being somewhere on time, even early when appropriate. I always had problems with getting myself going. "Like a cow being dragged to the slaughterhouse."

Of course, not every destination is a slaughterhouse. But my feelings for the destination never made a difference. I just cannot seem to readily accept that I have to go.

Take off.

On the other hand, I like the feeling of arrival. It is worth leaving just to arrive somewhere. I like the relief I feel from having been through with the transitional phase. And I like to encounter that vague familiarity from things that were once estranged from me. Arriving, whether it is a revisit or a visit that is brand new, always seems to leave me in wonder for the impossible marriage of contrasting feelings.

I feel

old and new,

forgotten and remembered,

rejected and embraced,

temporal,

and eternal.

Nothing replicates the feeling of arrival.

It is worth leaving just to arrive somewhere.

1:20 PM

I drown my oatmeal in water and simmer it until it softens. This makes it taste like porridge, Jook. I drizzle toasted perilla oil on disintegrated and watery oatmeal. I put a small plate of kimchi and changran jut on the side. My oatmeal tastes nothing like oatmeal. But it also does not taste like jook.

If done right with a radical lack of hesitation, the forced reinvention renders a miraculous transformation. *Didn't we make it better for them?* I swirl my spoon in the bowl. Oats look formless. Perilla oil intrudes into the decimated puddle. *They lack proper boundaries.*

I chew on the changran jut for a long time. My gut twists and turns from hunger even as I am eating. I check for how much oat and changran jut I have left in my kitchen. This will last for another month.

I stare at the microwave clock as I finish my lunch standing in my kitchen.

1:30 PM

A month after the lockdown I bought myself an espresso machine and a coffee grinder. The crazed Aeropress I had for four years was working fine, but I got frustrated with the circumstance. I think I wanted something shiny that resembles the feeling of buying a cup of cortado from a coffee shop.

I press ground coffee beans hard into the portafilter. I should probably start using my left hand for this. The tendons of my wrists and fingers whine annoyingly. It is likely that I am exacerbating my chronic tendonitis by holding up my phone for too long. But I cannot seem to fall asleep these days unless I spend enough time on my phone scrolling down a list of groceries, news, recipes, and Instagram. I am not sure how other people spend their nights. But I cannot seem to stop myself until my hands drop my phone right on my face due to intolerable pain. I feel pain. I stretch my knuckles as my espresso machine growls loudly.

I sip my iced latte. Heavy heels of my boots clunk as I step into the coffee shop across from my office. The pirate black colored wooden floor makes me feel like I am not expensive enough to enter. I hear her say, "Yeah, everyone in here is WAY TOO attractive." I giggle as I gaze at perfect blood-colored lips of a girl wearing a charcoal colored suede hat with a wide brim. As I receive a bright yellow cup of cortado from a woman who seems to appear as a perfect replica of Aidy Bryant, a flood of sunlight falls through the ceiling window and stuns me. I look up to witness the stream of light. The mock Aidy Bryant cheerfully informs me about the large circular ceiling light capable of automatically watering the planter atop. The greens are glowing from regimented water and light schedule. I tell her the light/planter is brilliant. She screams into my ear that she would rather die than wait for someone to change her diaper. I smell piss, shit, and Clorox...

I am clearly losing my grip. My latte hits the kitchen floor and it is shattered to pieces now. My feet are splattered with blood and coffee. I pull out a piece of glass from my big toe. "엄마!" The piece of glass punctures the tip of my index finger. Now I wish I had a glass to smash on the floor.

2:00 PM

I survey my feet with my phone flashlight. Occasionally, I find tiny speckles of shiny glass pieces on my feet. I put a needle in the flame of my gas stove. Some glass pieces are already beneath my skin. I poke and prick. I doubt I will get all of them.

She always brought up tetanus whenever I got a cut or a scrape. I did not even know I was already vaccinated until I saw my record. Come to think of it, she always brought up possibilities for losing limbs: frostbite, diabetes, tetanus, shrapnel, the list went on. I used to tell myself she is out of her mind, until I saw every case in a day, in a building.

"This country is some kind of glorious hell."

At least I can buy some hydrogen peroxide these days. I could not find it in my local drugstore during the first few months of lockdown. I never enjoyed the sight nor smell of it as a child. Now I can readily accept the sharp sting I feel as I dab my wound with it. The pain assures that I will be safe from a loss.

2:25 PM

I search for her name online. Maybe I did not see her last time. I try to read through the list of 100,000 names on the May 24th front page of the *New York Times* again. Maybe I will find her name this time. I cannot find her name.

She bellows while pounding her chest, "My mother never named me! My mother called me Female!" I try a different name. I try another name. I cannot find any of them.

I look at the image of the front page on my monitor from afar.

A god damn piece of visual art made of dead people's names. Of course, her name is not here. Of course.

...... What if she survived?

I hold my phone. I put it back down. It is already.

2:50 PM

I got to have two shots per day, and I lost some to the kitchen floor earlier. I make another shot of espresso. I sit in front of my iPad and sip my coffee. I make sure that the camera is not too close to my face and lower the brightness as much as I can. My eyes do not burn after work anymore though. I guess they got used to the increased screen time.

Or maybe I readily accept the pain now because

it merely assures that

I will be safe from loss.

3:30 PM

We sing and dance together in front of our cameras.

3:40 PM

We touch each other's face over the screen.

4:10 PM

We bring stuffed animals who hate cameras and growl at each other.

4:30 PM

We join a shared whiteboard online and draw many borders between two spaces.

4:40 PM

We destroy the borders mercilessly using colors, lines, erasers, and scissors.

4:45 PM

She screams at me, "DON'T LEAVE!" I stay with her until she angrily leaves.

5:45 PM

He lights up his cigarette and jokes about the end of our session coming too soon.

6:00 PM

We turn off our cameras to hear each other more closely.

7:00 PM

Her daughter holds her tight while whining, "Bedtime will not be the same without you."

7:45 PM

We say, "good night, see you next week."

II

"The most important step is to remove potential danger." She cuts its lips off swiftly with scissors. The fish looks rather dull without its teeth. I am astounded to witness its soft and white belly as she turns it over. She makes a small slit on its skin, then she tears it apart with her hands. She picks out a tender looking beige slab to let me know, "the liver is expensive." She scrapes off its small intestines and other organs, while leaving its stomach untouched. We stare at the way it is grotesquely expanded. She carefully cuts open the stomach, and we are stunned as it reveals a small pollock that is completely intact.

She tsks and says, "Poor thing must have been swallowed whole. Small ones have pitiful fate." She lays her eyes sadly on her dead rescue.

Dinner is a braised anglerfish and a grilled pollock.

8:22 PM

No scenery captures the great American desire better than the giant field of cut grass with a spectacular Manhattan skyline. A golden retriever approaches me with a stick in its mouth. It drags a long leash from its neon green collar that no one seems to be holding. The docile beast drops a stick in front of my feet and sticks its tongue out endearingly. A small girl dashes by me. She hugs the dog in her arms at last.

As soon as I sit on a park bench, I sink deep into her waiting room couch. I watch her ivory skirt caresses her legs gently as she calls me into her tummy. She turns around and I run after her. The green door shrinks into a narrow sliver. I walk sideways to squeeze myself through the entrance.

A beautiful glowing light dangles from her forehead. We are quiet. I notice a distinctive stench as she drools giant and heavy droplets into my mouth. My tongue stutters and mutters as I desperately whimper for a word.

"I fucking hate your rotten guts!"

I find her intestine and a pair of scissors in my hand. I must cut it clean right at her belly button, but my scissors look too sharp. Her mouth opens wide to cough up a burning pollock. She whispers, "*Didn't I make it better for you?*"

I wake up coughing for the air. People scurry away from me to avoid what I might have. The dusk fallen park is quiet. Colorful glowing lights enchant me from the horizon.

10:10 PM

I lay on my rooftop to greet the full moon. My vision is blurred by densely formed clouds, but I sit anyways. I have hopes of catching a glimpse of its great lure.

She desperately looks up at the sky with her hands clasped. As always, her devotion is visible on her entire being. Her nightgown moves fast in the wind. I sense the storm brewing in the air.

I hate watching her pray.

The Great American dream is to move forward until we settle on a patch of fresh cut lawn. We depart from everything that bled, everything that burnt, everything that died and leave them all behind.

We forget the moon

So we remember the sun

We leave the winter behind

So we embrace the summer

We let go of their dying breaths

So we make America great again.

Piss,

shit,

and Clorox

We will make vaccines

We will eradicate this too

We will make it better

Hate has no home here

Hate has no home here

I watch her pray until she is settled. I hear her singing the gospel from afar. Caged children bark and sing. We chant for revolution, as everything burns,

as everything burns.

I only left her to run into her again.

She only slapped me to hold me again.

How is it that some people have no problem

starting a brand-new day

every god damn morning?

I cannot seem to get going.

I cannot move forward.

I love you

and I hate you.

I will leave one day

Just to run into you again.

Good night,

See you next week.

The Empty Platter

Jeff Jackson

I had never seen many of the dishes that were served that night and I've never laid eyes on them again. The banquet was held at the back of the inn where customers were normally forbidden to enter. The private chamber was intimately candlelit. The town fathers insisted I take the seat at the head of the glass table. I was their guest of honor, so to speak.

The town fathers offered me the first choice of every dish and I sampled them dutifully. They explained each one, highlighting the rare breeds of fowl, the strangely colored vegetables, the foreign flavors and elaborate preparations. These must have been expensive delicacies because each dish made no more than two revolutions round the table before the empty plate exited the room in the hands of the waiter.

I cannot honestly say the food made much of an impression. Perhaps I'm a person of simple appetites, though I suppose we eat what we can afford. Perhaps I should have listened more closely to the town fathers' explanations and taken advantage of their obvious expertise and enthusiasm, but that night their words struck me as little more than distractions. I knew perfectly well why I was there.

As the hours passed, it became harder to conceal my nerves. I began to speak with a slight stammer. The waiter anticipated my request and informed me that no wine or spirits would be served during the meal. His firm tone made it clear there would be no exceptions.

When the boy finally appeared, he didn't announce himself. He stood in the doorway and waited for somebody to notice him. One by one our heads turned and conversation faded away. I observed my hosts' reflections in the table's glass surface. Their faces were flushed with expectation. Their silence was ceremonial.

The boy wasn't much older than my youngest daughter. He wore a tailored blue suit. His outstretched arms held a hand-carved wooden platter. At its center sat a perfectly formed oval wrapped in delicate gold leaf. Even in the room's subdued light, it glimmered.

He set the platter in front of me. This was the one dish the town fathers didn't bother to explain, though it was the most exotic. Inside the gold leaf was a freshly produced piece of excrement.

DOI: 10.4324/9781003335252-23

Beads of perspiration trickled down my forehead and stung my eyes. I gripped the fork in my right hand, but before I could do anything the boy began to sing.

His high voice was piercing in its purity. His face had an otherworldly expression as he lost himself in the haunting melody. It was an ancient psalm of praise, something sung in our region for hundreds of years. As much as I tried to resist it, it seized my heart.

As I watched the performance, I wondered if the boy was the origin of the object on the platter. I'd heard rumors that every year a child was selected from a remote village and fed a special diet for this purpose. It wouldn't surprise me if the town fathers put children through such a degrading regimen. Despite the elegant blue suit, I noticed the boy's feet were bare.

My hosts added their voices to the tune. As it rose toward the climax, the song swelled. The room's walls began to vibrate. I was touched they were serenading me, a gesture of encouragement which would make my task easier. But then I realized their faces were turned toward the piece of offal. They were singing to it, staring with an almost mystical reverence.

And I was staring at it, too. We were all mesmerized.

I reminded myself that I was lucky to be here. I had been chosen for this ritual, the town's form of jubilee where every year one citizen had their debts forgiven. All I had to do was eat this. The legend was that it would pass through my body and transform into gold, signifying the settlement of my obligations.

Of course, I didn't believe it was possible for my body to excrete gold. Neither did the town fathers. What remained of this ritual was a humiliation to be endured for the amusement of my rich benefactors. But it didn't matter. At the end of the night, my family wouldn't have to worry about our crippling loans and compounding interest. We would be citizens in good standing once again. We had no other options.

Once the song ended, the waiter refilled my water glass. No doubt my complete sobriety in this very moment was part of the ritual my hosts most relished.

I felt everyone's eyes upon me. I had a sensation that strong hands were shoving my head against the table and prying open my mouth, though of course they weren't. I shut my eyes and raised my fork.

I ate it. I don't wish to dwell on this. The consistency was unpleasantly soft. There was no smell, though it had a distinct aftertaste, as if spiced by a ghost herb. The tang of mown grass and fresh dill reappeared throughout the night.

There was a respectful silence as the boy removed the empty platter. The waiter reappeared with a bottle of champagne and poured everyone a glass. The Mayor offered a lengthy formal toast in my honor, but I barely listened. Instead, I counted the bubbles as they rose in the glass of golden liquid.

That's my last distinct memory of the banquet. Soon my head grew light and feverish, like a hot air balloon that threatened to float off into the night sky. Somehow, I must have found this sensation pleasant because I slipped into a state of euphoria.

I only recall shameful snippets of my behavior during the last portion of the banquet—singing traditional songs in a robust tenor, juggling a set of salt shakers, stripping off my shirt to display the scar I received as child from a foreman in the fields, an injury which would've killed most people.

None of the town fathers acted surprised by my foolishness. They seemed to enjoy the spectacle and even encouraged it. I picture them offering me a standing ovation, though what they were applauding remains unknown. My recollections are so dizzy they can barely stand on their own.

At some point, I passed out. I was carried to a room at the top of the inn and tucked under a thick quilt. I thrashed throughout the small hours in that unfamiliar bed. My dream that night was so vivid that it's continued to visit me over the years.

My young daughter was crying. She was stamping her feet and ripping apart the seams of the elegant blue dress she wore. "The Mayor tricked me," she sobbed. "He gave me a present of a bar of gold, so I let him kiss me. But as soon as he left, it turned to that!" She pointed at the floor and the stinking brown lump that was already attracting flies.

I woke from my dream with terrible cramps. My insides were grinding and churning. I was surprised to find the town fathers sitting on the floor around the four-poster bed. They stared up at me with bleary eyes and wicked smiles. They whispered among themselves as I clutched my stomach. They seemed to know what came next.

I leapt from the bed and lunged for the bathroom. I barely had time to fasten the latch behind me. As I perched on the toilet, my insides seized and contorted. It felt like my organs were turning themselves inside out.

The town fathers were still outside. I could sense them listening to the embarrassing gasps and shudders from my bowels, perhaps even with their ears pressed to the wooden door. This mortification seemed to be the climax of the ritual.

My exertions were so painful that I feared a grotesque gastric explosion, but instead there was a prolonged period of stillness as something passed from my body and dropped into the water below. It made the smallest sound, barely a splash.

I was relieved it was over. I climbed off the toilet and sat on the floor, exhausted and disoriented. My head was buzzing. My limbs felt strange, as if my body no longer belonged to me.

The Mayor unhooked the latch and led the town fathers into the bathroom. They tramped inside, reeking of alcohol and jostling each other for a position by the ceramic edifice. Together we lifted the lid and stared down into the calm waters. I shut my eyes several times, but it was still there each time I opened them.

Confronted by my present to them, the faces of the town fathers trembled. They were overcome by a hatred that I suspect even they didn't understand. Nobody spoke as we observed the unlikely lump. Resting at the bottom of the bowl, it shone with the unmistakable shimmer of gold.

Project Three

Talking About *Sexuality and Suffering or the Eew! Factor*

What's a Nice Vanilla Analyst to Do?

Project Three

Editor's Note

Stephen Hartman

Muse

Dimen, M. (2005). Sexuality and suffering: Or, the "Eew!" factor. *Studies in Gender and Sexuality*, 6: 1–18.

> *Writing about sex wobbles drunkenly among the celebratory, the didactic, and the disciplinary. Here is a darker path: the "Eew! Factor," that sexual moment when you go, "eew! That's disgusting!"*
>
> Dimen (2005).

Sex and affect; abjection; humiliation, narcissism, and sexual pain; embarrassment, racism, and disgust; shame, hatred, and sex: Dimen was not shy to chart the unspeakable. Nor was she afraid to raise multiple interrelated topics in a spree of insight, as these topic headings for her jaunty foray through squeamish territory portends. No surprise, Dimen leans on a wide range of authors for grounding citing an impressive roster of interlocutors whose thoughts on sexuality and suffering are filtered through her clinical and personal encounters highlighting how shame surfaces in enigmatic channels that demarcate interpersonal, intercultural, and intergenerational regimens of pleasure and disgust.

Readers

Talking about *it* and liking to talk about sex—these tasks are not one and the same. Context and power take the thrill out of *it* lickety-split. Dimen was keenly aware that shame and disgust co-construct much of the rubric that allows us to think about the factors in psychic and interpersonal commerce that give desire its name. *Eew*! is likely more potent in conversations about sexuality than excitement, particularly when a power dynamic and/or a family romance sets the stage for a conversation about *the birds and the bees*. This brave team, Lisa Buchberg and Emma Kaywin, write as parent and child, a psychoanalyst and a sex educator and activist. They take on the

DOI: 10.4324/9781003335252-25

challenge of talking about *it* as well as talking about them talking about *it* and the many important references Dimen leads them to along the way.

Form

Dimen's essay, like much of her work, takes the form of a patchwork. She charts landscapes with subtle shifts and dramatic twists and turns. An Escher reproduction that hung above Dimen's desk often comes to mind. She would refer to it to illustrate how recusivity knits interwoven ideas into a narrative. In responding to Dimen's stylistic manner of crafting a tour de force, the authors chose to work as a dyad, addressing each other as they parse Dimen's text in a manner that demonstrates Dimen's penchant for folding thoughts upon reflections and reflections upon thoughts. This co-written text is both a dialogue between a mother and daughter about sex, (Eew!), and a synthesis of subjectivities honoring Dimen's love/hate relationship with talking about *it*.

Bios

Lisa Buchberg, DMH, is a Training and Supervising Analyst at the San Francisco Center for Psychoanalysis and a Personal and Supervising Analyst at the Psychoanalytic Institute of Northern California. She lives in Berkeley, California.

Emma Kaywin, MA, is an educator focusing on sexual ethics and trauma working toward an EdD in health and behavior studies at Teachers College, Columbia University. They live in Brooklyn, New York.

Sexuality and Suffering, or the Eew! Factor

Muriel Dimen

Writing about sex wobbles drunkenly among the celebratory, the didactic, and the disciplinary. Here is a darker path: the "Eew! Factor,"[1] that sexual moment when you go, "Eew! that's disgusting!" The Eew! Factor is relative. Maybe yours has never been about sex at all. But like as not each clinician has felt this sexual disturbance—an excited disgust—at some time or another, which is this paper might be subtitled not "*the* clinician's sexual unease," but clinicians' sexual unease.

Sex and Affect

Although the disturbance of sex has many histories and manifestations, here I stress affect's role. The affects around sex make it difficult to think about. So when examining sex, it helps to weave theory and feeling together by splicing theoretical and philosophical reflections with clinical retrospection. The interleaved experiential and constitutive dimensions of the Eew! Factor's manifold and mingled aspects unfold when examined through the lens of sexual countertransference; sexual countertransference through affect, abjection, and intersubjectivity; and sex itself through all of them.

As I reexamine the three clinical moments I describe here, I ask your indulgence or, rather, effort. Please don't supervise these expired, not exactly successful, cases. Although I cannot control how you read, I hope that these cases do what I intend: spark discussion so the unspeakable can enter public discourse. My perspective is relational: neither psychic bedrock nor diagnostic sign, sex can be treated like any other clinical matter. "Sexual countertransference" designates any given clinician's responses to sexuality, including but not limited to, the desire marking erotic countertransference.

"Sex is a beautiful thing," soberly taught my parents—or, at least, my mother. Except it isn't—always. Donald Jones (1995) attributes to sex three different affects: excitement, enjoyment, and contentment, usually in that order. Missing, however, are anxiety, uneasiness, the Eew! Factor, dread—which is a little like anatomizing marriage without dissecting divorce.

DOI: 10.4324/9781003335252-26

Remember *The Joy of Sex*, whose author, the oddly but aptly named Alex Comfort (1972), might have penned instead *The Discomforts of Sex*, whose existence occasions, after all, his book's long life, Dr. Ruth's fame, and the success of David Reuben's (1969) *Everything You Always Wanted to Know about Sex but Were Afraid to Ask*. The 60s–70s sexual revolution contextualizing these media events emerged from the prudish 50s' naughty underside, itself a response to the sexual break-out of the 20s and 30s. But the Eew! Factor! lived on.

In countertransference, the affects accompanying sex tend to disturb. Charles Spezzano (1993) criticized a clinician who wrote about having interpreted as sexual his patient's experience of a haircut. But nothing that the patient said, complained Spezzano, allowed that interpretation. Apart from theoretical premises, the clinician had to have had *feeling:* his subjective experience, whatever its transference–countertransference sources, must have led to his understanding. But the clinician did not mention any countertransference affect.

Like all emotions, sexual feeling tends to be catching—I feel it, you feel it. Reporting on sexual matters in clinical space, Davies (1994), de Peyer (2002), and Samuels (1985), for example, record a profound if not surprising amount of personal discomfort. Among the many reasons for this unease, I want to emphasize affective contagion, which de Peyer's case shows especially well. Like all emotions, sexual feeling tends to be catching—I feel it, you feel it. "On the deepest level," wrote Steve Mitchell (2000), "affective states are transpersonal" (p. 61). Recent theory, for example, Ruth Stein's (1991), situates affect in the primal swirl of infant and caretaker. Feelings arrive at once corporeally and psychically, but corporeality is as much a two-person as a one-body phenomenon, standing, as we know, for both psychic and interpersonal reality (Fairbairn, 1954; Shapiro, 1996; Aron and Anderson, 1998; Harris, 1998; Dimen, 2000). To quote Mitchell (2000) again: "Questions like, 'Who started it?' and 'Who did what to whom?' tend to be meaningless when intense affective connections are involved, as in strong sexual attraction, terror, murderous rage, or joyous exhilaration" (p. 61).

What makes sexual affect special? "Sexual speech is inherently performative in that it materializes what it aims to describe," says Virginia Goldner (2003, p. 120), elucidating Foucault's take on psychoanalytic and confessional speech as "inscribed in an erotic circuit of scrutiny and disclosure." Because words are as visceral as psychosocial, and because, as Bakhtin's (1934–1935) theory of heteroglossia has it, my *parole,* or speech, is always already permeated by yours, sex talk is also sexy talk (Gallop, 1982; Dimen, 1999). Or at least it may be.

In the analytic situation, where sex comes to us in spoken words and body-language, even conversations that attempt to contain its excess and analyze its action-driven character are bathed in its heat, and [we] are thus always at risk of collapsing into a forced choice between "talking dirty" or not talking at all (Goldner, 2003).

Speaking sex, then, may threaten to violate ethics (Gabbard, 1989; Maroda, 1994) or catalyze the treatment (Samuels, 1985; Davies, 1994). You just don't know. The ambiguity is, currently, inherent.

Abjection

My effort to limn clinicians' sexual unease is part of a larger project, individual and collective, of reconsidering sexuality postclassically, beyond but not exclusive of the oedipal, inclusive of narcissism but registering culture too. Take, for example, a roundtable on developmental dialogues of sexuality held in 2002 at a New York City meeting of the Division of Psychoanalysis, American Psychological Association (Slavin et al., 2004). Ultimately the debate concerned whether sex was intersubjective (Seligman and Davies) or Other (Stein). Davies voiced the pull toward synthesis: the two sides, she insisted, were not so far apart. But, although I usually go for that third space too, this time I wanted the two sides to disagree more.

It is necessary to maintain a tension between sex as emerging in object relation and sex as Other. Although I cannot argue the point here, I want to explain why I take this stance. One reason is political: I fear that, if we imagine we can locate everything sexual in everything we know about intersubjectivity, it would not be too difficult to reduce sex to familiar forms of object relation that are overtly blessed, or damned, by social norms. The other, psychoanalytical, reason is cognate: there is more in heaven and earth than is dreamt of in normativity. Preserving sexuality as Other "stretches the clinical imagination about what patients' inner worlds are like and, given the chance, could be like" (Dimen, 2003, p. 178). In sex as in psychoanalysis, shouldn't there be room for discovery and invention, for surprise, if also disturbance?

In going for the sexual stretch, though, we are likely to come upon abjection. Before I turn to Julia Kristeva's (1982) ideas about this iffy state, I want to survey how the *OED* defines "abject" and its derivatives: to cast away, out, down; to reject, abase, lower; by implication, to feel discarded, rejected, dejected. Go further and you get to the affects that are, for Kristeva, abject central: humiliation, shame, and disgust. These affects arrive with a feeling of horror infusing what Kristeva deems abjection's primordial form, food loathing—or, as I call it, food alarm. One of my food alarms is seaweed. Seaweed in miso soup or sushi rolls, not to mention in the sea or on the shore—that's fine. But when, every year or so, I try a bite from a nice salad where that awful stuff, neither containing nor contained, sits on its plate, a siren screams silently and hyperventilation nears. Kristeva's evocation of "a massive and sudden emergence of uncanniness" (p. 2) is right on the money. Eew!

Abjection appears to be a one-person, one-body experience of Otherness. Implicitly, however, it is part of an intersubjective and developmental process. Kristeva's food loathing in reaction to "skin on milk's surface" leads to the thought: "'I' want none of that element, sign of [my parents'] desire" (pp. 2–3). Note her "I" in scare quotes, which alerts us to the developmental matter. If, Kristeva goes on, we think in terms of "subjective diachrony"—and what is that if not development?—abjection turns out to be "*a precondition of narcissism*" (p. 13), precondition as both prerequisite and prior stage. On the one hand, says Kristeva, "Even before being *like*, 'I' am not but do *separate, reject, ab-ject*."

Separating through rejecting and abjecting—that *is* who one is. On the other, the uncanniness, "familiar as it might have been in an opaque and forgotten life, now harries me as radically separate, loathsome." The abject state is "Not me. Not that. But not nothing, either. A 'something' that I do not recognize as a thing" (p. 2). Might we recognize here Sullivan's (1953) "not- me"?

Abjection's position on what Freud (1905) called "the frontier between the physical and the mental" (p. 168) locates it close to narcissism, which thereby takes on a new look. Narcissism as I am using it denotes "less a psychiatric character phenomenon and more a developmental position" (Ken Corbett, 2003, personal communication). The oneness with which it is usually endowed contains, as we know, the seeds of its own transformation. Inevitably corporeal and psychically inevitable, abjection registers that moment when one is not quite separate but no longer merged either. This uncertainty introduces to narcissism the discomforts of borders in the between spaces. "Abjection," says Kristeva (1982), "preserves what existed in the archaism of pre-objectal relationship, in the immemorial violence with which a body becomes separated from another body in order to be" (p. 10). Violence. Ungrounded affect. Loss. "The abject is the violence of mourning for an 'object' that has always already been lost" (p. 15). Would you have thought of transitional space as shot through with pain?

Abjection is desire before self and object have psychically cohered and, by so cohering, constituted each other (p. 5). In Kristeva's view, it renders narcissism a condition of torment and impossibility. No wonder abjection registers in liminal substances that evoke fascinated disgust—feces, to take the prime example, but urine, semen, vaginal fluids, menstrual blood, snot, pimples, pus, skin excrescences. These border materials, neither fully alive nor fully dead, signify what must be rejected in order that life exist—death—but that must exist in order that life exist (pp. 2–3). Abjection inhabits the space between deprivation and signification, as the Lacanians might put it. Finally, abjection signifies the breast, mother, and femininity, the disgust they inspire, and their consequent repudiation (Grosz, 1994).

Humiliation, Narcissism, and Sexual Pain

Let me try some of these musings out clinically. L, considerably younger than I, found me attractive. I responded in kind. At one point, I shared my feelings with him, to make the sexuality into what Ogden (1994), following Green, calls an object of knowledge or reflection. The disclosure relieved some anxiety, but an unease lingered that I would now name abjection because of the hovering shame and humiliation linked, for him, with maternal tantalization.

Sexual abjection is, to some extent, unspeakable, as de Peyer (2002), in a case study, has shown. The sexual disturbance between us—our Eew! Factor—was never fully translated into some other analytic pleasure, that is, analytic knowing. Rather, you might say that for years every session took place against a background of erotic unknowing. Did our muteness in fact help him to leave as he did, having regained his sexual potency? I want to claim success, even as I suspect failure. It is true that he continued in a state of abjection and gradually replaced me with another tantalizing object, the money he would win or lose at the track. Yet something shifted later, for he returned for a couple of visits to make sure I was still alive and to tell me that he wasn't gambling anymore.

You could say simply that L and I were frustrated: we couldn't do it, we could only sort of speak it. But frustration is more interesting than that. Think of its relation to abjection. Frustration marks sexual desire, as loss tinges attachment and pain, love. You may have a steady partner, but that does not always mean you get to have sex when or how you want it, or that you even want it now that it's available. When I spoke of these matters in Stockbridge in February 2002, Paul Lippmann alluded wistfully to "our efforts to have sexual lives." Sexual desire, Freud (1941) thought, is inherently unsatisfiable: "'*En attendant toujours quelque chose qui ne venait point* [Always waiting for something that never came]" (quoted by Green, 1996, p. 872). Concurring, Lacan (1977) saw satisfaction as a necessarily alluring impossibility critical to the crystalization of subjectivity, sanity, and culture. I don't know about this view of sexual satisfaction as an endlessly receding mirage, but it's not a useless perspective either, especially in a culture that means every sexual encounter to end atop Mt. Everest.

You could also locate the Eew! Factor between L and me in narcissism's unease—unstable identity, elemental uncertainty, fragility, spatial ambivalence, inability to distinguish inside from outside, pleasure from pain. What happens when sexual feeling enters? Required reading here would be Laplanche's (1976) account of the enigmatic message, sexuality as an unconscious transmission to the infant from the mother's or, as we might now emend it, the parental unconscious. Thus sexuality is always already an inarticulable mystery, an "alien internal entity."

Agreeing with but going beyond Laplanche, Stein (1998) limns the excess of sexuality, its transcendence and loss of self that contrast with and even contradict the state of mind required for ordinary life. Making a further distinction, Benjamin (1998) proposes to regard excess as a result of "failures in affective containment [that] may produce sexual tension rather than reflect some interpersonal transmission of unconscious sexual content" (p. 7). Davies (2001), unearthing yet another effect of the unmetabolizable spillover of parent–child intimacy, has suggested that parents' unavoidable silence about their children's sexual feeling will inevitably imbue sexuality with a sense of trauma. As she suggests, you may say to your child, "Oh you're so angry. I know what that's like," but you probably won't say, "Oh, you're turned on, aren't you?"

To return to the clinic, analysts may need to serve as containers for excess and trauma. But we need also to accept pain and discomfort's permanence in sex, hence in sexual transference– countertransference. Consider Kristeva's (1982) slant on "the edenic image of primary narcissism": "the archaic relation to the mother... is... of no solace. For the subject will always be marked by the uncertainty of his borders and of his affective valency as well" (p. 62). Cognate with this rather *undyllic* maternal relation is *jouissance*, which we generally read as orgasm in all its ineffability, but is sometimes pain or shame to the nth degree. "Freud's expansion of the sexual beyond the genital," explains Tim Dean (2001), "is redescribed by Lacan in terms of *jouissance*, a form of enjoyment so intense as to be barely distinguishable from suffering and pain" (p. 271).

Embarrassment, Racism, and Disgust

Think here of the French folk song: *Plaisir d'amour, Ne dure qu'un moment, Chagrin d'amour, Dure toute la vie. Chagrin d'amour* [the pleasure of love lasts but a moment. The sorrow of love lasts a lifetime.] or, at least, pain or suffering. That's what we need to add to our thinking about sexual countertransference and transference, even about sex itself, whatever that might be. With L, for instance, there was a congeries of emotions, shared and unshared, ranging from excitement and playfulness, to contemplative quietude, to fear, rage, disgust, and mortification. With A, in contrast, embarrassment ruled the clinical day. Probably both of us were embarrassed, but I was so locked in my discomfort that I never found hers. Once, for example, she picked up a minor celebrity. The morning after, he threw 50 bucks on the night table. "I took it," she shrugged with what I now see as an embarrassed laugh.

What's a nice vanilla analyst to do? I am trying to puzzle out my countertransference blind spot. A was a fledgling, temping for a living. I was a f ledgling too, conducting a once-weekly treatment early in my practice. Had we worked in the transference, I am sure I could have caught my reenactment of her mother's emotional abandonment of her. As it was, I failed to hear her plea that I see through her happy little mask to the frightened girl armed with a sexuality that she didn't know how to use. "Perhaps," I might have said, "you are asking me for something but you don't know what it is. I sense this encounter unsettled you, and you don't quite know how to think about it." But embarrassment? For enlightenment, let us turn to abjection's psychic and cultural ramifications. Since sexuality happens not only within but between psyches, its focus is not always clear. Sex may be for me, it may be for you; it may be for us, it may be for someone else. A source of both pleasure and pain, it may lead to self-gratification or other-gratification or both, and which goal governs any particular sexual encounter varies unpredictably from time to time, and person to person, even within any one coupling. Not only exploitation, but self-deception, is always possible. One person seems sexually gratified but is not: think faked orgasms. Another appears to feel love, or at least like, but actually feels indifference. Or disgust. You don't always know, even in a legitimated, long-term relationship, whether you are exploiting or being exploited or sharing; Kernberg (1995) almost prescribes part-object exploitation for conjugality.

A did not know how to negotiate this minefield. I didn't either. Who does? There is a great deal of pressure not to notice sexual abjection. Enter culture, which I introduce to pry open the closed-mindedness that exploits abjection.

Sex is value-laden, emotions are saturated with values, and values are emotionally charged (Jaggar, 1983; Stein, 1991; Spezzano, 1993; Tomkins, 1995). I have no doubt that A and I, even though we were from different subcultures and classes, shared a prevailing morality wedding sex to love and mutual respect, and in respect of which trading in sex, for example, is embarrassing.

At the same time, our subcultural differences worked on us, or at least me, insidiously, because this treatment never went deep or long enough for me to walk another conscious minefield of my own: racism. Looking back, I see that I believed that, in A's immiserated black and Latino subculture, exchanging sex for money stood on a continuum of acceptable behavior. Since this belief seemed to abject people of color and since I was ashamed of it, I could never make my way through it to see how embarrassed she was, to speculate on the transference implications, or to probe my countertransference by imagining myself as a hooker or resurrecting a hooker fantasy of my own. Was she embarrassed because I was the white middle-class lady doctor whom she paid for one-week stands as her one-night stand lover paid her? Because she sensed my abjecting racism? Because her need for care, so miserably unmet, left her begging for crumbs?

As I was drafting this article, however, I recalled Judith Walkowitz's (1980) feminist research on working-class Jewish women in New York City at the turn of the last century. Then and now, Walkowitz argues, dominant middle-class values have obscured the freedom with which some women have historically mined their own sexuality on their own behalf. In any given family of the group she studied, for example, there might have been one sister who married and reproduced right away; another who lived alone and worked in a factory or wrote books; one who did that and later married and had children; one who hooked and used her job to find the right man; and one who just ran a whorehouse (and, like Polly Adler, 1953, wrote a memoir). Indeed, I wonder if such a narrative might befit the cocotte in Freud's (1920) contemporaneous case of the psychogenesis of homosexuality in a woman. Could A's *mores* have been so described? I don't know. Maybe even suggesting so is offensive. The point is that a gendered and cultural, if not also personal, Eew! Factor prevented me from *thinking* about any of this then.

That psychoanalysis contributes to that familiar construction which filled my countertransference—sex belongs only in the region of intimacy—is a commonplace. The structure of *Three Essays*, Ethel Person (1986) has pointed out, begins in the wild sexual aberrations of adulthood. After having relished infancy's polymorphous perversity, the book finally narrows its prescriptions to the reproductive heterosexuality of maturity in which sexual health is defined as the release of semen into the vagina. But we know that sex was and remains far more multifaceted than that, and we are embarrassed by our own multiplicity, which, in cultural and psychoanalytic theory, turns out to consist of deviations.

This affectively complicated knowledge circles back to the first half of *Three Essays*. Sex, says Stein (Slavin et al., 2004), may be transgressive, transcendent, and transformative, but it is also r idiculous. Think, she suggests, about al l that embarrassing licking and slobbering. Now let's add the visual to the oral: who is pretty at the height of passion? Maya Angelou (1981) quipped about someone she didn't like: "She was utterly unable to make me ugly up my face between the sheets" (p. 102). Way back in 1915, Freud (1905) uneasily pondered the same problem. "There is in my mind," he confided in a footnote to *Three Essays*, "no doubt that the concept of 'beautiful' has its roots in sexual excitation and that its original meaning was 'sexually stimulating.'" Universalizing his unease, he added, "This is related to the fact that we never regard the genitals themselves, which produce the strongest sexual excitation, as really 'beautiful'" (p. 156 *n*. 2).

Note the word *really*. Genitals seem disgusting as well as beautiful. Stein (Slavin et al., 2004) was addressing what Freud knew, that sexual disgust is unavoidable and overcoming it is part of sexual experience. Sexual excitement transports you into bodily and sensory realms of abjection foreclosed long ago in the necessities of maturation. For one thing, you encounter the groinal odors and sensations that you learned to associate with the toilet and its privacy. To have sex, you have to climb psychic and symbolic, not to mention sensory, barriers established to civilize you and to render you and your caretakers happy and proud. "Libido," said Freud (1912) "thrives on obstacles" (p. 187) and "in its strength enjoys overriding... disgust" (1905, p. 152). Certainly disgust is one emotion you learn to employ for toilet training. No wonder it is embarrassing to talk of the pleasure/pain of sex. Think about the grunts, moans, and screams, the farts, the sound and feeling of sticky membrane on sticky membrane. And I haven't even mentioned taste. Eew!

Shame, Hatred, and Sex

It is not far from embarrassment to shame. Embarrassment, writes Andrew Morrison (1989), is a mild form of shame. In it, you feel exposed for some feeling or act that transgresses interpersonal or social morality but keeps you within the pale. Embarrassment may or may not snowball into shame, in which, in contrast, you feel that your core is corroded and that you should be excommunicated. Shame, perhaps, *is* the state of narcissistic injury. It is, Morrison suggests, the other side of self-regard (p. 42).

Shame spreads as easily as poison ivy. One patient calls it "wildfire": you tell of one moment of shame, then another comes back, and then another, and another, until all you are is shame. Shame self-replicates; if you near the shame feelings of someone with narcissistic injury, then that person feels, lo and behold, ashamed. Through its performativity, shame also oozes into intersubjective space, which in psychotherapy makes countertransference errors very easy. "The shame of patients is contagious," Morrison explains, "often resonating with the clinician's own shame experiences—the therapist's own sense of failure, self-deficiency, and life disappointments" (p. 6). I don't doubt that this contagion featured in my work with L and with A.

Shame, Kristeva (1982) holds, is core to abjection, but the reasons for this become clear only if we consider abjection relationally. You can see how this works in Fairbairn's (1954) take on frustration. Characteristically turning a classical concept on its head, Fairbairn argued that, in an object-relations as opposed to an impulse psychology, "frustration is always emotionally equivalent to rejection" (p. 13). This equivalence between frustration, on one hand, and exclusion and hurt, on the other, obtains because an object is always already present in psychic reality: "If the child is essentially object-seeking, frustration is inevitably experienced as rejection on the part of the object" (p. 13). If rejection comes, can humiliation and its cognate affect, shame, be far behind? Frustration being usual— whether in object seeking, in selfing, or in sex—shame partners pleasure from the getgo.

Talk about *chagrin d'amour.* When shame attends frustration, then disgust, hatred, and other effects of aggression are not far behind. How often, for example, we say, "making love" when we mean "having sex." Are we in reaction formation? Recall that Sándor Ferenczi (1933) concluded his amazing "The Confusion of Tongues" by referring to "the hate-impregnated love of adult mating" (p. 206). I cannot here deconstruct this fascinating, unsettling paradox of maturity, but will just note Stoller's (1975, 1979) thoughts on the subject and indicate its roots in paranoid-schizoid splitting and in abjection. Clearly, the achievement of ambivalence is necessary to negotiate it. But ambivalence is, as we know, unstable. I quote Meltzer's (1973) intriguing thought that a libidinal/object-relational "stage might be successfully traversed but... never truly dismantled" (p. 27). Having sexual feeling as adults, we always risk the shifting of positions—the return of abjection's unease and horror, of paranoid-schizoid suffering.

In my final clinical example, I track how excitement and revulsion attend the circulating affects of shame, hate, and love in transference and countertransference. W, a slender fellow with an ivory complexion, graceful black hair, green eyes, and a face I'd call chiseled, was not physically to my taste at all, but I could see how a girl could fall for him. And you can already see the war between my feelings for and against him. Tightly focused on his lucrative work, he was, if not exactly a mama's boy, fused to her in an underground sort of way.

As withholding from me as he was from his girlfriend (whose wishes for his commitment I was unable to grant; he'd been referred by his girlfriend's therapist), W had a sexual secret: he kept a lover on the side. Now, even though I do not escape the cultural belief that sex is a subset of intimacy, still I think that, adultery being as ubiquitous as French bistros, monogamy cannot really be a criterion for mental health and probity. But there was an Eew! Factor, perhaps, a hateful thrill he may have felt at withholding from his girlfriend and turning to a degraded lover. I wonder if, countertransferentially, I too felt that thrill, in complementary or concordant (Racker, 1968) fashion.

What really angered me was the degradation he effected, the disgust he felt, and the hatred he manifested—and the emergence of all those affects in me about him and about myself. W's lover was a woman whose lower status and dark skin, explicitly exciting for him, were also so embarrassing that he could not or would not reveal any of the identifying details. Was she Latina? Black? Indian? His silence, coupled with his eroticized racism and classism, offended me. Another hateful thrill: his treating all of us as part-objects. Looking back, I see that I felt humiliation, excluded like his lover, not to mention his girlfriend, who was, unlike him but like me, Jewish and as such may have already participated in the abjection necessary to his sexuality. (And here, in the land of part-objects, we might think back to A and to the Eew! of $50 tossed on the table and the corresponding Eew! of picking it up.)

Of course, we must suspect here W's own self-disgust, signaled by the occasional bulimic episode, as well as what, I speculate, may, in fact, have been his real sexual secret. Looking back, I wonder whether he was disguising not class and race, but gender. You see, as I was writing that monogamy could not be a criterion for mental health, I made a slip of the pen or, rather, of the keyboard. I had f irst written, not "monogamy," but "heterosexuality." If, then, heterosexuality could not be a criterion for mental health, then perhaps W was masking his lover's gender. Had I reflected on my heterosexual countertransference of humiliated, controlled, and hating female to his withholding, domineering, and hateful male, might I have been able to speculate about homosexual acts or wishes? Other features, after all, would have supported that hypothesis. After reading, in his girlfriend's diary, about her last boyfriend, he became so angry he would repeatedly grill her about her sexual past. Who was he interested in, his girl or her lover?

Yet another speculation forms. At issue was perhaps not object choice but his own gender or sexual identity. Recall his bulimia, more often than not what Louise Kaplan (1991) calls a "female perversion." When, for example, he would take his Maserati out of the garage, he would circle it several times, dramatizing his search for dings, not because he expected damage but to intimidate the garage attendants. "I don't like to do it," he explained, "but I have to." How hypermasculine, how hard edged, in contrast to the little boy whose mother found him so pretty that she would sit him on her lap in the bow window of their suburban home to show him off to the neighbors. How great was his struggle not to be her thing. Was his real secret a disgusting and shameful feminine identification projected and abjected onto a debased female lover, mistress, or analyst?

Conclusion

The hate that accompanies frustration, rejection, humiliating and shame is a prime cause of sexual suffering, whether at home or in the consulting room. Once inside the act, however, this disturbance evaporates. Space precludes further explanation, but I can share Goldner's (2003) observation of our reluctance to theorize good sex lest it fizzle. I do want to mention a friend's response to this thesis of the Eew! Factor. He shrugged. "You mean," I replied, "for you, it's all part of it?" So this Eew! Factor requires deconstruction. Do I—or, if you agree with me—*we* come to it because of a certain personal and professional, not to say theoretical, idealization of sex? The Eew! Factor, and certainly clinicians' sexual unease, may be multiply inflected by gender, sexual preference, time of life, character, cohabitational status, and certainly other features. Perhaps you know of Leo Bersani's (1988) one-liner: "There is a secret about sex: most people don't like it." Drawing on Bataille's notions of sex, death, and disgust, Bersani speaks of the shattering of the ego that constitutes *jouissance*, and that terrifies us and makes us want to forget to have sex. A culture theorist, Bersani writes in a one-person psychology. Add the two-person model and we would also have to think about how, when passion runs high, the balance between love and hate swings nauseatingly. Now hate is up, now love. You cannot predict. The depressive position, maturity, even sanity, and, as the Lacanians would have it, membership in the symbolic, human order, fail. We fall into dread and disgust. Journalist Amy Taubin (1994) writes about hate-fucking, an idea suggested to her by her maverick analyst, the late Ernst Pavel, which she sees registered in Mike Leigh's film *Naked*. But when hate pops out in sex, what happens to self-regard? Perhaps it turns to disgust. Eew!

Note

1 A term coined by Stephen Hartman.

References

Adler, P. (1953), *A House Is Not a Home*. New York: Rinehart.

Angelou, M. (1981), *The Heart of a Woman*. New York: Random House. Aron, L. & Anderson, F. S. (1998), *Relational Perspectives on the Body*. Hillsdale, NJ: The Analytic Press.

Aron, L. and Anderson, F. S. *Relational Perspectives on the Body*. Hillsdale, NJ: The Analytic Press.

Bakhtin, M. M. (1934–1935), Discourse of the novel. In: *The Dialogic Imagination: Four Essays by M. M. Bakhtin*, ed. M. Holquist (trans. C. Emerson & M. Holquist). Austin: University of Texas Press, 1981, pp. 259–420.

Benjamin, J. (1998), How intersubjective is sex? Keynote address at annual meeting of Division of Psychoanalysis (Div ision 39), American Psychological Association, Boston, April.

Bersani, L. (1988), Is the rectum a grave? In: *AIDS: Cultural Analysis, Cultural Activism*, ed. D. Crimp. Cambridge: MIT Press, pp. 197–222.

Comfort, A., ed. (1972), *The Joy of Sex*. New York: Simon & Schuster.

Davies, J. M. (1994), Love in the afternoon: A relational reconsideration of desire and dread in the countertransference. *Psychoanal. Dial.*, 4:153–170.

——— (2001), Erotic overstimulation and the co-construction of sexual meanings in transference and countertransference experience. *Psychoanal. Quart.*, 70:757–788.

Dean, T. (2001), *Beyond Sexuality*. Chicago: University of Chicago Press.

de Peyer, J. (2002), Private terrors: Sexualized aggression and a psychoanalyst's fear of her patient. *Psychoanal. Dial.*, 12:509–530.

Dimen, M. (1999), Between *lust* and libido: Sex, psychoanalysis, and the moment before. *Psychoanal. Dial.*, 9:415–440.

——— (2000), The body as Rorschach. *Studies Gender & Sexual.*, 1:9–39.

——— (2003), *Sexuality, Intimacy, Power.* Hillsdale, NJ: The Analytic Press.

Fairbairn, W. R. D. (1954), Observations on the nature of hysterical states. *Brit. J. Med. Psychol.*, 27:105–125.

Ferenczi, S. (1933), The confusion of tongues between adults and the child. *Contemp. Psychoanal.*, 24:196–206, 1988.

Freud, S. (1905), Three essays on the theory of sexuality. *Standard Edition,* 7:125–243. London: Hogarth Press, 1953.

——— (1912), On the universal tendency to debasement in the sphere of love, *Standard Edition,* 11:179–190. London: Hogarth Press, 1957.

——— (1920), The psychogenesis of a case of homosexuality in a woman. *Standard Edition,* 18:145–172. London: Hogarth Press, 1955.

Gabbard, G., ed. (1989), *Sexual Exploitation in Professional Relationships.* Washington, DC: American Psychiatric Press.

Gallop, J. (1982), *The Daughter's Seduction: Psychoanalysis and Feminism.* Ithaca, NY: Cornell University Press.

Goldner, V. (2003), Ironic gender/Authentic sex. *Studies in Gender & Sexual.*, 4:113–139.

Green, A. (1996), Has sexuality anything to do with psychoanalysis? *Internat. J. Psycho-Anal.*, 76:871–883.

Grosz, E. (1994), *Volatile Bodies.* New York: Routledge.

Harris, A. (1998), Psychic envelopes and sonorous baths: Siting the body relational theory and clinical practice. In: *Relational Perspectives on the Body,* ed. L. Aron & F. S. Anderson. Hillsdale, NJ: The Analytic Press, 2004, pp. 39–64.

Jaggar, A. B. (1983), *Feminist Politics and Human Nature.* Totowa, NJ: Rowman & Allenheld.

Jones, J. M. (1995), *Affects as Process.* Hillsdale, NJ: The Analytic Press. Kaplan, L. (1991), *Female Perversions.* New York: Anchor Books.

Kaplan, L. J. (1991), *Female Perversions.* New York: Anchor Books.

Kernberg, O. (1995), *Love Relations: Normality and Pathology.* New Haven: Yale University Press.

Kristeva, J. (1982), *Powers of Horror,* trans. L. Roudiez. New York: Columbia University Press.

Lancan, J. (1977), Écrits: *A Selection,* tr. A. Sheridan. London: Tavistock. Laplanche, J. (1976), *Life and Death in Psychoanalysis,* trans. J. Mehlman. Annapolis, MD: Johns Hopkins University Press.

Maroda, K. (1994), *The Power of Countertransference.* Hillsdale, NJ: The Analytic Press, 2004.

Meltzer, D. (1973), *Sexual States of Mind.* Perthshire, Scotland: Clunie Press, 1979.

Mitchell, S. A. (2000), *Relationality: From Attachment to Intersubjectivity.* Hillsdale, NJ: The Analytic Press.

Morrison, A. (1989), *Shame: The Underside of Narcissism.* Hillsdale, NJ: The Analytic Press.

Ogden, T. (1994), *Subjects of Analysis.* New York: Aronson.

Person, E. (1986), A psychoanalytic approach. In: *Theories of Sexuality,* ed. J. Geer & W. O'Donohue. New York: Plenum, pp. 385–410.

Racker, H. (1968), *Transference and Countertransference.* London: Hogarth Press.

Reuben, D. (1969), *Everything You Always Wanted to Know about Sex But Were Afraid to Ask.* New York: McKay.

Samuels, A. (1985), Symbolic dimensions of Eros in transference and countertransference. *Internat. Rev. Psychoanal.* 12:199–214.

Shapiro, S. A. (1996), The embodied analyst in the Victorian consulting room. *Gender & Psychoanal.*, 1:297–322.

Slavin, J. H., Oxenhandler, N., Seligman, S., Stein, R. & Davies, J. M. (2004) Roundtable: Dialogues on sexuality in development and treatment, *Studies Gender & Sexuality,* 5:371–418.

Spezzano, C. (1993), *Affect in Psychoanalysis.* Hillsdale, NJ: The Analytic Press.

Stein, R. E. (1991), *Psychoanalytic Theories of Affect.* New York: Praeger.

——— (1998), The poignant, the excessive and the enigmatic in sexuality. *Internat. J. Psycho-Anal.*, 79:253–268.

Stoller, R. (1975), *Perversion: The Erotic Form of Hatred.* Washington, DC: American Psychiatric Press.

——— (1979), *Sexual Excitement.* New York: Pantheon.

Sullivan, H. S. (1953), *The Interpersonal Theory of Psychiatry.* New York: Norton.

Taubin, A. (1994), Female trouble. *Village Voice,* April 15, p. 20.

Tomkins, S. S. (1995), *Exploring Affect: The Selected Writings of Silvan S. Tomkins*, ed. E. V. Demos. Paris: Maison des Sciences de l'Homme.

Walkowitz, J. (1980), Prostitution and Victorian Society: Women, Class, and the State.

What's a Nice Vanilla Analyst to Do?

An Intergenerational Conversation on Muriel Dimen's "The Eew Factor"

Lisa Buchberg and Emma Kaywin

EMMA: My mother and I have been invited by Stephen Hartman to discuss Muriel Dimen's paper, "*Sexuality and Suffering, Or the Eew! Factor.*" Our paper will be less of a formal discussion about the content of Dimen's formulation of the "eew!" and more a conversational mapping of our responses to the ideas she included in this article. Lisa will draw on her background of psychoanalytic theory and practice, while I'll be inviting in a patchwork of theories and ideas from a range of interdisciplinary areas, spanning sexuality, trauma, and horror genre theory.

LISA: I'll start my part with the obvious: Emma's and my relationship, announced in the title of this discussion. Dimen grounds her paper on Julia Kristeva's ideas of the abject as she works to locate the origin story of eew! Emma and I have lived this origin story together, "the immemorial violence with which a body becomes separated from another body in order to be" (Kristeva, 1982, p. 10; in Dimen, p. 6). Now we are composing a conversation that may meander, but nonetheless stays close to the topic: sex, with all its queasiness, liminal substances, excitements, pleasures, and disturbance. Perhaps you, our reader, will respond: eew!

Dimen is her own kind of meanderer, a psychoanalytic flaneur, strolling through the literature of sex, citing the best sights. On first reading her paper I found her references promiscuous but came to see them as carefully curated. She brings us to Kristeva, who isn't an easy read. "Even before being *like*, 'I' am not but do *separate, reject, ab-ject*" (Kristeva, 1982, p. 13; Dimen, p. 5) and, "The abject is the violence of mourning for an 'object' that has always already been lost" (Kristeva, 1982, p. 15; in Dimen, p. 6). The inverted commas do considerable work. I think we must take these words as familiar and unfamiliar. Separate, violence, mourning, object, lost. We know them, but as Kristeva uses them, they become strange. She defamiliarizes our language.[1]

I am particularly interested in the concept of the border, partly because I have some idea of what will capture Emma's attention on the topic and partly because it is crucial to the concept of abjection. Kristeva

DOI: 10.4324/9781003335252-27

tells us that "the subject will always be marked by the uncertainty of his borders" (Kristeva, 1982, p. 62; in Dimen, p. 8). The taint of abjection – the "border materials" – the ur eew – can become something to be gotten rid of and installed where it can be reviled, rendered less than human. "Not me. Not that. But not nothing, either. A 'something' that I do not recognize as a thing" (Kristeva, 1982, p. 2; quoted in Dimen, pp. 5–6). From this position, we seek psychic maneuvers to establish definition to the borders. Emma, I cede this territory to you.

EMMA: I understand your reading of abjection as one of creating borders, but borders that are in some sense uncanny or – to use Dimen's framing – disgusting. Eew! I want to take each of these topics in turn.

First up is the uncanny, which is an experience Freud describes as "that species of the frightening that goes back to what was once known and had long been familiar" (Freud, 2003, p. 124). Often we talk about fearing the unknown – the dark, the Other in the form of humans we don't know or who are not like us, etc. – but Freud's formulation of uncanny fear is that it is something we actually know, but (as is indicated in his use of the past tense) have lost to ourselves, repressed. In a sense, then, the uncanny is at its core a fear of the self – of what the self has repressed and therefore does not know of itself. Putting Kristeva and Freud into conversation, we get a fuller picture of what we fear in the uncanny: the parts of ourselves that we've shunted away through the process of abjection.

Now onto the concept of borders, because when we distinguish between self and not-self through abjection, what we are doing is constructing a border. Dimen argues that abjection is uniquely tied not just to borders, but specifically to feelings of disgust of the border and what lies on the other side:

> No wonder abjection registers in liminal substances that evoke fascinated disgust – feces, to take the prime example, but urine, semen, vaginal fluids, menstrual blood, snot, pimples, pus, skin excrescences. These border materials, neither fully alive nor fully dead, signify what must be rejected in order that life exist – death – but that must *exist* in order that life exist. (Dimen, 2005, p. 6)

This gets us to the topic of monsters. Yes, I mean vampires, zombies ("neither fully alive nor fully dead" as Dimen puts it), werewolves, witches, pick your favorite (or to be more in alignment with the abject and the eew, pick your least favorite). Horror genre theorists (an actual discipline) have done a lot of thinking and theorizing about why we create monsters, and more pointedly why we create *specific* monsters. For instance, why were vampires grotesque and terrifying in the days of *Dracula*, but are sexy and coveted (albeit often abusive) boyfriends now in *Twilight*, *The Vampire Diaries*, *True Blood*, and more?[2] The brief answer is: monsters are the embodiment of what we most fear in the current moment. This means we can read the body of the monster as an imprint of the fear-based imagination of a particular population at a particular time. For instance, popular culture historians have connected the hook nose and (blood)greed of the vampire in the 1922 German silent film *Nosferatu* as indicative of the anti-Semitism of the time (*See* Derman, 2017). More recently, in the 1980s, vampires morphed from nearly impossible-to-kill grotesque immortals to sexualized – and specifically queer – beings whose immortality was far more tenuous. See the 1983 cult classic *The Hunger* to see what I mean, and consider the timing of this film with the burgeoning AIDS epidemic.

Unfortunately, however, our fear doesn't stay put in the body of the monster, of the Other. Even as humans write (or draw, or direct) monsters to be *not-us*, monsters are "dangerous, a form suspended between forms that threatens to smash distinctions" (Cohen, 1997, p. 6). In Dimen's language, they are "border materials" – whether or not they are literally constructed of putrefying flesh, as in the case of Frankenstein's creature (p. 6). We can bring Jacques Lacan in here to say that monstrous bodies are bodies of the Real, insofar as they resist or are in excess of signification.

Putting this all together, I want to argue that the abject is in a sense monstrous – that what we abject, that which is not-us, we redefine as not just another thing we don't like but something we shouldn't like, have been told not to like. Because eew!

LISA: We arrive, then, at sexual monstrosities. Dimen's paper is packed with psychoanalytic references that speak in one way or another to the woes of sexual life. She tells us, "Having sexual feeling as adults, we always risk the shifting of positions – the return of abjection's unease and horror, of paranoid-schizoid suffering" (p. 13). In Kristeva's language: the uncanniness, "familiar as it might have been in an opaque and forgotten life, now harries me as radically separate, loathsome" (Kristeva, 1982, p. 2; quoted in Dimen, p. 5). That which was left behind – discarded, sealed off – spurns and persecutes, rendering the self monstrous. The abject lies in wait, available to infest the self's desire. This is Kristeva's shadow of the object – an abjection-drenched, melancholy story. Mourning is cast in violent language (and I will use a quote I introduced earlier) – "the abject is the violence of mourning for an 'object' that has always already been lost" (Kristeva, 1982, p. 15; in Dimen, p. 6) – but I think we must take it as 'mourning' – another familiar yet unfamiliar idea. Dimen's project is to "spark discussion so the unspeakable can enter public discourse" (Dimen, 2005, p. 2). Both she and Kristeva are attempting to speak about the unspeakable – the pre-symbolic – perhaps an undertaking that must remain elusive, lost in translation. "Eew!" is not a word; it is more a pre-linguistic eruption.

EMMA: What the concept of the "unspeakable" makes me think of is not just what can't be spoken but what is assumed doesn't need to be spoken. This brings us to the concept of norms. I'm specifically thinking about how the normal (and in turn the abnormal) is assumed, instead of being understood to be a boundary that is culturally and historically constructed. Any time I hear hints of something being "normal" or "natural", I get uneasy, and this is particularly true when it comes to the topic of sex, sexual desire, sexual activity, and the like. Normal *for whom*, is always the question I want to ask. Riffing on Hamlet, Dimen says: "there is more in heaven and earth than is dreamt of in normativity" (p. 5). Despite her joking tone, her point here is clear: I haven't dreamt (thought of, fantasized about) of it, so it's probably not normal. There is a particular power and privilege to being the one who names what is normal.

Judith Butler argues that "the 'norm' creates unity only through a strategy of exclusion" (Butler, 2004, p. 206). This sounds like abjection to me, or perhaps we could call it cultural abjection, through which a conglomeration of behaviors and identities is formulated as the norm. Regardless, it is important that when someone says "eew!" to a sexual act, or to anything really, it's not because they were born to feel that way. Quite the opposite – their engagement with the ubiquitous cultural messages that have surrounded them from birth have created their eew boundary, so to speak. "Vanilla" is in this sense an empty term, one constructed to mean "not kinky", but kinky sex is itself defined by particular historical moments. Read the *Kama Sutra* if you don't believe me. In contrast, Michael Warner, a daddy of the queer theory discipline, has defined queer sex as follows: "Sex is understood to be as various as the people who have it. It is not required to be tidy, normal, uniform, or authorized by the government" (Warner, 1999, p. 35). In essence, "normal" is a diverse, moving target, not the fixed definition we may assume it to be.

While norms are constructed by time- and space-specific cultural content, they have very real impacts on the lived experiences of actual humans. To borrow Dimen's language for my own (quite different) explanatory purposes, what and who we collectively say "eew" to is tied up in power disparities. This idea is paraphrased from Michel Foucault's argument that the categories of 'normal' and 'abnormal' are culturally constructed and that the category of 'abnormal' behavior is subject to surveillance in a way 'normal' behavior is not (Foucault 1978; 1977).

The easiest way to understand this argument is with an example. And my favorite example is sodomy. Sodomy is defined in law differently across states, but broadly it can be thought of as any sexual act that is non-procreative. Which means that technically, you likely are a sodomite, dear reader. However, the ways in which sodomy laws were *enacted* on actual human bodies in the legal system when anti-sodomy laws were on the books was overwhelmingly to punish the private sexual activities of homosexuals. In this example, an act that most people enjoyed in the privacy of their bedrooms or wherever they fucked was weaponized against only those already deemed sexually 'abnormal' by heteronormativity. This is the danger of the abject made law – that what we decide we aren't, can become what no one should be, and then we can feel justified in punishing people for the discrepancy.

LISA: Dimen gestures toward culture – the social unconscious – "to pry open the closed-mindedness that exploits abjection" (p. 10). Then, in a moment of confession, she conveys her own "clinicians' sexual unease": "What's a nice vanilla analyst to do?" (p. 9). Here she is both joking and dead serious – a moment of self-recognition. With this self-disclosure, she identifies received ideas (what my students call the "psychoanalytic police") that have infiltrated her countertransference: for example, "sex belongs only in the region of intimacy" (p. 11). Dimen tells us, "I have *no doubt* that A and I, even though we were from different subcultures and classes, shared a prevailing morality wedding sex to love and mutual respect, and in respect of which trading in sex, for example, is embarrassing" (p. 10, emphasis mine). The cocotte in Freud's case of the homosexual woman (the woman with no name) (Harris, 1991) provokes some uncertainty in Dimen, as does her historical review of working-class Jewish families at the turn of the century. Looking back, Dimen concludes that "a gendered and cultural, if not also personal, eew! factor prevented me from *thinking*" about her patient's acceptance of payment for sex (p. 11).

There is something subtle going on here, so subtle that I'm not clear whether I'm concocting it. On the one hand, Dimen has "no doubt" that her patient shared her view that trading in sex is embarrassing – so unquestioningly embarrassing that Dimen couldn't think about it at the time she was working with A. And then, in her paper, she reconsiders her countertransference. Trading in sex is something people do, have done, in plain sight, though maybe she hadn't known to look. Still, the "no doubt" remains, betraying something about her limits, her borders.

Race hovers around two of her cases and Dimen avows the shame in the "conscious minefield of my own racism" (p. 10), as well as the shame that traveled with her own dormant hooker fantasy. Let us take a moment to applaud Dimen's candor as she reviews her private self, and her clinical missteps. Who among us has not looked back at failure, whatever its countertransference contributions – a source of the analyst's suffering? (I would designate this as the oy! factor.)

Now Emma, I have a question for you here. Dimen says that analysts idealize sex and also speaks more generally about the idealization of sex, saying: "in a culture that means every sexual encounter to end atop Mt. Everest" (p. 7). I'm interested in your response to this.

EMMA: What this makes me think of first is sex education. Or to be more specific, the absolutely gutted situation laughably still called sex education in the United States. As of 2020, 21 states do not mandate any sex education, and only 17 mandate that the sex education provided be medically accurate. A total of 19 states require that sex education include instruction indicating that it's important to only have sex in the context of marriage (Guttmacher Institute, 2020). What is the chance that young people will learn about realistic sex in the classroom, given these guidelines?

Where young people (and let's be realistic, adults) learn about sex instead is through pornography, the ultimate Mt. Everest of sex. Fuck for hours! Never get soft! Deliver a pizza, land a gang bang! While of course pornography is technically sexual activity, insofar as body parts are put together in much the same way you might do it yourselves if so inclined, what is so often forgotten is that porn is fantasy. It's filmmaking. Consider a porn set. Consider all the people doing their jobs on the set who aren't the actors. There's the person sweating, holding the boom microphone. The person whose job it is to make sure there's wardrobe continuity between shots, so someone's top doesn't mysteriously pop back on halfway through a scene (the uncanniness of film). Actors present to camera to ensure certain body parts are viewable at the most enticing angles. Scenes are mapped out in advance (how many of you talk through all the sexual acts you plan on doing in a given night? And their order?[3]).

Without touching the ongoing porn wars argument (in brief, on one side: all porn is anti-feminist and rape; on the other: porn is a way for people to experience their fantasies and explore their sexualities) I would like to argue (and this is not an original idea) that porn often gives us a fantastical and idealized view of sex. Here I'm talking about commercial pornography – amateur and indie porn are doing a lot of work to show real people having real sex (usually in very low resolution, but I'll table that rant for now).

What we are left with is the issue of realism in sex, and to that I honestly don't have an answer because I have not seen all sex – none of us has. I think the point I would most want to make in response to Dimen is that even if you spend your entire life gathering stories of sexual encounters, whether in the clinical encounter or if you are miraculously Kinsey reincarnated, you are still just capturing a small slice of the diverse rainbow of sexual fantasy and experience enacted by people every day. There's an internet joke, "Rule 34", which is that if you can think of it, there's porn depicting it (Urban Dictionary, 2011). In this way, I think Dimen's concern of the idealization of sex brings us full circle (or perhaps it's a meandering loop) back to the concept of sexual norms and how they are essentially meaningless when placed next to the reality of sexual activity.

I seem to have gone off the rails but I hope I've answered your question. All this talk about idealization has me wondering about the idealization of the mother. Can you speak to that? (As my mother, who of course I idealize.)

LISA: I will speak to this but not as your mother, at least not at first. I'll get to that in a bit. I do want to say something about the cultural idealization of motherhood as it presents itself in the world with which I'm familiar. As Kristeva tells us, the time during and post birth is saturated with queasy stuff, none of which makes its way into the photographs of the new mother with her infant.

So, what is the provenance of the airbrushed version of motherhood? Here I want to bring in a talk I heard by Joan Raphael-Leff at the meeting of the 2019 International Psychoanalytic in London. Discussing the abject, she spoke about the intransigence of idealized images of maternity that represent an unconscious reification of intrauterine conditions: mothers are expected to reproduce placental functions of total care and sustenance. Inspired by her talk, I propose that *the idealization of motherhood is a veiled commandment.* The expectation of selfless devotion is imposed on a woman just as it is faithfully held by her: she is a good student of her culture. Idealized from the outside, she privately holds herself to severe account. Taking care of an infant can be fraught with severe anxiety, feelings of isolation and tedium. A mother can feel painfully torn between the infant she adores (if things go well) and the necessity/desire to pursue her work. I'm reminded of Maggie Nelson's words on the subject: "But here's the catch: I cannot hold my baby at the same time as I write" (Nelson, 2015, p. 45). But these experiences lie outside the frame of the perfect photograph. Maternal ambivalence becomes a matter of secret shame and failure. Further, mothers are well aware of what Claudia Lament argues in her 2015 article, the title of which speaks volumes: "A Misuse of Bion's 'Reverie-ing Mother': Another Weapon in the War against Women as Waged in the Consulting Room." Tasked (by psychoanalytic authority) with maternal reverie and containment, mothers face becoming the "'whipping boy' for her child's difficulties" (p. 59). Lament writes, "a woman [who decides to become a mother] is then subject to an automatically created unconscious construction: the culturally imposed vise that squeezes her between idealization and denigration" (p. 78). Another Madonna whore split.

At this point, if this conversation were a play, I would step to the side of the stage for a very brief soliloquy. I might say something like this:

"You may be wondering what it's like for me to talk with Emma about bodies, sex, porn, motherhood, and so on. We do a delicate dance in this conversation, and we contend with the potential awkwardness through one version of our separation and connection – by talking about ideas. As I learn about Emma's world, I return, as Dimen does in her paper, (p. 5) to Hamlet's admonition: 'There are more things in heaven and earth, Horatio, than are dreamt of in your philosophy.'"

Horatio, c'est moi.

EMMA: To respond to the soliloquy (and in so doing, break the fourth wall) I'd add that one of the ways mom and I have handled our intergenerational "eew", so to speak, of the difference between our lives, is through this form of sharing the heteroglossia of our academic backgrounds. I grew up with the language of psychoanalysis through my mother just as much as I was raised with her culture, her norms, her eew's, transmitted through maternal education and rearing. In collecting my own intellectual touchpoints, storing and cataloging my own challenges and concerns, and leading my own life through queerness and explosion of the gender binary, I have uncovered many of my mother's boundaries and eew factors. To be in love and partnership with another (an Other, my mother) and to discover we hold different boundaries – that where we place our "eews" are different – can be painful, and/or it can be instructive. We have and continue to work through these sticky points together.

Which brings me back to Dimen, specifically her raison d'etre for writing her paper – namely, the clinical relationship, and the ways in which analysts could or should be thinking about their own "eew!" reactions when they are working with patients whose boundaries are often if not always distinct from their own. I am not an analyst, so do you want to take this on?

LISA: I'll start to address the clinical with one of my favorite quotes, something Gabriel Garcia Marquez famously said to his biographer: "Everyone has three lives: a public life, a private life and a secret life" (Mathew, 2017). (To this I would add that there is a fourth life: the one we don't know about ourselves – another way of speaking about the unconscious.) The secret life is something that is often enveloped in shame. Shame and "eew!" are natural bedfellows.

For illumination about shame, Dimen turns to Ronald Fairbairn. He writes, "frustration is always emotionally equivalent to rejection," and then, "When shame attends frustration, then disgust, hatred, and other effects of aggression are not far behind" (Fairbairn, 1954, p. 13; in Dimen, p. 13). The signature Fairbairnian idea is that object seeking supplants instinctual gratification as primary. Shame, like rejection, always includes someone else; rejection/condemnation becomes engraved in a self who is unable to erase *the other who abjected.* One's privacy/secrecy is ongoingly transgressed; someone is always watching.

This inescapable shaming presence of the other can become a force of personal isolation. I would also say that the rejection, whenever it arises developmentally, *reawakens* the abject. The "opaque and forgotten life" (Kristeva, 1982, p. 2; in Dimen, p. 5) is a natural fit to the shame of rejection and abjection, and it makes a beeline to the body and its desires.

EMMA: I'm fascinated by the way shame is caught up in the cultural machine. An excellent example of this is in how the same act – having multiple sexual partners – is in men congratulated ("you're a stud") and in women shamed (which results in "slut-shaming"). This isn't just in language; it has very real impacts on how individuals are treated before the law as well. Many feminist legal theorists have described how female rape survivors are often interrogated during legal proceedings, as if they are the ones on trial for their own assault (why were you in that part of town at night, why were you drinking that much, why were you wearing *that*, etc.) (*See* Smart, 1989). This double standard, as it's so often termed in feminist theory, is completely culturally created; we are talking about literally the same behavior here, only the (perceived) gender of the participant is different.

This point is crucial when we think of what goes on in the clinical encounter. Sexual norms created by cultural abjection result in patients renaming their desires as distasteful or perhaps as supposed-to-be distasteful, shameful. Then, we add the layer of the analyst's (known or unknown) personal eew, constructed in a parallel manner. These eew! boundaries interact, often in a subterranean way. The patient gets the message, the analyst obfuscates the message, and this can lead to a spiral of misrecognition in which it looks as though the problem is solely the patient's. My friend and mom's friend and colleague, Samuel Gerson, on reading a draft of this conversation, wrote to us about the ways the analyst can obscure this intersubjective experience where the 'eew' has become the 'we-eew' (S. Gerson, personal communication, August 3, 2020). He chronicles this first-hand in an essay that describes an "intersubjective resistance" (Gerson, 1996); in other words, how a co-enacted eew forecloses thinking through the analyst's erotic countertransference.

LISA: An individual's personal eew can have as much to do with the culture of a family or a professional community as it does wider social norms, although these small and large contexts are not entirely separate, of course. A personal history doesn't take place within a standardized, miniature version of a wider, uniform culture. This is not a novel idea. Increasingly, however, I find that psychoanalytic theory is deficient in its understanding of history and culture and the ways in which they determine our basic principles. As the social link comes into view, I am less able to fall back on what I once believed were psychological universals. There may be some, but I no longer believe that I know what they are.

I will return to Dimen. In her conclusion, she writes, "The hate that accompanies frustration, rejection, humiliation and shame is a prime cause of sexual suffering" (p. 15). She goes on to qualify her claim by continuing: "Once inside the act, however, this disturbance evaporates" (p. 15). Then, her closing sentence: "But when hate pops out in sex, what happens to self-regard? Perhaps it turns to disgust. Eew!" (p. 16). In this, we find a seesaw of thoughts: hate, sexual suffering; then the insulation from disgust "once inside the act" (p. 15). And then disgust raises its eewy head.

What are we to learn from this lability of experience? I land by thinking that there is not one storyline for the cohabitation of eroticism and hate, abjection, and excitement. It can leave one, both, or all players with a scorched earth residue of self-hatred and isolation, excitement notwithstanding. Or, it can be the "suffering of pleasure": "an alternative exegesis of perverse sexuality" (Saketopoulou, 2014, p. 254) – one that carves out a developmental continuity and intimacy between pain and pleasure.

Attending to the clinical situation, Dimen writes, "analysts may need to serve as containers for excess and trauma. But we need also to accept pain and discomfort's permanence in sex, hence in sexual transference-countertransference" (p. 8).[4] She assumes we know what she means by containment, and here is how I unfold it. The hope/demand/need of the patient may be that shame, hate, secret excitements, and so on, can be brought into the analytic relationship, to be transformed by the non-abjecting response of the analyst – something that can't simply be performed. If the patient's inner life exceeds the analyst's comfort, this may get played out in the consulting room with an unending repetition of a hide and seek of secrets: an impasse of suffering. Then we come to Dimen's phrase, "pain and discomfort's permanence in sex" (p. 8). I take this as a challenge to what I will call the *idealization of cure*, an analog to the *idealization of sex*. Dimen cites Andrew Morrison, "The shame of patients is contagious, often resonating with the clinician's own shame experiences – the therapist's own sense of failure, self-deficiency, and life disappointments" (Morrison, 1989, p. 6; in Dimen, p. 12). I find that envy is left out of this account. Our patients may be having more fun in bed than we are; they may be more adventurous, less inhibited, with more access to erotic hate. The analyst's eew may be a cover for this envy. This is another dimension to Dimen's "pain and discomfort's permanence in sex," in countertransference. The permanent pain may live on both sides of the couch.

EMMA: So where does this leave us?

LISA: I will end with some thoughts about the task of being an analyst in 2022 and onward. Sex has lost its pride of place in a lot of contemporary analytic work. So, it's refreshing to have its place restored, even if it's burdened by the abject. I think that Dimen is making an important contribution to our understanding of why sex has once again been forgotten – exiled. Freud (1905) made his case; Dimen is making hers. Listening to sex described by a patient can be an alienating, squeamish, tantalizing business, just as hearing sex through the walls can be. When we combine this with shame, sexual desire and sexual practices can get sequestered – kept to the secret world; an entire analysis can slip by without this world getting breached. I take Dimen's paper as an admonition. When we analysts have an eew! reaction, an unexamined nerve has been struck and we would be wise to take it as a signal that we have our own internal work to do.

EMMA: Your last point is critical, and I would argue that so much of this conversation touches on not just the necessary internal work of the analyst, but of all humans. Our society is structured by norms that insidiously organize us into hierarchies, with an empty, unattainable normal "perfect" up top and the rest of us actually-not-all-that-normal people strewn in various states of disarray on the rungs below. Individuals may perform normality, but it isn't necessarily where they live. In the discussion of the abject and the disgust of the abnormal Other (and I think we can safely say that in the parlance of abjection, all "others" are in some sense abnormal), I see Dimen as landing on something essential to being human. I propose we take these insights beyond the couch to invite whoever is interested in the task to examine the roots of their disgust and their preconceptions of what they take to be the so-called "normal".

Notes

1 Some years ago, there was a quiz show called Who Wants to be a Millionaire? The show had something called the phone-a-friend lifeline that enabled a contestant, stuck on finding an answer, to make one phone call. In this spirit, I called my friend and colleague, Mitchell Wilson, with some questions I had about Kristeva. In a short space, he clarified some essentials about abjection for me. He wrote: "It's not about separation (which already is an abstraction) as it is the body of the mother birthing another being – that painful, messy, bloody, exhilarating, exhausting expulsion of another body. It's on that level that she's trying to speak to things that can't be spoken about." When I protested that pleasure and sensuality seem to be getting short shrift, he answered: "The abject doesn't prevent them or whatever. She's [Kristeva] trying to get at a 'pre-object' place, even before the 'semiotic,' the 'poetry' of early life with the mother (coos, songs, cries, humming, etc.)" (M. Wilson, personal communication, February 18, 2020).

2 In my academic inquiry into the monstrous, I focused on the figure of the vampire. As a result, I will be giving vampire-focused examples in the monster portion of this paper. This is a personal preference and in no way is designed to denigrate the other very interesting and important monsters, each of which has been constructed for their own specific purposes throughout history. I urge you

all to think about your favorite (or most reviled) monsters and consider what border(s) they police.

3 This practice of mapping out scenes in advance is often taken up in BDSM sexual encounters.

4 The "pain and discomfort's permanence in sex" (p. 8) to which Dimen refers must be paired with other clinically crucial inquiries: when disgust overwhelms pleasure and connection, how is it wielded? To what end? For an intelligent discussion of the interpersonal construction of disgust in couples, see Shelley Nathans' article, "Whose Disgust Is It Anyway? Projection and Projective Identification in the Couple Relationship."

References

Butler, J. (2004). *Undoing gender.* New York, NY: Routledge.

Cohen, J. J. (1997). *Monster theory: Reading culture.* Minneapolis: University of Minnesota Press.

Derman, U. (2017, September 27). The myth of the vampire Jew and blood libels. Retrieved from https://www.bh.org.il/blog-items/myth-vampire-jew-blood-libels/.

Dimen, M. (2005). Sexuality and suffering, or the eew! factor. *Studies in Gender and Sexuality, 6*(1), 1–18.

Fairbairn, W. R. D. (1954). Observations on the nature of hysterical states. *British Journal of Medical Psychology, 27,* 105–125.

Foucault, M. (1978). *The history of sexuality, vol 1: An introduction.* New York, NY: Vintage.

Foucault, M. (1977). *Discipline and punish: the birth of the prison.* New York, NY: Vintage.

Freud, S., McLintock, D., & Haughton, H. (2003). *The uncanny.* New York: Penguin.

Freud, S. (1905). Three essays on the theory of sexuality. *Standard Edition, 7,* 125–243. London: Hogarth Press.

Gerson, S. (1996). Neutrality, resistance, and self-disclosure in an intersubjective psychoanalysis. *Psychoanalytic Dialogues, 6*(5), 623–645.

The Guttmacher Institute. (2020, February 1). *Sex and hiv education.* Retrieved from https://www.guttmacher.org/state-policy/explore/sex-and-hiv-education.

Harris, A. (1991). Gender as contradiction: Psychoanalytic dialogues. *The International Journal of Relational Perspectives, 1*(2), 197–224.

Kristeva, J. (1982). *Powers of horror,* trans. L. Roudiez. New York, NY: Columbia University Press.

Lament, C. (2015). A misuse of Bion's "reverie-ing mother": Another weapon in the war against women as waged in the consulting room. *The Psychoanalytic Study of the Child, 69,* 59–82.

Mathew, P. (2017, October 22). Of public, private and secret lives. Retrieved from https://www.theweek.in/theweek/specials/of-public-private-and-secret-lives.html.

Morrison, A. (1989). *Shame: The underside of narcissism.* Hillsdale, NJ: The Analytic Press.

Nelson, M. (2015). *The Argonauts.* Minneapolis, MN: Graywolf Press.

Raphael-Leff, J. (2019, July 23–27). *Female embodied life as a site of violence and repudiation: A study in Kristeva's "abject"* [Conference presentation]. International Psychoanalytic Association 2019 Programme: The Feminine. London, UK.

Saketopoulou, A. (2014). To suffer pleasure: The shattering of the ego as the psychic labor of perverse sexuality. *Studies in Gender and Sexuality, 15*, 254–268.

Smart, C. (1989). *Feminism and the power of law.* London, England: Routledge.

Urban Dictionary. (2011). *Rule 34.* Retrieved from https://www.urbandictionary.com/define.php?term=Rule%2034.

Warner, M. (1999). *The trouble with normal: Sex, politics and the ethics of queer life.* Cambridge, MA: Harvard University Press.

Project Four

Wild Times/Wild Analysis/Wild Revolution

Project 4, Editor's note

Stephen Hartman

Muse

Dimen, M. (2014). Inside the revolution: Power, sex, and technique in Freud's "Wild Analysis." *Psychoanalytic Dialogues*, 24: 499–515.

Dimen first presented the paper, *Inside the Revolution: Power, Sex, and Technique in Freud's "'Wild' Analysis"* as a keynote lecture. Sprawling and mighty, Dimen positioned her essay on the wildness of psychoanalysis, as Freud did his, to be "a treatise both intellectual and political" (Dimen, 2014, p. 499). Recalling *Surviving Sexual Contradictions* (1986) appeal for nothing less than a revolution in gender, Dimen set her sights on a revolution in psychoanalysis. The paradox in so doing, she explains, is that psychoanalysis commands faith (in technique) yet leans on doubt as the font of creativity. Heterogeneity of thought and disciplinary practice, she explained, become bitter foes under the banner of revolution:

> And so a conundrum. The creation of a discipline requires discipline, a way both to decide who is well trained and to distinguish insiders from outsiders, those who know and those who do not. Yet must authoritative claims metamorphose into authoritarian fiat? (Dimen, 2014, p. 506)

In characteristic form, Dimen asks this important question such that current upheavals in politics and intellectual life may learn from past designs—including designs on revolution whose muddy ambitions obscured intersectional dynamics in and among persons in theory as in praxis.

Readers

Dimen was a remarkable teacher. Her unflagging effort to shepherd her students from writing groups and seminars to dais and print spoke to a priority on transition as much as it acknowledged the importance of institutions. The paradox of mentoring via supervision in psychoanalysis is that

DOI: 10.4324/9781003335252-29

hierarchy comes into view in the effort to be spread the word. Technical considerations become the ruse of authority. Originality suffers in turn, which has been a sore subject since Freud's days. Subject position and subject matter quickly align, and hierarchy too often rules the day. To amplify Dimen's commitment to intergenerational passages that feature generations learning from one another as a path forward is paved, I've chosen two thought leaders who are two generations apart to discuss Dimen's revolutionary quest, Daniel Butler and Ken Corbett.

Form

Dimen experimented constantly with form. In the last decade of her life, online colloquia became one of the most generative spaces for psychoanalysts to learn through debate and critique. She eagerly participated in online discussion threads as both primary author, interlocutor, and community member cognizant that for discussion threads to be a great equalizer, they must risk spinning out to become a pinwheel of ideas. An online discussion of her 2011 paper, *Lapsus Lingue, or a Slip of the Tongue?*, propelled the heretofore guarded discussion of boundary violations in a variety of directions that spanned well beyond Dimen's text (*See*, Levin, 2021a; 2021b). The mix of ruled and unruly gives the blog form its heft. Little has been written about the text thread and blog thread form as a psychoanalytic genre. To that end, I asked Corbett and Butler to engage in a blog thread correspondence over several months with the only caveat that they take up Dimen's *Wild Analysis* as muse rather than destination.

Bios

Daniel G. Butler, LMFT, is a PhD Candidate in History of Consciousness at the University of California, Santa Cruz. He is the recipient of multiple writing awards, including the Peter Loewenberg Award and the Alexandra and Martin Symonds Prize. His most recent publication, "Transitional Objects are Not Toys," appears in the October 2021 issue of *The Comparatist.*

Ken Corbett, Ph.D., is a Professor at the New York University Postdoctoral Program in Psychoanalysis and Psychotherapy. He is the author of *Boyhoods: Rethinking Masculinities*, and *A Murder Over A Girl: Justice, Gender Junior High.*

References

Levin, C. (2021a). *Sexual Boundary Trouble in Psychoanalysis: Clinical Perspectives on Muriel Dimen's Concept of the Primal Crime.* New York: Routledge.

Levin, C. (2021b). *Social Aspects of Sexual Boundary Trouble in Psychoanalysis.* New York; Routledge.

Inside the Revolution

Power, Sex, and Technique in Freud's "'Wild' Analysis"

Muriel Dimen

Freud's (1910g) "'Wild' Analysis" is a treatise both intellectual and political. It shares a basic concern with his "Five Lectures on Psycho-Analysis" (Freud, 1910a), also published in 1910: to lay out the elements of psychoanalytic technique, of the relationship between analyst and patient, and of the treatment of sexual suffering. At the same time, the two works differ in point and tone. Where the "Five Lectures" is reflective and wide-ranging, "'Wild' Analysis" drives fiercely forward, its destination revealed only upon arrival. Wanting to articulate the nature of his new discipline, Freud is also striving to create a movement, and the tension between these two goals makes "'Wild' Analysis" electrifying.

At once profound and full of holes, "'Wild' Analysis" simultaneously declares a revolution and forges an orthodoxy. In 1910, psychoanalysis was ahead of itself, too straight for its native immoderation. This *décalage* was no anomaly. Key to a contemporaneous cultural revolution and counterrevolution that, reciprocally, gave rise to it, psychoanalysis was living in interesting times: the arrival of modernism. A landmark in a historic movement, this essay, like the story it tells, was at the same time an effect of social and cultural transformation.

Accordingly, I situate "'Wild' Analysis" in its local and global histories, even while reading it for what it can tell us about psychoanalysis now. I take this marvelous and annoying essay on its own terms. But I also use it as a means to consider psychoanalysis as host to crucial tensions, its ideas and their relation to technique, its traffic in power, and sexuality and the primal crime. My argument, illustrated by a clinical vignette, shall be that the heterogeneity and multiplicity inherent to psychoanalysis are a gift to us, even if they made trouble for Freud. In celebration and critique, I look, in effect, at where Freud was and where we are now.

A False Memory

Many people seem to believe that "'Wild' Analysis" is where Freud tells analysts not to have sex with their patients. Given psychoanalytic history, it makes sense to assume he was tackling the problem that won't go away. After all,

DOI: 10.4324/9781003335252-30

psychoanalysis was already tormented by sexual misconduct—think Ferenczi, Jones, Stekel, Gross, and of course Jung (*See* Kerr, 1993 [although Kerr doubts Jung had sex with Spielrein]; Makari, 2008). However, while this particular fantasy about "'Wild' Analysis" has meaning (see below), the essay itself is as much about power as about sex (to which power matters, but that comes later).

That is, sex and technique lead to several linked power questions: Who defines psychoanalysis? Who authorizes the claim to be an analyst? And who, as Phillips (2002, p. xvii) asks, "legitimates the legitimators?" We misremember "'Wild' Analysis," I propose, because we no more care to think about regulatory practice—the policing of ideas—than about sexual infraction. Yet institutional power matters. Indeed, as Makari's (2008) *Revolution in Mind* demonstrates, "'Wild' Analysis" decided a battle that, in 1910, allowed Freud to win a "war."

Power

"'Wild' Analysis" shows its cards only at the end, yet all along the reader can sense a tacit sub- text. The essay begins with a clinical story about a 40-something woman who consults Freud. Divorced, she has been suffering panic attacks, for which a young physician—a fledgling—has diagnosed sexual frustration and prescribed one of three remedies: reconcile, take a lover, or masturbate. None of these suiting her, the neophyte suggested she confer with Dr. Freud, who, he told her, had discovered the cause of anxiety: sexual unhappiness. Meanwhile, this still desirable woman has in tow "an older, dried-up and unhealthy-looking"[1] friend who asks Freud to negate the novice's advice, for she herself, a widow of some years, has remained "respectable without suffering any anxiety" (Freud, 1910h, p 3).

I read this account, like the essay, on its face, for its clinical and cultural resonance, and I track the clinical revolution it maps out. At the same time, cued toward irony by the scare quotes encasing the adjective "Wild," I treat it as a crafted story. Note then its curious next move: the essay shifts its sights from patient to tenderfoot doctor. Freud's overt intent is to correct certain misapprehensions of psychosexual theory and psychoanalytic technique. Yet his argument, inci- sive and at times cutting, seems tendentious. Short shrifting the patient's autonomous reasons for rejecting her doctor, Freud states his hope that, if he uses this case to critique "wild" analysis, the good he does—protecting patients—will absolve him of any injustice he does the physician.

The fledgling's first error lay in his diagnosis. Like a layperson, he seemed to believe "that sexual needs merely consist of the urge to coitus, or analogous measures for procuring an orgasm or voiding sexual fluids" (Freud, 1910h, p. 4). Freud authoritatively restates his key contribution: psychoanalysis is about *psycho*sexuality—sexual desire as *mentally* registered, expressed, and inhibited. Indeed, "emotional frustration with all its consequences, can persist even where there is no lack of normal sexual intercourse" (Freud, 1910h, p. 5). Then his tone shifts from the pedagogical to the authoritarian: "A practitioner who does not subscribe to this conception of psychosexuality has no right to invoke these principles of psychoanalysis that deal with the causal significance of sexuality" (Freud, 1910h, p. 5).

Strong stuff. Someone has "no right to invoke" certain principles? With these provocative words, Freud appears to be trying to regulate who can say what.

And indeed he is. "'Wild' Analysis," Makari (2008, pp. 258–262) attest, served as a way for Freud to create a face-off with Adler in a newly and highly competitive situation. In 1909–1910, the Vienna Psychoanalytic Society was growing: more students, more analysts, more potential adherents. A lot was at stake. In 1909, Adler's theory of masculine protest had begun to compete with Freud's theory of psychosexuality. Adler emphasized not a sexual but "an aggressive instinct, which, then repressed, led to *feelings* of inferiority and neurosis" (Makari 2008, p. 258) that in turn manifested consciously in what we would now call gender dysphoria. Adler's schema was threatening because it was reassuring: its clarity, finitude, and emphasis on consciousness contrasted starkly with Freud's intricate, unsettling, and evolving vision of unconscious desire and unhappiness.

So if we see "'Wild' Analysis" as aiming, in part, to stem a reductive trend, then its turn toward conflict makes perfect sense. Ensuring we get just how dim the doctor—read Adler—was, Freud asks what, in fact, was the point of the man's advice at all. Surely, he coolly observes, the patient is mature enough to know that she can heal her sexual frustration by masturbating or finding a lover. Then the sarcastic jab, another hint that this essay's target exceeds the anonymous physician whom Freud indicts: "Or does the physician think that a woman of over forty is unaware that one can take a lover, or does he over-estimate his influence so much as to think that she could never decide upon such a step without medical approval?" (Freud, 1910g, p. 223).

The patient's problem, missed by this junior clinician, is that she fails to connect her anxiety to her frustration because she cannot know what only psychoanalysis can reveal: she is *conflicted* about her desire. The inglorious novice should know what the well-known Adler defied: "the psychoanalytical tenet that neurotic symptoms arise from a conflict between two forces, a libido (usually unduly enlarged), and an over-powerful sexual denial or repression" (Freud, 1910h, p. 5). If only the absence of sexual activity caused neurosis, then the sex drive's strength "would show... the way to satisfaction, even without [a] doctor's encouragement" (Freud, 1910h, p. 5).

Even as "'Wild' Analysis" trenchantly states elemental and profound psychoanalytic principles, it was also a tactic in a strategy by which an embattled Freud trounced the enemy. If psychoanalysis was gaining cachet as profession and treatment, it was institutionalizing itself too. The creation of a movement, whether professional or political, is a process of power as well as ideas. It entails jockeying and elbowing, triumph and loss, and the flip and flop of friends and enemies and comrades-in-arms. Earlier in 1910, Freud had tried to mollify Adler, as well as Stekel, by ceding them control of the Vienna Psychoanalytic Society. As they went on to avenge still earlier wounds, Freud began to worry that his former comrade's challenge would amplify the doubts of adherents as well as opponents. And so after the essay's appearance in December 1910, Freud set Adler up: he invited his rival to give two lectures, then proceeded to denounce them. The ensuing vicious debate culminated in Steiner's accusal that, although they "had come together to study the unconscious and libido,... Adler had turned to consciousness and aggression" (Makari, 2008, p. 261). And, he charged, Freud should have stepped in sooner. Adler and Stekel later resigned, and Freud resumed leadership of the Vienna Psychoanalytic Society.

Interesting Times

Still, guild politics did not set this charge alone. "'Wild' Analysis" swirled in a cultural tornado. Weirdly, the essay came out in the very month named by Virginia Woolf's famous, retrospective proclamation of 1924:

"On or about December 1910, human character changed. I am not saying that one went out, as one might into a garden, and there saw that a rose had flowered, or that a hen had laid an egg. The change was not sudden and definite like that. But a change there was, nevertheless; and, since one must be arbitrary, let us date it about the year 1910" (as cited in Kern, 2003, p. 183).

Her phrasing's quiet extremism conveys cataclysm—"the disintegration of late Victorian Europe," which may have been "the defining experience of [her] lifetime" (Judt, 2009, p. 86).

While Freud and Adler were duking it out, in other words, the cultural ground was shifting beneath their feet. In the arts, consider that, just the year before, in 1909, James Joyce had both opened Dublin's first cinema and begun to write the oneiric fragmentation of linear time known as *Ulysses*. Cubism's multiperspectival reevaluation of positive and negative space was already holding its brief dominion. And, three years later, Stravinsky's *Rite of Spring* was to premiere to the old guard's derision. At the same time, political creations—the rise of socialism and anarchism—and revolutions in knowledge—Einstein's renovation of space-time, Freud's invention of psychoanalysis—were agitating the taken-for-granted homogeneity and stability of place, person, and meaning in a period when the pith of Western life had been indelibly altered by electricity and powered flight. All were one with "sweeping changes in technology and culture [that] created distinctive new modes of thinking about and experiencing time and space [in the West]" (Kern, 2003, p. 1).

A Crazy Mixed-Up Theory of Sex

As modernism was taking hold, the nineteenth-century grand narrative was losing its grip, a long, slow process to which psychoanalysis was, paradoxically, vital. "'Wild' Analysis" arrived in an epoch of "'multiplicity and indeterminancy,'" in von Hoffmannsthal's 1905 phrase (Kern, 2003, p. 182). This wording, as familiar to twenty-first-century (relational) psychoanalysis as it was foreign to

Freud's scientific ambitions, helps situate the contradictions, discrepancies, and disharmonies in the psychoanalysis of the time and hence of this enigmatic essay.

Psychoanalysis then was like an exuberant plant, leafing idea upon idea, theory upon theory, practice upon practice. This fecundity, proper not only to Freud but to the discipline itself, was—and is—both a wonder and a burden. Freud, like Marx, was a "founder of discursivity," as Foucault puts it (Rabinow, 1984), his *oeuvre* a fount to which we return repeatedly. Carrying that bounty forward, psychoanalysis is "a probe that constantly expands the field that it explores" (Ferro, 2005, p. 92). Such expansion, being unpredictable, is ill-suited to an Enlightenment or scientific psychoanalysis. It is both outcome and cause of a "fundamental ambiguity" (Baranger, 2005, p. 59) whose clinical and theoretical power psychoanalysis would not begin to mine until much later in the twentieth century; concepts like multiplicity and ambiguity, it is fair to say, were mostly footnotes to Freud's thought.

How striking then that the two topics on which "'Wild' Analysis" focuses, sex and technique, should themselves be home to a great deal of prodigality, excitement, confusion, and ambiguity.

Both are similarly recalcitrant: neither submits readily to control, whether intellectual, instru- mental, or moral. Not only does sexuality, to take up the first, backfire in the face of the most elaborately coded moralities, as Freud (1908) observed. It regularly exceeds the concepts used to wrangle it, as I have argued elsewhere (Dimen, 2003). What a mess for Freud, whose thinking about it was, after all, nascent.

Consider that his admirably complicated scheme of psychosexuality, already in formation for 15 years, was less than halfway done by the time of this essay: 1909 saw "Little Hans" (Freud, 1909), while in 1910 came "Contributions to the Psychology of Love, I-III" (Freud 1910c, 1910d, 1910e) and "Leonardo" (Freud, 1910b). Still to arrive were transference-love and masturbation; femininity; the incest taboo and the Oedipus complex; Eros and Thanatos; and so on. Given Adler's challenge to his unfolding signature theory of sexuality, repression, and illness, it is hard not to read Freud's polemic in "'Wild' Analysis" as also preemptively protective; similarly, he would jump the gun in 1924–1925 by rushing into print his yet unfinished conception of feminine sexuality in order to block Karen Horney's strong critique of phallic monism (Fliegel, 1986).

To return to the story told by "'Wild' Analysis," one can, considering how preliminary were Freud's theories of sex, actually sympathize with the straw man physician, and not just because he has been shamed and excommunicated. After all, he comes honestly by his belief that the sex act—the body—has something to do with mental health. Nor did he have to get it from Adler's theory of organ defects. He had only to encounter the magisterial *Three Essays*'s (Freud, 1905b) vacillation on whether sex is about body or mind, act or desire. And even just two years before "'Wild' Analysis," in "'Civilized' Sexual Morality and Modern Nervous Illness," Freud (1908) had positioned coitus in a mordant dialectic: sex as the bane we cannot live without.

No wonder the early consulting rooms flooded with sexual errors. Sex is too much to think: it always registers as both, mind *and* body, act *and* desire. What appears as conceptual chaos is actually a sign of sex's semiotic and lived excess, which, to draw on culture theorist Bhabha (1994), demands a hybridity of theory that thrives on ambiguity. If the contradictions within Freud's sexual ideas did not, happily, stop him from theorizing, still he lacked a systematic way to use them—to see them as signs of the subject matter, as products of sexual experience itself, not as flaws in his theory. Such reflexivity is, I will suggest later, key for addressing the primal crime.

Technique

If, in the matter of sexuality, Freud is telling his readers what to think, in regard to technique he is telling them what to do. In so doing, he faced a couple of problems. For one thing, he is trying to rein in and reign over something that would not exist for another decade: technique as imparted by a rigorous system of training (Makari, 2008, pp. 369 ff.). For another, although the technique of psychotherapy cannot be laid out in an instruction manual, in "'Wild' Analysis" Freud writes as if it could even while resisting such manualization (Phillips, 2002, *passim*).

Three technical matters trouble him. Writing with his now familiar alternation between reason and passion, instruction and contempt, he addresses the most remediable error first. He illustrates the danger of "ignorance" via the unidentified physician's confusion of a physical disorder with a mental illness. This neophyte had not learned enough to consider "the possibility of [...] anxiety hysteria" (Freud, 1910g, p. 225) instead of anxiety neurosis. So, "neglect[ing] the mental factors" (Freud, 1910g, p. 225), he prescribed a physical therapy—sex—not a psychological one.

With disdain for this "lazy-minded misconception" (Freud, 1910g, p. 225), Freud's next daz- zling strike names his second main concern: "Oddly enough, the three therapeutic alternatives of this so-called psycho-analyst leave no room for—psycho-analysis!" (Freud, 1910g, p. 225). As a reader, one shakes one's head as if freed from a daze: of course! Starting to think, one recalls how hard it is to maintain the discipline demanded by clinical psychoanalysis: surely all analysts have tried to fix something for a patient, do something, act; even Freud fed and lent money to the Wolf Man. Life's excessiveness regularly overtakes us—as Freud (1930 p. 75) himself knew—rendering technique so elusive as to create doubt even in the minds of those who have learned it. Freud gets the dilemma, yet at the same time he envisions technique as a uniform method or a consistent set of methods designed for an isolable problem.

However, the scientific suit of clothes into which he tried to pack the stuff of clinical life is bursting at the seams. Freud's final instruction says what a clinician should not do, then unsays it, and so leaves the reader at a loss. The novice's main technical error was to rely on the outmoded view that patients suffer from ignorance and therefore need teaching: he told the patient that her pain came from sexual dissatisfaction. Psychic suffering, Freud counters, grows not from an informational void, but instead, once again, from conflict: "the *inner resistances*" (S225) to knowledge. Next, in what begins to feel like a shell game, he goes back on himself. Of *course*, he continues, patients need educating about the unconscious. Since, however, this education is painful, it requires time and finesse. Unlike the greenhorn who plucked an interpretation out of nowhere, the analyst must wait until, first, the repressed material nears awareness, and, second, the patient's "attachment to the doctor (through *transference*)—has become strong enough to create an emotional relationship that rules out further flight" (Freud, 1910h, p. 7).

Here, under the pressure of its two divergent aims, "'Wild' Analysis" approaches a low point, ignoring elemental questions: How does one know when the material is approaching conscious- ness? When the emotional attachment has cured sufficiently for one to speak? What to do while waiting? All Freud says is that regression in turn demands "prolonged contact" between analyst and patient. It is not that he believed things are as simple as either teaching or waiting: psycho- education and psychoanalysis are evidently compatible. Rather, I would argue, based on my read of the structure of this compact and fertile essay, Freud could not spend time expatiating on technique because his political goal was urgent.

Putting on the Brakes

I want to stop briefly to review the paradoxical historical context for this essay and the intellectual and disciplinary struggles at play in its pages. Here was the principal contradiction: the discipline of psychoanalysis was taking shape in a period when the very idea of shape was in question. As German sociologist G. Simmel capsules the matter on the eve of World War I: "'we are experiencing… a struggle of life against form *as such*, against the principle of form'" (as cited in Kern, 2003, p. 182). Truly, the exuberance of psychoanalytic ideas matched the intellectual wildness of the times. At the same time, though, it suited neither the intellectual stature to which Freud aspired nor the political stability required by the movement, the two goals depending on one another.

One can discern, in "'Wild' Analysis," a rift in Freud's allegiances. With ferocity, he defends his new *Wissenschaft*, an untranslatable term that I use to signify what Freud saw himself creating: both a "science," which is what *Wissenschaft* technically denotes, and a body of scholarly knowl- edge with its own intellectual and technical processes, which is what the word more generally connotes. Grasping, however, that his creation is endangered by it runaway success, he puts on the brakes. At least, that is how I read both his animus for the wretched physician and the essay's next, and abrupt, shift, which at first sight surprises, but on second look makes sense, because it explains the subtext hinted at from the start by the essay's tension between emotion and reason. In all likelihood,

Freud's impulse to slow things down leads to the unearned conviction with which he concludes his discussion of technique: "Following the *clear* [emphasis added] rules of psychoanalytic technique is a substitute for that mysterious 'medical tact' that is demanded of the practitioner" (Freud, 1910h, p. 8).

Let us take it for granted that "tact" was and remains overdue for demystification. The critical point is that Freud's assertion of psychoanalytic technique's clarity contradicts what he goes on to show: whatever rules of psychoanalytic method exist, they are not and never have been and cannot be clear. Technique cannot be picked up from a book, any more than patients can cure themselves by reading a text. It cannot in fact be written down in a book. Rather, adepts acquire it only "by sacrificing much time, effort, and success" at the feet of "accomplished practitioners" (Freud, 1910h, p. 8). The acquisition of psychoanalytic technique is contingent, because it needs to be absorbed in the idiosyncratic medium of personality as lived in the intersubjective spaces of analysis and supervision.

When Freud arrives at his destination, the reader understands that this contradiction was in fact a canny move necessary to the polemic animating "'Wild' Analysis." Nearing the end, Freud sniffs,

"It is a matter of some significance, therefore, in forming a judgment on the incident which I took as a starting-point for these remarks, that I am not acquainted with the physician who is said to have given the lady such advice and have never heard his name" (Freud, 1910g, p. 226).

And if he has not heard of the man, then it means the fellow has no credibility whatsoever. For had the tyro been properly trained in the highly personal system of training that existed at the time, he would have been in the informal network of analysts all of whom were linked to Freud and whom he would have known.

This informality, however, was too fragile a structure to gird a flourishing professional move- ment. Hence the essay's startling climax: in March 1910, Freud announces, he, along with his friends and colleagues founded an International Psycho-Analytical Association, to which its members declare their adherence by the publication of their names, *in order to be able to repudiate responsibility for what is done by those who do not belong to us* and yet call their medical procedure "psycho-analysis" (Freud, 1910g, p. 227).

"'Wild' Analysis," an essay on a method for treating patients suffering from sexual disorders, turns out to contain an engraved announcement for the method's institutionalization. "'Wild' Analysis" in effect sent a signal round the world announcing a single psychoanalysis.

With this event, the tension between politics and ideas took another form. Once, the political problem was the war between competing claims to intellectual dominance. Now the problem was the relation between the many varieties of psychoanalytic practice and a centralized idea about what psychoanalysis was supposed to be. "'Wild' Analysis," a disquisition on key theoretical and clinical practices, shares its centenary with a gatekeeper, the International

Psychoanalytic Association—a home *and* a panopticon, preserving *and* policing. Whether this be paradox or contradiction remains to be seen.

For sure, though, it raises questions of ongoing relevance to psychoanalytic politics. It is possible to appreciate Freud's indignation that an improperly trained person was passing himself off as legitimate, and still be concerned that his manner of speaking laid down the law in a stentorian, if possibly intimidating way that suited an institution monitoring the method he is teaching. At stake is the fine line between two stances, "authoritative," or trustworthy, reliable, and therefore commanding, and "authoritarian," or favoring obedience at the cost of autonomy. The frequent confusion of the two adjectives in ordinary speech, or the substitution of one for the other, reflects what often obtains in ordinary life: a person or institution embodying authority slips without much notice into the wielding of power inherent to authoritarianism.

There is a conundrum. The creation of a discipline requires discipline, a way both to decide who is well trained and to distinguish insiders from outsiders, those who know and those who do not. Yet, must authoritative claims metamorphose into authoritarian fiat? Perhaps even Freud recognizes the conundrum when he introduces his justification for the IPA by saying how dis-agreeable he finds it "to claim a monopoly… in the use of a medical technique" (Freud, 1910g, p. 227). That one cannot quite trust the sincerity of his reluctance may be a sign of what one senses in the essay's structure and tone, a slide from the authoritative to the authoritarian.

Yet perhaps what "'Wild' Analysis" manifests is the problem faced by any movement. How does a movement form? At a movement's intellectual and practical nascence, are there not always swings between creativity and control? How is this formation accomplished without rules regarding who does what, and who belongs and who is excluded? In the course of what sociologist Weber (1947) called the "routinization" of institutions, rigidity and dullness set in; over the years, Kernberg (1986, 1996) has concerned himself with this problem in psychoanalytic education and organizational structure and process. Informally, many criticize the frequency with which the "usual suspects" dominate the tables of contents of learned journals, including this one. At the heart of the dilemma is the inevitable drift toward regulatory power (Foucault, 1976/1980), that is, the control of ideas and bodies in the service of maintaining institutions.

Toward a Cubist Psychoanalysis, Or One Thing to do While Waiting

A return to the historical context for "'Wild' Analysis" will enrich a view of these tensions as they populate psychoanalysis now. For all the intensity of its internal political crisis, psychoanalysis then was not alone in its drive toward centralization, control, and institutionalization. From 1909 to 1914, for example, some 230 other international professional entities formed. One could ascribe this and other rationalizations of knowledge (classification, museum collecting, etc.)

to industrial capitalism and colonialism. Yet such an approach would miss the centrifugal/centripetal dialectics of the historical moment (Kern, 1983/2003, *passim*): as forms were multiplying—superimpositions and juxtapositions latticing, chaos looming (as some saw it)—impulses toward integration, consolidation, and homogeneity were taking organizational shape too, as though, in a whirling world, stabilization beckoned.

As culture and technology gyrated and counterpoises materialized, paradoxes abounded. The world in which psychoanalysis found itself in 1910 was "at once uniform and incomprehensible from a single perspective," as Steven Rosenheck (personal communication, June 10, 2009) put it. Intrinsic to this vertigo was, says Kern (2003), "the [cultural] affirmation of a plurality of times and spaces" (p. 8). Here psychoanalysis is in step with its coeval disciplines: think of Freud's invention of a heterogeneous internal universe alongside Bergson's "reality of private time," flux in Proust's *In Search of Lost Time*, the ephemeral dear to Impressionism, and cubism's perspectival revolution. All parts of this galaxy may, in turn, be said to have manifested "simultaneity," that is, "the property of two events happening at the same time in at least one frame of reference," a concept that may illume the technical multiplicity found in contemporary psychoanalysis (*See* Cooper, 2010, and below).

Psychoanalysis then and now smacks of these conditions, in which difference is both proliferating and becoming networked. Consider, as a concrete example, how the telephone, which, invented in 1876 at the cusp of modernism, freed any given pair of individuals to be together "in two [different] places at the same time" (p. 69). Consider something more abstract, how the global diversity of time itself would be retained while being wrangled by a single system. In 1870, for example, if one traveled by rail from Washington, DC, to San Francisco, one's would have reset one's watch over 200 times (Kern, 1983/2003, p. 11; *See* also Schivelbusch, 1977, pp. 42–44). In contrast, 40 years later and three years post "'Wild' Analysis," time-setting everywhere submitted to an overarching calculus: on July 1, 1913, at 10 a.m., the Eiffel Tower beamed a wireless signal synching clocks in all time zones 'round the motley world; from now on, if it was 10 a.m. in Paris, everyone knew it was (Daylight Savings Time apart) 4 p.m. the same day in New York and 11 p.m. the next day in Beijing. Thus was set in place a shared global frame for communication, trade, and meaning (and no doubt the current digital revolution will have parallel effects).

Inside the revolution, all had become one even as all were not one at all. With universal time and the telephone, people could speak to one another simultaneously from utterly different places and cultures, at literally different yet entirely knowable times that seem to be, but are not the same moment. Likewise in psychoanalysis: even as Freud is at times set on a single psychoanalytic voice, still, Makari (2008, pp. 467–486) rightly insists, a diversity of ideas and practice marks not only his evolving thought, but psychoanalysis itself before 1910 as well as between the wars.

To make the point in a different register: *Pace* the end result of "'Wild' Analysis"—a homogeneous conception of sex, a unitary theory of technique, a single allegiance—psychoanalysis had dreamed up a multidimensional interior world at once *sui generis* and, ultimately, impossible to understand from a single perspective. Psychoanalysis construed mental life as a set of diverse worlds spinning simultaneously on discordant axes and timetables, each of which was equally central to understanding and treating troubled minds—consciousness, unconsciousness, the preconscious. Or take dreams, fantasies, slips of the tongue, and jokes—to which should now be added enactments—together, their varied, juxtaposed notes and rhythms create their own meaningful dissonance.

In "'Wild' Analysis," for example, Freud speaks of "the mental factor" (S 223). However, at least for now if not forever, this factor seems impossible to grasp from any one viewpoint. In 1910, it was located only in single minds. Today, some analysts think of an unconscious between and among minds (Bass, 2001; Gerson, 2004). Others reference mirror neurons (Schore, 2011), so that we might imagine the mental factor as situated in the body too. To extend the point, still others—for example, the International Association of Relational Psychoanalysis and Psychotherapy—deem approaches to mind "historical, linguistic, political, and contextual" (IARPP, n.d.). Consider also Widlöcher's (2001) view that "the same mental state can be interpreted according to two different strategies" (pp. 30–31); he was, of course, anticipated by Harry Stack Sullivan (1953), who advised analysts to entertain two hypotheses about any single clinical moment.

In this light, the battle between Freud and Adler takes on a new meaning. The political pressures Freud felt (in addition to whatever competitiveness or grandiosity he may have felt, about which I cannot and do not mean to speculate) seem to have led to his derogation of his rival. However, seen from a multiperspectival rather than a monist vantage point, Adler's position on gender shows up in a more favorable light. Perhaps his crude notions of masculinity and femininity, and their role in psychic suffering, were avant-garde, not erroneous. From the perspective of feminist and psychoanalytic gender theory, women's rejection of femininity and men's drive toward omnipotence do not seem so peculiar. Could it be that what seemed like an error issued from a metatheoretical lacuna, not stupidity? In psychoanalysis as Freud was driving it in 1910, there was to be only one correct view, a position to which he perhaps had to hold rather tight given the discipline's near anarchistic fecundity and the cultural challenges to it.

In psychoanalysis, I would like to argue, heterogeneity and discipline are always in contest. In "'Wild' Analysis," theory and technique live parallel if also matching lives: a one-person theory of mind, a one-person theory of technique—except, of course, that it is a technique for two, in which one acts on or has effects on or influences the other. Relational psychoanalysis proposes a dialectical resolution of that contradiction: a theory of mind-formed-in-relation that goes hand-in-hand with a theory of treatment as the joint analysis of a relationship.

Yet even here discipline resurges. Relational psychoanalysis formed under a big-tent banner, inclusive of approaches from Freudian object-relations to self-psychology. Still, despite the absence of formal, unified statements of relational technique, there have cohered certain informal notions of what constitutes relationality. I limit myself to one anecdote: A patient, herself a relational analyst, asked with a conspiratorial smile, "Are we allowed to say 'I' in relational psychoanalysis?" The "analytic police" are everywhere, we giggled, almost as though, having momentarily escaped the panopticon, we felt it wicked to imagine our canon's limits.[2]

I discern in this moment, when my patient and I playfully critiqued the reification of relational psychoanalytic principles, the way regulatory practice kindles the opposition it douses. Even where hegemony is overtly disavowed—as in relational psychoanalysis's openness to a multiplicity of perspectives—a central tendency toward a correct and reductive line of theory emerges. Hence, even though my patient and I "know" better, we experienced a pull, at once syntonic and dystonic, to believe that intersubjectivity is all, which inclines us to feel—not think, but feel—that we can never say "I," only "we." We felt governed by an unspoken rule, which somehow seems to be the whole story even if it is itself only half. Regulation may come from a single authority—for example, Freud—or it may come from the tendency of discourses to fold in on themselves, of groups to close ranks in self-creation.

Our giggle may be the most important moment in this anecdote. It signifies the tension I am pointing to now, that between the tendency toward uniformity and the pull of heterogeneity. How can we keep this tension in mind? I am beginning to think cubism may tell us something about it. I'm not really being funny. Consider negative space or, as Kern (1983, p. 179) calls it, "positive negative space." This idea follows on the Einsteinian proposition that the space between objects is, albeit named negative, not empty at all. Hence the negative space in cubist imagery as full, not vacant. An example is Escher's fascinating dilemma: which is foreground, which background? Cubism's adventure in trying to collapse them—all as foreground—parallels a contemporary adventure in clinical space. Once the patient was foreground while the analyst was background—or negative space. Now both matter equally if differently, at least in certain quarters.

This recognition, initially found in interpersonalism's emphasis on the analyst's person, currently shows up in diverse schools of psychoanalytic thought. I offer two examples. According to the late James McLaughlin's (2006) account of his evolution from a rigidly classical stance, he gradually came to hear the analyst's silenced subjectivity as one of the loudest sounds in the room. As Steven Cooper (2010), from the next generation of a related lineage, views the new synthesis, analysts, who are no longer transparent, benefit from taking patients' views of them as seriously as theirs of patients. (By-the-by, this technical innovation mitigates the way analysts' expertise once justified a claim on absolute authority, our authoritarianism.)

This habit of mind—analyst and patient as same and different, their relationship as both mutual and asymmetrical—is a feat of simultaneity. It can be limned in John Keats's phrase of 1817, "negative capability," about which many analysts, most famously Bion (1970, p. 125), have written. In this reflective state, one "is capable of being in uncertainties, Mysteries, doubts without any irritable reaching after fact & reason" ("Negative Capability," n.d.), making it possible, desirable, and expectable to bear irresolution, or what you might call "unknowing." This uncomfortable state of mind was not one embraced by Freud, a rejection that contributed toward the regulatory politics he was instituting in "'Wild' Analysis." However, it frames the uncertainty or, better, the "unknowing" (Corbett, 2009, p. 12) that infuses psychoanalytic work and that, recognized, might militate against rigidity. Queer theorist Salamon (2010, pp. 5–7) expands this view: unknowing is not not-knowing. It is an active state: "to unknow is to revise or undo knowledge" one already has. It is not just to withhold judgment, to "mark... the limits of knowledge," but to "engage... something beyond that marking of limits." A path to the doing and undoing of the clinical hierarchy between analyst and patient, unknowing affirms that one is "no longer within the regime of knowledge, but... engaged in something else too."

That something else is a congeries of emotions and mental states, including feeling, thinking, sensing, imagining. Let me illustrate with some reflections about my work with the patient whose critique of relational psychoanalysis I shared. As I wait and engage these mentations with her, I know and unknow various assessments of what is transpiring. I contemplate one, let it go when it thins, circle to another, and so on. With her, I imagine the transference/countertransference: is her chummy joke her idealization of me? her identification with my contrariness? her nascent appreciation of her own mind that might have an origin in my idealization of her? Then the inter- subjective: are we repairing the mutual hurt, humiliation, and fear, distrust, anger, and felt betrayal circulating between us for two or three years? Wondering about resistance/counterresistance, I reflect on the Law against which we are marshaling our aggression by, for example, together betraying relational psychoanalysis or by sharing our emotions without, as yet, making symbolic meaning.

Given this new matrix—clinical and theoretical meaning as held in negative capability and hybridity—the great breakthroughs now and to come likely issue less from the traditional apparatus of technique and knowing that "'Wild' Analysis" privileged, and more from, on the contrary, the rich, fertile, and uncharted territory of unknowing, negative space, and excess. Once there was a metatheory of psychoanalytic technique. Like all normal science, it evolved a set of rules about what-to-do-when that concretized over time. However, such a method has gone by the board, and so has the idea behind it, and nothing has replaced it.

Heterogeneity within one frame of reference needs a metatheory to hold it. The one I am identifying suits a view of technique as a set of contingent intellectual and clinical practices, for example, Chefetz's (2008) brilliant vision of technique as that which is negotiated in the evolution of each embodied clinical pairing. To say, for example, that I do not know which way I might go with my patient, would be disingenuous because, since she has read *my* words in order to allow me to use *hers*, what I do next depends on her response, already in the works. An instance of heteroglossia (Bakhtin, 1934–1935), for sure. With another patient not in the field and/or about whom I would not be writing, my tack would inevitably differ.

Hybridity, I am suggesting, crosses diverse psychoanalytic schools of thought. Maybe, as Makari (2008, p. 430) claimed, a heterogeneity of thought and technique, whose last hurrah occurred during the interwar years, is native to psychoanalysis. In these exhilarating postclassical times, perhaps we can begin to recoup some of the wild exuberance with which psychoanalysis began. Certainly, from the '70s onward, McLaughlin (2006) was keeping to himself such heterodox thoughts as "analytic knowing... must evolve within the dyad through searching interaction and negotiation between two separate realities, both claiming their own validity and both idiosyncratically shaped by separate developmental pasts" (p. 35). As though taking McLaughlin's struggle with psychoanalytic binaries one step further, Cooper (2010) proposed diverse ways of thinking about and linking theories of mind and theories of technique. He juxtaposed fundamental clinical differences: "I have never understood why there needs be an antipathy between a constructivist approach to symptoms and an interest in describing symptoms from an intrapsychic perspective" (p. 38). We are far from the vague strictures of "'Wild' Analysis."

But What about Sexual Boundary Violations?

Prepare for a U-turn. In this exegesis of an iconic essay, I have considered power in psycho- analysis as an institution, psychoanalysis's place in a cultural revolution, sexuality's threat to a fledgling profession, and technique as a hybrid creature. Yet, at the rather anticlimatic close of "'Wild' Analysis," one more hot topic steps up, and I want to meet it as a way to conclude, even tie up, these wide-ranging reflections.

In the essay's dénouement, Freud seems spent, his interest in his patient flags, his priorities become disconcertingly clear. And the lady in question? It's as though he has loved and left her! At first, his feeling for her was lively, if voiced in the muted tones of "the embodied analyst in the Victorian consulting room" (Shapiro, 1996): "In the second half of her forties, [she was] quite well preserved and *obviously* not past her prime as a woman." Now, though, "the lady whose complaint against her physician we have heard" (Freud, 1910g, p. 227) seems of no more interest to him than her shadow self, that old biddy toward whom he felt a repulsion as visceral as his excitement for her friend.

His passion is psychoanalysis, and to preserve it he will sacrifice the clarity of his own thought. Having uneasily justified his support for a monopoly, he ends by saying, "the truth is that these wild analysts do more harm to the cause than to individual patients" (Freud, 1910h, p. 8). Even bad psychoanalysis surpasses any other treatment: "the wild analyst did more for [her] than any highly rated specialist who would have told her that she was suffering from a 'vasomotor neuro-sis'" (Freud, 1910h, p. 8). But how? "He directed her attention to the real cause of her trouble, or at least to the right area" (Freud, 1910h, p. 8). "And," he goes on, "in spite of all her opposition this intervention of his cannot be without some favourable results" (Freud, 1910g, p. 227). I italicize for emphasis: "The *real* cause"? "The *right* area"? "*Cannot be without?*" Is Freud here accepting the inevitability of compromise? Or trying to have it both ways? That he could have plumbed further what he meant by "real" and "right" and by the vague "*cannot be without*" (the German reads, "*nicht ohne günstige Folgen bleiben*" [Freud, 1910, p. 125]) suggests he has lost interest in the clinical dimension of his argument.

"'Wild' Analysis" looms large. Its big presence contrasts with its brevity, a mere 7.5 pages. There's no doubt the power of Freud's prose, like the clever structure of the essay and its ability to do so much in so small a span, registers as magnitude. I think, though, there's another reason for its impression of bigness, and it has to do with the heterogeneity and the anxiety it bears, which, in its organizational drive, it tries to erase. This magnification is a variant of a collective psychoanalytic wish for some authority—what Lacanians call "the subject-supposed-to-know" (Lacan, 1977)—to ease the expectable discomfort of unknowing, to tell us what to do, and thereby to dispel the anxious mysteries of sex and technique.

And to stop us from having sex with our patients. Although sexual boundary violation is literally absent from the text of "'Wild' Analysis," it nevertheless haunts the essay. I make this claim by applying to the text Lévi-Strauss's (1963) principle that each version of a myth, including interpretations, is valid. I read our shared fantasy about this remarkable essay—for I too mis-remembered it as the place where Freud instructs analysts to refrain from sexual congress with their patients[3]—as part of the text. And what I detect is a collective *wish* for regulation implicit in what one may call the essay's textual unconscious, in Freud's opinion that the neophyte's sexual speech may have been a bit frank for a lady.

Really, his concern here seems rather strange. After all, five years earlier, he said that when analysts speak of sex with patients—even teenage girls—they are to be direct, frank, fearless, and medically dry (1905a). Does this disjuncture stem from Freud's wish to continue humiliating the incompetent analyst? Or does it also betray an underlying anxiety that sex will slip into the consulting room? Curiously, at the very moment Freud claims to speak most straightforwardly, he takes what Gallop (1982, p. 140) slyly terms a "French detour": "I call bodily organs and processes by their technical names, and I tell these to the patient if they—the names, I mean—happen to be unknown to her. *'J'appelle un chat un chat'*" (Freud, 1905a, p. 48). The proper doctor becomes, Gallop cleverly suggests, flirtatious, even titillating, simultaneously prurient and puritan: Freud, unconsciously using the French vulgarity for female genitalia (*chat* or *chatte*), "calls a pussy a pussy" (Gallop, 1982, p. 140). A slip of this order, even if occurring just with his reader and not his patient, suggests a dread that we ourselves can recognize to this day.

Given that now, as opposed to then, we can talk about the primal crime—the conversation has already begun (e.g., Burka, 2008; Celenza, 2007; Cornell, 2009; Dimen, 2011; Gabbard, 1989)—I want to return to the essay's ostensive topics—sex and technique—and ask, rhetorically: Is there any technique to help us with the problem of sexual boundary violations? Short answer: No. Or, rather, the only technique we know—exhortation, or "Don't!"—has failed; like most super-ego solutions, it likely inflames the problem it means to solve. Sexual boundary violation is no more about to disappear than incest. Indeed, as Celenza and Gabbard (2003) argued, it is an occupational hazard. Maybe we are stymied because our anxiety and shame about this act impel us to stop it—to act, not think (like the perp). Could be, then, that thinking is just what the doctor ordered. For what is theory but a way of thinking?

Perhaps it would help undo our primal dilemma to refigure sexuality with hybridity, empha- sizing its mixture and irregularity as opposed to its normative consistency.[4] It seems especially crucial to remove sexual infraction from a discourse positing a homogeneous problem fixable by one technical solution. Consider that not all those who are objects (and subjects) of this transgression find it damaging. Too, sex inhabits all mental registers, so sometimes, to modify Ferenczi's (1933/1988) teaching, the coin of one realm is mistaken for that of another. Negative capability might help psychoanalysis mine such "fertile confusion," to adapt Laplanche's (1995, p. 678) phrase, which is, in fact, what already permits us to construe sexuality as shifting tensions instead of mutually exclusive binaries (Blechner, 2009; Corbett, 2009; Dimen, 2003; Dimen & Goldner, 2005).

Boundary transgression being a collective problem, thinking together about how to make sexu- ality *qua* sex grist for the analytic mill again seems like a no-brainer. This means as well to render sexuality grist for the training and supervision mills, the peer group and lecture hall mills, and so on (See also Green, 1996, 1997; Shalev & Yerushalmi, 2009). I am aware that, in wondering how to steal a march on sexual harm, I may seem, at the end of this critique of Freud's regulatory thrust, to be calling in the cops myself. Yet surely there is another way to create stability besides a power move. Really the cops are us, we are our own authority. If we can't make us the ethical people we want to be, who can?

Conclusion: Hybridity and Doubt

"'Wild' Analysis" created a still center in an exploding theory of mind, and established a dis- cipline in a kaleidescoping world.[5] Yet its goal, a regime of sexual and technical knowledge founded on disdain for disagreement, set a disturbing tone that reverberates still. Freud's con- temptuous attacks on his junior colleague are entertaining, but I find myself wondering whether they bode the traditional psychoanalytic mode of assault, especially on candidates and super- visees. And I wonder too whether this shaming play of hierarchy, described by Buechler (2008) and Kernberg (1996), reappears precisely in psychoanalysis's primal crime, as clinicians in the penumbra of patriarchy internalize the aggressor (Freud, 1966) and take it out on the low-in-the-analytic-food-chain patient.

Psychoanalysis's excessiveness also occasions another occupational hazard: doubt. Faith and doubt, though, partner well. They make room for negative capability and the negotiation of the hybridity that is inevitable when two people and all their thirds are in a room together. Indeed, hybridity means a continual effort at integrating related, but differently languaged registers of experience (*See* also Cooper, 2010, p. 85). As such, psychoanalysis is neither art nor science. Rather, like other disciplines whose data talk back, it is a third, still evolving practice, which it is too soon to name.

Notes

1 A note on quotation and translation: I am relying heavily on verbatim quotes from "'Wild' Analysis." Given that Freud wrote in German, this not uncommon practice runs a risk for the Anglophone readers: translators can and do make mistakes. Perhaps this risk is mitigated here by my reliance on two translations, Strachey (referred to as S) and Bance (referred to as B), between which I have selected the version that seems to me the more accurate in its context.
2 The foregoing statements belong to a larger argument about relational psychoanalysis and technique that I lack the scope to make in this context.
3 As did a colleague in an entirely different field, who'd read it in graduate school.
4 Here I join Widlöcher's (2001) critique of the necessity "for theoretical coherence, which is what led Freud to join the 'presexual' and biological sexuality" (p. 23).
5 The question of "wild" analysis endured: even "in 1920 at the International Conference at The Hague, many analysts were shocked by Groddeck's describing himself as a 'wild analyst' and by his associating freely, instead of reading his prepared paper. Only a few—among them Rank, Ferenczi, Horney, Fromm-Reichmann, and Simmel—shared Freud's interest and affection" (Alexander, Eisenstein, & Grotjahn, 1966, p. 211).

References

Alexander, F., Eisenstein, S., & Grotjahn, M. (1966). *Psychoanalytic pioneers*. New York, NY: Basic Books.

Bakhtin, M. M. (1934–1935). Discourse of the novel. In M. Holquist (Ed.), *The dialogic imagination: Four essays by M. M. Bakhtin* (C. Emerson & M. Holquist, Trans., pp. 259–420). Austin: University of Texas Press. (Original work published 1981)

Baranger, M. (2005). Field theory. In S. Lewkowicz & S. Flechner (Eds.), *Truth, reality, and the psychoanalyst* (pp. 49–71). London, UK: International Psychoanalytic Association.

Bass, A. (2001). It takes one to know one; or, Whose unconscious is it anyway? *Psychoanalytic Dialogues, 11*, 683–702.

Bhabha, H. (1994). *The location of culture*. New York, NY: Routledge.

Bion, W. R. (1970). *Attention and interpretation*. London, UK: Tavistock.

Blechner, M. (2009). *Sex changes: Transformations in society and psychoanalysis*. New York, NY: Taylor & Francis. Buechler, S. (2008). The legacies of shaming psychoanalytic candidates. *Contemporary Psychoanalysis, 44*, 56–64. Burka, J. (2008). Psychic fallout from breach of confidentiality: A patient/analyst's perspective. *Contemporary Psychoanalysis, 44*, 177–198.

Celenza, A. (2007). *Sexual boundary violations: Therapeutic, supervisory, and academic contexts*. New York, NY: Aronson.

Celenza, A., & Gabbard, G. O. (2003). Analysts who commit sexual boundary violations: A lost cause? *Journal of the American Psychoanalytic Association, 51*, 617–636.

Chefetz, R. A. (2008, December 12). The unique negotiation of technique [Web log post]. IARPP-COLLOQUIUM, IARPP-Colloquium Series: No. 13, 12/1/08 to 12/14/08. Retrieved January 25, 2014.

Cooper, S. (2010). *A disturbance in the field: Essays in transference-countertransference engagement*. New York, NY: Routledge.

Corbett, K. (2009). *Boy hoods*. New Haven, CT: Yale University Press.

Cornell, W. F. (2009). Loves and losses: Enactments in the disavowal of intimate desires. In D. Mann & V. Cunningham (Eds.), *The past in the present: Therapy enactments and the return of trauma* (pp. 82–101). New York, NY: Routledge.

Dimen, M. (2003). *Sexuality, intimacy, power*. Hillsdale, NJ: The Analytic Press.

Dimen, M. (2011). *Lapsus linguae*, Or a slip of the tongue? A sexual violation in an analytic treatment and its personal and theoretical aftermath. *Contemporary Psychoanalysis, 47*, 36–79.

Dimen, M., & Goldner, V. (2005). Gender and sexuality. In A. Cooper, G. Gabbard, & E. Person (Eds.), *American Psychiatric Association publishing textbook of psychoanalysis* (pp. 93–114). Washington, DC: American Psychiatric Publishing.

Ferenczi, S. (1988). The confusion of tongues between adults and children. *Contemporary Psychoanalysis, 24*, 196–206. (Original work published 1933)

Ferro, A. (2005). Commentary. In S. Lewkowicz & S. Flechner (Eds.), *Truth, reality, and the psychoanalyst* (pp. 87–96). London, UK: International Psychoanalytic Association.

Fliegel, Z. O. (1986). Women's development in analytic theory. In J. L. Alpert (Ed.), *Psychoanalysis and women: Contemporary reappraisals* (pp. 3–31). Hillsdale, NJ: The Analytic Press.

Foucault, M. (1980). *The history of sexuality*, Vol. *I* (R. Hurley, Trans.). New York, NY: Vintage. (Original work published 1976)

Freud, A. (1966). *The ego and the mechanisms of defense*. New York, NY: International Universities Press.

Freud, S. (1905a). Fragment of an analysis of a case of hysteria. *Standard Edition, 7*, 7–122. Translated and edited by Strachey J. London, UK: Hogarth Press, 1953.

Freud, S. (1905b). Three essays on the theory of sexuality. *Standard Edition, 7*, 125–243. Translated and edited by Strachey J. London, UK: Hogarth Press, 1953.

Freud, S. (1908). "Civilized" sexual morality and modern nervous illness. *Standard Edition, 9*, 177–204. Translated and edited by Strachey J. London, UK: Hogarth Press, 1959.

Freud, S. (1909). Analysis of a phobia in a five-year-old boy. *Standard Edition, XX*, 3–149. Translated and edited by Strachey J. London, UK: Hogarth Press, 1955.

Freud, S. (1910a). Five lectures on psycho-analysis. *Standard Edition, 11*, 3–56. Translated and edited by Strachey J. London, UK: Hogarth Press, 1957.

Freud, S. (1910b). Leonardo da Vinci and a memory of his childhood. *Standard Edition, 11*, 63–137. Translated and edited by Strachey J. London, UK: Hogarth Press, 1957.

Freud, S. (1910c). A special type of choice of object made by men (Contributions to the psychology of love I). *Standard Edition, 11*, 163–175. Translated and edited by Strachey J. London, UK: Hogarth Press, 1957.

Freud, S. (1910d). The taboo of virginity (Contributions to the psychology of love III). *Standard Edition of the Complete Psychological works of Sigmund Freud.* Translated and edited by Strachey J. London, UK: Hogarth Press, 1957.

Freud, S. (1910e). On the universal tendency to debasement in the sphere of love (Contributions to the psychology of love II). *Standard Edition, 11*, 177–190. Translated and edited by Strachey J. London, UK: Hogarth Press, 1957.

Freud, S. (1910f). Über Wilde Psychoanalyse. Gesammelte Werke: VIII, 118–125.

Freud, S. (1910g). "Wild" Psycho-analysis. *Standard Edition, 11*, 219–227. Translated and edited by Strachey J. London, UK: Hogarth Press, 1957.

Freud, S. (1910h). "Wild" Psycho-analysis. In A. Phillips (Ed.), *Sigmund Freud: Wild analysis* (A. Bance, Trans., pp. 1–10). New York, NY: Penguin.

Freud, S. (1930). Civilization and its discontents. *Standard Edition, 21*, 64–146. London, UK: Hogarth Press, 1961. Gabbard, G. (Ed.). (1989). *Sexual exploitation in professional relationships.* Washington, DC: American Psychiatric Press.

Gallop, J. (1982). *The daughter's seduction: Psychoanalysis and feminism.* Ithaca, NY: Cornell University Press. Gerson, S. (2004). The relational unconscious. *Psychoanalytic Quarterly, 73*, 63–98.

Green, A. (1996). Has sexuality anything to do with psychoanalysis? *International Journal of Psychoanalysis, 76*, 871–883.

Green, A. (1997). Opening remarks to a discussion of sexuality. *International Journal of Psychoanalysis, 77*, 345–350. IARPP. (n.d.). Who we are. Retrieved from http://iarpp.net/who-we-are/what-we-do/.

Judt, T. (2009). What is living and what is dead in social democracy? *New York Review of Books*, p. 86.

Kern, S. (1983/2003). *The culture of time and space: 1880–1918.* Cambridge, MA: Harvard University Press.

Kernberg, O. F. (1986). Institutional problems of psychoanalytic education. *Journal of the American Psychoanalytic Association, 34*, 799–834.

Kernberg, O. F. (1996). Thirty methods to destroy the creativity of psychoanalytic candidates. *International Journal of Psycho-Analysis, 77*, 1031–1040.

Kerr, J. (1993). *A most dangerous method.* New York, NY: Knopf. Lacan, J. (1977). Écrits: A selection. New York, NY: Norton.

Laplanche, J. (1995). Seduction, persecution, revelation. *International Journal of Psycho-Analysis, 76*, 663–682.

Lévi-Strauss, C. (1963). The structural study of myth. In C. Lévi-Strauss (Ed.), *Structural Anthropology* (C. Jacobson & B. G. Schoepf, Trans., pp. 206–231). New York, NY: Basic Books. Makari, G. (2008). *Revolution in mind.* New York, NY: Harper Perennial.

McLaughlin, J. T. (2006). *The healer's bent: Solitude and dialogue in the clinical encounter.* Hillsdale, NJ: The Analytic Press.

Negative Capability. (n.d.). *Wikipedia.* Retrieved January 25, 2014, from http://en.wikipedia.org/wiki/ Negative_capability.

Phillips, A. (2002). Introduction. In A. Phillips (Ed.), *Sigmund Freud: Wild analysis* (pp. vii–xxv). New York, NY: Penguin.

Rabinow, P. (1984) *The Foucault reader.* New York, NY: Pantheon. Salamon, G. (2010). *Unknowing the other.* Unpublished manuscript.

Schivelbusch, W. (1977). *The railway journey: The industrialization of time and space in the 19th century*. Berkeley, CA: University of California Press.
Schore, A. N. (2011). Tthe right brain implicit self lies at the core of psychoanalysis. *Psychoanalytic Dialogues, 21*, 75–100.
Shalev, O., & Yerushalmi, H. (2009). Status of sexuality in contemporary psychoanalytic psychoterhapy as reported by therapists. *Psychoanalytic Psychology, 26*, 343–361.
Shapiro, S. A. (1996). The embodied analyst in the Victorian consulting room. *Gender & Psychoanalysis, 1*, 297–322. Sullivan, H. S. (1953). *The interpersonal theory of psychiatry* (H. S. Perry & M. L. Gawel, Eds.). New York, NY: Norton. Weber, M. (1947). *The theory of economic and social organization*. Glencoe, IL: Free Press.
Widlöcher, D. (2001). *Infantile sexuality and attachment*. New York, NY: The Other Press

The Wild, the Revolution, the Abject Social Imaginary, the Racialized Psychoanalytic Setting a Conversation between Daniel G. Butler and Ken Corbett Inspired by Muriel Dimen's Contemplation of the Wild and the Heterodox in Sigmund Freud's Wild Analysis Held Amidst the 2020 American Summer of Social Discontent

Daniel G. Butler and Ken Corbett

Daniel G. Butler
dangreeleybutler@gmail.com
Wednesday, March 25th, 2020

I'm wanting to think about revolution within psychoanalysis, perhaps along the lines of paradigm shifts and psychoanalysis's epistemic unruliness, especially since this is close to the manifest meaning of Muriel's paper. But I'm also inclined to think about the plurality of revolutions (social, psychical, political), and the notion of revolution itself as a kind of psychopolitical space. The spatiality of revolution is, of course, evident in Muriel's title. I like the idea of being "inside the revolution"; and yet, I have to say, it sounds like a difficult place to stay. One thing I've been reminded of, especially lately with the University of California Wildcat Strike,[1] is how dissociative this historical conjuncture is. Neoliberal and neocolonial societies are seemingly designed to make any revolutionary fervor wane, not by coopting unconscious desire as much as by occupying attention, perception, and capacities to associate (Stiegler, 2010). That's definitely what I've experienced during the strike. The University's strikebreaking is rarely a direct show of police violence, although that's there too. The majority of it

DOI: 10.4324/9781003335252-31

is an intervention into time, space, and the digital, a slowing of the COLA (Cost of Living Adjustment) Movement, the creation of gaps in email communications, gaps into which our desire to stay 'inside' might lapse. Even as a clinician (and perhaps especially as an early clinician), I struggle to stay close to psychoanalytic psychotherapy as a modality in which I believe and am trained. I have to return to psychoanalysis over and over, almost to the point that I don't know – for better and worse – what it is. Perhaps 'getting inside' is a praxis, and while Muriel is right that psychoanalysis is a revolution that's ineluctable by design (the identity of psychoanalysis itself being undecidable), 'getting inside' of that revolution would seem to take a particular kind of work that just isn't easy.

In sum, I guess I'm left wondering how one 'gets inside' the revolution. But I'm also wondering what the feat of 'getting inside' might tell us about the 'wild' in wild analysis. Sometimes I wonder if the inside is actually *out there*, somewhere *in* the wild or the great outdoors, where different generations of theorists and philosophers radically depart from orthodoxy only to find themselves penning it anew. Or perhaps the heterodox impulse between generations introduces paradigm shifts that actually break with such repetitions, however subtly, to generate something novel in psychoanalysis and allied fields, even while retaining the moniker of those disciplines from which they broke away?

Anxiously quarantined in San Francisco – and quarantined after being tested for COVID-19 – our historical conjuncture certainly feels 'wild,' but in this case, I don't know that I'm inside of something so much as I am subject to it. Summoned to revolt, my quarantined self is labile, doubtlessly wild, symptomatically swinging psychically and somatically, often overwhelmed by fear. Sometimes I have difficulty breathing, and I'm often thinking about death. If I'm inside a revolution of sorts, the revolt is against some indwelling being, a virus perhaps, but without that being, at least in this moment, I have no inside to speak of. This virus is libidinal in a way that it can only be following AIDS, but also because it similarly attacks an imperious ego or self that Bersani (2010a) considers the basis of social violence. In Bersani's early work, to be at war with oneself is to choose – or be chosen by – death. Psychoanalysis – and psychoanalytic practitioners – may indeed be at war, albeit playfully in an ideal situation, a point the later Bersani (2010b, 2018) gets. If psychoanalysis always seems to be dying – a truism that many would agree with – I guess we've chosen a dying art as our work. But hopefully, to invoke Montaigne (1993; cf. Critchley, 2020), that choice has also taught us something about dying as an artful form of breakdown. Perhaps acceding to such death is the price of entry to psychoanalysis, and perhaps this accession is a kind of play, even if it takes unsettling material forms (e.g. my quixotic daydream of free psychoanalytic training, which could spell the 'death' of institutional psychoanalysis).

After the long nineteenth century and the so-called Age of Revolution, and the birth of modernism that Muriel wants us to think about, the concept of revolution is deadened by a determinism and historicism that leaves little room for failure, experimentation, and excess – in short, for the play and festivity – that constitutes the "LIFE" (Winnicott, 1975) of the demos. Revolution, in the modernist sense, is either successful or not – the odds aren't great. Dashed upon the rocks of productively repressive power that so often seems to reconstitute itself in the image of its opponent, revolution also seems to give way to terror and savagery that petrifies groups and individuals who otherwise might become revolutionary actors. This stilling of social action (Harcourt, 2017) has perhaps sounded the death knell for revolution, such that it's no longer a concept around which people easily mobilize, just as radical psychic transformation is a notion that can easily send new patients running to the hills if introduced prematurely.

Freud (1910) intuits this in "Wild Psycho-Analysis." The interpretation of the repressed is timed when "the patient has reached the neighborhood of what he has repressed," but the patient "must have formed a sufficient attachment to (transference) to the physician for his emotional relationship to him to make a fresh flight impossible" (p. 226). This fresh flight is not into the wild but back to the tame. The wild would seem to involve some encounter with the repressed, but "Wild Analysis" is about practitioners whose superficial knowledge and application of psychoanalysis impedes precisely such an encounter. As Muriel clearly gets, Freud's "Wild Analysis" is thus a defense of psychoanalysis as, ironically, an entrée to the wild (i.e. the unconscious). The modernist concept of revolution with its 50/50 odds is thereby complicated. Such calculations falter in the anti-science of psychoanalysis. For Freud, Muriel, and psychoanalytic practitioners generally, the answer to "what is revolution" has to possess a psychic dimension, such that revolution is always already shot through with timelessness, displacement, condensation, replacement of external by internal reality, and the absence of mutual contradiction that we associate with a dynamic unconscious. Non-Freudian models also apply here. My point is that social and political revolutions are necessarily refracted through projection, introjection, splitting, repression, dissociation, reverie, and so on, none of which they could do without.

Ken Corbett
kencorbett@kencorbett.com
Sunday May 31, 2020

I begin with your thoughts about being "inside a revolution," and how you imagine it to be a difficult place to stay. Muriel, I believe, found her way into that difficulty, feet first. One might say that her feet led, and her pen followed, as she challenged what you reference as the "heterodox impulse(s)" of her own generation with particular attention to matters of sex and shame (Dimen, 1986, 1991). Later in life with feet and pen, Muriel joined forces with the generation of analysts she helped to educate, as they began to re-imagine the inner/outer blend of psychic lives, with an emphasis on sociopolitical forces (Dimen et al., 2011).

As I read *Inside the Revolution: Power, Sex, and Technique in Freud's 'Wild' Analysis* (Dimen, 2014), I find that once again it is the inter-implication of her political/clinical feet and her scholarly pen that forge what I take to be the major claim of the paper: Psychoanalysis is a praxis of unknowing, that makes "room for negative capability and the negotiation of the hybridity that is inevitable when two people and all their thirds are in a room together" (p. 512). I follow here with some thoughts about how Muriel found her way along this crowded (all those thirds!), unknowing, hybrid path. I do so in response to some of the points you raise in your initial post, and with the hope that we might think toward how one stays inside the revolution, and within the complex daily work of the psychoanalyst.

I think it is fair to say that Muriel cut her revolutionary teeth in the trenches of second-wave feminism, a story that she narrates in her 1986 book, *Surviving Sexual Contradictions*. I have recently watched a few episodes of *Mrs. America* (2020), the television series that depicts the lives of prominent second-wave feminists and their detractors. I have longed to talk with Muriel about it, sure that she have would have had just the right way to skewer the wig work and actress-y camp of the pop drama as it playacts women's liberation. Although, at the same time, if you squint hard enough, and don't go in search of too much depth, *Mrs. America*, like *Sexual Contradictions*, dramatizes the conflicts women faced in staying within the revolution; power, homogeneity, envy, rigidity, gatekeepers, and racism challenge the best of coalitions, and wigs.

Muriel brought these challenges into her early psychoanalytic work and writing, in a manner similar to her later challenge of Freud's efforts to define/claim psychoanalytic technique and orthodoxy in *'Wild' Analysis*. The inside of a revolution, Muriel (2014) reminds us, "is a process of power as well as ideas. It entails jockeying and elbowing, triumph and loss, and the flip and flop of friends and enemies and comrades-in-arms" (p. 500). Having shared an office suite with Muriel for 25 years, I was keenly aware of her elbows and her kindness, her enemies and her friends; she sharpened her eye on power. She never closed a door; she swung it open, and let it slam.

I miss that slam, even though it made me jump for 25 years. But even more, I miss her mental dexterity, as she kept perplexed, hybrid ideas in play with scholarly rigor and discipline. My favorite part of her *'Wild' Analysis*, follows on her examination of giggling with a patient about whether relational psychoanalysts can say "I." Isn't "we," the third person plural more proper? We watch as she employs that moment to examine the "tendency toward uniformity and the pull of heterogeneity" (p. 507). But she does not stop there. She also subtly employs this moment to show us how one can make use of the rupture (the gigglement [a word that ruptured spell check]) of play. Moving with her clinical feet, she pens her plea for the kind of negative capability and unknowing that unfolds in play. Muriel, following on Gayle Salamon (2010), argues that psychoanalysis and revolutions are processes that seek to actively [revolutionarily] undo knowledge, "a path of doing and undoing of the clinical hierarchy between analyst and patient, unknowing affirms that one is 'no longer with the regime of knowledge [per Foucault], but … engaged in something else too" (Salamon, p. 7). Muriel paid particular attention to the unknowing and re-thinking that can happen when one attends to matters of "hierarchy" and "regime." Her clinical work bore the mark of her signature commitment to the sociopolitical inter-implications that cannot be untangled from the affect and desire to which psychoanalysts' routinely attend. "I" and "we" bear desire, but they also carry social-political history. In the "I"/"we" example that Muriel provides, she and her patient were musing on the history of the psychoanalytic guild, specifically the relational wing of the guild, and the power such societies wield in making a mind.

Unknowing is not simply a matter of nothingness, it is a praxis (Corbett, 2014a). One that I would suggest opens onto Salamon's "something else too," which, following on Donald Winnicott (1971), we could call potential space (the capacity to imagine a future). I hold that this praxis of unknowing may allow one to stay in the revolution, joining and countering its "terror and savagery," to which you point. This is not to suggest that futures are utopian, for surely they are not. But just as surely we can cruise them (as per José Muñoz, 2009) looking for the hybrid, the poly-vocal, the contested, the converging, the bloody, the glittered, the paranoid, the negotiated. Without the potential of a future, how do we rend the kinds of ruptures necessary to create change? How do we grab hold of the openings that may afford movement and growth?

We correspond against the backdrop of a vicious virus that has to date claimed the lives of 367,000 people worldwide, primarily those whose lives are seen as not having a future worth preserving (J. Butler, 2020). [I was relieved to learn in a separate post that you tested negative for Covid-19, and you are feeling better.] We correspond as yet another black man was deemed unworthy of breath. We correspond as our country is on fire, with a president who fans the flames. I make my plea for potential space, with the hope that we don't simply stop and settle in the white house of the depressive position: the implied temperance of mourning, the too often hasty repair of splitting that ignores social subjection, the reach for the balance of good and bad that may not match the sociopolitical reality for any given subject.

Perhaps that which is wild in psychoanalysis is our capacity to listen for the ruptures of improvisation, even tinged by mania, that shake the chains of material reality and historical consequence. It is our job – one might say, our ethical charge – to hone in on those breaks where life may be otherwise livable, where life may be better, but to listen as well to how those ruptures are summoning a better world in a form we cannot yet imagine.

Daniel G. Butler
dangreeleybutler@gmail.com
Thursday June 4, 2020

It's a bit uncanny to resume this dialogue on wildness and revolution amidst what could be the social and political eschaton of our time. While this moment feels exceptional to me, for some it might not differ so much from the everyday of their socially disposable lives. Teetering on the brink isn't generally a universal condition of social life, but a feeling of "on-the-brinkness" (Valayden, 2019) has nevertheless spread globally since we last spoke. We resume after the deaths of Ahmaud Arbery, George Floyd, and Breonna Taylor; after Covid-19 claimed almost three times as many black lives as non-black lives; after numerous police vehicles and even a Minneapolis police station were set ablaze. My erstwhile breathlessness now seems racialized, but of course it was then too. Breath itself has come to signify anti-blackness. What does it mean that I can breathe with the confidence that my respiratory system is not under state-sanctioned threat?

Elsewhere I've written about the racialization of clinical and national settings, and about how the violence of the setting is both concealed and revealed in the setting's rupture (cf. Butler, 2019). Prior to this most recent rupture, many (non-blacks) who take our national setting for granted never had to wonder if breath itself commits an ontological violence against those black subjects who, in the afterlife of slavery (Hartman, 2008), only exist for us, albeit unconsciously, as things or abjects whose breath and mortality are negligible. Why would black subjects need breath and protection from gratuitous violence, asks an anti-black national setting, if said subjects are already socially dead (cf. Wilderson, 2010, 2017)?

As Muriel knew, it's impossible to think about sex without race (Dimen, 2011a), which means that if "sex is too much to think" (Dimen, 2014, p. 503), race is too. Perhaps race could be the phantom organ that supports sex as the so-called heart of the psychoanalytic revolution. For Marriott (2018), denigrated blackness is condensed with the sexuality and aggression of the drive, thus functioning as the social embodiment of perversion and criminality. Gratuitous, indiscriminate violence is only a step away: because black skin, if not breath, signifies transgression *par excellence*, it must be snuffed out. There's a difference here, it seems, between sex and/or race as a *feature* of the subject rather than that subject's *essence*. In the former, "what appears as conceptual chaos is… a sign of… semiotic and lived excess" (Dimen, 2014, p. 503), whereas in the latter that excess cannot be semiotically lived. The latter bodies are marked as defects, and all they can do is take up the marks they're given. Surely living on scraps is a devitalizing life, albeit one that might spawn para-ontologies from within a space of social death (Sexton, 2011; Chandler, 2013).

But how might such a creation, let alone revolution, unfold psychoanalytically? Perhaps one has to be vitalized enough to get inside the revolution (cf. Alvarez, 1988). Perhaps one has to know "something else" before encountering the "something else" that they've unknown. Perhaps this expresses a paradox of the unknowing you, Muriel, and Salamon write about, namely that the "something else" already haunts the inside and that what's outside the revolution is, in some ways, as inside as one can get. From the position of an outside, then, one might be even better placed to mount a revolution, even if through the "gigglement" that acknowledges the panopticon without needing to somehow expose its regulatory power.

Getting inside would thus mean staying outside, existing contiguously, and this might tell us something about the "tension… between the tendency toward uniformity and the pull of hetereogeneity" that Muriel sees in psychoanalysis (p. 508). This tension is certainly something that I can imagine; it's a going-on-being of sorts, a potential space, one of flow, becoming, process. And yet, maybe it could also be connected to Muriel's door that slams, to the giggle that trails off into a cry, or to the twilight of a better future as the necessary crucible for any future to be birthed at all. This might be a cryptic way of revisiting the role of sexuality and aggression in relational thought, where the drive that slams severs the tension between uniformity and heterogeneity so as to reassert that tension anew. Here breakdowns and *im*potential become central to psychoanalysis as revolution. Disaster becomes a psychic and ontological premise. That would mean we have nothing to lose, nothing to sacrifice, and that the unsacrificeable (Nancy, 1991) could manifest equally in a setting on fire (Butler, 2019) or a giggle that momentarily seems to stop the world, an infant's giggle to be sure.

What I'm saying is something that haunts me as a clinician and writer. Hope for a better future is absolutely necessary, especially in midst of abject despair, but I also wonder if the inability to imagine the future is simply a prerequisite for the radically new to emerge. There's something about living in breakdown that potentially instills hope, right? Can we cruise the breakdown, even if the breakdown sunders the "we" who cruise? Is breakdown a non-place, a nothingness, from which "phantastic phallicism" (Corbett, 2011) can sometimes miraculously burst forth? Is this a moment of aliveness, that "new beginning," at the edge of Balint's (1992) basic fault? Sounds impossible – sounds like wild analysis! – and so does revolution in the face of a seemingly indomitable oppression. I agree with the importance of imagining a praxis by which a better future might unfold, and I also wonder if it's equally important for imagination and sociality to falter, such that there's nothing we can do in the wake of a social imaginary's disrepair. That nothing might induce ennui, but it also might invite a giggle... or even a revolution. Especially at this historical conjuncture, an espousal of nothingness and doing nothing can sound morally reprehensible, but perhaps some kind of stillness and indifference to death, to the suspension of the "we," is crucial for the revolutionary praxis of unknowing to recharge. Perhaps a more radical "I-ness" (or Otherness) in intersubjectivity, something like the object of Muriel-and-patient's giggle, could distill yet transform the relational thought that we've inherited from Muriel and others.

Freud couldn't easily tolerate such stillness, let alone the distillation of psychoanalytic concepts to the point that they transform into something else; it was too much to imagine that *his* revolution might fail. Almost counterphobically, Freud insisted on the tragic in defiance of Adler's optimism (Dimen, 2014). Freud's dogged return to conflict as the basis of psychoanalysis foreclosed further dialogue. To varying degrees, this struggle is replayed time and again in psychoanalysis – even between us? – which is perhaps why Muriel (2014) ends the paper with such an enlivening and prophetic cliff-hanger, namely that psychoanalysis is a "third, still evolving practice, which is too soon to name" (p. 513). Like revolution, psychoanalysis is untimely, and perhaps the only way to be inside of it is to be outside of it, to become subject to a Promethean kind of thought that exceeds yet anticipates the thinker, a thought not unlike like Ferenczi's (1994) "happy" and iconoclastic "inspiration" (p. 129). I think this is the psychoanalysis that Muriel's oeuvre gives us.

Ken Corbett
kencorbett@kencorbett.com
Sunday, June 14, 2020

As I begin this final installment of our conversation, I want to note that some readers might feel we have moved far afield from Muriel's (2014) *Wild Analysis*. Indeed we have moved or, more properly, we have *been* moved to discuss what you describe as that which, "could be the social and political eschaton of our time," namely the forceful and unremitting opposition to anti-blackness, white supremacy, policing, and the national setting. In keeping with these considerations, we also address the radicalized psychoanalytic setting. In so doing, we have moved from the revolution of feminism and the sexual setting, which was Muriel's domain, and within which she was an esteemed contributor. Muriel (2014) reads Freud's original *Wild Analysis* as his simultaneous declaration of "a revolution [that also] forges an orthodoxy" (p. 499). She pays particular heed to what she calls the "crucial tensions" that compose psychoanalysis: "its traffic in power, and sexuality and the primal crime" (p. 499). In our correspondence, we have primarily turned to questions about the character of revolution, the nature of that which is called a future, and in this last exchange to black/anti-black antipathy, black bodies, and denigrated blackness as it is fused with sexuality, aggression, perversion, and criminality. We consider blackness and anti-blackness as they live outside and inside the social order, along with the ways in which anti-black and black subjects do and do not imagine the future; we ask how these matters might transform the psychoanalytic revolution, including the traditional psychoanalytic setting.

I can say with unwavering certainty that Muriel would have wholeheartedly supported this exchange. In years prior to Muriel's untimely death, she actively organized and participated in discussions about race and psychoanalysis. This support can also be noted in her 2011 book, *With Culture in Mind*, a collection of essays written by students with whom she had been working for at least a decade. *With Culture in Mind* can be read in many different ways, but one way that I read the book is as an act of mentoring, an act of futurity. Like any serious scholar, Muriel wanted her ideas to live; she wanted the collection of papers that compose this book to be published. But she also believed strongly in something you mentioned at the opening of this correspondence: "Perhaps the heterodox impulse between generations introduces paradigm shifts that actually break [orthodox] repetitions, however subtly, to generate something novel in psychoanalysis and allied fields, even while retaining the monikers of disciplines from which they broke away?" So, in that spirit: into the streets, and onto the page.

I begin with your reference to the "uncanny" resumption of our correspondence as protests stream by my windows, pulling me down to the streets, chanting and shouting, while helicopters rasp and whirl overhead. I share your experience of the exceptional aspect of our discussion about revolution and wildness, as our fellow citizens from New York to Paducah are calling for the transformation of our social and political order. At the same time, I am mindful of how the "uncanny" is also used to describe the experience of something strangely familiar, rather than simply extraordinary. Notably, Freud (1919) intertwined the strange familiarity of uncanny experience with the repetition compulsion, repeating events over and over, events that simultaneously unsettle and reinstate the repressed.

The repressed is nothing if not repeating, as the primitive paranoia of white supremacy circles and repeats the chokehold. Consider how James Baldwin, in 1950, when he was 26 years old, left America and sought exile in Paris, where he lived for nearly a decade. He later told Robert Cole in 1977, "I had to leave; I needed to be in a place where I could breathe and not feel someone's hand on my throat" (*New York Times*, July 31). Baldwin not only presaged George Floyd and Eric Garner, he reanimated the hand at the throat of slavery, as he went in search of life, and lungs that could take in air.

Baldwin, in keeping with your thoughts about revolution as a mode of "staying outside," schools us: *Get Out*. The getting out is not simply a matter of running, or running as a progress narrative, but running as an act of pursuit, even as the horizon may be uncertain. Running in search of transitional and potential spaces where a mind can be made, made up, and a future can be imagined. Baldwin emphatically and fabulously failed to reproduce the white American progress narrative, with its anxiously regulating racial, sexual, and property norms. In Paris, Baldwin was not only freer to be black; he was freer to be queer. Baldwin, AB Huber (2018) takes note, did not only know "the past corporeally in ways that exceed reason [the hand at the throat of slavery], he also knew the future in ways that exceed reason, if by reasonable we mean history as progressive and normative" (personal communication).

Under such conditions, dis-identification becomes a key mode of refusing the polity of whiteness, and the power of citizens who sustain whiteness through non-thought, non-thinking, non: not doing, not involved with, not of that kind. The dis-identification currently animating our streets seeks to undo the paradigm of policing as a juridical methodology, and mode of governance ("Hands Up!"); the police are an anti-black law unto themselves, laying claim to breath as white.

I read your posts as living within the register of dis-identification, but at the same time, understandably wary of ideas that pivot on the concept of identity; ideas in which we can wrap ourselves, and optimistically try to close the gaps between pain and repair. As Lacan (1973) reminded us, any fixed claim on realness, especially when it is tied to identity, also has a finger in psychosis. Premature moves toward the 'realness' of empathy, either in the form of identification or self-consciously employed dis-identification, can serve to undervalue or obliterate the suffering of the other (Hartman, 1997). Or seek to repair alienation, in a manner through which it reenacts the violence of "being for the captor" (Wilderson, 2017). Or ignores the ways in which blackness as a condition for enslavement matters more than efforts to deconstruct the freedom of whiteness, fragile or otherwise.

These kinds of psychic traffic were the dynamics that Muriel was keen to observe (Dimen, 2003, 2011a). In this respect, I am sure she would have been eager to hear more of your thoughts about how "denigrated blackness is condensed with the sexuality and aggression of the drive, thus functioning as the social embodiment of perversion and criminality." Jeremy Harris's (2019) *Slave Play* works similar terrain, taking us to the brink of the chokehold-climax of natal alienation and ontological death as the black object yields in sexual intercourse with the anti-black other. The inter-racial couples that populate Harris's play variously depict the structural violence that maintained slavery (subjugation, domination, terror), and point to the ways in which notions of mutuality, consent, and recognition slyly prey upon black bodies to simultaneously shape and undo desires intensified by dynamics of subjection and aggression (Hartman, 1997; Saketopoulou, 2020a, 2020b). The excess and enigma of sexuality-race-class point to the need to revisit "the role of sexuality and aggression in relational thought" (as per your last post), a revisiting that is at least partially underway (Dimen, 2003, 2017; Goldner, 2020; Guralnik, 2011, 2020; Saketopoulou, 2020; Stein, 2008).

But if I understand you correctly, I think you are seeking a revisiting that reasserts the creative tension of negation (as per Fanon) or what might be called the pulsing of 'going-on-not-being.' You speak of "breakdowns," "impotential," "disaster," "nothing to lose," and "setting fire." On face, one might read this plea as nihilistic, but that would be to misread and underestimate your argument, which follows on your elaborated claim as to the violence of the traditional psychoanalytic setting (Butler, 2019a):

> While psychoanalysis is sensitive to breaches in the setting, an exclusively psychical presentation of such breaches risks painting a malformed picture, for the breach is not just psychical or even psychosocial, but onto- and psychopolitical in its contention that one's *potential* for being is vulnerable both politically and psychologically, with the two domains being inextricable but irreducible to the other. If the setting as a heuristic is taken to be politically neutral, presuming as it does that all bodies bear the same *potential* for existence, the setting's violence remains unchecked. Similarly, if the setting as a political phenomenon is taken to be purely sociological, the psychical dimension of the onto-political fails to be understood. (p. 156; emphasis added)

I have emphasized your use of "potential" in this summation of your claim, in order to return to the work of potential as a feature of psychoanalysis and revolution. I do so in order to ask, how do we think about potential for those who have not been granted the futurity that potential implies? (J. Butler, 2018, 2020).

There are many ways to approach this question, including the need for structural change at the level of the psychoanalytic institution, including who gets to be a psychoanalyst, the curriculum that structures their education, and how they afford the costs of so becoming. (In this respect, the work being done at Psychoanalytic Institute of Northern California is exemplary, and a model for the larger psychoanalytic community.) We need to query the traditional customs of practice, like the consulting room, the 50-minute hour, the fee. (Again, work being done with respect to these matters at PINC, under the visionary eye of Julie Levitt, should be noted.) We need to question the traditional two-person model (analyst/analysand), moving into the community and into groups, following on Francisco Gonzalez (2019), who has called upon us to "count beyond two." Also, in this respect, consider Orna Guralnik's work on the documentary television series, "Couples Therapy" (Kriegman, J., Steinberg, E., Despres, E., 2020, 2021), as she and the creative team behind the series break the fourth wall, and thereby widen both the frame of therapy and community.

We also need to examine the anti-black frame through which the setting has been constructed. In this respect, I share your critique of Winnicott's color blindness, "decorat[ed]," as you point out, by an abundance of present progressive participles: "holding," "communicating," "living," "dreaming," "being," etc. (2019a, p. 149). It is enough to lead one to declare that the present progressive is white. I also share your critique of the ways in which Winnicott's generally nuanced redress of trauma lacks a way to consider "trauma's onto-political depths," or the "effacement, splintering, and atomization of blackness" (2019a, p. 151). And let us not go down the road of his misogyny.

Yet, I cannot do without him. In an effort to try to find my way, I sometimes imagine Winnicott in conversation with José Muñoz, who, like Winnicott, draws us toward thinking about the psychic action of illusion, fictive improvisation, rupture, and the aesthetic freedom that playing affords. They both wrote about the ways in which play upends time and space producing aesthetic experiments in living otherwise. They both prized the ways in which a good story and "the logic of play," as per Michael Parsons (1999), augments and exceeds the satisfactions of reason.

Muñoz and Winnicott were stalwarts in their belief in play as serious business, including breakdowns, fire setting, murder, wilding, effacement, non-belonging, disaster, and disillusion. The slow work of potential only follows on the hard-won work of establishing transitional space. There are long periods of waiting and stillness, moments, as you indicate, within which one is "held in a time of suspense, unplaced and ungrounded." There are equally long periods wherein, as you suggest, "imagination and relationality falter, such that there's nothing we can do in the wake of the social imaginary's disrepair".

The potential of potential space does not jump the shark of abjection, more often it follows on the bereaved inability to imagine; play and potential are lost, found, re-found, and unfound, in the interstices of transitional space. The relational landscape of transitional space falters, over and over. Hence, the unknowing that seeks to follow, as opposed to the knowing that hastily offers misplaced empathy, premature interpretations, or lame identifications as a means of repairing the faltering, the aggression, the paranoia, the ruination, the despair.

I imagine Muñoz and Winnicott squiggling, Winnicott giggling despite the miserable morality of his internal Protestant protestations, and Muñoz (1999) delighting in pointing out how squiggled "hybrid transformations" draw minority subjects into being (p. 5). I hear Muñoz telling Winnicott that "being with" another vs. "going on being" is the atomistic engine of queer transport and brown futurity. I picture Muñoz challenging Winnicott to consider the social and political conditions that limit entrée into potential space: the broken streetlights, the breakfast to which the poor do not wake, the fag bashing, the future which is too often foreclosed, the pepper spray that takes breath away, the carceral powers that arrest and assassinate.

Muñoz (2009) would tell Winnicott that, "The here and now is a prison house. We must strive, in the face of the here and now's totalizing rendering of reality, to think and tell *a then and there*. Some will say that all we have are the pleasures of the moment, but we must never settle for that minimal transport; we must dream and enact new and better pleasures, other ways of being in the world, and ultimately new worlds" (p. 1). I like to think that just as Winnicott could look upon the runaway adolescent as the child who needed to be found, the child who broke from that which was unbearable, he could hear Muñoz to be making a relational bid, not only for new psychopolitical imaginaries, but for a dismantling of the old: old specters, old imaginaries, old whiteness.

I don't believe Muriel found the same inspiration in Winnicott as do I. All of that waiting, likely tried her patience. Muriel preferred to lean into her countertransference, and to move from the kind of relational/Frenczian "inspiration," you note. She unquestionably held a position similar to yours with respect to Winnicott's insufficient address of the social, and the social imaginary's disrepair. Not to mention the ways in which Winnicott's engagement with sexuality would have felt tepid and insufficient to her. Although, I do think she would have found interest in your (D. Butler, 2019) and Scarfone's (2012) recent invigoration of Winnicott and the infantile sexual. I am saddened that you and she never met; she would have enjoyed your mind and good company.

Still, I think that Muriel would have been more than happy to join Muñoz, in my imagination, when he knocks on the patriarch's door.

Note

1 The 2020 UC Santa Cruz Wildcat Strike began after the Executive Vice Chancellor sent a campus-wide email explaining administration's refusal to consider a Cost of Living Adjustment (COLA) for UCSC graduate students. A highly public email exchange between graduate students and the Executive Vice Chancellor followed. A graduate student challenged the Chancellor's explanation, and administration responded to the student's challenge with the threat of disciplinary action. This set off a chain of angry emails from fellow graduate students, who one by one called for a wildcat strike (or a strike unsanctioned by the UAW 2865, the official union body for all UC graduate students). As a result, graduates, undergraduates, and faculty joined in what became one of the largest worker-led strike actions in recent UC history. 17 students were arrested, and 82 students were fired. Graduate students throughout the UC system also joined the strike, and sympathy strike actions were taken at universities across the country.

References

Alvarez, A. (1988). Beyond the unpleasure principle: Some preconditions for thinking through play. *Journal of Child Psychotherapy*, 14, 1–13.

Balint, M. (1992). *Basic Faults: Therapeutic Aspects of Regression.* Chicago, IL: Northwestern University Press.

Bersani, L. (2010a). Is the rectum a grave? *Is the Rectum a Grave? And Other Essays.* Chicago, IL: University of Chicago Press.

Bersani, L. (2010b). Sociability and Cruising. *Is the Rectum a Grave? And Other Essays.* Chicago, IL: University of Chicago Press.

Bersani, L. (2018). *Receptive Bodies.* Chicago, IL: University of Chicago Press.

Bulter, D.G. (2019a). Racialized bodies and the violence of the setting. *Studies in Gender and Sexuality*, 20(3), 146–158.

Butler, D.G. (2019b). Riding instincts, even to die. *Studies in Gender and Sexuality*, 20, 106–118.

Chandler, N. (2013). *X – The Problem of the Negro as a Problem for Thought.* New York: American Literatures Initiative.

Cole, R. (1977). James Baldwin Back Home. Interview in the *New York Times*, July, 31.

Couples Therapy. Created by Josh Kriegman and Elyse Steinberg. Showtime, 2020–2021.

Corbett, K. (2011). *Boyhoods: Rethinking Masculinities.* New Haven, CT: Yale University Press.

Corbett, K. (2014a). The analyst's private space: Spontaneity, ritual, psychotherapeutic action, and self-care. *Psychoanalytic Dialogues*, 24(6): 637–647.

Critchley, S. (2020). To philosophize is to learn how to die. *New York Times.* April 11th, 2020.

Dimen, M. (1986). *Surviving Sexual Contradictions.* New York: Macmillan.

Dimen, M. (1991). Deconstructing difference: Gender, splitting, and transitional space. *Psychoanalytic Dialogues*, 1 (3): 335–352.

Dimen, M. (2003). *Sexuality, Intimacy, Power.* New York: Routledge.

Dimen, M. (2011a). The mystery of hysteria and the crossroads of power: Commentary on paper by Sam Gerson. *Psychoanalytic Dialogues*, 21(5): 531–537.

Dimen, M. Ed. (2011b). *With Culture in Mind.* New York: Routledge.

Dimen, M. (2014). Inside the revolution: Power, Sex, and Technique in Freud's 'Wild' Analysis. *Psychoanalytic Dialogues*, 24(5): 499–515.

Ferenczi, S. (1994). Child analysis in the analysis of adults. *Final Contributions to Psychoanalysis.* Ed. Michael Balint. Trans. Eric Mosbacher and others. London: Karnac.

Freud, S. (1910). Wild psycho-analysis. *The Standard Edition XI, Five Lectures, Leonardo da Vinci, and Other Works.* 219–228.

Freud, S. (1919). The 'Uncanny'. *The Standard Edition XVII.* 217–256.

Goldner, G. (2020). Pleasure can hurt: The erotic politics of sexual coercion. *Psychoanalytic Dialogues*, 30: 239–250.

Guralnik, O. (2011). Ede: Race, the Law, and I, in Dimen [Ed.], 2011, *With Culture in Mind.* New York: Routledge.

Guralnik, O. (2020) #Me Too, I Was Interpellated. Psychoanalytic Dial., 30: [x].

Harcourt, B. (2017). On revolution: An introduction. *Modalities of Revolt.* Conference at Columbia University. Retrieved online.

Hartman, S. (2008). Lose Your Mother: A Journey Along the African Slave Route. New York: Farrar, Straus, and Giroux.
Hartman, S. (1997). *Scenes of Subjection: Terror, Slavery, and Self-Making in Nineteenth-Century America*. Oxford: Oxford University Press.
Huber, A.B. (2018). Personal communication.
Harris, J. (2019). *Slave Play*. New York: Theater Communications Group.
Lacan, J. (1973) [1981]. *The Four Fundamental Concepts of Psychoanalysis*. New York: Norton.
Marriott, D. (2018). *Whither Fanon: Studies in the Blackness of Being*. Stanford, CA: Stanford University Press.
Montaigne, M. (1993). *The Complete Essays*. Trans. Charles Cotton. New York: Penguin.
Muñoz, J. (1999). *Disidentifications: Queers of Color and the Performance of Politics*. Minneapolis: University of Minnesota Press.
Muñoz, J. (2009). *Cruising Utopia: The Then and There of Queer Futurity*. New York: NYU Press.
Mrs. America. Created by Davhi Waller. FX, 2020.
Parsons, M. (1999). The logic of play in psychoanalysis. *Int. J. Psycho-Anal.*, 80(5): 871–884.
Salamon, G. (2010). Unknowing the Other: A Response to Ken Corbett's Queer Childhood. Unpublished. February 2010, University of California, Berkeley.
Saketopoulou, A. (2020a). Risking sexuality beyond consent: Overwhelm and traumatisms that incite. *Psychoanalytic Quarterly* 89: 771–811.
Saketopoulou, A. (2020b). #consentsowhite: On the Erotics of Slave Play in *Slave Play. Los Angeles Review of Books*.
Sexton, J. (2011). The social life of social death: On afro-pessimism and black optimism. *InTensions*, (5). https://doi.org/10.25071/1913-5874/37359
Scarfone, D. (2012). Winnicott: Early Libido and the Deep Sexual. *Canadian Journal of Psychoanalysis*, 20, 3–16.
Stein, R. (2008). The otherness of sexuality: Excess. *Journal of the American Psychoanalytic Association*, 56, 43–71.
Stiegler, B. (2010). *Taking Care of Youth and Generations*. Trans. Stephen Barker. Stanford: Stanford University Press.
Valayden, D. (2019). States of Attrition. *Poor Theory in Three Movements*. https://uchri.org/foundry/states-of-attrition/
Wilderson, F. (2017). *Afropessimism: An Introduction*. Free PDF|connect: rackedanddispatched.noblogs.org racked&dispatched@riseup.net.
Winnicott, D.W. (1971) Playing: A theoretical statement, in *Playing and Reality*. New York: Penguin Books.
Winnicott, D.W. (1975). The manic defense. *Through Pediatrics to Psychoanalysis*. London: Tavistock.

Suggested Reading

Butler, J. (2018). Solidary/Susceptibility, *Social Text* 137, 36(4), 1–20.
Butler, J. (2020). *The Force of Non-Violence*. Verso: London.
Corbett, K., Dimen M., Goldner, V., Harris, A. (2014b). Talking Sex, Talking Gender – A Roundtable. *Studies in Gender and Sexuality*, 15(4): 295–317.

Dimen, M. (2016). Rotten Apples and Ambivalence: Sexual Boundary Violations through a Psychocultural Lens. *Journal of the American Psychoanalytic Association*, 64 (2). 361–373.

Goñzalez, F. (2019). When Recognition Fails, We Recognize History. Plenary Address, Div. 39 of the American Psychological Association, Philadelphia, April 2019.

Nancy, J.L. (1999). The unsacrificeable. *Yale French Studies No. 79: Literature and the Ethical Question*. New Haven: Yale University Press.

Schjeldahl, P. (2020). Edward Hooper and American Solitude. *The New Yorker*, June 8 & 15, 2020.

Wilderson, F. (2010). *Red, White, & Black: Cinema and the Struggle of U.S. Antagonisms*. Durham, NC: Duke University Press.

Project Five

Rotten Apples – Talking About It/Them/Us

Project Five

Editor's Note

Stephen Hartman

Muse

Dimen, M. (2016). Rotten apples and ambivalence: Sexual boundary violations through a psychocultural lens. *Journal of the American Psychoanalytic Association*, 63: 361–373.

After Dimen's *Lapsus Lingue, or, a Slip of the Tongue?* was published in 2011, the topic of sexual boundary violations moved from the margins of psychoanalytic conversation front and center. At conferences and in institutes, Dimen's moment of self-disclosure opened a reckoning with sexual improprieties in the field that brought questions of accountability and ethics to the forefront of collective inquiry. I think it is fair to say that, in no small part, Dimen's challenge to the unspeakable in psychoanalysis paved an opening to more recent conversations about racial microaggressions and structural dynamics in the practice of psychoanalysis that confirm inequities in society at large. In Dimen's words:

> The phenomenon of sexual transgression between analyst and patient, I am suggesting, is insufficiently addressed as long as it is only deemed psychological. Since it is also a social matter, as I am insisting, then it needs to be understood via social as well as psychological concepts. And given that it is a group matter, it must be addressed by the group of which it is a property (Dimen, 2016, p. 2).

Readers

In tribute to Dimen in 2017 at the NYU Postdoctoral Program in Psychoanalysis and Psychotherapy, Velleda Ceccoli presented a paper that closely read Dimen's posthumously published paper, "Rotten Apples and Ambivalence: Sexual Boundary Violations through a Psychocultural Lens," illustrating how discussions often begin with a precis and then branch out to follow an author's leads to new conclusions. Ann Pellegrini responded with a discussion that is, in true Dimenesque form, a discussion of a discussion as a paper in and of itself. Taking Dimen's text as a starting point, Pellegrini

DOI: 10.4324/9781003335252-33

broaches a broad interdisciplinary conversation about the sexuality of groups. Both discussants chart the form in a manner that salutes "the paper" intertextually allowing the reader to appreciate Dimen's lifelong effort to broaden and deepen the conversation.

Form

Discussion of authors' papers and author's replies to discussions are the mainstay of psychoanalytic conferences and publications. Yet discussions and replies are rarely cataloged among an author's major work. Remember that in volume 1 of *Psychoanalytic Dialogues,* Dimen (1991b, pp. 359–360) risked a heated discussion about gender and sexuality with a discussant no less formidable than Stephen Mitchell, the journal's founding editor. "I do not believe that repeated appeal to Freud (one of Mitchell's rhetorical strategies) adjudicates any given argument" begins Dimen's snappy reply.

Dimen was herself the author of more than a dozen published discussions and the interlocutor on at least twice that many conference panels. The discussion/reply format offered Dimen (as writer and as journal editor) the opportunity to bring junior colleagues and students to print. It also provided a medium to contest the positions of colleagues—comrade and foe—within a traditional frame as a means to challenge disciplinary framing.

Here, two of Dimen's beloved colleagues reprise their 2017 presentation/discussion of "Rotten Apples and Ambivalence: Sexual Boundary Violations through a Psychocultural Lens." These are discussions of the traditional sort, but with a twist. To draw attention to the discussion (and reply) as an undertheorized genre, Ceccoli and Pellegini read and write for, as, and with Dimen.

Bios

Velleda C. Ceccoli, Ph.D. is a psychologist and psychoanalyst in private practice in New York City, New York. She is on the faculty of NYU Postdoctoral Program in Psychotherapy and Psychoanalysis, the Stephen Mitchell Center for Relational Studies, the Institute for Contemporary Psychoanalysis and the Institute for Self-Psychology and Relational Psychoanalysis in Milan, Italy. Dr. Ceccoli is on the editorial board of *Psychoanalytic Dialogues* and *Studies on Gender and Sexuality*, and writes a psychoanalytic blog called *Out of My Mind.*

Ann Pellegrini, Ph.D., is Professor of Performance Studies & Social and Cultural Analysis at New York University, and a psychoanalyst in private practice in New York City. Their books include: *Performance Anxieties: Staging Psychoanalysis, Staging Race*; *Love the Sin: Sexual Regulation and the Limits of Religious Tolerance* (coauthored with Janet R. Jakobsen); and *Queer Theory and the Jewish Question* (coedited with Daniel Boyarin and Daniel Itzkovitz).

Rotten Apples and Ambivalence

Sexual Boundary Violations through a Psychocultural Lens

Muriel Dimen

Sexual boundary violations ferry analysts and patients from thought to action, from the symbolic toward the materiality of life. They bring the outside in. Yes, they are enactments of fantasy. At the same time, though, sexual transgressions are workings of power and vehicles of culture. They evoke the social context for psychoanalysis, its rules, politics, and disciplinary power, its ethics committees, the legal systems that license and regulate training and clinicians, define and punish breaches of sexual boundaries by the licensed. Sexual boundary violations make trouble for any group. And they are a problem *of* the group too.

Most psychoanalytic thinking about this problem tends to take an inside view. I am going to do so too, but I am also going to view it from the outside in. Thinking as an anthropologist, I consider psychoanalysis an institution that, like any other social unit, has a structure, history, rules, and beliefs. Since, I am, of course, an insider, I can in no way claim objectivity. Nor would I want to. But my frame in this paper is different: a multiperspectival approach to this enigma, a position I am naturally inclined to take since in fact I approach sexual boundary violations in several capacities: psychoanalyst, anthropologist, whistle-blower.

I am suggesting that the phenomenon of sexual transgression between analyst and patient is insufficiently addressed as long as it is deemed to be exclusively psychological. Since it is also a social matter, as I am insisting, it needs to be understood by means of social as well as psychological concepts. And given that it is a group matter, it must be addressed by the group of which it is a property. On this score, though, muteness seems to reign, in groups but also as a paradoxical way to hold the problem in mind. It is hard to have a thoughtful conversation about this particular aspect of group life. Sexual transgressions generate a great and contagious anxiety prompted by how they pollute and stigmatize anyone and anything in their vicinity.

The impulse to silence is fertile soil for intergenerational transmissions, that is, for the repetition of trauma. As one colleague said to me, "If I know my colleague knows of a violation, that knowledge makes me so anxious about my beloved profession and makes me so fearful I will be tainted, that I want to put distance between me and that known knower even if that person never speaks of it to me." Such terrors render sexual boundary violations unmentalizable, a

DOI: 10.4324/9781003335252-34

hush that welcomes action as the only form of speech available. In other words, don't ask, don't tell, just enact. And so we come full, vicious circle. Breaking into it, I am saying, depends on thinking socially as well as psychologically.

I am quite taken with the phrase "the privatization of damage," by which the Latin American Institute for Mental Health and Human Rights (ILAS) aims to conceptualize how therapists might work with patients traumatized by the Pinochet regime in Chile. As I hear this motto, it calls into question the conventional psychoanalytic view that ascribes suffering only to interior processes and reduces political reference to a defense. Power structures, ILAS contends, must be regarded as an independent cause of psychic difficulty and trauma. The pain and anguish they occasion are a shared group concern, a public concern, and must be taken up as such.

Implicitly, then, ILAS's phrase indicates the way psychoanalysis tends to erase the cultural roots of individual difficulty. When it comes to sexual transgressions, for example, analysts, in keeping with their expertise, have historically preferred to focus on the unique individuality of suffering: perpetrators are ill, patients are seductive, exceptions occur, apples rot, throw them out. By the same token, familiar methods of the sort found in daily, noninstitutional group life are used to eliminate the disturbance: perpetrators are excommunicated, victims discredited or pitied, whistle-blowers isolated, apples tossed.

Yet thinking socially can partner with thinking psychically. One sort of social thought has to do with how groups preserve themselves. Every group, large or small, has a set of mechanisms that function to help it stay as it is, to maintain its institutions and beliefs and customs and power structures unchanged. Chief among these are ways of knowing and unknowing that discourage critical reflection on the group's fundamental premises, whether manifest or implicit. Here I would class the unspeakability of sexual boundary violations. Such an institutionalized shared disinclination—whether we would call it unconscious or unthought-known—functions to preserve the group's standing as a good object, but interferes with thinking about its problems and flaws: in this case, the phenomenon of sexual boundary violations. What will make such critical thought possible, I suggest, is to acknowledge ambivalence about the group, which itself hinges on some grasp of this phenomenon's place in psychoanalysis as a social institution.

The Folk Theory of Sexual Boundary Violations

I want to highlight the efforts to understand and treat sexual boundary violators that have preceded mine and on which I build. This ongoing original research and theorization regarding the narcissistic pathology of serial predators (See, e.g., Gabbard 1989) and the lovesick one-time offender (Celenza and Gabbard 2003; Celenza 2007) provide a remarkably sound foundation for further thought. However, this crucial work needs a more complex intellectual context. Our current discourse is what one might call a folk theory, captured in the saying "One rotten apple spoils the barrel." There's nothing wrong with the other apples. They are good. It's just that one susceptible apple has contracted those nasty mold spores that will travel to and ruin the others. Guided by this folk wisdom, psychoanalysis repeatedly pitches the bad apple, only to find that, lo and behold, another rots.

Various responses to this repetitiousness are possible. One is to think, rightly, that we have not reached the bottom of the matter, whether you call it pathology, crime, felony, ethical breach, or transgression. Another is to wonder whether in fact all the apples in the barrel have it in them to spoil, which, as Gabbard observes, is also likely the case. A third, my point here, is that maybe we need to check out the barrel or, to follow Bion, the container itself.

For the aphorism I have chosen as a guide is a bit ambiguous: does the rotten apple spoil only the other apples, or is it thought to spoil the container too? It could be that one reason for chucking the bad apples over and over again is to safeguard the container that is psychoanalysis itself. Here might be one of those social functions performed by individual acts that together amount to another, unconsciously collective way of keeping the social unit just the way it always was. Since there's nothing wrong with the barrel, goes the premise, all that needs to be done is to eliminate the apple. But this solution invites a question: is the container endangered by the apple's mold spores, or does it also generate rot on its own?

It's my intent not to throw out the rotten-apple theory but rather to recycle it. So in this paper I am risking a mix of psychoanalytic and cultural ideas in order to advance a common concern: we have an institutional problem on our hands that requires collective thought because it exceeds any single analyst and any single patient, and exists at a level that cannot be reached by psychotherapy, supervision, rehabilitation, rules, New Year's resolutions, or even the buddy system that some psychoanalytic communities have adopted so that analysts may keep each other on track.

Psychoanalysis as a Sexual Field: Beta Elements and –K

For starters, consider psychoanalysis as a sexual field, "a matrix of sexual meanings, discourses, and practices embedded in social institutions [linked] to individual sexual scripts" (Green 2014, p. 10). It is, however, an odd sexual field, for its brand is not a recognized practice like heterosexuality or barebacking. Rather, its brand is no-sex. "Psychoanalysis," quips Adam Phillips, "is about what two people can say to each other if they agree not to have sex" (Bersani and Phillips 2008, p. 1). Don't even *think* about it, analysts double-bindingly tell patients. Open yourself to your desire and of course you will want sex with me, but do not imagine it will ever materialize, a prohibition that of course incites the forbidden longing. Don't get my irony wrong: this injunction is necessary, but it's also crazy-making. Or, better, it has interesting sequelae.

The taboo on sex between analyst and patient is foundational to psychoanalysis. Carrying on the Hippocratic tradition, it substitutes the meeting of minds for the embrace of mucous membranes. It creates an absence that widens, even generates, potential space. The gap also functions, in my view, somewhat like Bion's "preconception" (1962), an unstatable expectation of something not yet formed, neither cognized nor cognizable, a placeholder for the possibility psychoanalysis potentiates. Insofar as this preconception is fundamental, its violation sends shudders right down to the DNA of the psychoanalytic edifice.

This alarm might be said to be in the realm of beta elements. Unthinkable, these tremors show up, as Bion proposes, in the form of projective identifications. "Why is she doing this to us?" asked one person after listening to me give a lecture on a sexual breach I'd experienced in analysis, making me wonder whether I was harmful and, if so, what harm I'd done. What is shaken to its very foundation by the revelation of sexual boundary violations is the container, but the whistle-blower is made into the problem instead. I do not take such a response personally. I do not blame or pathologize the hearer. I interpret it rather as a sign of a shared, elemental refusal, –K in the service of protecting the container (Bion 1962). Yes, everyone "knows" sexual boundary violations occur. But this knowledge is somehow compartmentalized and one-dimensionalized. It is a truth in the head, not in bones and hearts.

When knowledge enters the bones, however, it is more dangerous. Thus do I read the hostility in the question—not an inquiry at all, it was an accusation as much as a complaint. Perhaps when a colleague is straightforward, the fact of sexual transgression begins to percolate through multiple registers of knowledge, entering the empathic space that allows shared thought. When it thus gets under the skin, however, it also excites hostility, much as someone shoving you on the subway inclines you to shove back. A retaliation for what is perceived as an attack on the group's cherished belief—analyst and patient do not have sex—this hostility strikes back at the contagion that travels through the ether of empathy.

Psychoanalysis as a Cultural Institution: Purity and Pollution

Reenter the rotten apple, which I now want to reframe as a cultural problem, that of pollution. Switching, then, from Bion to anthropology, I draw on Mary Douglas (1966), who in *Purity and Danger* argues that all human cultures create an opposition between the pure and the impure that functions to preserve culture by keeping order. The polarity arises, Douglas argues, in response to human life's inherent and culturally dysregulating untidiness: rotten apples being routine, the cultural problem is how to restore order when they show up.

Dirt is Douglas's signal example. Dirt is dangerous—impure—because, like all pollutants, it threatens to spoil everything: "Dirt [is] matter out of place" (p. 48). Dirt is "dirt" only relative to what is considered clean. Ubiquitous, it "is never a unique, isolated event." Rather, dirtiness and cleanliness are part of a system. "Dirt is the []by-product of a systematic ordering and classification of matter, [] in so far as ordering involves rejecting inappropriate elements" (p. 48). Then we get to dirt's power to pollute, and the rules to undermine it. "Shoes are not dirty in themselves, but it is dirty to place them on the dining table" (p. 48). What is contaminating is not the item of clothing but its being in the wrong place; "food is not dirty in itself, but it is dirty to leave cooking utensils in the bedroom, or food bespattered on clothing..." (p. 48). There is always dirt, but if each thing has its place and is kept in or returned to its place, purity will prevail.

When there are systems of classification, however, anomalies are inevitable. Not everything fits the either/or of binaries: think, for example, of how those people once called hermaphrodites, now intersex, confound the neat divide of male from female, and needed to be hidden away so their presence would not pollute everyone else. In anticipation of such problems, each culture has institutionalized solutions to restore order before disorder snowballs and poisons what is sacred, which is the group itself. In every culture are found ways to demarcate and separate the clean and the unclean—meat from milk, say, or beef from pork. Yes, beliefs and rituals dividing pure from impure foods may be shown to have salubrious effects. That they do so, however, does not mean they cannot also function to maintain, by iteration, cultural health, that is, the identity, structure, and existence of the group, which also must be preserved at all costs.

By the same token, every culture has ways to repair the contamination caused by crossing such boundaries. There are usually very simple remedies for the effects of most mistakes. For example, if you accidentally put meat in the milk pot, you just re-kosher the pot. In rarer instances, though, transgressions are punished rather than remedied, the penalties cautioning against future occurrences, especially when it comes to sex. Some adulterers, for example, are branded forever (think Hester Prynne), sometimes they are excommunicated (Adam and Eve), and sometimes they are stoned to death or, like Anna Karenina, kill themselves. A measure of the group's sanctity, such actions, from the mundane to the catastrophic, function in the long run to maintain an ongoingly reliable structure for life: "rituals of purity and impurity create unity in experience," Douglas writes (p. 13). That such rules and practices of maintenance are also regulatory, serving as well to shore up a structure of power is not within Douglas's purview, though it should be within ours.

Seen in anthropological perspective, the proscription on sexual action between analyst and patient appears to play a role in maintaining the life of the institution. That this taboo is clinically and therapeutically crucial does not keep it from also serving a ritual and ideological function: as a premise, it is an emblem of the identity, integrity, and sanctity of psychoanalysis. Along with the requirement for personal analysis, it is one of the regulations by which psychoanalysis distinguishes itself among therapies. Its breach pollutes: sex out of place—sex in the consulting room—contaminates not only the parties to it or those nearby, but, I am suggesting, the entire institutional order of psychoanalysis.

Consider the way sexual boundary violations have traditionally been responded to, that is, by rituals of purification: the perpetrator is ill, so kick him out. Consider, too, how others are spoiled by the perpetrator's offense, like the victim, who, if she has participated in the sex, may be deemed seductive, so that her complaint becomes dismissible, and her perpetrator's act is expunged. Or take a bystander, like Sue von Baeyer of the San Francisco Center for Psychoanalysis. As she reported in a paper she presented at the Wounds of History conference in New York, after the news broke that her training analyst, Dan Greenson, had committed a sexual boundary violation, she experienced feeling tainted by the refusal of training analysts from her institute to take her into treatment (personal communication, February 2, 2016). A line between purity and danger is drawn between us, the clean, the good—and them: the dirty, impure, contagious.

Let me accept the charge: like our founder, I bring you the plague. But in what way? The questioner who asked, "Why is she doing this to us?" felt polluted by my story, because I refused to protect psychoanalysis from a necessary deep knowing: sexual transgressions perdure. In deprivatizing damage, my public discussion threatened the field's integration, purity, and unity: a kinsperson in the tribe we call psychoanalysis had violated a basic tenet, and, we are reminded, he wasn't unique. He has an estimable genealogy going back to Ferenczi, Jones, Stekel, Gross, and, of course, Jung, not to mention the many, many others lost in veils of secrecy and memory. No wonder sexual boundary violations belong to what Freud (1919) called "the uncanny... that class of the frightening which leads back to what is known of old and long familiar" (p. 220). Such a lineage can only prompt the scary question: Is it something about psychoanalysis? Is whatever keeps this phenomenon going connected to what keeps psychoanalysis going?

The Vulnerability of Psychoanalysis

Perpetrator, victim, and whistle-blower, their bodies marked by sexual boundary violations, recall the vulnerabilities of psychoanalysis itself. Analysts' and patients' bodies are carefully monitored, not only because of the Hippocratic oath but because, observes Douglas, the body's form, in particular its imperfectly closed borders, are quite apt for representing the aporias and incompletions of culture. By the same token, the body is quite suitable for rituals of purification. Psychoanalysis itself, a mortal institution populated by mortal human beings, has weaknesses. There is the rule against sex between doctor and patient that triggers the impulse to break it. There is desire, without which analysts cannot work, but which has no certain home in the work. There is the memory desire carries: sex tends to reignite unresolved incestuous frustrations and longings alongside quotidian but painful regrets about the failures and losses in love and sex. This incompletion intensifies the vulnerability to unrequited love that, under pressure of grief or tragedy (the lovesick analyst) or pathology (the serial or narcissistic predator) leap from representation to act, from Symbolic to Real.

The policing of analytic bodies takes on urgency for other reasons as well. It is not uncommon, says Douglas, for anxiety about the body to show up when a society is in trouble. Insofar as notions of purity and pollution and their associated rituals "express anxiety about the body's orifices, the sociological counterpart of this anxiety is a care to protect the political and cultural unity of a minority group" (p. 148). To the degree that bodies can represent the relation between parts of society, ideas about sexual danger in particular mirror patterns of hierarchy or symmetry found in the larger system (p. 14). In other words, anxiety about analysts' and patients' erotic orifices may be deeply implicated in the struggle of psychoanalysis for existence, which has been in question from the initial effort to establish the field, right up to the current battle to maintain its standing in public opinion and the marketplace. If purity is vital to social acceptability, then an unstained reputation is crucial. "Aren't you afraid you will hurt psychoanalysis?" asked a Canadian colleague about the paper I was writing. Already weakened, it needs perhaps to be in quarantine.

As the stain of stains, the violation of the analytic incest taboo may therefore be responsible for a task to which it is unsuited. If someone who happens to be an analyst and someone who happens to be a patient—of a different analyst—meet in a bar and go on to a sexual liaison, their encounter breaks no rule. Nor does their sexual relationship have the power to pollute: no boundaries having been drawn, none are violated. No order is disturbed, no pollution caused.

Between Social and Psychological: Rotten Apples and Stigma

If what I have been saying so far about the social construction of sexual transgression and pollution holds any water, still it remains to think about how we get from cultural to personal experience. For this, I turn to Erving Goffman (1963), an ethnomethodologist who studied stigma, which he defined as "spoiled identity." If pollution threatens the whole social group, the threat of stigma divides it into two unequal parts, the discredited and the discreditable. Each of these has its own dilemma in the context of shared but tacit premises about normality, revealing stigma to be a regulatory practice in the operation of power.

These two groups are the inverse of each other. The discredited are those who carry the stigma of otherness: their differentness shows. Bodies marked by, say, the wrong skin color or a disfigurement or a disability, their lives are informed by the presumption that everyone knows about their discrediting feature. The discreditable, in contrast, are those whose stigma is neither known nor immediately perceptible. Only they themselves are aware of the potential discredit in which they live. These people are the normals, the majority who live in fear of being found out, of acquiring stigma.

Here is Goffman's remarkable insight: most people are discreditable. Most of the time, most people live with the fear of being outed for one or another potentially discrediting behavior or thought or thing—secret eating, for instance, or out-of-the-ordinary sexual practices (let alone fantasies about, say, having sex with a child or a patient), or politically incorrect beliefs, or maskable body parts that seem or are weird. Stigma is a set of social practices fueled by shame and a hierarchy of power that divides the acceptable from the unacceptable. As a system, it creates a truth out of a lie: the discreditable have something to hide, but their majority status renders them pure and normal.

In psychoanalysis, then, you could say that those who have not been involved in sexual boundary violations are the normals. This does not mean, however, that they have nothing to discredit them, just that they may not be discreditable by sexual transgression. But most have something in their lives that they don't want others to know. This discreditability is an unpleasant fact of life of which they are reminded when one of those with whom they identify—a colleague, or a colleague who is a friend—is stigmatized by connection to sexual transgression. This revelation in turn evokes everyone else's unvoiced terror of being outed and consequently discredited for a secret personal truth. Since, however, the discreditable cannot, or are not about to, get rid of their private dishonor, they prefer, by means of projection, to self-purify by eliminating those who cannot hide theirs. They erase the offender and the offended and the whistle-blower, and lo, the stigmatizing event that stains their beloved and precious profession never was.

To put it more generally, psychoanalytic life is burdened by a routine dissociation that is broken through when news of a sexual boundary violation breaks or when the phenomenon itself breaks into conversation. At such a moment, everyone in the group becomes stigmatized: the stigma carried by those involved in the sexual transgression travels to all the others as in a contagious process. But here is the truth: the stigma is, and has always been, latent in everyone. Perpetrator, victim, and whistle-blower may be treated as Typhoid Marys, but in fact they are catalysts, for they prompt the ordinarily dissociated knowledge of what is already there. The fear and attribution of contagion mask the certain, and discreditable, knowledge that all analysts are already polluted. As long as the routine presence of sexual boundary violations in psychoanalysis is dissociated, the field needs to live in fear of being discredited.

Sexual boundary violations and those immediately touched by them evoke the irony built into human culture. Purity and pollution are a system. Evoking one conjures the other. If, as you must, you insist on keeping things clean, you are re-creating, with each act of cleanliness, the notion of dirt. If you insist on the rule of no-sex, *as you must*, you are insisting on purity, which then reinforces the notion, and possibility, and lure, of sex and pollution. As you identify and try to eliminate that which is polluting, you are implicitly identifying and trying to value that which is pure.

Hatred, Idealization, Ambivalence

How do you do something about which you can do nothing? The risk of stigma constitutes a profound fault line in psychoanalysis, and it is one of the rigors that generates analysts' hatred of their discipline. This hatred, argues von Baeyer, is a cause of sexual boundary violations themselves. Drawing on literature arguing various aspects of this thesis, she wonders if some aspect of sexual boundary violations may not be about "disavowed aggression [that] gets split-off and works insidiously as a hatred of psychoanalysis,... the law,... the principles that make psychoanalysis possible" (von Baeyer 2013, p. 10). Convincingly, she details various dynamic and characterological processes, flaws, and illnesses leading to the expression of this hatred.

The problem, though, is not that we hate psychoanalysis but that we *may* not hate it. Let me explain. What von Baeyer does not illuminate is the phenomenon's systemic nature: however much individual pathology destroys a given analytic pair's capacity to think, which would normally keep sexual desire in the realm of representation and not in action, this approach does not shed any more light on sexual boundary violation as a recurrent problem of the group. For example, it does not explain the runaway anxiety that impels the normals, the discreditable, to act without thinking and eject the stigmatized and discredited.

I am about to go out on a limb here. So let me bring Winnicott along with me. Like him, I love psychoanalysis. But remember what he was brave enough to say in "Hate in the Countertransference" (1958): hatred is a routine, discreditable aspect of the work. The guilty are not the only ones who hate psychoanalysis, even if, in acting out, they act on that hatred in ways that, as Gabbard as noted, may incite envy and retaliation. Winnicott told us those 18 reasons mothers hate their babies to illustrate why analysts hate their patients and, I am adding, their work. Nor will I detail the economic instability, the endlessly deferred and inconsistent personal gratification, the disciplinary hierarchies—where there's power, there will be hate—and the mental labor so layered and intricate you often cannot even remember who and where you are. I want to get to Winnicott's intent that we incorporate the hatred with our love for our patients, our work, ourselves; that analysts, like mothers, need thus to take on the ambivalence that is the core of our psychoanalytic heritage.

However, in regard to psychoanalysis itself, this stance feels as hard to hold as it is to achieve. It's one thing to diagnose the incestuous failures of the rotten apple who lets her destructiveness rip. And it's another to understand that the social body of psychoanalysis, like our unconscious development, seems to demand an idealization that is necessarily unstable. While Douglas, following Durkheim, says that the group is sacred, psychoanalysis calls it idealization. Whatever term you use, it does not admit of hatred. According to both institutional rules of purity and the unconscious need to idealize, psychoanalysis merits only love.

It is as though the psychoanalytic body is too fragile to bear hatred. As if it is so vulnerable to contamination and stigma that it cannot withstand searching inquiry into its inevitable flaws—for example, the nuttiness of a sexual field defined by a ban on sex. Could it be that the prohibition on institutional hatred also issues from the unresolved idealization of our elders that is built into the processes of training analysis and supervision and that maintain the profession's hierarchical structures? Maybe these ordinary parts of the psychoanalytic institution are the most palpable manifestation of an intergenerationally transmitted idealization that rolls all the way back to our totemic ancestor, the patriarch of the primal psychoanalytic horde, the one who analyzed the analytic great-grandparent of anyone who analyzed you. But where there's idealization, there is hatred, and therefore pollution.

Psychoanalysis, like any institution, entails endless rituals of purification, ongoing acts of idealization. Every conference, for example, must end with an affirmation of the discipline's absolute value. So must every paper, including, perhaps, this one. If you participate in these obligatory acts of purification, though, you also have a hard time thinking about the pollution that requires remedy, for example, about sexual boundary violations, because then you have to think endemic impurity, fault lines, stigma. How, given this stricture, is it possible to sustain ambivalence for anything, a posture that is necessary in order that neither hate nor love manifest as action, in order to maintain an atmosphere of K?

Thinking and knowing at all levels, in heart and mind and bones, inside and together, is necessary in order to reduce the incidence of apple rot. To think about anything in this full way, however, you need to hold it in ambivalence: maybe it's good, maybe it's bad. You need a critical faculty, to entertain skepticism about the thing, the work, the institution whose perfection is so unstable. It's not hatred of psychoanalysis that's the problem. It's the difficulty of ambivalence about it.

This is perhaps another way of saying that my concern is to move sexual boundary violations into the realm of K, to transform our responses to them into alpha elements.

References

Bersani L. & Phillips A. (2008). *Intimacies*. Chicago, IL: University of Chicago Press.

Bion W.R. (1962). *Learning from Experience*. London: Karnac Books, 1984.

Celenza A. (2007). *Sexual Boundary Violations: Therapeutic, Supervisory, Academic Contexts*. Lanham, MD: Aronson.

Celenza A., Gabbard G.O. (2003). Analysts who commit sexual boundary violations: A lost cause? *Journal of the American Psychoanalytic Association* 51:617–636.

Douglas M. (1966). *Purity and Danger: An Analysis of Concepts of Pollution and Taboo*. London: Penguin Books.

Freud S. (1919). The uncanny. *Standard Edition* 17:217–256.

Gabbard G.O. ED. (1989). *Sexual Exploitation in Professional Relationships*. Washington, DC: American Psychiatric Press.

Goffman E. (1963). *Stigma: Notes on the Management of Spoiled Identity*. Englewood Cliffs, NJ: Prentice-Hall.

Green A.I. (2014). *Sexual Fields: Toward a Sociology of Collective Sexual Life*. Chicago, IL: University of Chicago Press.

von Baeyer S. (2013). Sexual boundary violations: A hatred of psychoanalysis. *Paper presented at the Wounds of History conference*, New York, March 1–3.

Winnicott D.W. (1958). Hate in the counter-transference. In *Collected Papers: Through Paediatrics to Psycho-Analysis*. New York: Basic Books, pp. 194–203.

Paradise Lost

What Is Most Dangerous About Our Method – Muriel Dimen's "Rotten Apples and Ambivalence: Sexual Boundary Violations through a Psychocultural Lens"

Velleda C. Ceccoli

A First Bite

Speaking to the individual and the collective, Muriel Dimen's *Rotten Apples and Ambivalence: Sexual Boundary Violations through a Psychocultural Lens* (2017),[1] addresses sexual boundary violations in psychoanalysis from a dialogic and interdisciplinary perspective. In this essay, Dimen moves beyond the dynamic components of the psychoanalytic couple and what breaks down in the analyst, the analytic process, and the patient when sexual boundary violations occur, instead speaking as both insider and *other*, and bringing her anthropological lens to psychoanalysis, inviting us to think as a group about our beloved profession and its ongoing struggles with the sexual and the violation of the taboo proscribed by Freud on touch and sexual relations with patients.

In discussing her paper, I will argue that sexual boundary violations stem from an inability to navigate the intricacies of intimacy both on the personal level as well as the group level, and that such inability perverts the intimate nature of our work by attacking the very basis of therapeutic action. And further, that sex and sexuality have a dysregulating effect on everyone, and that our ability to navigate within such states determines our boundaries and their permeability to transgressions. I am going to attempt to engage you, the reader, in a conversation about sex, and the fact that it is rarely spoken about in relation to sexual boundary violations. In so doing I hope to highlight Dimen's revolutionary ideas about sex and boundary violations within the culture of psychoanalysis and her insistence that we must engage collectively on this topic, in spirit and flesh.

From Apples to Orchards

The thorny issue of sexual boundary violations has haunted psychoanalysis since its beginnings, leading to a host of papers in the analytic literature that

DOI: 10.4324/9781003335252-35

focus on the perpetrator and/or the victim, the doer and the done to, and the behavioral and dynamic preamble and sequelae of sexual boundary violations (i.e., Celenza, 2007, Gabbard, 1989). Curiously, none of the literature questions the culture of psychoanalysis. Nor are psychoanalysts understood to be inter-implicated in relation to sex, despite the fact that Celenza and Gabbard each insist on sexuality as bedrock to identity. Even as these and other authors struggle with all things sexual and take account of the pull toward action and transgression that the sexual realm evokes, there is no sense that psychoanalysis is a culture of sex.

Until Dimen's *Rotten Apples*, the literature on this topic had focused on what Dimen identifies as folk theory: "one rotten apple spoils the barrel," since it threatens to contaminate the rest and must be expunged. Boundary violations were delimited by the wayward actions of individual perpetrators. Dimen considers a different option: What if all the apples have it in them to spoil? And further, what if we need to check out the container? Ought we not think only about rotten apples in terms of orchards? And, particularly since rotten apples tend to fall very close to the tree, ought we not explore a deeper understanding of rot?

Beginning with her breakout paper: *Lapsus Linguae, or a Slip of the Tongue? A Sexual Violation in an Analytic Treatment and Its Personal and Theoretical Aftermath* (2011), Dimen takes boundary violations on in her indomitable style – where the personal (spoiler alert: her analyst tongue kissed her while getting a hard on) – becomes the entryway to a deep, thoughtful theoretical exploration of the misuse of power, the shattering of the analytic promise of safety, and the question of how psychoanalysis can work with the sexual with words. And yes, she also speaks to the reality of transference and countertransference while examining the impact on her own psyche – the dissociated event, its ongoing shadow on the self, the rationalizations, the self-doubt and the shame that such transgressions bring about. *Lapsus Linguae* was 20 years in the making and 7 years in the writing, remaining in a dissociated lacunea which continued to haunt Dimen,[2] and finally made it to paper as she found the words to say it *and* think about it – as victim, survivor, psychoanalyst and theoretician. And further, as both an outcast and a member of the collective of psychoanalysis.

When she was finished with her writing and ready to go public, many analytic presses passed on publishing it. Her psychoanalytic cohort was shocked, incredulous, frightened and unwilling. One of the many issues that Dimen raises in *Rotten Apples* – the group's tendency to punish the victim and whistle blower, of sealing the container tightly so that the rot is expunged and visible only on the one and not the many. Where the group's silence somehow reflects the absence of symbolization, the denial of the event, the erasure of the experience, *as if* it has not taken place. Where the group encourages a binding silence, making it necessary for the victim to forget, be confounded and remain mute so that the many can continue *as if* all is well. Dimen would say *as if* all is cleansed and remains pure so that the phenomena of contagion anxiety that sexual boundaries engender, is silenced so as to not pollute or stigmatize anyone in the vicinity. She views such fears as rendering action the only form of speech: don't ask, don't tell, just enact. I would add that there is something about sex and the sexual that makes language fail in its symbolic function, and further, that when we add boundary violations to what is already un-mentalizable (sex) we are indeed in the land of the flesh, the unspeakable Real and no longer in an area where reflection is possible. It is here, that Dimen's assertion that we need to be thinking socially as well as psychologically begins. But I get ahead of myself.

After Lapsus Linguae

Lapsus Linguae was the beginning of Dimen's work and focus on psychoanalysis as culture and social group, and *Rotten Apples and Ambivalence: Sexual Boundary Violations through a Psychocultural Lens* develops this. True to her anthropological roots, the Dimen method was to consider ideas from as many points of view as possible, inside and out, around the edges, and only then, to write them down in both *personal and theoretical* voices, a dialogue she shared in her presentations and published work. Thereafter, she would observe the reaction to her ideas, and the impact of her personal, theoretical narrative on the *o*ther, and (re)incorporate this in her thinking. Thus, *Rotten Apples*, includes Dimen's commentary and theoretical observations to the responses of the psychoanalytic community to her first paper, *Lapsus Linguae*.

Building on the aftermath and sequelae of her published personal experience in *Lapsus, Rotten Apples* speaks to the culture of psychoanalysis, the relationship between the social and the individual, and the sexual nature of both ourselves and psychoanalysis as a discipline. In this essay, Dimen continues her deliberate and focused consideration on the subject of sexual boundary violations, opening up an *O*ther space (think capital O: as in the Bionian *O* and the Lacanian big *O*) to think together beyond the individual/dyadic psychology we know so well as psychoanalysts (beyond perpetrator and victim), and onto psychoanalysis itself – as culture and group. A culture and group that embodies the sexual yet continues to struggle with sexual transgressions. She is concerned with the ongoing occurrence of boundary crossings, at the individual and group level; with migrations of the flesh into psychic territory and consequently, with transgressions that violate the very nature of psychoanalytic work and collapse the space that psychoanalysis prides itself on creating.

Dimen takes on the culture of psychoanalysis, the container itself, and in so doing she moves the discussion from the psychological to the social, from the one, the intrapsychic, the interpersonal, the dyad, to the many, the social, the group, the collective of psychoanalysis. It is not just the person(s) it is also the field, she tells us, and our failure to consider the field while focusing on the individual has everything to do with the repeated incidence of sexual boundary violations. We have not looked widely enough she tells us, and in our myopia we have missed the proverbial forest – or apple orchard in this case. We might be chucking out the bad apples to safeguard the container – performing a (perhaps unconscious) collective function of keeping the container pure. She queries: Is the container endangered by the apple's mold spores, or does it also generate rot on its own? In answering she engages us in a conversation between psychoanalysis, sociology and anthropology, as well as between the individual and the group.

Dimen views sexual boundary violations as corporeal events that bring the outside into the consulting room enacting fantasy and collapsing the symbolic function of psychoanalysis. She considers them not only as sexual transgressions but as vehicles of power and of culture, evoking the social context of psychoanalysis and its rules, politics, ethics and disciplinary committees. Dimen looks at how psychoanalysis as an institution negotiates and regulates its identity and function. In so doing, she highlights the complicity of all of the systems within psychoanalysis that license and regulate training and clinicians. She tells us to consider them a problem of the group – our group. Wearing Dimen's anthropological hardhat, we walk through the processes and structures that help groups preserve their utility and stability and find that critical reflection of the group's essential premises might be discouraged in favor of helping the group endure. Thus, sexual boundary violations are at the heart of psychoanalysis's disinclination to think critically – and at the heart of our problem. Dimen suggests that acknowledging ambivalence about the group might allow for the necessary space that critical thinking requires. She is asking us to consider the distinction between thought and action, reflection and representation. Where does reflection give way? Whenever the sexual enters say I, and she agrees. But she goes further: when it comes to actions, and patterns of actions (*something we as psychoanalysts should know a great deal about*) and institutions that cause harm repeatedly, she insists that we must ask why? And do so collectively.

What Dimen wants us to know is that there are vectors of power and pleasure that shape our social beings as well as our deeper erotic strivings. These are inter-imbricated, so we must ask: how do these contingencies of desire push us to hurt, silence and harm repeatedly (2017b, p. 144). How indeed? When these questions are asked by not one but many, there is the possibility for reflection and, she tells us, that when we agree to listen collectively we are engaging in reflection as an action. A group action that might begin to build a safe enough container for the affective intensity that sexual boundary violations generate in all of us.

The Personal, the Collective, I, Thou, Us and Sex

It stands to reason and analytic curiosity that any discussion about sexual boundary violations would include sex. Yet talking about sex is hard. Sex makes everyone uncomfortable when it creeps up. IT is *R*eal, and in its *R*eality makes all of us nervous. In life such discomfort is usually *acted* on. The immediacy of the physical overwhelming all else, people get turned on by each other and they have sex. Sex collapses everything into the physical, into the envelope of skin and mucous surfaces with the highest density of nerve endings capable of giving us pleasure. Sex lives in the realm of the body and its senses, and connects us to our primordial nature, our animal self, our non-speaking, non-thinking-just-feeling self. Sex is about the interpenetration of bodies and interpenetration necessarily transgresses boundaries, at best suspending them momentarily, at worst, violating them entirely. The tension that sexual desire thrives on, the discomfort of containing it, dissipates in the act. Sex is necessarily a transgressive act, and *when that transgression occurs in the psychoanalytic setting it turns perverse.* I will return to this point.

The psychoanalytic literature on sexual boundary violations has typically focused on areas of theoretical ambiguity, the perpetrator and the victim and the character of transference and countertransference. The question of transference love as real is hypothetical of course – all feelings that arise within the transference are real in so much as they are expressions of personal desires and wishes seeking a resolution. This is particularly true of erotic feelings, because of their early relational, sensual and somatic resonance. So if we agree that transference defines what is real in the psychoanalytic situation, and relates to a "...particularly intense mode of relating induced... (by the power asymmetry of the psychoanalytic situation) ...so that (such feelings) necessarily harken back to our earliest conditions of loving, desiring and fantasy production" (Celenza, 2015), then we need to consider how once we have seduced our patients with our method, and rendered them vulnerable to their previously unknown or unspoken desires, we are to deal with such desires in a way that helps them get on with their lives.

The Words to Say IT

As psychoanalysts we are in the business of words because they signify experience. The talking cure, while rich in the intricacies of transference, enactments and play, is a relationship which ultimately relies on language – the intimate language created between analyst and patient – to restructure the ego. However, *sexuality and eroticism come alive precisely through a disruption of language in their ongoing elaboration. They come to be through the language of the senses and the body, which resonates with the affective echo of early intimacy, thus making it difficult to capture and articulate.* You have to feel it.

With Eros we encounter desire in all of its sensual and imaginary potentialities, so it is no wonder that it interrupts our ongoing narrative and thoughts, and speaks to us through our senses: we *feel it* first and then struggle with how to understand it and talk about it. The *critical* difference between psychoanalytic relationships and other relationships is that we do not *do, we talk*. Talking sex, no matter how descriptive the talk is not doing sex. Dimen and I part ways here, as I believe that there is a crucial distinction between talking and doing which is necessary for symbolization to take place. Talking keeps it in the imaginary realm, corporeality brings it into felt reality – perhaps in an attempt to achieve symbolization – but action moves it into the Reality of the Thing. With Eros there are bodies in question, and it is the body that ultimately articulates erotic desire in its sensual inscriptions. As psychoanalysts we are always pressed to find a way to translate intense emotions into language and words, and sex and erotic experience are perhaps the most intense.

So if the sexual disrupts and fragments language, in what language can we speak of sexual boundary violations? What is our discourse, Dimen asks, for something drenched in affect, and embedded in personal and group experience? Where we are at a loss for words and a narrative that captures and describes the event(s) and sequelae, for an articulated account that might initiate and actual dialogue with the one and the many rather than remain a cover story. Part of the problem, is that sex speaks through the body and its particular desires and enigmas, if there is any symbolization at all, it perhaps it occurs through the corporeality of the sexual, through the arousal (read intense affect) that pushes for action and consummation. As psychoanalysts we must make room for this through renunciation and containment.

What is the role of language here? This place where words fail and the intensity of the Thing takes over. In thinking of how to respond to her scandalized colleagues, Dimen broods: "Am I only to think, reflect, consider, ponder, contemplate? …I feel the impulse to correct, drain the affect from the words, to separate remonstration from a reasoned inquiry into history and dynamics... Of course, because thinking, reflecting, considering, pondering and contemplating *all drain affect out of experience,* (my italics) only to perhaps return it to experience in more modulated form through language." (2017, p. 145) Indeed, return it to experience through language in a more modulated form! Here we have what psychoanalysis, arguably, does best: it (re)turns intense, unmodulated affective experience to the experiencer in words. In the talking cure, it is language that helps to modulate internal states. Ours and our patients.

Perverse Cleansing: Promises, Seduction and Renunciation

Psychoanalysis as a discipline offers guidelines on technique and ethical practice, but it does not parse the intricacies of intimate negotiations for us.

Aside from the prohibition of thou shall not, few psychoanalysts take sexuality and Eros on directly as it is felt and embodied by the analyst and in the dyad. Dimen is among the few to wrestle with the knotty topics of sex, desire and the breaking of boundaries and essential promises in the psychoanalytic setting. She understood that, when our bodies are the register of another's communication, clarity is not always immediate or forthcoming – and we must be able to live with our discomfort, sometimes for long periods of time, before such powerful experiences can be processed and understood. In that space, language is likely to lose its hold on us and speak instead through sensorial and affective experience, captured in relationship to another and his/her evocation through us.

At such times sustaining a certain level of arousal can be analytically useful. When it comes to Eros, we must be willing to be *turned on* and find a way to understand our arousal and what it conveys about our patient within a self-contained space. And then, we must find a way to translate this experience and its potential meanings into words that initiate an authentic dialogue. It is impossible to do this without a seductive element, as it is an invitation to the other to talk and explore sexuality *a deux*, but with the promise that analytic boundaries will be maintained. Such a promise is precisely what is seductive in the analytic setting, as it makes it possible for patients to want out loud with us (Celenza, 2015). But ever since Eve's sharing of the proverbial apple with Adam, seduction is a dirty word, one that many analysts struggle with because it implicates them in the process of eliciting desire. One of those stained, impure words, Dimen might say. Yet, if seduction is built into the method, are we not speaking of some kind of perverse therapeutic system wherein we are in the omnipotent position of eliciting desire, shaping reality through the transference and restraining our own desire while utilizing it to "invite the emergence of unrestrained, and relatively undefended desires of the patient"?

There is a built-in equivocation in the psychoanalytic method: And it is the fact that although we acknowledge that we are first and foremost sexual beings, we expect that as analysts we can overcome our sexual nature. Be surgically removed from it, as Freud (1912) instructed. Sex, unless it remains theoretical makes psychoanalysts uncomfortable. Dimen knew that sexual bodies in their flesh make psychoanalysts uncomfortable, and in her writing she brought us into the carnal.

Yet we remain neutered by our theory, our technique, and the idealized historical transmission that Dimen alerts us to. Our cleansing remains As If, leaving only the rotten apples to figure out this dangerous territory.

While reminding us that psychoanalysis substitutes "the meeting of the minds for that of mucous membranes" generating potential space, Dimen engages Bion's (1962) notion of preconception,[3] where the taboo on sex serves as a fundamental 'preconception' and its violation fragments the institution of psychoanalysis. Further, she thinks that the alarms that sexual transgressions generate are in the realm of beta elements, where their unthinkable fragments show up as projective identifications – the whistle blower is made into the problem so that the container can be safeguarded. She views this as a "shared elemental refusal, – K in the service of protecting the container".

Dimen's use of language, and in particular, her metaphors and dialogue activate our senses, engaging and speaking to us in our 'bones and hearts' as well as our heads. To wit, her use of Mary Douglas's *Purity and Danger* (1966) a text Dimen introduced me to during a conversation about the dysregulation that accompanies sex and the erotic. Here, Dimen uses Douglas's thesis that life is inherently and culturally untidy and that this in itself is dysregulating, leading to the implementation of systems of order and classification that aim to restore homeostasis. Since rotten apples are routine Dimen tells us, our problem as a culture is how to restore purity and order. As long as there is order, a place for everything to be (re)stored before disorder hits, there is no danger to the group.

Every culture, including psychoanalysis, has ways to repair and cleanse the contamination caused by the transgression of its boundaries. These usually involve punishment rather than remediation, particularly when they involve sex. For Dimen this is the point: the fact that the proscription on sex between analyst and patient not only serves a therapeutic and clinical function, it also plays a powerful role in maintaining the life of psychoanalysis as an institution. Thus, sexual boundary violations contaminate not only the individuals involved and those close to them, but "the entire institutional order of psychoanalysis." When we throw out the rotten apple we are engaging in a purification ritual, one meant to keep the rest of us clean and separate us from the dirty and dangerous. The beauty of the dialogue between Dimen and Douglas's is that they both address the corporeality of the body and its dangers in ways that intersect and complement: Dimen via human desire and Douglas's through the body's form and its open orifices. Our (psychoanalytic) anxiety and discomfort with the body also shows up when a society is in trouble – as per Douglas – so that ideas about sexual danger mirror patterns of hierarchy found in the larger system. If purity is vital to the social acceptability of the group then an unstained reputation is crucial. Rotten apples out!

Much of Dimen's essay is devoted to creating a theoretical foundation for us so that we might be able to consider the social and begin to build a collective space for critical thinking as well as experiencing. An astute observer of the group as well as the individual, Dimen builds a bridge between the social construction of sexual boundary violations and personal experience. Here, she calls upon Goffman (1963) and his studies on spoiled identity and stigma. Still working across lines, stepping into the dirty and the clean, she describes Goffman's ideas on stigma as divided into two equal parts: the discredited – who represent stigma through their otherness, and the discreditable, the normals who pass and whose stigma is yet to be discerned or known. Dimen identifies stigma as a regulatory practice in the operation of power, and it is this latter function that applies most perniciously to psychoanalysis. Since, Goffman tells us, most people are discreditable, they live in fear of being found out and/or outed.

Dimen brings this insight into sharp relief when it comes to psychoanalysis and sexual boundary violations: the fear and anxiety of the group has to do with our own vulnerability to rot, to being discreditable and found out. Stigma is latent in everyone. This makes dissociation a necessary part of the process of dealing (or not) with the problem of sexual boundary violations. We know in the head but not in the bones as Dimen would say. I would add that what is known in the head can be modified by the power of the group. Cleansed so that purity can prevail.

But let us not forget that purity and pollution are a system – strange bedfellows they might be, but they travel together, in groups and individually. Dimen views the risk of stigma as a profound fault line in psychoanalysis because it generates feelings of hatred toward the discipline. Enter the need for idealization so that psychoanalysis and its fragile body can be loved and only loved; so that rot might not be discernible despite the questionable status of the container. Here Dimen is nodding to history, and to our profession's need to retain the elders of psychoanalysis, many of whom where transgressors themselves, in an idealized status that reifies the hierarchical structures involved in our group maintaining it stability and value to society.

Always working herself out of binaries and polarities, Dimen calls for a space where ambiguity can reside so that we can hold both our love and hate, for our patients, for our method, for ourselves. Those of us that have followed her writing know that ambiguity and ambivalence have always been central to her work. Holding the clean with the dirty, the good with the bad amounts to what she has previously and in another context called "a state of grace" (Dimen, 1999). A state of grace indeed, as perhaps in the garden of Eden and the proverbial bite of the apple that ushered sex and copulation, and ambivalence as a state of being. Indeed, Dimen's essay makes me think that perhaps Eden was always meant to hold us in such a "state of grace", a place where the good lives alongside the bad and the apples are shared.

Encircling Intimacy

Negotiating intimacy, including analytic intimacy requires being able to deal with our ambivalence on a regular basis. Are we in or are we out? What and who do we need to be and do to stay in? What makes us want to get out? The intimacy that analytic work requires is hard on both participants. For the analyst, it requires not only self-analysis and discipline, but also a container: a group, colleagues, supervision, theory – those things and people that support, nurture and validate us, helping us to entertain the fact that we may all be tempted by the dangers in our method as fellow potential transgressors. Potentially rotten one and all, we must engage collectively together and *not* with our patients.

Desire holds an inherent tension between having and wanting, fantasy and the corpo*reality* of bodies, satisfaction and misery, and the affective maelstrom involved. It is precisely the tension between pleasure and the inherent pain of wanting that powers the sexual and drives us *out* of our minds and *into* our bodies. So it is how we manage our own individual jouissance, our own wants, embodied and felt, and our own ability to negotiate this intimately with others, that determines how available we will be to engage with our patients' erotic experience and sexuality – *without acting out*. The analyst's act of renunciation, and his ability to mourn the loss of the Real, here serves as a potential bridge to symbolization: we hold back so the patient can move on. To this individual responsibility, Dimen adds the power of the group and its collective function as container for the loss, renunciation and affective dysregulation that our work requires.

What I am suggesting is the emotional counterpart to the critical ability to think and hold ambivalence that Dimen is writing about. Intimacy requires that we constantly assess where we are, what we feel and why we feel it in relation to another person. If we can successfully hold those "not me" parts of ourselves, the "dirty, impure" ones while at the same time being, or at least not losing sight of, our best selves while being with another, we are working within an intimate zone: one that allows both parties to experience affective honesty and authenticity in all areas. In this space it is possible to acknowledge the sexuality of both parties, without having to act on it. Intimacy entails the ability of holding a mutual space where the other is recognized, felt, and known without an impingement, demand or violation of their subjectivity. Transgressions, if or when they occur must be acknowledged, articulated and reflected upon individually, interpersonally, and most importantly interpersonally.

Dimen's focus on the group as container thus highlights its function as reflective surface; where our 'not me's', our bad and dirty self states are exposed and held by the many, opening up the opportunity for self/other reflection. Psychoanalysis is hard work, and intimacy is even harder. Sexual boundary violations collapse the Symbolic into the Real, by stripping the signifier of meaning, and reducing it to a thing in itself, destroying thought and foreclosing the ability for full object use. In fact, when we enact being the actual object of desire for our patients we collude with them in the disavowal of their desire. This is, without question, what Dimen hoped we would understand and take heed of.

Theoretically psychoanalysis is equipped to deal with sexuality (although both Dimen and I are arguing that in reality it is not) yet within the intimacy that can exist in the analysts' office, our theoretical equipment often fails. Because Eros speaks to us by engaging the body and tantalizing the mind it disrupts reason by engaging us sensually with the language and affect of early intimacy. Our body and our senses carry the traces of that early intimacy, as well as a profusion of representations of self and other as engageable in specific and particular ways. Eros makes its presence ***felt*** in the analytic situation: intensely, passionately even, because it implores for consummation where it cannot. As an over-affectation, erotic experience speaks through the senses and the body in an effort to achieve symbolization: *not through consummation but through object use. And as analysts we are the potential object of use*. Experiencing the others' sexuality- is a form of thinking and a pathway to signification.

All of Us Fallen Apples – Rot or Not

As a method that aims to understand the human condition, psychoanalysis appeals to many who are interpersonally wounded and are seeking a way to re-negotiate relationships. This applies to both patients *and* analysts. Ours is a field filled with many who struggle to negotiate intimacy in their own lives and find it in their work: One-way intimacy which keeps the analyst safe while the patient is vulnerable. A *perversion* of intimacy, which I think, is our dirty little secret. Some of the bacteria that Dimen speaks of. The kind that grows under the conditions she elaborates.

As analysts **we** individually establish the boundaries that demarcate the space as safe enough for our patients to unfold and be in. The way that we negotiate intimacy helps to define those boundaries and create a container (the way I hold myself, the way I hold the space and the way I hold you) from the outset. Psychoanalytic space turns perverse when there is an effort to create the illusion of the *self's mastery over its instincts*. In an effort to manifest the immateriality of psychic life, perversion gives sexuality a permanent and locatable character. It thus creates a false mastery, based on a sense of omnipotence that limits behavior and ensnares desire. In effect, perversions' are attempts to provide very tight and bound containers for desire, and many negotiate intimacy in this way.

There is a chemical interaction between the container and what it contains. To attempt to add disinfectant here is hazardous. It will engender a split between those that do and those that don't, between the discredited and the discreditable, between the pure and the stained, not to mention foster the need for group secrecy, and dissociation. It will collapse the space that intimacy requires on its way to full object use.

There is no "pure" container for sexuality, no person no thing, no group. This is a most dangerous method we work in. Psychoanalysis *is* a sexual field. It attempts to work with sexuality with words when sexuality cries out for action. So perhaps what requires our collective thought is the fact that *sex and sexuality dysregulates us, all of us*. That no amount of support, whether from a primary intimate relationship, or from other relationships can inoculate us to such dysregulation, and that *it is our own individual ability to navigate such dysregulation and negotiate intimacy which determines our boundaries and their permeability.* It determines our anxiety over being discovered, stigmatized by the nature of our over-affectation and our attempts to contain and metabolize it without injuring the patient.

Is the assumption that we can contain our sexual instincts and impulses in a situation that aims to intensify them, in and of itself perverse? Yes! I hear Dimen answering, and indeed, she might add that since we are all perverse when it comes to the sexual (ala LaPlanche) it behooves us to examine the container on an ongoing basis as a group.

What if sexuality and sex will necessarily create leaks in any container, and as analysts we must be able to work with the leaks and the uncertainty and potential mess they create?

What if some will necessarily fall, like Adam to Eve's inviting apple?

What if we were always meant to work in purgatory and not paradise?

Can we play in that space without turning the play perverse?

Can we live and navigate within the "state of grace" that Dimen is arguing for?

Notes

1 Dimen was particularly proud of this essay. She presented it as part of a panel for the International Association for Relational Psychoanalysis and Psychotherapy, in Toronto 2015, where I was honored to discuss it. In January of 2016, it was read by Levin and discussed by Saketopoulou and Gabbard at the meetings of the American Psychoanalytic Association, and subsequently published in their journal. In 2017, I read and discussed it, along with Ann Pellegrini at NYU.

2 We are haunted as much by what is not said (silence) as by what is done (Dimen, 2016).

3 "Dimen defines preconception as an unstatable expectation of something not yet formed, neither cognized nor cognizable, a placeholder for the possibility psychoanalysis potentiates".

References

Bion, W.R. (1962). *Learning from Experience.* London: Karnac Books, 1984.

Celenza, A. (2015) *Lessons On or About the Couch: What Sexual Boundary Transgressions Can Teach Us About Everyday Practice.* Paper presented At the 2015 IARPP conference, Toronto, Canada, June 28, 2015.

Celenza, A. (2007). *Sexual Boundary Violations: Therapeutic, Supervisory, Academic Contexts.* Lanham, MD: Aronson.

Dimen, M. (1999) In the Zone of Ambivalence: A Feminist Journal of Competition. In, *Sexuality, Intimacy Power*, New York: Routledge, pp.223–256.

Dimen, M. (2011) *Lapsus Linguae, Or a Slip of the Tongue? A Sexual Violation in an Analytic Treatment And Its Personal And Theoretical Aftermath.* Contemporary Psychoanalysis, Vol. 47, No. 1.

Dimen, M. (2017a) Eight topics: A conversation on sexual boundary violations between Charles Amrhein and Muriel Dimen. *Psychoanalytic Psychology*, Vol. 34, No. 2, Apr 2017, 169–174.

Dimen, M. (2017b) Ghosts and the Sexual Boundary Violation – The Limits of an Idea. In A. Harris, M. Kalb, & S. Klebanoff, *Demons in the Consulting Room: Echoes of Genocide, Slavery, and Extreme Trauma in Psychoanalytic Practice*, Oxon: Routledge, Ch. 7, p.141–147.

Freud, S. (1912) Recommendations for Physicians on the Psycho-Analytic Method of Treatment. In *Collected Papers*, Vol. II, Ed., (1948), pp.323–333.

Douglas, M. (1966). *Purity and Danger: An Analysis of Concepts of Pollution and Taboo.* London: Penguin Books.

Gabbard, G.O., Ed. (1989). *Sexual Exploitation in Professional Relationships.* Washington, DC: American Psychiatric Press.

Goffman, E. (1963). *Stigma: Notes on the Management of Spoiled Identity.* Englewood Cliffs, NJ: Prentice-Hall.

No Sex, Please. We're Psychoanalysts*

Ann Pellegrini

Muriel Dimen's "Rotten Apples and Ambivalence: Sexual Boundary Violations through a Psychocultural Lens" (2017) was, and remains, a call to the psychoanalytic collective to listen and respond beyond defensiveness. She even suggests that we all already *are* responding to the specter of sexual boundary violations. One of these responses is to fall mute, an "impulse to silence" that does not quiet the problem, but does leave it "unmentalizable" (Dimen 2017, 362). She prods and challenges us to respond differently. "Thinking socially can partner with thinking psychically," Dimen writes (2017, 363), suggesting that responding differently will involve tracking the interimplication of the psychic and the social. This was certainly one of her great gifts: to draw across the social and the psychological, to draw *on* social and psychological theories, as a way to think between the group and individual. She was in many regards herself an in-between, coming to psychoanalysis as an outsider: an anthropologist, a woman, a feminist, whistle-blower.

Although she did eventually become a psychoanalytic insider, Dimen never ceased to think with the outside, and in multiple ways. In "Rotten Apples," she turns to resources provided by non-analytic theories of the social, specifically to anthropologist Mary Douglas's *Purity and Danger* (1966) and sociologist Erving Goffman's study of *Stigma* (1963), in order to explore psychoanalysis as "an institution that, like any other social unit, has a structure, history, rules, and beliefs" (Dimen 2017, 361). Using critical vistas from *outside* psychoanalysis, she aims to understand the internal functioning *of* psychoanalysis. She also invites us to think outside in, to explore, that is, how the outside comes inside and maybe even provides the sense of having—or being?—an inside, a closed and boundaried self at all. If sexual boundary violations bring the outside in, as she argues, it is because the outside is always already in: inside the consulting room, inside each of us.[1] The boundaried selves we imagine ourselves to be are always threatened with collapse: any body's multiple openings to the world, ports for intake and outtake, betray (and offer) as much. Betrayal and offering: bad news and good news at once.

DOI: 10.4324/9781003335252-36

Dimen's double status, inside and outside the institution, surely contributed to her ability—her audacity—to blow the whistle (Dimen 2017, 362; Dimen 2011, 69). As someone who has also come to psychoanalysis from the academic outside, in the rest of this essay I turn to the resources of one of my interdisciplinary homes—queer theory—to explore the relationship between knowing (what and how we know) and no-ing (what we say no to). In particular, I want to ask what conceptual and clinical resources Michel Foucault's path-breaking, counter-intuitive, and historically grounded arguments about the way sex gets put into discourse—and put into bodies—as "the" secret of secrets might offer to psychoanalysis.

There is a certain irony, if not scandal, in suggesting that Foucault might be a resource to psychoanalysis. He was a profound critic of psychoanalysis, psychiatry, and other psychological disciplines. The term "discipline" is not idly made. Foucault urged us to take this term seriously; it even appears in the title of one of his most famous books, the 1975 study *Discipline and Punish: The Birth of the Prison*. We divide forms of knowledge into academic disciplines. We also use the term "discipline" to refer to the cultivation of desired habits and styles of life such that they come to feel like second nature: as in self-discipline. Related to this is discipline in the sense of correction or punishment directed at "delinquencies" of various sorts (Foucault 1975). Foucault saw the psysciences as crucial technologies through which "disciplinary power" is exerted (Foucault 1976). Disciplinary power refers to the array of institutional and cultural practices that have produced individuals *as* individuals, investing them with particular beliefs about and commitments to their inner selves, the core of their beings. Disciplinary power does not do its work on pre-existing individuals; it is rather the method through which the experience of being a particular kind of individual is solicited and takes shape. I'll come back to this solicitation momentarily.

Keep in mind here that disciplines are not primarily methods of correction or punishment, though they are also that. They are, rather, fundamentally *productive*: methods of power that organize behavior, churning, in some instances, acts into identity. "The sodomite had been a temporary aberration," Foucault writes, "the homosexual was…a species" (1976, 43). As such, disciplines normalize individuals, and generate a sense of bounded interiority. In western modernity, Foucault argues, this sense of interiority has been embedded, "produced," specifically by discourses of sexuality and by the embodied and embodying practices that teach us that "sex" is at our core. Whether conceived as natural force to be regulated or as life source to be de-repressed and liberated, sex-as-truth functions, in both instances, as a "ruse of power," convincing us that nothing less than our future is at stake. In the first volume of his *History of Sexuality* Foucault offers a pressing criticism of the historical, analytical, and political short-comings of the "repressive hypothesis." He concedes that some sexual acts and actors have indeed been repressed, although there is important historical and cultural variation as to which acts and which actors have been repressed. Nevertheless, Foucault is arguing against the habit of mind that sees the relationship between sex and power as fundamentally negative. This model of power and of power's relation to sex is historically inaccurate, he counters, not because sex has not been repressed, but because the argument of its repression, what Foucault called the "repressive hypothesis" (1976), overlooks the ways sex has also been given a lot of airtime *as long as certain conditions are met for its air rights.* The repressive hypothesis carries forward an understanding of power on the model of law. Power, according to this line of thinking, is a centralized possession that operates top-down in the form of censorship, prohibition, nay-saying of all kinds. This view of the matter makes repression out to be the defining feature of the relationship between power and sex. When it comes to sex, Power (and why not capitalize this kind of totalizing Power) says N-O. Seeing power as essentially negative and repressive in turn generates a politics focused on confronting power's "no" with a revolutionary "yes," in which we turn the tables, flip our middle fingers, or maybe even flip the couch—as Dimen so delightfully did in the consulting room of the infamous Dr. O (Dimen 2011, 52).

Although he is sometimes described as a theorist of quote unquote "sexuality," Foucault was not. He was interested in sex and in sexuality not as positivities, concrete and discoverable "truths" of the self, but as discursive productions with profoundly material effects. The original French title of Volume I of *History of Sexuality* better gets at his argument for the way discourses of "sex" and "sexuality" conduct power and incite subjects to know themselves: *La Volonté de savoir*, usually translated as "the will to knowledge." An interest in the relation between power and knowledge threads throughout his books, interviews, and posthumously published lectures.

Foucault presents psychoanalysis as a paradigmatic secular site (a shift from "soul" to "psyche") for the disciplinary production of modern sexuality: we no longer confess our sins to God's intermediary; instead, we spill out our secrets to ears for hire. And there is always more to say; the notion of *unconscious* sexual repression turns the process of uncovering sex-as-truth into the interminability of the analytic process. Even if you say everything you know, you can't possibly know everything about your unconscious, and hence there's always more to reveal, to confess, to share. Moreover, sex becomes a super conductor, gathering into its orbit things that need not go together: "the notion of 'sex' made it possible to group together, in an artificial unity, anatomical elements, biological functions, conducts, sensations, and pleasures, and it enabled one to make use of this fictitious unity as a causal principle, an omnipresent meaning, a secret to be discovered elsewhere" (Foucault 1976, 154–55). The truth is out there, says agent Mulder; the truth is in there, aver the vast new agencies of the human sciences.

The spilling of secrets, the collecting of secrets, their exchange, and their shared, if also asymmetrical, examination: none of this takes place under the sign of coercion. Instead—and this is one of Foucault's profound prompts for thinking and re-thinking politics—we are willingly conscripted into our ongoing subjectivation and do so in the name of freedom and liberation (Jakobsen 2005). Not only that, to the pairing power-knowledge he adds a crucial third term: *pleasure* and the many solicitations to talking about sex in the consulting room and elsewhere:

> The pleasure that comes of exercising a power that questions, monitors, watches, spies, searches out, palpates, brings to light; and on the other hand, the pleasure that kindles at having to evade this power, flee from it, fool it, or travesty it. The power that lets itself be invaded by the pleasure it is pursuing; and opposite it, power asserting itself in the pleasure of showing off, scandalizing, or resisting. Capture and seduction, confrontation and mutual reinforcement: parents and children, adults and adolescents, educator and students, doctors and patients, the psychiatrist with his hysterics and his perverts, all have played this game continually since the nineteenth century. These attractions, these evasions, these circular incitements have traced around bodies and sexes not boundaries to be crossed but *perpetual spirals of power and pleasure.* (1976, 45; italics in original)

The discourse of sexuality materializes in bodies and in the spaces occupied by them—by *us*. Foucault specifically discusses the new architecture of the nineteenth-century home (1976, 46), which took root first among the bourgeoisie but would expand to working class homes as well: bedrooms segregated by sex (sons in one room, daughters in another) and by generation (parents' and children's bedrooms strictly segregated, the better to set the parents' sex off from view behind another shut door). Far from shutting out primal scenes, this spatial segregation primed the pump: just what is going on behind that closed door?

The physical arrangements of the consulting room have their incitements, too. The treatment choreographs bodily experience and invites excitement and anxiety: from the literal spacing between couch and chair, the angles of vision open and closed, to the amount and placement of lights (it is a fine line between interrogation and seduction), to the door whose closing and opening convert space into time (tick tock, tick tock, time's up for today, and then the rush to the doorknob). Psychoanalytic treatments are "architected" to promote a strange kind of seductive intimacy (Saketopoulou 2021). But architecture is more than metaphor; in the consulting room, the arrangements of couch and chair literally *stage* intimacy. And yet, despite—or because of?—the fact that psychoanalysis is organized to kindle intimacy and reopen enigma, thus, reawakening the "infantile sexual" (Laplanche, 1987), psychoanalysis and psychoanalytic institutes are continually taken by surprise whenever sexual boundary violations happen. This surprise is also a group anxiety (the worry that "our" institute or psychoanalysis in general will be discredited by this violation) and by individual worries (what does this say about me?). Dimen's "Rotten Apples" sit precisely on this precipice between the inner and the outer; no sex is allowed, but sexuality is incited. This is the Foucauldian bull's-eye.

Dimen certainly knew Foucault's *History of Sexuality*. But he is not an interlocutor for "Rotten Apples." She makes nimble use of Goffman's *Stigma* (1963), to dramatize "the routine dissociation that is broken through when news of a sexual boundary violation breaks or when the phenomenon itself breaks into conversation" (Dimen 2017, 370). The key distinction she is mining in Goffman's work is between the *discredited person or persons*, whose stigma as other is supposedly known/knowable at a glance, and the *discreditable*, those "passing" subjects who are able, mostly, to cover up their stigmatizing otherness. Goffman argues that the degree of worry and self-consciousness is magnified by intimacy. That is, we feel most at risk of exposure the closer we are to someone. What do they know about me now and what would they think about me, if they knew? Do I disclose? If so, when? How much? Although there are obvious exceptions to this, in general we do not have the same degree of self-consciousness in interactions with strangers. The closed door of the consulting room opens the possibility of intimacies, yes, and thus also the risk of discrediting disclosure—on couch and chair. But it also overflows the bounds of the consulting room. Here it might be helpful to consider the relation and difference between discreditability and *discretion*. The latter is a crucial promise we make to patients: what is said in the consulting room stays in the consulting room, sorta. After all, we do talk with supervisors and present anonymized versions of our patients to colleagues. But discretion and its undersides (gossip? anxiety? the sense of my secret and yours?) electrify any analytic institute, in which one person's training analyst is another's supervisor, who was analyzed by so-and-so, who may have been seated next to you at the lecture you attended last night.

An analyst's unvoiced terror of being "outed" for her own "sins" may be stirred up by the revelation, or just the gossiped about conjecture, that a colleague, psychically often a sibling substitute, with whom she identifies has committed a "sexual boundary violation." Purging the offender—the rotten apple—from the community intends to purify the barrel, Dimen argues, but it also aims to purify the remaining individual apples whose enduring discrediting "secret" or "secrets" are overshadowed by the attention given to the bigger transgression. Still, Dimen highlights, this does not diminish the fact that even as the rotten apple is tossed, the "hot potato" of the anxiety of discreditability remains. I am reminded here that the French term for potato is *pomme de terre*, literally: apple of the earth, with all the subterranean and, even, shitty associations of earthiness. The apple come to earth also suggests the gravitational pull of shared and culturally "hot" knowledge. Cue Eve's curiosity and the fall of and into flesh. Cue also perpetual spirals of power and pleasure.

Still, there is forbidden knowledge and there is forbidden knowledge: "Everyone knows that sexual boundary violations occur. But this knowledge is somehow compartmentalized and one-dimensionalized. It is a truth in the head, not in bones and hearts," Dimen writes (2017, 365). This inability or refusal to "know" in the bones and hearts makes sense; it is connected to a longstanding disconnect in western culture between mind and flesh, a splitting elevated as divine principle in much western philosophy and Christian theology. This splitting gets played out in the dyad; the patient has a body; I have her speech; I am speech, all in mind, nothing enfleshed. I am here following the arc of Saketopoulou's argument (2021) about the pervasive and, possibly, defensive, de-sexualization of the erotic in clinical literature and discussions of erotic counter-transference. Saketopoulou flags how hard it is for analysts to think about, let alone talk or write about, how their bodies respond to their patient's bodies, to their patients' words, to their flesh made words. It is not simply that talk about sex can be very, very sexy. Good talk—about anything—can prick up desire in excess of the words or topic per se.

Which sends me back to French. Language exceeds the will to use it, to control it, to communicate ourselves and our intentions through it. That's the risk; that is also the pleasure of intercourse. I am referring here to what we do with words and what words do with us. I am beside myself in language. Is this the moment to peel back the hilarious onion skin of intertexts Dimen invokes when she accepts the charge of bringing the plague? She references a line that Freud is famously said to have uttered when he "arrived in New York harbor" for his one and only trip to America, and—with Jung at his side—"they caught their first glimpse of the famous statue illuminating the universe, *'They don't realize we're bringing them the plague'*" (Lacan 1955, 116; italics added). The story is passed to us by Lacan in an essay announcing "the meaning of the return to Freud." "I have it from Jung's own mouth," Lacan says (1955, 116). Indeed. I roar at the sly way Dimen thus returns us to the many slips of the tongue that disturb the scene of psychoanalysis, underscoring the impurity ever in our midst: "like our founder, I bring you the plague" (2017, 367).

Let me dare my own return to Freud, specifically to the preface of his "Fragment of an Analysis of a Case of Hysteria" (1905), where he anticipates the objections of "medical readers," who will be scandalized by the frank ways he talked about sex with his young female patient, "Dora." The best way to talk about such things, he says is to be "dry and direct" and to avoid the "prurience" that shades such subjects in "'society,'" a term he ironizes with scare quotes (1905, 48). Curiously, his example of how to do sexual straight-talking is, "*J'appelle un chat un chat*" (1905, 48; italics in original). Literally: "I call a cat a cat," but sometimes a pussy cat is not just a pussy cat. Whether we see this as ultimate Freudian slip, or a case of the literary Freud besting Freud the man of science, this punning eruption of French into the German text doesn't just bust the linguistic frame; it also exposes as fantasy the claim that talk about sex could ever be dry, direct, easily contained.[2] In both "Rotten Apples," Dimen points out that "straightforward" talk about sexual boundary violation isn't exactly welcome either. Where sex talk is concerned, it's complicated.

Alright already, but with my Foucauldian hat back on, I want to ask, why sex? Adam Phillips describes psychoanalysis as "what two people can say to each other if they agree not to have sex." Dimen quotes him in her essay (2017, 364), though she, unlike Phillips, doesn't downplay "the nuttiness of a sexual field defined by a ban on sex" (2017, 372). Condensed in Phillips' seductive *bon mots* is a positive/prescriptive and negative/proscriptive version of the fundamental rule of psychoanalysis. The prescription: for the patient, say whatever comes into your mind without censor; for the analyst, listen openly without pre-determining what you are listening for. But this to-do list is undergirded by a fundamental *pro*scription: no sex. The command to the impossible (free associate) is conditioned by another command to the impossible (no sex). At minimum, the frequency of the violation of the no sex rule, and from the earliest days of psychoanalysis (Levine 2010, Blechner 2014), suggests its impossibility. This does not, however, disqualify it is an ideal any more than the impossibility of free association means we should give up failing at it. And fail we will. But there is so much to be made out of failure.

Nevertheless, why is sex the privileged thing analysts must not do with their patients (Pellegrini 2021)? Is this due to something inherent in sex or is it rather produced through the cultural and psychic meanings loaded upon sexual relations, the way sex comes to stand in for a host of other scary, pleasurable, life-threatening, and life-preserving things people already do or might do with each other? It may well be that psychoanalysis poses Phillips's question "what two people can say to each other if they agree not to have sex." But what about all the other precious and preciously intimate things analysts agree not to do with their patients? Do analysts—should analysts—have dinner with a patient? Write *with* a patient, and not just *about* one? What links the nos, or delinks the yeses, to any of these questions from the great big NO—and KNOW—demanded of sex?

I worry how to even ask these questions without setting in motion an expanding moral panic. Before, we policed sex between analyst and patient (and between analyst and former patient). Are we now to police every possible interaction between patients and analysts, current and former, in every possible context,[3] stamping out "rogue interpretive moments" (Bass 2007, 7)?

That is not my aim. Certainly, questions concerning the expandability and negotiability of the frame and just how far the analyst's "acts of freedom" (Symington 1983) may properly go are not new to psychoanalysis. But I worry that the focus on sex as the act of acts analysts and patients (current and former) must not do with each other preserves sex as "the secret" to be ferreted out. The fixation on sex may also block thinking and talking about the other lively, sensuous, embodied intimacies that the analytic dyad generates in the room and enables outside it, as well. To be clear: I neither wish to treat those "other" intimacies as somehow "sex equivalents" (it's just like sex, oh no!), nor am I making an argument about sublimation (it's sex transformed, hooray!). Nor am I implying that the prohibition to sexual relations should be lifted. Rather, I want to take these other intimacies, which we feel deep in bones and heart, very seriously as life-sustaining, pleasure-giving intimacies, in a way that the dominant culture of marital sexuality (straight and gay) tends not to.[4]

To the frustration of many readers, and to the delight of many others, Foucault refuses to offer blueprints, to answer the question: now what? That is, having offered an expansive and counter-intuitive conception of the way power works, he does not tell us how we might get elsewhere or become otherwise in relation to power. Instead, he ends *The History of Sexuality* with an enigmatic call to the future: "perhaps, in a different economy of bodies and pleasures, people will no longer quite understand how the ruses of sexuality, and the power that sustains its organization, were able to subject us to that austere monarchy of sex, so that we became dedicated to the endless task of forcing its secret, of exacting the truest of confessions from a shadow" (1976, 159). Foucault's criticisms of psychoanalysis and of the way it turned sex into discourse notwithstanding, I am myself not ready to give up talking or thinking about sex. Nor could I. Exactly, says Foucault, and therein lies the rub. But can we rub the words otherwise—including the words said and not-said in psychoanalysis—to move us toward "a different economy of bodies and pleasures"? Here it seems to me that we need to put some air between sex as "the secret" and sex (the sexual) as "enigma." This air may well be dense with unmetabolized feeling, with the bodily ooze of categories that will not stay put, and words that hit and miss their mark time and again. Including words like "sex," "sexuality," "my body," and "yours." I'm a queer theorist; I can't think without sex. Sometimes I can't think because of it.

Call me conflicted or call me greedy, but I want my Freud and I want my Foucault, too. One of the many lessons I have learned from Muriel Dimen is that I don't have to choose. Embrace your ambivalence, she tells us in an essay that has the word "ambivalence" in its title and whose concluding subsection is entitled "Hatred, Idealization, Ambivalence" (2017, 371). Certainly, our ambivalence is always already embracing us! Psychoanalysis is richer for its communications with outsider theories. It was once itself an outsider theory that brought the plague. Maybe it still can.

Notes

* I wrote and "talked" the first version of this essay for an April 2017 forum on Muriel Dimen's "Rotten Apples and Ambivalence," which was hosted by NYU's Postdoctoral Program in Psychotherapy and Psychoanalysis. I was lucky to be in conversation that night with Velleda Ceccoli, and I'm grateful to Stephen Hartman for the chance to reprise my remarks in written form for this volume. Avgi Saketopoulou carefully read and commented on this essay; it's far the better for her critical attentions.

1 Dimen was here thinking about social contents, which might well take the form of fantasies, but are in any case representable. But, with Laplanche we could also consider another sense in which the outside comes into and, even, becomes an inside: through the intervention of the other and their infantile sexual, which gets under the psychophysiological skin like a "splinter" (Laplanche 1992, 209). This content-less transmission, which Laplanche somewhat unhelpfully called an "enigmatic message," thereby implying some positive content (a "message") to be translated (Scarfone 2019), generates the drive to respond to and interpret the alien intrusions of the parental other. These intrusions are doubly alien: they come from another into the infant, but they are also alien to the consciousness of the adult whose unconscious "infantile sexual" (Laplanche 1987) parasites communications with the child.

2 For a related discussion of this French turn, *See* Gallop (1985, 208–209).

3 This expanding "line of penetration" (Foucault 1976), the way that "sex" and worries over it, move into spaces far removed from it to saturate and manage those spaces, too, was even among Foucault's worries about the productive power of sex-as-discourse.

4 In a 1981 interview on "The Social Triumph of the Sexual Will," Foucault poignantly calls for an expanded "relational fabric." "In effect," he says, "we live in a legal, social, and institutional world where the only relations possible are extremely few, extremely simplified, and extremely poor. There is, of course, the relation of marriage, and the relations of family, but how many other relations should exist…!" A page later, he continues, "institutions make insufficient and necessarily rare all relations that one could have with someone else and could be intense, rich—even if they were provisional—even and especially if they took place outside the frame of marriage" (1981, 158–159).

Works Cited

Bass, A. (2007). When the Frame Doesn't Fit the Picture. *Psychoanalytic Dialogues* 17:1–27.

Blechner, M. (2014). Dissociation among Psychoanalysts about Sexual Boundary Violations. *Contemporary Psychoanalysis* 50:23–33.

Dimen, M. (2011). *Lapsus Linguae*, or A Slip of the Tongue? A Sexual Violation in an Analytic Treatment and Its Personal and Theoretical Aftermath. *Contemporary Psychoanalysis* 47:35–79.

Dimen, M. (2017). Rotten Apples and Ambivalence: Sexual Boundary Violations through a Psychocultural Lens. *Journal of the American Psychoanalytic Association* 64:361–373.

Douglas, M. (1966). *Purity and Danger: An Analysis of Concepts of Purity and Taboo.* London: Penguin Books.

Foucault, M. (1975). *Discipline and Punish: The Birth of the Prison*, trans. Alan Sheridan. New York: Vintage, 1979.

Foucault, M. (1976). *The History of Sexuality*, Volume I: *An Introduction*, trans. Robert Hurley. New York: Vintage, 1990.

Foucault, M. (1981). The Social Triumph of the Sexual Will. In: *Ethics: Subjectivity and Truth*, ed. Paul Rabinow. New York: The New Press, 1997.

Freud, S. (1905 [1901]). Fragment of an Analysis of a Case of Hysteria. *Standard Edition* 7:3–122.

Gallop, J. (1985). Keys to Dora. In: *In Dora's Case: Freud, Hysteria, Feminism*, ed. Charles Bernheimer and Claire Kahane. London: Virago.

Goffman, E. (1963). *Stigma: Notes on the Management of Spoiled Identity*. Englewood Cliffs, NJ: Prentice-Hall.

Jakobsen, J.R. (2005). Sex + Freedom = Regulation: Why? *Social Text* 84–85:285–308.

Lacan, J. (1955). The Freudian thing, or the meaning of the return to Freud in psychoanalysis. In: Écrits: A Selection, trans. Alan Sheridan. New York: W.W. Norton, 1977.

Laplanche, J. (1987). *New Foundations for Psychoanalysis*, ed. Jonathan House. New York, Unconscious in Translation, 2016.

Laplanche, J. (1992). Masochism and the General Theory of Seduction. In: *Essays on Otherness*, ed. John Fletcher. London: Routledge, 1999.

Levine, H. (2010). Sexual Boundary Violations: A Psychoanalytic Perspective. *British Journal of Psychotherapy* 26:50–63.

Pellegrini, A. (2021). From no to know: Charting the "Space Between." In: *Social Aspects of Sexual Boundary Trouble in Psychoanalysis: Responses to the Work of Muriel Dimen*, ed. Charles Levin. London and New York: Routledge.

Saketopoulou, A. (2021). Does sexuality have anything to do with sexual boundary violations? In: *Social Aspects of Sexual Boundary Trouble in Psychoanalysis: Responses to the Work of Muriel Dimen*, ed. Charles Levin. London and New York: Routledge.

Scarfone, D. (2019). The feminine, the analyst and the child theorist. *The International Journal of Psychoanalysis* 100:567–575.

Symington, N. (1983). The Analyst's Act of Freedom and Agent of Therapeutic Change. *International Review of Psychoanalysis* 10:283–291.

Project Six

Of Ghosts and Groups

Project Six

Editor's Note

Stephen Hartman

Muse

Dimen, M. (2015). Ghosts and the sexual boundary violation: The limits of an idea. Unpublished manuscript.

Dimen's unpublished manuscript, *Ghosts and the Sexual Boundary Violation* (2015), is one of her most intimate papers. It is also one of her most raw. At once private and public, the paper illustrates Dimen's lifelong quest to theorize socially from personal data. In this paper, she takes up the experience of outing herself the "victim" of a sexual boundary violation among colleagues. She documents how the experience haunted her before and after going public. In the act of writing about "the unspeakable crime of sexual boundary violation", as in *Surviving Sexual Contradictions* (1986), Dimen fears being *ghosted* by her colleagues as whistleblowers often are. She describes the isolation felt by the survivor, and allows herself to voice anger, disappointment, and confusion. At the same time, she licks her wounds and redoubles her convictions to offer an impassioned plea for repair embracing ambivalence and its transformational value.

Readers

Many psychoanalytic authors vet early drafts of their papers in writing groups. Often these groups become home base even after careers evolve, paths diverge, and groups morph. At times, groups fray. Even when they do, the sound of the group's influence echoes and reverberates in writers' internal monologues. Dimen found herself constantly in conversation with *Muriel* who she experienced herself to be in and for the many groups that nurtured (and sometimes frustrated) her. She brought this mode of self-scrutiny to the writing groups that she led. And, aware how painful this process of finding oneself in relation to the group can be, and how challenging it can be to juggle the frictions and frissons of group process given authors' vulnerability to criticism, Dimen guided her much beloved writing groups with the proviso that group members were to help their colleagues reach their destination, wherever that may be, rather than offer critique.

DOI: 10.4324/9781003335252-38

She describes this method with great care in her introduction to *With Culture in Mind* (2006), a collection of short essays on allied topics produced by a writing group that Dimen led for several years. I was fortunate to learn and grow in the group's strong embrace.

Nowadays, I cherish being part of a writing group known among its members as LOC 148 (a reference to a fragment of graffiti that is the backdrop for a group portrait in Buenos Aires). I turned to my writing group for this reading and writing experiment. We are accustomed to helping our comrades develop their work but, prior to this experiment, we had never collaborated on a group text. Some of us had very close personal relationships with Dimen; others knew her as a teacher and scholar. Part of our task was to navigate different qualities of intimacy in the effort to find a collective voice.

Form

While writing groups often present together on panels at conferences, and sometimes produce publications that feature individual members' work, writing groups rarely if ever write collaboratively as a group. For this project, LOC 148 read Dimen's unpublished text out loud as a group. We then spent several meetings trying to decide how to best write about the essay (which is a meditation on group dynamics as much as it is an introspective anatomy of writing; it charts the culture of "the group" as much as it is a story about the ghostliness of a boundary violation). We decided to reread the text and transcribe every session interweaving the original text and our discussion. The edited "roundtable" would be our finished project.

Easier said than done. It took almost a year for the group to live with Dimen's paper. To edit can quickly become a form of ghosting all its own, and we struggled to balance homage and critique against the backdrop of vulnerability and boundary violation. Hundreds of pages of transcript later, and many meaningful conversations about what it means to write as a group later, we offer this result.

Unlike the other projects in this book, *Ghosts and the Sexual Boundary Violation* was never published. Perhaps because it is such a raw text? Perhaps because ambivalence acquires many shades over time? As I mentioned earlier, Dimen wanted this text to be published in this collection even without sufficient time gone by for her to revise and reconsider (as she often did, copiously crafting her essays in multiple drafts). Given the task of imagining how Dimen might have lived with this text over time, it seemed necessary to LOC 148 to hold Dimen near even as she was painfully absent. Much as Dimen at times seems to be a ghost haunting Muriel in the text, she was as much a spectral writer of our text as we were uncanny readers of hers. Hence, the decision to join Dimen's text and our own. We make this ambivalent gesture to our process with deep admiration for the risks Dimen took to inscribe this deeply personal text with a generative admixture of sorrow and love.

Bios

Francisco González, M.D. is a Personal and Supervising Analyst, Community Psychoanalysis Supervising Analyst, and faculty at the Psychoanalytic Institute of Northern California (PINC) where he is also co-director of the Community Psychoanalysis Track. He practices privately in San Francisco and Oakland, and publicly at Instituto Familiar de la Raza in San Francisco.

Orna Guralnik, Psy.D. is a clinical psychologist and psychoanalyst who serves on the faculty of NYU PostDoc, National Institute for the Psychotherapies, the Stephen Mitchel Center, and the editorial boards of *Psychoanalytic Dialogues* and *Studies in Gender & Sexuality.* Her writing centers on the intersection of psychoanalysis, dissociation, and cultural studies. She co-founded the Center for the Study of Dissociation and Depersonalization at the Mount Sinai Medical School and is a graduate of NYU PostDoc's analytic program. She has completed the filming of four seasons of the Docu-series *Couples Therapy*, airing on Showtime.

Stephen Hartman, Ph.D., is a joint editor-in-chief of *Psychoanalytic Dialogues* and formerly editor of *Studies in Gender and Sexuality.* He teaches at the Psychoanalytic Institute of Northern California and at NYU Postdoc in the relational track. His writing on technology investigates how a nascent sense of being *at-risk* joins hashtaggers in political endeavors. Stephen practices in San Francisco and New York commuting via Zoom. His road bike and yoga mat are parked in Brooklyn.

Julie Leavitt, M.D., is past President of the Psychoanalytic Institute of Northern California, and co-coordinator of the PINC-allied Race Working Group. She organizes, teaches, and writes about combatting institutional racial projects/whiteness, and about queering psychoanalysis: clinical activism, alter-theory and poetic unlearning.

Jade McGleughlin, M.S.W. L.I.C.S.W., is past president, personal and supervising analyst, board member, and faculty member of the Massachusetts Institute for Psychoanalysis. She is on the editorial boards of *Psychoanalytic Dialogues* and *Studies in Gender and Sexuality.* She is in private practice in Cambridge, MA, providing consultation, supervision, psychotherapy and psychoanalysis to children and adults. Her writing focuses on gender, the negative, the analysts' necessary nonsovereignty, and uses of visual art to articulate problems in representation. She is a portrait painter.

Eyal Rozmarin, Ph.D., is a co-editor of the book series *Relational Perspectives in Psychoanalysis* and associate editor of the journals *Studies in Gender and Sexuality* and *Psychoanalytic Dialogues.* He writes, teaches in various psychoanalytic institutes, and practices out of New York.

Ghosts and the Sexual Boundary Violation

The Limits of an Idea

By Muriel Dimen (unpublished manuscript, 2015) with discussion by the writing group known as LOC 148: Francisco Gonzalez; Orna Guralnik; Stephen Hartman; Julie Leavitt; Jade McGleuphlin; and Eyal Rozmarin (section headings in BOLD CAPS were placed by LOC; italicized section headers were placed by Dimen).

GHOSTS AND GHOSTING

Muriel Dimen

In the intimate sphere, the ghostly carries a certain heft. In the public domain, not so much. A metaphor goes only so far.

Orna Guralnik

I think we have to ponder about this first sentence.

Francisco Gonzalez

I already have questions. The idea that the ghostly does not carry heft in the public domain seems antithetical to the way I think about something like the intergenerational transmission of trauma. I would think that today we would imagine the ghostly is very much a part of the public domain.

Julie Leavitt

I was thinking she was saying that we think of ghosts haunting us personally, but ghosts are public: that we don't think enough about ghosts being in the public domain.

DOI: 10.4324/9781003335252-39

Jade McGleuphlin

We do think a lot more about ghosts in a public domain now. Let's say ghosts of slavery that underlay and haunt all aspects of race relations or economics. Or the way whiteness haunts us. Our ghosts are coming out of the closet.

Orna Guralnik

In Israel, it's a long-standing idea; the Holocaust haunts everyday culture.

Francisco Gonzalez

She's setting up two ghostly spheres: one of fear and one of the public domain.

Jade McGleuphlin

But it's an artificial divide. Those spheres are...imbricated, always informing each other and creating the other. The inextricability of the public and private domains makes her story our story, too.

Stephen Hartman

Let's remember that most of Muriel's work involves recursion. The idea that the public makes the private, the private makes the public, and the public makes the private and so on.

THE WOODEN: PRIVATE, PUBLIC, RECURSION

Muriel Dimen

Intimate

The sexual boundary violation that came my way was, like any self-respecting golem, inanimate, amorphous, an anthropomorphic figure of rock and clay. A haint, it ghosted me, I see now. I was unaware of it, though. All I had was petrified knowledge.

It's not that I didn't try to speak. But even when I described the injury to my women's group, it remained a story made of wood. I confided in a Zen priest, who, moved, wrote a poem about me telling him. I told my second analyst but did not feel that my bewilderment made an imprint. I kept trying to spill the beans, I see now. But the thing had no voice.

It did not speak until writing made it alive.

There is a step between writing and life though, at least in this case: listening. Or rather seeing. Or perhaps synesthesia. A witness who, hearing me, discerned the eerieness I lived with. Someone who could sense the lost soul in the golem.

Orna Guralnik

I find the writing gorgeous. There are many stories or things that are in us, but they have the quality of a wooden, non-usable thing, that is there, somewhere. I'm assuming she's going to talk about how things become less wooden as they develop in between self and others.

Jade McGleuphlin

How does that recursion work with writing and speaking? Is there a kind of separation between the story and her? She tries to voice her story, but she tells us the story was petrified, that the story had no voice even when she told her women's group. Somehow even in the telling she couldn't get her story heard. She says the writing gave her a greater sense of being heard. But why? And, what makes a story dead or wooden?

Stephen Hartman

Right: a story "made of wood."

Jade McGleuphlin

She says, "*it* didn't speak until writing made it alive. And that step, at least in this case, is listening or seeing." Something comes alive in the telling of the story in writing that didn't happen for her in speaking once close attention is paid.

Julie Leavitt

We need the public actually, in order to make these wooden things speakable so they can come to life.

Francisco Gonzalez

Yes, I thought there was something really interesting along those lines. A story doesn't live until it circulates, until the collective aspect of your personal story becomes something that's heard by others. And I also thought that there was something interesting here about writing. Because writing is already something that's haunted by absence. There's a kind of listening that happens in live presence: they're here, and they hear it. But writing is always already kind of ghostly. It's sent out to a presence that isn't there. There's something in writing that is hollowed out.

Stephen Hartman

It raises the interesting question about the reader, the place of the reader when you write...

Julie Leavitt

or the listener, or the witness...

Stephen Hartman

which seems to be suggesting that the Other, the listener/reader in your head when you write, listens more carefully than the reader in the real world because it's your own imaginary reader.

Francisco Gonzalez

It does, and there's a question of context: is she writing for a talk or for publication? Context shapes so much about how something opens up.

Orna Guralnik

There are many things that exist in us, between us, that do not start off wooden, elements that we do not actually need the collective to liberate. Sometimes the collective, or the imagined collective, is what makes things wooden. So, with boundary violations, there's a collective injunction to *not know* (perhaps a refusal to hear). And maybe when you're writing, you find some kind of intermediary zone between yourself and some imagined other, the way Stephen is describing it, where you can find some space between different parts of *me*.

Stephen Hartman

It's like Bromberg's idea of *standing in the spaces* because there's a third, but the third is conversing with an Other in your own mind.

Orna Guralnik

Maybe you can imagine a better third.

Julie Leavitt

Yeah, there are collectives that are always going to be scrutinizing and denying, but there are other collectives that actually are helpful. Maybe as an analyst one is a single person but also a member of a group and so the "I" oscillates in and out of a collective.

Francisco Gonzalez

One way that it oscillates is that those collectives are not just outside. The idea of a one-to-many relationship involves a whole history of one's relationship to many others, and those kinds of internal templates are inside, shaping what one imagines possible in collectives. Then there are real collectives that interact with that internal history and shape it in all sorts of different ways for good and ill.

Jade McGleuphlin

Beautifully put. For one thing, there is the whispered whole history of boundary violations in psychoanalysis that lives as background but a movement that propels the story forward. Still, I don't think the actual collective(s) and the internalized historical collective(s) can be separated out. I am interested though in this idea of intermediary space inside you and when and how that functions. Clinically, we see there can be a kind of separation between trauma and the story we tell about it which seems operative in some of this writing. There is a voicing of something, the "story," but to survive, the affect has been split off from the narrative. Unless there is genuine witness. I don't know if Muriel is saying that her experience remained wooden or became wooden in her telling or in its reception or at all, but it's interesting that for her it's writing that creates the bridge when, so often, especially in academic writing, there is some kind of dissociation or disconnect from affect. She is saying that something came alive in the writing when she had the internal sense of a deep listener or seer. Maybe her own metabolizing of something.

Orna Guralnik

But usually when people talk about dissociation from affect, if you look closely, it's not dissociation from affect but from all the different layers of experience that make it feel like 'me-happening-right-now'.

Julie Leavitt

Well, maybe you're both talking about the same thing. There is something about the link to the emotional. I get what you mean Jade, about watching people tell a story of trauma and then start to connect with it on an affective level. The telling definitely brings it into a different register, brings it alive.

Stephen Hartman

Muriel wrote this very soon before she died, and she was very steeped in Laplanche in those last years. You can really hear the echo of Laplanche here in the enigmas and haunts.

Orna Guralnik

How aware was she of her imminent death?

Stephen Hartman

I don't think she was as ill as she would become. But she knew she had terminal cancer.

Muriel Dimen

The golem had to become a ghost. Not a thing in the darkness but a message from the past that could be read and reread, its meaning emergent, legible only when the elixir of close attention falls on the invisible ink in which it is written.

I do not really know how I came to know I could speak. Once again, I can recount the sequence of events. But the emotional process remains illegible.

*****

Jade McGleuphlin

There's something about that. It's the ghost that then becomes the entity that can live, not the illegible Golem. I think that is interesting.

Orna Guralnik

Very interesting, right? The Golem needs to be transformed into a ghost.

Francisco Gonzalez

I love this figure Muriel gives us of the ghost on the one hand, the haunting, and on the other hand, the Golem that never lived. Those two different figures or characters would be interesting to think more deeply about. How are they related to one another? How they're really different from one another and how they occupy the text.

Julie Leavitt

I'm thinking about it like "the real" and "the symbolic," this idea of invisible ink and the Golem. Something has to come into being from nothing or from a place of illegibility. It's fascinating. I love the way she's writing. Synesthesia comes to mind, such a cool idea to think about how the senses all kind of mash together in confusion, and then they start to take shape.

Francisco Gonzalez

I guess a Golem has never been alive. So, a ghost is something that's been alive and then has died.

Julie Leavitt

Well, and she's bringing in time, which I think is really important. History. Ghost, specter – I think there's something too about the way that all of this stuff collapses in a time-space…

Jade McGleughlin

…Right: the intergenerational transmission of trauma not being a one-person passage.

Francisco Gonzalez

And how about the Golem? That's such an interesting figure. It's the manifestation…

Jade McGleughlin

…on the individual level. I thought she was trying to say it is a kind of dissociation. Something petrified has to be brought to life and animated. The Golem is not yet anything but dead. Maybe she wants to say that the Golem becomes a ghost once it is made alive, once it comes into speech and writing, into the collective, into our consciousness? She is critical of the language of ghosts because she thinks it dodges responsibility. When we just stay in the language of ghosts, no one's taking responsibility in life: I hear her saying "I want some responsibility. I want people to own this and be responsible for it!"

Julie Leavitt

She writes, "The Golem had to become a ghost. Not a thing in the darkness but a message from the past that could be read and reread, its meaning emerging legible only when the elixir of close attention falls on the invisible ink in which it is written." So, I'm thinking the opposite of what you're saying, Jade. There's something about that becoming in the "elixir of close attention" that is invisible, but that can't *not* be taken up? I'm reading it as forcing us to take responsibility. That it's meaning comes through even when you cannot see it.

Jade McGleughlin

But I think she thinks that never quite happens when she writes, "*the ghost metaphor no longer cuts much ice. Begged are questions of personal and collective responsibility; one's relation toward these who are called here "ghosts"; gender; and power.*" She wants us to take responsibility.

THE STORY

Muriel Dimen

By the same token, I don't know how much I should speak here. Think of it as ghosts interfering with me. Having recounted the sexual boundary violation that I was subject of and to (Dimen 2011), I wonder whether I ought repeat it here. Will I bore my readers with (what may seem) a stale saga? For those who have not read that original essay and/or heard me speak of the events at various venues, will I be saying too little? Providing insufficient context? Perhaps you will hear me as too attached to the secondary gains of victimhood. Perhaps you will think I am self-centered. Perhaps I am.

I can't figure it out. So, I will proceed as I did in the first place when I decided to speak: just do it.

In 1968, at the age of 26 and a graduate student in another field and mostly illiterate in psychoanalytic process and history, I entered treatment with an impeccably credentialed psychoanalyst. Five years later, I was an assistant professor about to attend an annual conference and set on sleeping with a man I'd met the previous year. Off and on, I'd been sharing my exciting, guilty plan with Dr. O. Though I'd often discussed sex, I see, looking back, that this was the first time I owned my sexual intentionality.

The session ended, Dr. O walked me to the door, I said, "I'm scared, I want a hug." (This was not the first hug: when, after I'd sat up on the couch at another session's end, I was weeping about my father's death the previous year, Dr. O had sat next to me and put his arm around my shoulders.) As I was ending this embrace, I kissed his cheek; I don't think there'd been a kiss before. And then he said, and this was a definite first—and last—"No, how about a real kiss?" So—it wasn't even a question, because, as the quip goes, there's a "trance" in "transference"—I kissed his mouth. He returned the favor with his tongue—at which point, I recall a feeling of shock, and then a feeling of ignoring the shock. He chuckled: "Oops, I'm getting a hard-on, I better stop." In me, nothing or, rather, awareness of nothing. Call it a confusion of tongues.

I left, went to the conference, had disappointing intercourse, never saw the guy again, returned to analysis, did not speak of hug or hard-on or French kiss, and never did anything like it again in a treatment that lasted for seven more years. Dr. O did not mention it either.

*****

For years, I wanted to write about this most peculiar sexual encounter with my first analyst, but could never find the first line. Ghosts of past, present, and future obtruded everywhere. But then, 31 years later, in 2004, my opportunity arrived: an invitation to speak on a panel about infidelity and its clinical ramifications. As I was picking up the phone to decline on the grounds of lacking clinical material, the lights went on: after all, did I not have a clinical account of infidelity? Did Dr. O not violate the trust of his patient, his troth to his wife, the ethics of his profession? Did I not betray the bonds of marriage?

And so I accepted. Because speakers had to turn their papers in 6 weeks before the conference, however, the organizing committee knew my topic in advance: I fully expected a phone call disinviting me, but that specter wasn't to appear until the next conference (See Dimen, 2011).

I grasped my stroke of luck in the midst of two intense life passages. An overlong love affair had finally ended, leaving an unpleasant ghost in its wake. And, in the third analysis I'd begun in hopes of averting that inevitability, I was being listened to and seen in a way that had not previously graced me: I felt contained as if by a friendly ghost from so early in my preverbal past as not to count as my past at all. Hence, when the sun of good fortune finally rose, my story was ready to burst into dark flower. The passion and rupture of loss had made room for the torrents of anger, grief and guilt.

Public I

But what if we consider also that I was bearing a story that was not mine? Certainly in my tellings I sensed the ownership I was taking. And, believe me, it was hard to do: the self-focus felt inappropriate, unprofessional. Yet I felt driven to do it. No doubt the drive was personal, a healing effected by an exorcism, a turning of the golem into a ghost so that I would no longer be haunted by the fear of fury and remorse but could live in the present with sadness from the past.

It feels equally self-aggrandizing to speculate that the force which kept me writing was also larger, or other, than me. Yet, it is a premise of this collection that presences from the past accompany us as we make our ways forward. Call it haunting. As much as we are our scars, are we not also our histories? In taking psychoanalysis in, in opening my body to Dr. O in the year I'd decided to become an analyst, did I not also open to its legacy of bads as well as goods?

The intergenerational transmission of trauma is not a one-person passage: Dr. O and I cut a fine, but entirely traditional figure: the patriarchal couple, the older, virile man and the younger, sexy woman. But we did not get there by ourselves. Each of us lived by unconscious forces, we were also conducted into this combo of enactment and acting out by heterosexuality and its cultural imperatives, compulsions, and symbols.

Authors of their lives, people are always also authored by cultural and historical forces as they engage with the world to which they are heirs. Patriarchy is particularly culpable in this instance: Dr. O summons me back into the realm of the transferential erotic just as I am about to have sex with another man. As in other sexual trangressions, this incestuous act – a combination of enactment and acting-out – created the selfsame backdrop of loss against which SBVs tend to occur.

If, in speaking of the sexual transgression, I detect the weight of a past that has become mine since that time, wasn't Dr. O, in taking advantage of an erotic windfall, bearing that past too, albeit one that I cannot imagine as a conscious presence in his mind? To be sure, this repetition of a hidden and largely unspoken analytic history was also a repetition of professional infidelity – albeit with difference, since, after all, a tongue in the mouth – or even an unfelt hard-on – is not the same as the genital encounters that have baptized many an analytic couch, like Ferenczi's treatment of and affair with his patient's daughter (whom he married at Freud's encouragement), or the sexual delinquencies of Gross and Stekel and, perhaps, Jung (Makari 2008), and, later, Horney (Falzeder 2005–2006) and, to arrive at the now, Smith (Herman 2012).

History passed through us that day. Lacan's Third, the Law, was absent from the room, its position occupied instead by a ghost trying to speak but lacking a voice. Or, better, listeners? And the silence that followed was of a piece with all the other silencings of all the other sexual boundary violations that preceded our sad act, all the sexual violations that are taking place in and outside the consulting room every day right now.

Shall I emphasize that point? When you read about a sexual boundary violation, it has already happened: you read about something in the past. But violations of sexual ethics feature ongoingly in the institutions you belong to, knowledge of which is more often held in the breach. And it is within such a silence that a golem is made and remade. Together. The intergenerational transmission of trauma happens between as well as within persons, in intersubjective as well as social and historical space. We are haunted as much by what is not said as by what is done.

My experience of telling this story in its various iterations bears a bit of the uncanny too. When I tried to present it a second time, for example, I was nearly disinvited: what specter could have led a conference committee to declare that, as a patient recounting a transgression, I was in ethical breach because my (deceased) analyst – whom I have never publicly named – could not defend himself on grounds of having to keep confidentiality? What specter could have then caused a prominent psychoanalytic journal to "lose" a game-changing paper (Dimen 2011) that both recounted the story of the transgression and analyzed the situation of sexual boundary violation in psychoanalysis? What specter could have even later brought down a conference planned to honor that very paper? that turned a collection of papers dedicated to discussion of that selfsame paper into an anthology about the problem as a whole? What specter could subsequently cause another committee to acknowledge receipt of a new paper on the entire topic and then never announce they'd turned me down? Was it the same specter that, the next year, succeeded in disinviting the author of these works – me – from a keynote address?

THE ACT OF VIOLATION: WHO IS DR O? WHAT IS PSYCHOANALYSIS?

Jade McGleuphlin

She is trying to offer her own story to intervene into the silence of boundary violations in psychoanalysis but it's recursive. She is in the outrage and pain of how that silencing happens to her and she has to figure out how to write that without risking more vulnerability. How does a writer imagine the listener, and manage the fears that occur in the process of writing and imagining the other? Is it useful to give voice to a possible response or is it alienating to the reader? I totally identified with the need to share her internal process and fears with us as a writing device, but also feel some ambivalence about that as "technique" when I do it. I am not sure it translates.

Orna Guralnik

I don't like this level of self-questioning she is sharing with us.

Francisco Gonzalez

I end up feeling quite unsettled...

Julie Leavitt

I was unsettled too, but I actually was unsettled in a way that I find fascinating because being unsettled is necessary to knowing someone. This being-unsettled is so much a part of our culture that when someone comes forward with their own story about having been victimized, there's always that awkward and indulgent feeling of a confession – and it gets confused with *my* confession. I really appreciated her bringing us into that problem and making it our problem – a collective problem. And she's wondering, "am I going to be scrutinized?" People are going to say, "Oh, you've told the story a million times. What do you want from us? You're just going on about it." I really appreciated that she brought us into this dilemma (the boundary violation and its confession) even though I also felt unsettled about it.

Jade McGleuphlin

And it is the sexual abuse victim's plight. There is no good way to tell the story.

Orna Guralnik

Can I move us to the business of having something like this happen to you? Because, you know, I was in Muriel's writing group when she started writing about all this. And she shared a lot of this writing with the group, as well as her struggles with it. I remember one of the things that kept driving me crazy about it, and I did ask her on it repeatedly, was, for example, her refusal to name him which I for the life of me could not understand. Why is she protecting him? And, you know, when I read this thing, I'm thinking: Oh, my God What a sociopath. He just exploited her. He took something from her. For himself. He's just a jerk. What a betrayal. And why is *she* sacked with the shame? How does that work? That it's somehow *her* shame that she has to hide and burrow by various acts of concealment.

Jade McGleuphlin

The aggressed on are always left with the shame.

Julie Leavitt

Muriel may be protecting him, but she is also protecting herself because she's the one who has to live with this story. And he's dead, so she has to take all the scrutiny from the outside world by telling a story about someone who is revered – who may even symbolize "psychoanalysis" for some people. And some people might not even consider this wrong, they might consider this something that was part of the transference-countertransference or she "brought it on herself." People are going to think all kinds of things. There is something too about just feeling protective as the person telling the story.

Francisco Gonzalez

I think that this comes back to a very critical question of what writing is. There's an editing process in writing, which is different from speaking where you don't get to edit things out. Things get said and they've been said, you don't get to delete from a conversation.

Muriel Dimen

Public 2

And yet. I must say that when it comes to the social dimensions of this weirdness, the ghost metaphor no longer cuts much ice. Begged are questions of personal and collective responsibility; one's relation toward these who are called here "ghosts"; gender; and power. Here we are in an area of much uncertainty for analysts.

The ghost made me, him, them do it? I don't think so. Writing of the false memory "syndrome" used to discredit those who have recovered memories of sexual abuse, Adrienne Harris (1996) says: "The demands made on the analyst to think, feel, reason, and process within a social field (the transference and countertransference phenomena) are anchored on a determination not to act but to reflect" (184).

Perhaps. But the distinction between action and reflection does not always hold. When it comes to actions, and patterns of action, and institutions that harm repeatedly, one wants to know how this nasty stuff happens, and how people come to it, and how one hurts another and how one enters into hurt. How does one enter the taboo, breaking laws willy-nilly? How does one opt for silence and erasure? How do groups do it? How do those who listen opt to do so? What are the vectors of power and pleasure in which our private and social beings take shape? How do these contingencies of desire pinball each of us into the infliction and reception of pain?

More. When these questions are asked by not one but many, is reflection no longer an action? When we agree to listen collectively, or just happen to do so, are we not also engaging an act? I do not know how to think this through alone. If you think it through with me, are we not also acting? Here goes.

Let me say it straightforwardly, even though to begin a paragraph this way is to be somewhat indirect: colleagues hurt me, but – is this worse? – they may not have even registered how. And it embarrasses me to note these facts: in acknowledging the hurt,

I am showing you something I'd rather you not see. Sometimes to acknowledge hurt risks seeming one-down, even sometimes a sense of abjection.

Still, if there is any purchase in the idea that the past lingers, then I am honor-bound to take that risk. "Why did you do that?" This is what I want to ask each of those who injured me in some way around this dilemma. My question is as much accusation as inquiry. Obscurely, though, I feel I am not supposed to accuse. I am only to think, reflect, consider, ponder, contemplate. And so I feel the impulse to drain the affect from these words, separate remonstration and indignation from reasoned inquiry into history and dynamics.

But perhaps separating the personal from the political, or the professional, is a stupid move. The ghosts of personal life meet the historical forces of public life, and they power each other. They animate the transgression, its excitement and guilt and pain. They vivify the objection, the protest, the outrage. As fascinated as one is by the haunting hurt and its jouissance, one still wants to, and must, say, even in the face of the unconscious: No.

Of course, I must blame each of the individuals who had some hand in these disappointing and sometimes shocking erasures. And yet so many smart and even compassionate people have acted like fools, as well as foolishly – and here I include Dr. O, and me too – that anyone with a sense of historical and cultural and psychological context must wonder what patterns are being relived despite our intent. Are these patterns historical? Social? Personal? All of the above, I think.

A "specter is haunting Europe." So wrote Karl Marx and Friedrich Engels about what they saw as a good thing, the communism that would create social justice and that society feared in the nineteenth century. But likening the ghosts of sexual boundary violations to "the specter of communism" doesn't quite work. After all, The Communist Manifesto *is a work of irony, anger, passion: the "specter" Marx and Engels fingered was, in their view, desirable.*

Can one write and speak with irony about sexual transgression? What would the equivalent specter be? Incest, of course, brims with desire. The wish for it, ever unresolved, spooks us at the oddest moments. It endures because the craving for the ecstasy that halos the violation of this universal taboo never abates (my own personal participation in which was stolen by Dr. O). Yet, speaking in the name of the law, decency, and what one is forced to call "mental health," incest stands outside the category of the desirable.

We face this problem with helplessness, irony beyond our shared reach, except of course in the gallows humor of the injured, in the jokes that cannot be told in front of them. Maybe it's better to think here of enigmas rather than golems, ghosts, specters, the uncanny. Perhaps we face an enigma: a specter is haunting psychoanalysis, the specter of enigma, enigma being inevitable and, perhaps, desirable in the work.

No. I don't think that works either.

"Don't mourn, organize!" This exhortation, attributed to the organizer Joe Hill executed for murder in 1915, capsules the problem.

Not that one either.

For psychoanalysis, can the ghost of sexual boundary violations become, one day, an ancestor (Loewald 1960)? There is, of course, the problem that this sort of transgression is a contemporary, not a forebear: as I have been emphasizing, it inhabits the present as well as the past, and in all likelihood has a long, if maybe less robust future ahead. Many quote or render their own versions of Santayana's "Those who cannot remember the past are condemned to repeat it." In googling his aphorism, I ran into Kurt Vonnegut, who quips, "I've got news for Mr. Santayana: we're doomed to repeat the past no matter what. That's what it is to be alive"

(http://www.goodreads.com/quotes/tag/doomed-to-repeat-it October 20, 2014).

Julie Leavitt

I hear Muriel struggling with the problem that when analysts themselves bring up their own trauma, or anything personal, it creates a wave of anxiety. Especially around sexual boundary violations. I mean, what she's describing isn't new, this stuff has been going on since long before Freud. The transgressions within the field get buried. We're all vulnerable to transgressions. And we are both titillated by the hard-on and completely scared off by it.

Jade McGleughlin

I think that's why she didn't want to name Dr. O. Her point was about what happens when there's an account of a sexual boundary violation. When she describes the transgression itself, does it feel shocking? Does it feel ordinary? I wondered what people's experience of her telling us about this thing that happened to her was as they read it?

Francisco Gonzalez

To me it feels shocking. When he slips her the tongue and gets a boner. Is that what you mean? Jade?

Jade McGleughlin

Yes. I mean, when she discloses what happened to her. Does it evoke the terror of that moment, or does it defuse it?

Julie Leavitt

I think it does both. I was both shocked and struck by its mundane quality. And, so late after the incident, and a part of me just kind of rolls my eyes with the mundaneness: like, "Oh, yeah, this happens. This could happen to me. It just happens in our field. It happens all the time, actually."

That's one of the things she's grappling with. Her story causes this shockwave to the point where silence happens, where things don't get published or the writer gets hystericized. Perhaps, she didn't name Dr. O. because, if she had, we could just go after *him*. That's what happens. The individual becomes the person of study rather than, as you're saying Francisco, the group. To me that's where the shock is. We can sit around and reflect on this because we've been reflecting on it for 100 years, and it's still happening with great frequency.

Jade McGleughlin

And she wants us to know: not only did I not experience empathy and sisterhood and collectivity of my closest colleagues and friends, I felt shunned at the very moment that I needed everyone to accompany me and bring this alive. She's not feeling empathy or being witnessed which is one reason to write. A kind of mourning to manage the ongoing melancholia.

Stephen Hartman

I agree. I think that she is trying to do what you say Francisco, to write about how the group speaks through a person but then add that the writing doesn't help that person hurt any less. It doesn't take that hurt away from her and may even magnify it. It's interesting because, Jade, you asked "did we find the writing shocking?" For me, Muriel's hurt and her anger at her close colleagues was more shocking than the event itself. The hug and the hard-on has been retold enough times now that it has taken on a repetitive quality that is voiced as, "oh, yeah, I heard this already. Why must you keep bringing it up?" I think the answer is because it is the currency of the hurt, of being disinvited, of feeling shut down in the aftermath of a telling that shocks.

Julie Leavitt

She's telling a personal story, and she's appealing to the group around her that responded in a particular way. I hear her saying that the field purports to want to understand these things and actually does want to effect change in people, but that we as a group get caught in a vortex. The distinction between action and reflection does not always hold when it comes to actions and patterns of action and institutions that harm repeatedly. One wants to know how this nasty stuff happens between analyst and patient.

Muriel Dimen (repeated)

How does one enter the taboo, breaking laws willy-nilly? How do groups do it? How do those who listen do so? What are the vectors of power and pleasure in which our private and social beings take shape? How do these contingencies of desire pinball each of us into the infliction and reception of pain?

LOCATING "THE GROUP"

Julie Leavitt

I mean, to me, that's the key. She's challenging the group, which is psychoanalysis, to use her as a foil, to use her experience, not just to say, "I was done wrong" but to ask, "what is our responsibility and accountability?" And how do we take this up as a group, and how do we understand the way that the personal is always political? Even in psychoanalysis, even the last bastion of an institutional pact that continues to demand that we're not political!

Francisco Gonzalez

I really agree with that. It's where you can hear that the individual is actually speaking for the group. It makes a huge difference as to the reception that an individual gets. That's the condition, I would say, that allows a kind of empathy. It's the way that groups think and speak through action. Groups don't reflect like individuals reflect, but groups reflect through doing things. It's a very different level than the level of the individual. So it's not just that we might understand what Muriel says as speaking for a group. It's that I cannot act as a *we*, collectively; *we* have to act. And so is it a good analogy, again shocking as it is mundane, that Black men keep getting killed over and over and over again in this country? We've heard it a million times. It's shocking, but it's also completely predictable. And at a certain point, when George Floyd is killed, there is a huge group response, an uprising (and not for the first time).

Eyal Rozmarin

But what is the collective that is acting on the street? What is the psychoanalytic collective? I think part of the problem is figuring out who and what is the group that we're seeing move on the streets. We're seeing parts of groups, but is there a collective that's actually forming?

Francisco Gonzalez

Just like who is the self that speaks? We never really know that either. It's a contingent kind of thing.

Eyal Rozmarin

But if Muriel is talking to a group, maybe it's important to understand what is the group that she has in mind? And also, what is the group that we are talking about? What is the group of psychoanalysis? I don't know that actually.

Jade McGleughlin

There was a whole history of organizing by people of color and some white people before a larger group could no longer deny that the murder of a Black person was not an individual event but a result of the aftermath of slavery and the systemic dehumanization of Black people. Muriel wants to speak to what happened to her in the larger context of what happens in the power relations of psychoanalysis. She is asking us to think together as a form of action that we can use. Now the group is us.

Stephen Hartman

The group is always changing. And you don't always know who the group is. It forms and morphs on many levels. So, for instance, the Arab Spring is credited to Mohammed Bouazissi's act of self-immolation after a policeman tipped over his vegetable cart; it ignited something through much of the world. There was briefly some clear sense of who that collective was, but it became other collectives as it morphed in different contexts. Just as George Floyd taps into a variety of collectives: the character who speaks for the group is not one person; it's not a stable location.

Julie Leavitt

Well, and I would even say Stephen, to dovetail on that because I agree with you, that the wish to identify a group is itself part of the problem, part of what happens where we get collapsed into groups. Even to say like white suburban people are doing this or that, isn't really speaking in actuality. It's generalizing. That's where we can fall into helplessness and name calling and whatever else. So, to me, there's something about not getting pulled into thinking that Muriel is speaking to one group. She names a group, but she also is addressing other groups. That pull is something itself to interrogate? Why is it that we keep thinking that we need to know who's doing this or that as if the collective can't be this very complex, everyday thing of interconnections that happens. I mean, my discussions with my mother yesterday about starting to read about race and to talk to her friends about it, that kind of conversation is very different than my conversations with people at PINC about race, which is again different than my conversations here with you guys.

Francisco Gonzalez

The collective is as much a fiction as the individual self is a fiction – just at a different level. I would say it doesn't matter who Muriel thinks the group is. In a way the group is speaking through Muriel, using Muriel to speak. It is using her personal difficulties to speak. And it's the confusion between those two levels – Muriel as individual, Muriel as the voice of a collective – where Muriel can get caught and torn apart in a certain way, because if there isn't a group that can really hear *itself* through individuals, groups eat up or annihilate individuals.

Eyal Rozmarin

That's very interesting to reflect on as the source of psychological trouble. You don't understand what is *yourself*; because you don't understand what is, what are the groups that are speaking through you.

Jade McGleughlin

I feel like there's something here that would be so interesting for us to tease out in more depth.

Because I think Muriel's saying another thing as well. I think it's because I was just reading *Scenes of Subjection* by Saidiya Hartman where she's really saying "don't lose the person" by your imagined identification with them. It potentially erases the other with your own experience. Although the intention is good to use Muriel to speak for the group, a different problem is created. We lose Muriel. Muriel knows and says the ghosts of the personal can't be separated from the political but she is also struggling with how *she* can be personally angry.

She writes, "I must blame each of the individuals who had some hand in disappointing and sometimes shocking erasures." I think she's saying I am angry and I don't have a way to express it. And each time I try my internal voices say, don't sound like that, I can't be like that. But actually, there are people I want to hold accountable. And it's not just some vague group or collective. I have a grievance. But there is something about moving to the collective that can counter accountability. I think the move out to the group is also a move away from the pain and the affect and also the level of responsibility...

Stephen Hartman

...Individually *and* collectively.

Francisco Gonzalez

Jade I really agree with what you're saying. I think of it as two really different levels. When the collective speaks through individuals, there's always a violence involved no matter how it's speaking because it really does wrap its talons around and tear apart the individual. No matter how beautifully they are speaking, there is always something that gets erased in one's individual sovereignty when the collective is speaking through them.

And so there is something important about trying to identify with the individual pain so that it doesn't get lost. It's not an either/or. I think both modes are happening at the same time, and that my identifying with Muriel in one way is dis-identifying with all sorts of other people in other ways. There's always this kind of tearing apart that's happening between these two levels: of an identification of an individual self and the fiction of a collective self. Those are two completely different registers that operate under very different logics.

THE GROUP'S PLACE IN GRIEVANCE

Jade McGleughlin

But how we use them is political. As is our response to a certain kind of grievance and affect.

Eyal Rozmarin

It is putting yourself in the classic position of the scapegoat. Like Jesus, you know, you get killed to make a point. That's the sad truth of these kinds of rituals. If you don't die, you don't get to make a point. That's Jesus, that's George Floyd, that's that man who started the Arab Spring in Tunisia. That's Muriel in a way. You have to be there and there has to be violence or you don't have a point somehow.

Julie Leavitt

Maybe we could stop separating these things out? Francisco, I agree with you that they're really different, but they are so interrelated. People die, but they die within a group too. They die individually. And I mean, Jesus died and then it reverberated or, you know, Floyd died, and now the group forms. There's an interconnection there. I don't think Saidiya Hartman is just saying we should look at the individual. She's saying that within the scene of subjection, there is both a subject who needs to be named and a scene. We too often use the word *slave*, for example, instead of actually naming people. But in the naming of the person, we also take responsibility for the collective, for what's happening in terms of how this stuff comes down and becomes an affliction against people, not just against a person by people. To live within that dichotomy is the task. I think it is really important to figure out how to not make it one or the other.

Jade McGleughlin

I think Hartman wants to say that the way certain white people tried to persuade other slave owners about the horrors of slavery, was to imaginatively put themselves in the position of the slave to evoke empathy; to say, "if I was treated in this way, it would be so horrible, can you imagine?" She was cautioning against that way of using identification. She argues that it eradicates the enslaved person's own voice such as we could know it. That's what I had in mind when I was asking you in the beginning, how did people hear Muriel's own voice?

Do they identify with her? Do they disagree with her? Do you know what I mean? Is there a way of listening that is not appropriative or is that the nature of empathy? And what about when there are power differences, because there's something about Muriel's own words getting to be her words.

Stephen Hartman

It's both things: her words are individual and social. Her words convey both the subject position of the person who is hurt and their political effect. It moves toward a collective subjectification of that person's role. At the same time, it's painful that there is no ambivalent stance for Muriel to take there. Because her words are operating on many levels at the same time; it isn't comfortable to be in any one position.

Francisco Gonzalez

They're always intersectional. What I would say, as I think you're saying right now, Stephen, is just as even Jesus says, "take this cup away from me. I do not want to do this." George Floyd may resonate with the uprisings, but I would imagine he would prefer to be alive. His story resonates through the uprising but I am sure he would rather be alive What it means for the group to speak through you is that you are in some way effaced. There's something of your individual subjectivity that is killed when the group speaks through you. That is a painful thing to bear as an individual. It happens constantly, which is why even right now, any one of us can only hold one position, can only say something at any given time. But between all six of us, we're able to say something else. That's operating in a different order that is more complex. It requires the multiplicity of the group, and for us to listen to *us* as opposed to me listening to *me*. When those two levels cross through each other, there can be a certain violence.

Orna Guralnik

I do not resonate with the distinction between the collective speaking and the individual. I find that the collective is always in the *me* who speaks. I don't even know how to begin to separate them. The collective is huge, it's there as some kind of bigness, too muchness or excess, and as far as a felt experience of being an individual, and being an individual for the collective, I don't see much of a difference.

Francisco Gonzalez

There is never subjectivity that it does not happen at the intersection of those two levels. There's no such thing as subjectivity outside of the intersection of the individual and the collective.

Orna Guralnik

I would say that there's no subjectivity that is not also collectivity.

There is no place in language where one can have an *individual* experience that is not collective. I know that I've never had that.

Francisco Gonzalez

Subjectivity *is* the intersection of the individual with the collective. There is an individual that is grounded in the body and then there's another register that's grounded at the level of the group and the history of groups. Only at the intersection of these do we have what we call "subjectivity." But I believe that the logic of the organism or body, which is where traditional psychoanalysis grounded itself, and the logic of the group beyond that body, are two very different logics. They cannot be reduced to one another. And that intersection is highly problematic, painful, violent, necessary.

Julie Leavitt

This idea of an intersection, it's not such a clear-cut thing to me. It's like two hands reaching, not two lines crossing at some clear vector. The group has a different logic than the individual no doubt. But then how, at what place, whatever we call it semantically, how can we determine what's happening there? Who's responsible? How are we accountable? That's what we're facing right now as white people in America. Like, how do I personally become accountable, not just for the ways that I harm – internally and outwardly – but that I am part of a group that harms. That's not a discrete self-identity at a discrete intersection with the group.

Stephen Hartman

Muriel always used the term "recursive" or "the recursive node" or "the point of recursion" for what you're calling "the intersection." She believed that you can't discuss one thing without the other, the individual without the collective, because they are in a constant relation, each making the other as each comes into view.

Francisco Gonzalez

Yes, we're both particles and waves. It's not just two lines. It's nodes, a network of multiple nodes or densities.

GETTING PERSONAL

Eyal Rozmarin

I'm thinking again through the concept of the scapegoat, the one who is doing the work for the group by taking on some kind of collective problem and getting exiled or killed with/for it. But then there are those who refuse to go away or die and still insist on talking *to* the group.

I'm thinking about the very thankless position of someone like Tarana Burke, who launched the #MeToo movement. You're calling out something and you're attacked for it? Either you're calling out something by having died like George Floyd or Jesus, or you're calling out something and you are still alive. And what happens to you then?

I think Muriel is speaking from that position. She doesn't want to die. She's not planning to die. And, or maybe yes, she knows she is going to die. But she's talking from the position of the one who accuses in life. I think it is very important to factor this position into the levels of engagement that we're talking about, because there's a person who's hurting, who's not willing to just live with the idea that "I'm the conveyor of collective ghosts." Something happened to me, and I accuse you. She's writing on that level. She wants a reply. I think that's what this paper is. She wants a reply. She's writing a very, very theoretical but also very personal paper, again and again, because she wants some kind of reply that she's not getting.

Jade McGleughlin

I hear Muriel in that very same way. I think about enactments with one's patients. They want you to say, not that, you know, you're sorry they felt that way. But you did it, you hurt them. To acknowledge it and say that you are sorry...

Stephen Hartman

...because it needs to happen for there to be a future.

But I think Muriel is also saying that the repair is not likely to happen.

Julie Leavitt

Well, right. I think she's problematizing it. I think she's saying, "Yeah, anyone would want that. But it's not possible," that we're caught up in too many vectors of meaning for a collective to have to face the anxiety of fully taking on reparation.

Eyal Rozmarin

I think it's an ethical question. She's doing two things right toward the end: mourning what she is not going to get, (but asking the audience of readers to answer her wish to be recognized?) and she is assuming the role of accuser. There's a complex and, for me, also an ethical question. As the reader of this, what am I responding to? Because she's both accusing – and she's doing wonderful things that are diffusing the accusation by giving us other things to think about.

Francisco Gonzalez

At this moment, I'm thinking about what it would have been like to be in that analysis for all those years after this thing happened, and how disturbing and isolating. How every moment after that would have already been a mindfuck, you know, and would have been so incredibly painful. And then in thinking and reflecting on that, like when I started to actually feel that pain in my body, then I thought somebody needed to say to Muriel, "psychoanalysis failed you, we failed you." We, our profession, failed you." There is something that she didn't hear back from us in her lifetime.

Sometimes, I feel like I'm living the intergenerational transmission of trauma: something that happened to Muriel and to her cohort or generation, but specifically to her in a way that I feel has a lot to do with this line between what's really personal and what's, third-personal, or *writerly*. It's something that feels very…

Julie Leavitt

fraught…

I think Muriel was aware that *she is what she writes*. Consider this passage:

Muriel Dimen (repeated):

"By the same token, I don't know how much I should speak here. Think of it as ghosts interfering with me, having recounted the sexual boundary violation that I was subject of and to, I wonder whether I ought to repeat it here, while I bore my readers with what may seem a stale saga for those who have not read that original essay or heard me speak of the events at various venues, will I be saying too little, providing insufficient context? Perhaps you will hear me as too attached to the secondary gains of victimhood. Perhaps you will think I am self centered. Perhaps I am."

Orna Guralnik

Muriel gets very caught up in her standing in the community. This preoccupation takes us readers to another dimension of why people write, and what are we supposed to do as readers? But then, suddenly, you're far away from the story itself and you're in a 'scene'. I often said to her: why don't you just tell the story?

Julie Leavitt

You know, it's interesting. It's reminding me of this paper, this short paper I gave on a panel at APsAA a couple of years ago about race and about whiteness. I spoke very personally about an experience I had had where I was called out in a very kind of intense way by a colleague of color. The chair of the panel was really concerned about my paper, about me exposing my vulnerability. The guy was like, "you know, I think maybe we just shouldn't publish this. I think maybe it's okay just to have that be, you know, something that happened as a one-time thing." I couldn't help but think that he couldn't quite figure out what my paper was trying to do, because the other papers were very academic, distancing in that way sympathy can be expressed from a safe distance, without accountability.

Jade McGleughlin

Can you even separate out the personal "story" that way? Because what Muriel is saying, I think, is, "I have this story, and I want to say this piece of it now but I need to bring you along with me". Those are the kinds of dilemmas both of a writer and someone who endured a sexual transgression. Right. You know what I mean? Like both of those things…

Eyal Rozmarin

…are how to give your testimony. I think it's important to actually reflect during the testimony about the possibility of giving testimony, about the conditions of giving testimony and so on.

Francisco Gonzalez

This has me thinking, when do we feel that we know the truth and have a duty to warn if we know of an analyst who has perpetrated a violation on a patient? We talk only about more extreme conditions where the violation becomes clearer. But then as we start to pull back from that, it gets fuzzier and more confusing, right?

Julie Leavitt

Well, it's that need to know. This is the thing – it really shakes up the whole question of truth. Like one thing I learned when participating on an ethics task force during a boundary violation inquiry at my Institute is: I don't know what happened in that room. Probably the people who were in that room don't even any longer know what happened, because it was a traumatic transgression. It's when we get into these legalistic, duty to warn things that analysis really breaks down, you know, where it's no longer analysis. It's this need to know and need to hold on to a truth. And so how does one preserve the negative capability, so to speak, of an analysis? It's through not knowing. It's through having some understanding of what happened, but then being able to think about that, and not going to this place of having to know a single truth. That's a very hard balance. It's a human conundrum. It's an ethical conundrum, really.

Jade McGleughlin

It's where the naming becomes important and treacherous. When there is a boundary violation in the community, there are other people in analysis with that person. Likely, when the story comes out, many feel that their analyst could not be the same analyst who was having sex with a patient.

Eyal Rozmarin

That's a big problem, the more time goes by, I remember in the beginning also, not understanding why Muriel was not naming him. But the more I think about it, the more it seems to me a complicated and maybe even a correct decision.

Orna Guralnik

How so?

Eyal Rozmarin

Because there's a lot of collateral damage. It raises the question that there may have been a lot of people that had a perfectly good analysis with Dr. O. and did not have this kind of experience. Even Muriel continued seeing him for ten years after the incident. And, so, what role do you take on when you disclose something damning in a community?

And what is exactly the meaning of "disclosure?" I don't wish to make everything relative, and definitely not to protect criminals and abusers, but isn't it also our most basic premise in psychoanalysis, that every story told is part of a fantasy, a transference, that it always has more meaning than its manifest content? This gets even more complicated when you try to make sense of things on the frontier of the subjective-collective. I think that for us, as holders of the constitutional ambiguity of the human condition, we must remain suspicious about the certainties of collective mindsets, and how they draw the lines and boundaries at any given time.

Julie Leavitt

Well, yes. Would you want to know if your analyst had committed a murder or had raped somebody or had done some pretty major transgression?

Eyal Rozmarin

Yes, murder and rape. Yes.

Julie Leavitt

Yes, but not a sexual boundary violation – you wouldn't want to know that?

Eyal Rozmarin

I'm just thinking. Suppose my analyst had an affair and cheated on her husband. Do I need to know that?

Julie Leavitt

No, but I'm not talking about that.

Eyal Rozmarin

So, you're making a distinction between rape and infidelity?

Orna Guralnik

No! We're talking about when it pertains to the work of analysis. It's not "what kind of art do they like? Do they like horrible art or good art?" This is about the work of analysis.

Eyal Rozmarin

Yes, yes.

Stephen Hartman

It's interestingly about the boundary of self in a way, because what I thought you were going to say, Eyal, was: "just because my analyst is having an affair with a patient, does that necessarily mean my analyst is violating me?" There is clearly a way in which we could imagine that a violation against one patient is by definition a violation against all patients because it becomes a hot potato that is up for grabs. Everyone is potentially violated by its reverberation in the community as the news tosses around.

Eyal Rozmarin

For me, this feels too general.

Julie Leavitt

But I think it's important to think about it this way specifically because this is what our minds do. When we learned that someone that we trusted implicitly with our minds, with our unconscious, with our lives, and then we learned that they did something unethical and transgressive, it is hugely impactful. And, so we do all kinds of things with that. We try to categorize it. We try to say, "well, it wasn't rape, but it was maybe somewhere between rape and an affair." We try to make it something so that we can think about it precisely because it is impactful. And I agree with you, Stephen, that it causes these terrible reverberations. I would want to know if my analyst had aggressed someone, personally, because I would not want to leave the analysis saying, "Oh, my God, he could have done that to me" without having had the opportunity to talk to him about it.

Orna Guralnik

And to know…

Julie Leavitt

…yeah, if we think that we're operating in a field that positions us in the liminal space between the individual and the group. I mean, this is where it lands. Like, this is where the rubber hits the road.

Jade McGleughlin

We can't quite know what we're dealing with. I mean, we might not know…

Julie Leavitt

…that. No, we can't know, you're right, Jade, we can't.

Jade McGleughlin

That's a little bit of an illusion.

Julie Leavitt

Yes, we don't know exactly how to explore it. We can start by trying to think about it. And that's really hard to do in the face of trauma, and I think that any sexual boundary violation is a trauma. But then how do we start to think around it, particularly when it's our analyst?

Francisco Gonzalez

I really appreciate this kind of complexity and the dilemma that we're talking about. I'm thinking about how to contain it. As far as I understand, Dr. O is dead. So, it's one thing, say, if I were in analysis with someone, and I could talk with them about it. Even if I had ended analysis with them, I could still talk with them. And then there's this other case in which they're no longer alive. That complicates the question of revealing the identity. With someone who is dead and is no longer seeing patients, how do you then complete the analysis after such a disclosure?

SELF-DISCLOSURE

Jade McGleughlin

Can we take a quick detour back to the tension between self-focus, which Muriel names as can something that feels inappropriate and unprofessional, and the wish to keep the bigger meaning that can feel self-aggrandizing and grandiose? I feel like that's a tension that people who identify as women struggle with as they write out their stories. Of course, everybody likely does, but not everyone discloses it in their writing. It's that I am trying to call attention to... But I'm just curious about whether people feel an identification with that tension she's trying to talk about and talk about in writing, and would they write that in? Right there. At another level, she is writing about the dilemmas in speaking or writing about one's own experience.

Stephen Hartman

I'm not sure that it is gendered. When you're very identified with what you're disclosing and you know that it is controversial, there's a slippage between your ideas and a sense of safety in your own mind, especially when you are a whistleblower.

Julie Leavitt

Self-focus is a very particular thing for a whistleblower. It's not like, "Oh, I did this great thing, and I want all the attention." It's like, this really awful thing happened. And I'm having to talk about it, because it's my story. I can imagine the layers of how that gets tense and deeply rooted in a person's being to do that. But I think this thing about relating this to gender, Jade, it's always risky business to go there. I'm imagining you might be talking something about a certain kind of masculine defensiveness that doesn't feel threatened or doesn't allow oneself to feel – because I think I can do both of these things, depending on how open I am to my vulnerability, which is, you know, kind of socially considered? Girls get socialized to think.??? feel? Right? And be able to express it and also to be self-conscious and self-loathing about it.

Jade McGleughlin

Right. But I was also talking about incorporating that into analytic writing. It's the self-consciousness and self-loathing maybe. Eyal, Francisco, Stephen, do you feel identification with this dilemma?

Eyal Rozmarin

Yes or no from me. Yes or No. I know what Muriel's talking about. I understand it. But not exactly. Not exactly that way. But I don't know if it's a gender thing.

Stephen Hartman

As opposed to…?

Eyal Rozmarin

Just difference between people. But back to the woman who finds herself in this impossible dilemma where if she critiques power, it's one kind of trouble, and if she doesn't, it's another kind of trouble…

Julie Leavitt

…Which is very much about the body. Muriel talks about her body opening: "in opening my body to Dr. O in the year I decided to become an analyst." I think that dilemma has very much to do with the way the female body is projected onto by public enemy number one (Trump). That's interesting to me. That's kind of haunting to me and also enraging.

Eyal Rozmarin

So that's the position she finds herself in. And she writes this paper and other papers where she's compelled to talk, but she feels judged both by herself and potentially by others for doing so. But she can't not do it. This is the dilemma that keeps being expressed in her papers.

Julie Leavitt

Yeah, exactly.

OPENING UP HER BODY?

Orna Guralnik

Speaking of *opening up her body*: it really bothered me, in a way that provoked me to deeply dis-identify with what she's trying to convey. I keep thinking not only about Muriel, but about women in these situations. I'm not talking about women like Blassey Ford, but rather about situations where part of the reason women participate in the scene (this is in addition to misogyny and all of that) is that there's a different aspect of sexuality and desire at work there. Like, what if we think of Muriel's actual desire for her analyst, and about her exerting power as a desiring woman. She may *want* him sexually, and she may even also want something of his that she was describing earlier – his work ability, or his power. There's a power grab in the act. Men work hard to get and keep that power to themselves. I mean, I hate it. But women are also working hard to get it. It's not easy to establish power. And perhaps there's some kind of power grab on women's part in these scenes.

What about the act of associating yourself with a powerful man, getting something through that. I know this is a very unpopular way of describing things, but I feel compelled to say it. It's a vicarious route to power. You get to steal something from the powerful man.

Stephen Hartman

It's interesting to look at the sentence again in this regard, as to what you're saying Orna, because "in opening my body to Dr. O in the year I decided to become an analyst" written many years after the incident is actually very tricky. It is laden with hindsight. It isn't just the kiss and the hard-on at this point, but Muriel's whole body that is laid out before the psychoanalytic patriarchy that is eager to penetrate her completely. And before her readers as well.

Orna Guralnik

Actually, no that takes the sting out. What I'm saying is that it's not only an act of being penetrated; it's also an act of going and getting something that she wants.

Stephen Hartman

Yes: I'm going to be an analyst. She has to strip herself bare to take a bite of the psychoanalytic apple but at a hefty price.

Julie Leavit

Yes, taking the bite. It makes me think about haunting again, about melancholia, because I think the same – it's an impossible position to be in. It's a position of suicidally scripted powerlessness to want power. And then to waste a ton of time going after it the wrong way, only to find yourself up against the quest again and again, against this wall, and then to try to just swallow that fucking bitter pill. I agree with you, Orna. I actually do think this is a really complicated thing. And there's the impossibility of the true relative powerlessness. But then how *do* you go after power?

Eyal Rozmarin

This is how Muriel wants to describe the backdrop of the loss of power against which sexual boundary violations tend to occur.

Stephen Hartman

it's an Oedipal mess, right? Because in the moment that she's going to take a lover the father takes her.

Eyal Rozmarin

Because it's also a loss for him, the father/analyst.

Stephen Hartman

Yeah, this the backdrop of loss, the loss of the Other who you can't have. But, also the loss of power that she is being stripped of.

Eyal Rozmarin

I don't know. So, he's losing her if he's giving her to a younger man. He's losing her. She's losing him.

Stephen Hartman

Yes. And he's refuting that loss, which is a dirty trick. The nature of the transgression is to forget about the power difference between the analyst and the patient and then reoccupy that power as if its disruption had no significance. It's perverse because that loss of power is disavowed.

Julie Leavitt

That's how I read this – as a disavowal of loss.

Orna Guralnik

It is the loss of lawfulness.

Eyal Rozmarin

So the father...

Stephen Hartman

Well, there is no father any longer, Muriel is saying. There's no role for the father at this juncture. The Father has become, for better or worse, consciously or unwittingly, through acting-out and enactment, the embodiment of loss in a triadic configuration. It's a perverse disavowal of any difference that would allow meaning.

Jade McGleughlin

I think about it as Dr. O reasserts himself at the moment of Muriel's separation to be with another man…

Julie Leavitt

Yes. I think that's what Stephen is referring to around a lack of difference. In traditional psychoanalytic theory, perversion is all about refusing to see the difference.

Stephen Hartman

There is no father in the room because the father has become a perpetrator.

Eyal Rozmarin

So, there is a father.

Francisco Gonzalez

Yeah, I read that a little bit differently. I think that she's talking about patriarchy. So, there's specifically the legacy of the Father and the father's ownership of the daughter that patriarchy implies: "I own her body, I can marry her off to somebody else for my gain." It's the "traffic in women": it amounts to a declaration of ownership. I think that when she says that there is no law, but I think that there is a law there, you know? It is this kind of brutal, patriarchal law of the Father.

Eyal Rozmarin

And the son, by the way. This is the basis of Roman law. The father owns everything, on to the daughters, on to the sons, on to the slaves. You can rape them, you can kill them, you can give them away.

Orna Guralnik

So, to me, again, it is about the loss of lawfulness.

Francisco Gonzalez

Yeah. That's what makes it a transgression. Right.

Stephen Hartman

Through disavowal, clearly through disavowal. And it becomes a trap; it goes back to what we have been saying: can't win for losing. If Muriel speaks out, she risks judgment and censure; if Muriel doesn't write about the transgression, then she enters a kind of a perverse pact with the Law.

Eyal Rozmarin

Or the means to avoid…?

Francisco Gonzalez

…the transgression of the Law when…

Stephen Hartman

…when she speaks of the transgression.

Orna Guralnik

All these roles are mythical.

Stephen Hartman

Yes. The Father has the obligation, the ethical obligation, to not have sex with his children. Like most founding myths, the duty that empowers corrupts.

Eyal Rozmarin

Freud turned this into a theory of what the person is, which is kind of interesting.

Jade McGleughlin

So, then, can we just unpack this phrase: "detect the weight of a past that has become mine since that time?" What does she mean?

Eyal Rozmarin

It's her story.

Julie Leavitt

Well, but it also links her to the legacy of boundary violations in psychoanalysis. I think that she keeps linking to a legacy that preceded her, and then she enters into that legacy.

Eyal Rozmarin

Or, no…that (in carrying this legacy) she is also a father? By writing this history, she adopts the position of parent also. Maybe that's what she means. That she is also in the parental position…

Stephen Hartman

…which grants power and influence to her story if not to Muriel as author, but also this traumatizing dilemma of being the whistleblower: that was horrible for her as a person.

THE SEXUAL BOUNDARY VIOLATION: DISCOURSE AND HARD-ON

Eyal Rozmarin

Let me ask you, those of you who are familiar with this concept more than I am: the concept of "sexual boundary violation" did the concept exist at the time that she's describing, did it?. Did people refer to "sexual sexual boundary violations" in the 1980s?

Orna Guralnik

As opposed to calling it something else?

Eyal Rozmarin

Yes. Yes. As opposed to having a different way of – or not having a different way of – describing it?

Julie Leavitt

Yes. It was called sexual abuse in the 80s.

Eyal Rozmarin

As I recall, the idea of a *boundary violation* seems to me a rather new…

Julie Leavitt

...it would be interesting to look that up in earlier analytic literature to see how it was described then versus now.

Eyal Rozmarin

I'm pretty sure it didn't exist.

Jade McGleughlin

I was at Children's Hospital on a sexual abuse treatment team in the 80s. We definitely talked about sexual boundary violations.

Eyal Rozmarin

Was the concept of *boundary* already in use then?

Jade McGleughlin

Yes, body boundary. A child's body boundary...but that wasn't the psychoanalytic literature.

Eyal Rozmarin

It's referring to when a child is transgressed, but not an adult? Or was the adult also party to the boundary? I mean, was rape conceived as a boundary violation?

Stephen Hartman

What was it called? With Clinton and Monica Lewinsky? Do you remember? Was it called a boundary violation? I think it was called abuse of power or something like that.

Eyal Rozmarin

I'm just curious about this because this is rather contemporary language, which is applied to something that happened 30 years before. And I'm wondering to what degree it is the present that is signifying the past? Not that it didn't happen or that it wasn't traumatic, but that something about how we come to think about certain things is very often reconceived, recoloring and re-signifying what happened, and flattening it also at the same time. You know, what Freud called Nachträglichkeit. So, I'm wondering if this is happening as Muriel writes about her experience, if in bringing it to the present she and all of us are missing something.

Stephen Hartman

An interesting thing about this essay is that Muriel writes in very different temporalities at the same time. I think she's saying that "I'm carrying the past of the history of sexual boundary violations" (which may be the pre-history of attention to what we call "sexual boundary violations") as well as "this particular violation happened" as well as "a violation that could have or did happen in the past can reoccur in the future."

Julie Leavitt

Steven Cooper wrote a paper about preferring the term "sexual misconduct," because he talks about how "sexual boundary violation" brings in this whole complicated and kind of flattened idea of boundary violation. It's very clinical and doesn't really get to the fact of the behavior, of the actual conduct.

Eyal Rozmarin

Yeah, it's kind of boundary skirmishes. It's like the *New York Times* reporting about some boundary skirmishes somewhere in the world without giving you the background of what actually is happening and why people are people.

Francisco Gonzalez

We as a field are having difficulty in taking ownership, that this is our legacy that we've *baptized* many an analytic encounter through precisely this kind of thing.

Stephen Hartman

And this idea that it *baptized* many an analytic encounter: it focuses our lens on how a "boundary skirmish" lends gravitas – harkening back to that sentence about the body that we were talking about, that she has to open her body to him. There is this way in which we are baptized in the unsavory rituals of the couch.

Eyal Rozmarin

I'm curious what's happened to her all these years with the memory of his erection? I want to know where his hard-on was all those years?

Julie Leavitt

Well, it's interesting because even just in that paragraph where she mentions it, I was thinking about how the "sexual boundary violation" becomes very disembodied.

Eyal Rozmarin

And flattened and flat. To call it a "sexual" boundary violation is of course an element of it. But the term somehow actually erases the sexual. I'm assuming that the same way we're sitting on Zoom now and our patients know what some of our rooms look like, that will not disappear when we go back to the office. Muriel knows that he has a hard-on and she felt it, and she felt his tongue in her mouth. I would have wanted her to write about the hard-on, what it did to her? If it disgusted her? This is what's evoked for me, where are all those things that got flattened...

Orna Guralnik

I'm interested in how we fix the nature of an event to an experience. A lot depends on the time in which the 'doing' happened, and the collective discourse around it. There's no fixity. As with a word in a sentence, or paragraph; there's no way to hold on to the absolute meaning of any word if you take a real constructivist, postmodern approach to meaning making.

And, so, what about the "hard-on?" One way to hear Eyal's question is that the hard-on itself has some kind of absolute value. But that is the most phallocentric idea of where meaning sits. What about: What the fuck! The hard-on is nothing. Who cares about the hard-on??

Muriel Dimen

Repetition does not exclude the new. Lives are hybrid, the past relived, the past corrected, the new created, the old uploaded, the seeds of the new secreted in the past. And suddenly one day, after decades and centuries of hard work, slavery is outlawed, women get the vote, health care becomes a public good, psychoanalysis joins the fray. That slavery endures elsewhere, that women remain disenfranchised somewhere else, that the public good is not as good as it should be and anyway is always under attack – that harm resurges simply gives us more work to do.

What is the right way? Of litigation around sexual abuse, Harris (1996) has also written, "Whatever the many vicissitudes for a patient who has been abused and is attempting to come to terms with her or his experience, the goal of treatment in analysis is mourning a loss that cannot be undone with retribution nor perhaps even with justice" (166). Mourning, as opposed to melancholia, is classically thought to dispel the ghosts, but, as Judith Butler has argued (1995), Freud was wrong: mourning is most always melancholia. Imbued with trauma, it is never really done, and so we survive in its penumbra of sadness, which serves as the somber gray sky against which the slanting sun looks ever more piercingly beautiful.

Afterword

Adrienne Harris

So many tugs and worries get in the way of this writing. In some eerie way, the writing of an afterword and indeed this wonderful compilation of Muriel Dimen's work appearing in print makes her death more real. An afterword comes as her voice – in print and in life – stops.

Has stopped, Will be stopping. Stops. What grammar is right for this impossible thought?

My predicament, which I am finally articulating in this set of notes, is clearer and clearer to me. Shouldn't she have the last word? I say this because I witnessed with such anguish, how deeply Muriel wanted to be living, how much she feared and hated her illness, that fate handed her. "Do not go gentle into that good night." She did not.

So, an afterword seems partially an affront, an evasion of what she felt and wanted as she was dying, a place of helplessness that she was living at the end of her life all too massively.

I see in this writing that I need to speak of the anguish for her and her friends and companions in order to get to the place of pleasure and excitement.

Most pleasurably, I have just been teaching a course in ethics to a new generation of students who reading Dimen on Rotten Apples, felt transformed. Actually, what was striking is that they felt both transformed and vindicated. For this new generation, reading her work for the first time, they felt that excitement of her ability to speak to the accountability of the institution as well as the individual and to object to the privatization of damage. I would say that this experience of freshness and intense meaning at the collective and individual level is all over this book. She is having not the last word, but a next word, of interest and meaning to old and young, analysts, students, patients, and scholars.

DOI: 10.4324/9781003335252-40

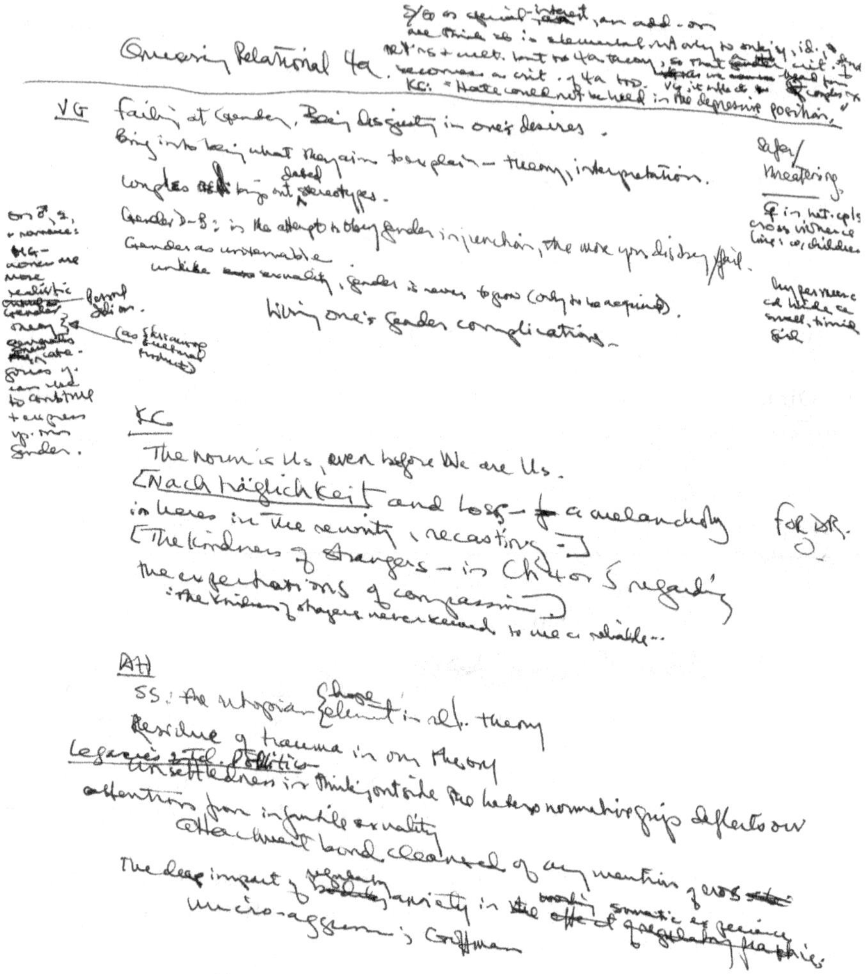
Queering Relational Ψa

KC: Hate could not be held in the depressive position.

VG failing at Gender, Being disgusting in one's desires.

Bring into being what they aim to explain — theory, interpretation.

Gender as untenable

unlike sexuality, gender is never to grow (only to be acquired).

Living one's gender complications.

KC

The norm is Us, even before We are Us.

[Nachträglichkeit and loss — a melancholy inheres in the security recasting.]

[The kindness of strangers — in Ch. 4 or 5 regarding the expectations of compassion]

AH

SS: the utopian element in rel. theory

Residue of trauma in our theory

Legacies of rel. politics

Unsettledness in thinking outside the heteronormative grip deflects our attention from infantile sexuality

Attachment bond cleansed of any mention of eros

micro-aggression; Goffman

Index

Note: Page numbers followed by "n" denote endnotes.

"abject," defined 139
abjection 20, 192, 193, 257; border and 150–152; culture and 142–143, 153, 154, 158; disgust and 139, 140, 151, 160; frustration and 141, 145; Kristeva and 152, 158, 160n1; Mitchell Wilson on 160n1; mourning and 140, 150, 152; overview and nature of 139–140; potential space and 198; rejection and 157, 158; sexuality and 139–140, 142–144, 146, 159–160; shame and 139, 140, 143, 145, 157
Abraham, Karl 96
action and reflection, relationship between 257
activists 49, 75; *see also* feminist activism and activists
Adler, Alfred 169–171, 177, 194
affect 13; defenses against 250; language and 223, 224; sex and 137–138, 141, 143, 223; *see also specific topics*
Ahmed, Sara 14, 21
alienation: class, money, and 104–105, 109–110; Freud on 104, 105, 117
alpha elements 216
ambivalence 38, 105, 226, 227, 244, 255; about groups 208, 221; acknowledgment of 208, 221; embracing of 238, 243; Freud on love, hate, and 118; hatred, idealization, and 214–216; maternal 156; maturity and 145; as unstable 145; *see also* "Rotten Apples and Ambivalence"
American-ness and political correctness 58–60
American Psychiatric Publishing Textbook of Psychoanalysis (Dimen and Goldner) 19
anal eroticism 96, 108
analytic bodies, policing of 213
analytic frame 116
analytic third *see* third
anxiety 102–104; contagious/contagion 207, 220 (*see also* contagion); money and 101, 102, 104, 106–108; orifices, the body, and 213
Aron, Lewis 12, 96
At the Crossroads (Dimen) 18–19
auto-criticism 18

Baldwin, James 195–196
Balint, Michael 193
Benjamin, Jessica 11, 141
Bersani, Leo 147, 188
beta elements 210, 225
Bion, Wilfred R. 209, 210, 224–225; container/contained and 16, 209, 210, 225; on preconception 210, 224
Bionian Field Theory 16–18
black feminism 67
blackness: denigrated 192–193, 195, 196–197; perversion and 192, 195, 196
bodies: economy of pleasures and 238; ownership of girls' and women's 277
body boundary 280; *see also* sexual boundary violations
border and abjection 150–152
boundary: history of the concept of 280; *see also* sexual boundary violations
Bourdieu, P. 6
Brazil 71–73
breath and anti-blackness 192–193
Buchberg, Lisa 19, 20

Butler, Daniel G. 20
Butler, Judith 153, 282

campaigns and political correctness 71–74
cases: Dr. French 95, 96, 106, 108; Dr. O. 253, 254, 258, 259, 270, 272, 274, 275, 277; Ms. Rose 114–117
Celenza, A. 182, 219, 222
Chefetz, Richard A. 179
"cisgender" 76, 77
class: Bourdieu on 6; countertransference, alienation, and 103–105; definition and nature of 103; feminism and 75; Freud and 98, 103–104, 117; professional-managerial 102–103, 107; psychoanalysis and 98–100, 102, 103; race and 6, 44–47
classism 104, 146
Cobb, Jonathan 110
collective action 49–50
collective unconscious 5
collective(s): Eyal Rozmarin on 261, 262, 266, 270; Francisco Gonzalez on 248–250, 261–267, 270; I, thou, us, sex, the personal, and the 222; Jade McGleuphlin on 250, 252, 260, 263; Julie Leavitt on 249, 256, 260–262, 264, 266, 267; Orna Guralnik on 249, 265; Stephen Hartman on 262–264, 266
communes 32
community psychoanalysis 22n1
compoundedness of identity: consciousness and 5; denial of 3
"confusion of tongues" 145, 253
contagion 210, 212, 214; affective 138; anxiety and 207, 220; shame and 144, 159
container/contained 16; Bion and 16, 209, 210, 225; group as container 226–229; nature of 228; perversions and 228; psychoanalysis as a container 209, 220–221, 226; recursion and 17; rotten apple metaphor and 209, 219, 221, 228; sexual boundary violations and 210, 221, 225; sexuality and 141, 159, 222–224, 228–229; trauma, excess, and 141, 159
Cooper, Steven 178, 180, 281
Corbett, Ken 13, 19, 20
corporeality 138, 140, 196, 221; of body 225, 227; of sexual 223
countertransference 138, 141, 158–159, 179; class, alienation, and 103–105; erotic/sexual 137, 138, 142, 158, 236; money and 97, 100–104, 117; pain/suffering and 142
creative tension 14, 17, 197
Crenshaw, Kimberlee 3, 5, 47n3, 83
cultural capital 6
culture and abjection 142–143, 153, 154, 158
cure, idealization of 159

Davies, Jody Messler 138, 141
de Peyer, J. 138, 140
de-westernisation 79
Dean, Tim 142
decolonisation in South Africa, calls for 78–81
depression *see* melancholia
Dimen, Muriel 1, 10, 135, 165–166; approaches 12–14; championing innovation 14–15; on the perspective of everywoman 2, 3, 5; *see also specific topics*
dirt, notion of 210–211, 214
dis-identification 196, 263
disciplinary power 207, 232
discipline 11, 13, 16, 69; Foucault on 232; heterogeneity and 165, 177–178; rotten apples metaphor and 206, 215, 216, 226; wild analysis, wild revolution, and 172, 173, 175
discreditability and discretion 235
discredited *vs.* discreditable persons 235
disgust 139, 142, 144–147; abjection and 139, 140, 151, 160; Freud on 144; normality, the abnormal, and 160; sexuality and 135, 137, 140, 142, 144, 146, 147, 159, 161n4; shame and 135, 139, 145, 157
dissociation 17, 49, 50, 219, 250; sexual boundary violations and 214, 226, 235
domesticity 6, 7
Dora, Freud's case of 117
Douglas, Mary 210–213, 225, 231
Durkheim, Émile 100

eco-feminists 84–85
Eew! Factor: intergenerational conversation on 150–160; sexuality and 137–147
Ehrenreich, Barbara 102–103
ELA (English Language Arts) 44–46

embarrassment: racism, disgust, and 142–144; sex and 142–144, 154; shame and 144
Engels, Friedrich 258
English Language Arts (ELA) 44–46
Eros 223, 224, 227–228
ethics *see* moral judgments
experimentation 2, 7, 9, 11–13; *see also* reading and writing experiments

Fairbairn, W. Ronald D. 145, 157
false consciousness 38–39, 55, 67, 89
Fanon, Franz 1, 13
fathers 130–132; sexual boundary violations by 276–278; *see also* patriarchy
Fear of Falling (Ehrenreich) 102–103
female perversion 146
female sexuality 41
feminism 1, 7, 10, 41, 90, 177; cyberfeminist campaigns 71–74; Eew! Factor and 143, 158; individualism and 32–33; intersectionality and 83–85; liberal 68–69; Marxist 75; patriarchy and 33, 68, 77, 80, 85; political correctness and 32–33, 37, 75, 77; political incorrectness of, and decolonisation in South Africa 78–81; radical 42, 66, 67; second-wave 2, 3, 190; sexuality and 33, 38, 39, 42; *Surviving Sexual Contradictions* (Dimen) and 1, 165, 190; third-wave 3, 56; as unAfrican 78–81; whiteness and 41, 42, 68–69
feminist activism and activists 41, 42, 75, 80
Fenichel, Otto 96
Ferenczi, Sándor 96, 145, 182, 194
"field of its own" (Dimen) 16, 17
field theory: Bionian 16, 18; Dimen's 14–17
Floyd, George 192, 261, 262, 264–266
folk theory 219
form 166
Foucault, Michel 234, 238; on disciplinary power 232; on Freud and discursivity 171; *History of Sexuality* 232, 233, 235, 238; on "normal" *vs.* "abnormal" 153; psychoanalysis and 232, 233, 238; on psychoanalytic and confessional speech 138; on relational fabric 239n4; on repressive hypothesis 232–233; sexuality and 153, 232–235, 238, 239nn3–4
Freud, Sigmund 98, 100, 194, 236; abjection and 140; on alienation 104, 105, 117; authoritarianism and relations with colleagues 169–170 (*see also* Adler, Alfred); class and 98, 103–104, 117; as a "founder of discursivity" 171; on love and hate 118; Masud Khan on 105; money and 95–98, 100, 101, 104–106, 108, 109, 114, 116–117; on sexuality 141, 143–144, 168–169, 171, 181 (*see also* "Wild Analysis"); on technique 172–173; terminology 181; on the uncanny 151, 195, 212; writings 167, 171 (*see also* "Wild Analysis"): case histories 116–117, 143, 154, 236; *Three Essays on the Theory of Sexuality* 143–144, 171
frustration: abjection and 141, 145; Fairbairn on 145, 157; Freud on 168, 169; hate and 145, 146, 157, 159; nature of 141, 145, 157; sexuality and 141, 159, 168, 169; shame and 145, 157

Gabbard, Glen O. 182, 209, 215, 219
Gauttari, Félix 69
gender 3, 4, 6–7; race and 5, 7, 14, 16; *see also specific topics*
general-purpose money 110, 111
General Theory of Seduction (Laplanche) 12, 16
generations 19–20, 166; hierarchies and 9, 20, 166
Gentile, Katie 13–14, 19, 28
Gerson, Samuel 158
Ghent, Emmanuel 3–4, 12, 115, 118
ghosting 243, 244, 246, 247, 263, 268; collective 267
ghostly, the 246–248; Francisco Gonzalez on 246–248, 251; Jade McGleuphlin on 247, 248, 251, 252; Julie Leavitt on 246, 248–252; Orna Guralnik on 246, 247, 251
ghosts 246–247, 253–255, 257, 258; golems and 251, 252, 254; language of 252; mourning and 282; nature of 251; *see also* ghostly
Ghosts and the Sexual Boundary Violation (Dimen) 243, 244
Goffman, Erving 213, 225–226, 231, 235

Goldner, Virginia 19, 138, 146
golems 247, 251, 252, 254, 255
Gonzalez, Francisco J. 9, 256, 257, 259, 261, 265, 272–273, 281; on collective(s) 248–250, 261–268, 270; on context 249; on the ghostly 246–248, 251; on Golem 251, 252; on patriarchy 277; on sexual boundary violations 267–269; on subjectivity 265–266; on transgression 277, 278
grace, state of 226, 229
Greenson, Dan 212
group process 243
groups 260–262, 265–266; as containers 226–229; *see also* collective(s); writing groups
Guntrip, Harry J.S. 113
Guralnik, Orna 250, 255, 268, 271, 282; on the collective 249, 265; couples therapy and 197–198; on the ghostly 246, 247, 251; on power 17, 274–275; on sexual boundary violations 249, 256, 268, 271, 274–279, 282; on the wooden 248, 249

habitus, psyche as 6
Harris, Adrienne 11, 19, 22, 257, 282
Harris, Jeremy 196
Hartman, Saidiya 263, 264
Hartman, Stephen 248–251, 260, 262, 281; on the collective 262–266; on power 276, 278–280; on recursion 247, 266; on sexual boundary violations 263–264, 267, 271, 273–278, 280–281
hate-fucking 147
hatred 159; frustration and 145, 146, 157, 159; idealization, ambivalence, and 214–216
Herron, W.G. 100
heterogeneity 167, 176; discipline and 165, 177–178; technique and 179–180; uniformity and 190, 193
heteroglossia 138, 180
heterosexual privilege. 4
heterosexual zone, of safety 4
heterosexuality 146
hierarchies 6, 11–12, 103–104, 160; generational 20; generations and 9, 166; patriarchy and 6, 85, 183; of privilege 103; rotten apples metaphor and 214, 215, 225, 226; wild analysis, wild revolution, and 166, 179, 183, 191
History of Sexuality (Foucault) 232, 233, 235, 238
homophobia 4
homosexuality 35, 154; *see also* lesbianism
hooks, bell 67
Horney, Karen 171
humiliation 52, 83, 131; Eew! Factor and 139, 145, 146, 154; narcissism, sexual pain, and 140–142

idealization 103; hatred, ambivalence, and 214–216; of motherhood 156; psychoanalysis and 117, 216, 226; of sex 147, 155–156, 159
identification 263, 264, 273; *see also* dis-identification
identity 102, 196; spoiled 213 (*see also* stigma)
identity intersectionality 3–4; *see also* intersectionality
ILAS (Institute for Mental Health and Human Rights) 208
imaginary, the 223; *see also* social imaginary
incest 213, 258, 276–278
India 87–90
infantile sexual 234, 239n1
Inside the Revolution: Power, Sex, and Technique in Freud's 'Wild' Analysis (Dimen) 165, 190
Institute for Mental Health and Human Rights (ILAS) 208
interpellation 17
intersectional frame, plea for an 75–76
intersectionality 3, 14, 47, 83, 265–266; in feminist discourse, politically correct and incorrectness of 83–85; identity 3–4; political correctness and 75–77
intersubjective resistance 158
intersubjectivity 139, 178, 179; sexuality and 139
intimacy 4, 244; analytic 226; embodied 238; encircling 226–228; nature of 227; negotiation of 228, 229; one-way 228; perversion of 228; rotten apples metaphor and 218, 222, 235; seductive 234; sexual 35; shared 15
Israel and political correctness 51–53

Jacobson, Edith 96
Jones, Annie Lee 68

jouissance 142, 147
Jung, Carl Gustav 236

K (knowledge) 216
-K (opposite of knowledge) 225
Kaywin, Emma 19, 20
Khan, Masud M.R. 105, 113–114
kinky sex 153
Klein, Melanie 103, 112, 113
Kristeva, Julia: abjection and 139–140, 145, 150–152, 158, 160n1; on narcissism 139–141; on shame 139, 145; on uncanniness and the uncanny 139, 140, 151, 152

Lacan, Jacques 152, 236; on *jouissance* 142; on realness 196 (*see also* Real); on satisfaction 141; *see also* Symbolic and the Real
Landlady of Time approach and money 114–116
Language: affect and 223, 224; sexuality and 222, 223; *see also* English Language Arts
Laplanche, Jean 13, 16, 141, 239n1, 250; General Theory of Seduction 12, 16; on sexuality 141, 239n1
Lapsus Lingue, or a Slip of the Tongue? (Dimen) 19, 166, 205, 219; after 220–221
Leavitt, Julie 259–262, 264, 266, 267; on collective(s) 249, 256, 260–262, 264, 266, 267; on the ghostly 246, 248–252; on power 275; on race 268–269; on sexual boundary violations 256–257, 259, 260, 268–280, 281
left-wing ideology vs. moral judgment 51–53
lesbianism 4, 35, 56, 63; "The Psychogenesis of a Case of Homosexuality in a Woman" (Freud) 143, 154
Lévi-Strauss, Claude 181
listservs, professional 48n11
LOC 148 (writing group) 21–22, 244, 246
longing, state of 39
Lorde, Audre 67
love: contradiction between money and 108–112; paradox between hate and 112–116, 118

Makari 168, 169, 176, 180
Mallory, Tamika 76
March On (organization) 76
Marx, Karl 105, 109, 111, 258
Marxist feminists 75
maternal ambivalence 156
McGleuphlin, Jade 247, 248, 250, 260, 263, 264, 267, 272, 273; on the collective 250, 252, 260, 263; on the ghostly 247, 248, 251, 252; on power 252, 262, 264; on race 261, 264; on sexual boundary violations 250, 252, 255, 256, 259, 260, 269–271, 280
McLaughlin, James T. 178, 180
melancholia, mourning and 4, 260, 282
Meltzer, Donald W. 145
mental factor 177
mental states 177; *see also* states of mind; *specific states*
#MeToo campaign 72–74
microaggressions 5, 7
Mitchell, Stephen A. 138, 206
money: anxiety related to 101, 102, 104, 106–108; case studies (*see* cases); commerce and psychoanalysis 105–108; contradiction between love and 108–112; countertransference and 97, 100–104, 117; defined 106; as Devil's gold 108–110, 115; disturbance of 100–103; Freud and 95–98, 100, 101, 104–106, 108, 109, 114, 116–117; gender differences and 107; Landlady of Time approach and 114–116; as last taboo (in psychoanalysis) 98; and the paradox between love and hate 112–116, 118; psychoanalytic discourse about 95; psychoanalytic fees 105–107; in psychoanalytic question 98–100; psychosexuality of 95–98; *see also* class
Money, Love and Hate in the Countertransference (Dimen) 20
monsters 151–152; nature of 152
moral judgments 32, 34, 51; feminism and 79; left wing ideology and 52–53
moralism 42–43, 52
Morrison, Andrew P. 144, 159
mourning 282; abjection and 140, 150, 152; melancholia and 4, 260, 282
Mrs. America (television series) 190
MsAfropolitan (Minna Salami) 80
multiple points of view 2
multiplicity 52, 143, 265; psychoanalysis and 143, 167, 170, 171, 176, 178

Muñoz, José 198–199
#MyFirstHarrassment campaign 71
#MySecretSanta campaign 71–72
myth 181, 278

narcissism 141; abjection and 139–140; Kristeva on 139–141; money and 112; nature of 140
narcissistic injury and shame 144
Nation of Islam (NOI) 76
negative capability 179
Nelson, Maggie 156
"non-racialism" 49
normative unconscious 17
normativity 6, 57, 139, 153; Foucault on 153; history and 196; politics and 67; psychoanalysis and 14; sexuality and 14, 139, 153 (*see also* perversion); *see also* Otherness

Ogden, Thomas H. 16, 140
"one rotten apple spoils the barrel" 208–209, 219
Otherness 16–17, 220, 249; abjection and 139, 151, 157–158, 160; abnormality and 160; fear of 151, 152; loss of 276; self and 16; sexuality and 139

Palestine/Israel conflict 52; *see also* Israel and political correctness
Palestinians 52, 66
paradox 118
patriarchy 68, 254, 277; colonialism and 80; feminism, feminists, and 33, 68, 77, 80, 85; hierarchies and 6, 85, 183; psychoanalytic 216, 275; sexuality and 35, 41, 254
Pavel, Ernst 147
Perez, Carmen 76
performative allyship 66
Person, Ethel S. 143
personal life, importance of 1–2
personal power, quest for 7
perverse cleaning 223–226
perversion 14, 15, 159, 222, 228, 229; blackness and 192, 195, 196; difference and 277; disavowal and 277, 278
Phillips, Adam 168, 209, 237
play 188–191, 198
Pleasure and Danger: Exploring Female Sexuality (Vance) 27, 41
pleasure and power 234, 236
political correctness (PC) 83–85, 87–90; accessibility to life and 61–64; American-ness and 58–60; as bad 34–39; campaigns and 71–74; collective action and 49–50; defining 27, 31–32, 51; as dual defense 65–69; as good 33; ideology and behavior of 33; intersectionality and 75–77; in Israeli context 51–53; origin of the term 75; people implementing 33; political incorrectness of feminism and decolonisation in South Africa 78–81; politics of inclusion and 49; as psychological foot-binding 75; queer politics and 56–57; sexuality and 34–39; White Monopoly Capital (WMC) and 54–55
politically correct ideology and behavior 32–34, 49
Politically Correct? Politically Incorrect? (Dimen) 73
pornography 31, 41, 155
positive negative space 178
potential 197
potential space 191, 193, 196, 198–199, 210
power: disciplinary 207, 232; emancipation and 42; intimacy and 10, 15; Jade McGleuphlin on 252, 262, 264; knowledge and 233, 234; loss of 275, 276; money and 110, 117; Orna Guralnik on 17, 274–275; personal 7; pleasure and 234, 236; political 6, 33, 35, 42, 49, 55, 67, 71, 79, 103, 110; political correctness and 65–68; privilege and 54, 153; psychoanalysis and 168; regulatory 175, 193; repressive 189; revolution and 190–194; rotten apples metaphor and 207, 213–215, 221, 238, 239n3; sex and 5, 168–170, 233, 234, 274–275 (*see also Sexuality, Intimacy, Power*); Stephen Hartman on 276, 278–280; stigma and 226; "Wild Analysis" (Freud) and 168–170
power asymmetry in analytic relationship 93, 179, 222
power relations 10, 262
power structures 208, 211
preconception: defined 210, 229n3; notion of 210, 224–225
privatization of sexual experience, critique of 34–35

privilege 3, 6, 11, 56, 103; heterosexual 4; Lionel Shriver on 76; nature of 77; perspectives on 76–77; political 49; racial 6, 14; willed obliviousness of 76
professional-managerial class 102–103, 107
projective identification 210, 225
psychoanalysis: analysts' hatred of their discipline 214–216; class and 98–100, 102, 103; as a container 209, 220–221, 226; as a cultural institution 210–212; hatred of 214–216; as a praxis of unknowing 190; as a sexual field 209–210; vulnerability of 212–213; *see also specific topics*
Psychoanalytic Institute of Northern California (PINC) 197
psychoanalytic institutes 8, 197
psychoanalytic technique, Freud on 172–173
purity: and danger 212; and pollution 210–212
Purity and Danger (Douglas) 210, 225, 231; *see also* Douglas, Mary

queer sex 153
queer theory 232
queers 56, 57

race 6, 7, 9, 11, 54–55; class and 6, 44–47; gender and 5, 7, 14, 16; Jade McGleuphlin on 261, 264; Julie Leavitt on 268–269; sexuality and 55, 146, 192; shame and 154; as socially contextualised 55; *see also specific topics*
racial oppression 54, 55
racial privilege 6, 14
racism 48, 49, 88; anti-blackness 192–193, 195; embarrassment, disgust, and 142–144; *see also* Floyd, George; white supremacy
reading and writing 1, 2, 12, 18, 21; *see also specific topics*
reading and writing experiments 5, 8, 18–21, 244; *see also* experimentation
Real, the 152 *see also* Symbolic and the Real
recursion 12, 13, 17, 247, 248, 266; nature of 17; Stephen Hartman on 247, 266
Reflections on Cure (Dimen) 19
Reich, Wilhelm 96
rejection 157–159; abjection and 139–140, 157, 158; Fairbairn on frustration and 145; Kristeva on 139–140; shame and 157–159
relational psychoanalysis 177–179
relational space 16
relationality 17, 145, 178, 197–199
repression and the repressed 189, 195, 233
repressive hypothesis 232–233
revolution 188–195; inside of 176, 187–190, 193; in modernist sense 189; nature of 187, 189; psychoanalysis and 187–195: potential as a feature of 197; spatiality of 187; as staying outside 193, 195–196; unknowing as praxis and 191, 194; wildness and 190–192
Riviere, Joan 103, 112, 113
rotten apple metaphor 209, 224, 225; from apples to orchards 218–220; container/contained and 209, 219, 221, 228; eroticism and 213, 221–223, 225, 227, 228; a first bite 218; purity and pollution 210–212; stigma and 213–214; *see also* "Rotten Apples and Ambivalence"
"Rotten Apples and Ambivalence: Sexual Boundary Violations through a Psychocultural Lens" (Dimen) 205–206, 218–220, 231, 235, 237, 283; on the social 220–221, 225, 231; *see also* rotten apple metaphor
Rozmarin, Eyal: on the collective 261, 262, 266, 270; on scapegoats 264, 266; on sexual boundary violations 269–271, 274–282

Saketopoulou, Avgi 159, 236
Salami, Minna (MsAfropolitan) 80
Salamon, Gayle 179, 191
scapegoats 264, 266
seduction: psychoanalysis as 117–118; sexuality and 224; *see also under* Laplanche, Jean
self-consciousness 235, 273
self-disclosure 273–274
self-disgust 146; *see also* disgust
self-righteousness, danger of 52
self states 227
Sennett, Richard 110

sex: a crazy mixed-up theory of 170–172; idealization of 147, 155–156, 159; as Other 139; part and whole relations and 37–38; shame, hatred, and 144–146, 159, 160; talking about 222–223; *see also* sexuality; *specific topics*
Sexual Boundary Trouble in Psychoanalysis (Dimen) 19
sexual boundary violations 180–182; analytic literature on 279–280; container/contained and 210, 221, 225; dissociation and 214, 226, 235; Eyal Rozmarin on 269–271, 274–282; by fathers 276–282 (*see also* incest); folk theory of 208–209, 219; Francisco Gonzalez on 267–269; hatred, idealization, ambivalence and 214–216; Jade McGleuphlin on 250, 252, 255, 256, 259, 260, 269–270, 280; Julie Leavitt on 256–257, 259, 268–279, 281; Orna Guralnik on 249, 256, 268, 271, 274–280, 282; power structures and 208; psychoanalysis as a sexual field and 209–210; rotten apples metaphor and 205, 213–214, 231, 234–235, 237; Stephen Hartman on 263–264, 267, 271, 273–279, 280–281; terminology 279, 281; through psychocultural lens 207–216, 218–229; and the uncanny 212; vulnerability of psychoanalysis and 212–213; "Wild Analysis" (Freud) and 180–182
sexual contradictions *see Surviving Sexual Contradictions*
sexual frustration 141, 168, 169
sexual intimacy and political correctness 35
sexual monstrosities 152–153
sexual transgression *see* sexual boundary violations
sexuality 2–3, 14; abjection and 139–140, 142–144, 146, 159–160; as ambiguous 36–38; container/contained and 141, 159, 222–224, 228–229; denigrated blackness and 192, 195–197; disgust and 135, 137, 140, 142, 144, 146, 147, 159, 161n4; Eew! Factor and 137–147; feminism and 33, 38, 39, 42; Foucault and 153, 232–235, 238, 239nn3–4; Freud on 141, 143–144, 168–169, 171, 181 (*see also* "Wild Analysis"); language and 222, 223; normativity and 14, 139, 153 (*see also* perversion); politically correct ideology and behavior and 34–39; power and 5, 168–170, 233, 234, 274–275 (*see also* sexuality, intimacy, power*);* as socially contextualised 34, 55; *see also* sex; *specific topics*
Sexuality, Intimacy, Power (Dimen) 10, 18
shame 154, 157–159, 219, 256; abjection and 139, 140, 143, 145, 157; contagion and 144, 159; disgust and 135, 139, 145, 157; frustration and 145, 157; gender, race, and 5, 6; Kristeva on 139, 145; rejection and 157–159; sex, hatred, and 144–146, 159, 160; stigma and 214
Sheehi, Lara 13–15
Simmel, G. 173
Slave Play (Harris) 196
sliding scales 107
social, the 9, 49, 199; recursion and 17; "Rotten Apples and Ambivalence" (Dimen) and 220–221, 225, 231; sexual transgressions and 221, 225
social imaginary: disrepair of the 194, 198, 199; *see also* imaginary
social unconscious 17, 154
sodomy 154; defined 153–154; Foucault and 153, 232
South Africa: political correctness and 54–55; political incorrectness and decolonisation in 78–81
special-purpose money 110–111
Spezzano, Charles 138
spoiled identity 213; *see also* stigma
"state of grace" 226
states of mind 141, 179; *see also* mental states; *specific states*
Stein, Ruth E. 138, 141, 143–144
stigma 216, 229, 231, 235; defined 213; discredited persons and 235; division of 225–226; Goffman on 213–214, 225–226, 231, 235; risk of 214–215; rotten apples theory and 213–214
"stupid" 63
subjective diachrony 139
subjectivity 178; as intersection of the individual and collective 265–266; *see also* intersubjectivity
suffering: countertransference and 142; psychic 173, 177
suicide 61–63

Sullivan, Harry Stack 140, 177
Surviving Sexual Contradictions (Dimen) 4, 7–8, 11, 13; auto-criticism and 18; boundary violations and 243; feminism and 1, 165, 190
Symbolic and the Real, the 207, 212, 227, 251
symbolic space 33
symbolization 223, 227, 228

technique, Freud on 172–173
temporal tensegrity 13–14, 16
Theorizing a Field (Dimen) 14
Theorizing Social Reproduction (Dimen) 19
therapization of America 99
third 183, 190, 249, 255
Three Essays on the Theory of Sexuality (Freud) 143–144, 171
transference 222; erotic/sexual 97, 141, 142, 222, 253, 254
transgenderism 56–57, 66; *see also* "cisgender"
transitional space 140, 196, 198
trauma 208, 272; analyst as container for 141, 159; intergenerational transmission of 207, 246, 252, 254, 255, 268; political correctness (PC) and 52; stories of 250; Winnicott on 198; *see also* sexual boundary violations

ultrapsychic register 8
uncanniness and the uncanny 195, 255; Freud on 151, 195, 212; Kristeva on 139, 140, 151, 152; sexual boundary violations and 212; uncanny fear 151
unconscious 12, 177; collective 5; normative 17; social 17, 154; textual 181; unknowable 16
University of California Wildcat Strike 187, 199n1
unknowable unconscious 16
unknowing 179, 181, 193, 198; erotic 140; nature of 179, 191; praxis of 190, 191, 194

Vaughans, Kirkland 67
Vienna Psychoanalytic Society 169, 170

whistle-blower(s) 273; and the container 219, 225; Dimen as 231, 232, 243, 279; made into the problem 210, 225, 243; self-focus and 273
white liberal discourse, limitations of 65–69
white liberal progressives 66–68
White Monopoly Capital (WMC) 54–55
white supremacy 41, 42, 67, 69, 76, 195
whiteness 48n10, 69; dis-identification and 196; feminism and 41, 42, 68–69; *see also* race
Widlöcher, D. 177
"Wild Analysis" (Freud) 167, 189, 194; a false memory 167–168; hybridity, doubt, and 182–183; inside of revolution and 190–191; *Inside the Revolution: Power, Sex, and Technique in Freud's 'Wild' Analysis* (Dimen) 165, 190; interesting times 170; mixed-up theory of sex and 170–172; power and 168–170; putting on the brakes 173–175; sexual boundary violations and 180–182; technique and 172–173; toward a cubist psychoanalysis 175–180;
Wilson, Mitchell 160n1
Winnicott, Donald W. 113, 191, 198–199, 215
Wissenschaft, concept of 173
With Culture in Mind, Psychoanalytic Stories (Dimen) 21, 195, 244
WMC *see* White Monopoly Capital
wokeness, concept of 80, 81n3
Woolf, Virginia 170
writing and reading *see* reading and writing
writing groups 243–244, 256; *see also* LOC 148

For Product Safety Concerns and Information please contact our EU
representative GPSR@taylorandfrancis.com
Taylor & Francis Verlag GmbH, Kaufingerstraße 24, 80331 München, Germany

www.ingramcontent.com/pod-product-compliance
Lightning Source LLC
Chambersburg PA
CBHW071411290326
41932CB00047B/2575

9781032370873